Thomas William Allies

Thomas William Allies
portrait at the age of 17
by Mary Carpenter

The Life of

Thomas William Allies

1813–1903

'A soul temper'd with fire'

Michael Trott

GRACEWING

First published in England in 2022
by
Gracewing
2 Southern Avenue
Leominster
Herefordshire HR6 0QF
United Kingdom
www.gracewing.co.uk

No part of this publication may be reproduced, stored in a retrieval system, or transmitted in any form or by any means, electronic, mechanical, photocopying, recording or otherwise, without the written permission of the publisher.

The right of Michael Trott to be identified as the author of this work has been asserted in accordance with the Copyright, Designs and Patents Act 1988.

© 2022 Michael Trott

ISBN 978 085244 982 0

Typeset by Word and Page, Chester, UK

Cover design by Bernardita Peña Hurtado

CONTENTS

Preface	vii
1. The Making of a Controversialist	1
2. The Tractarian Whirlwind	55
3. The Church of England is not in Schism	101
4. The Process of Disillusionment	143
5. Crossing the Tiber	203
6. A New Life	241
7. Home and Family	365
Notes	385
Bibliography of the Works of Thomas William Allies	445
Index	449

PREFACE

Allies first became an absorbing interest many years ago when I spotted his manuscript diary for 1839 in a bookseller's catalogue. I had recently completed a biography of Richard Waldo Sibthorp—an Anglican clergyman who converted to Roman Catholicism in 1841—and remained fascinated by the intellectual journeys of the many other Victorian converts. I discovered that there was no biography of Allies besides that published by his daughter Mary in 1907, and because she had quoted extensively from his diaries no academic library had expressed an interest in acquiring the one for sale. As well as the diary there was also a commonplace book he had kept during the 1850s and 1860s, following his appointment as reader in the philosophy of history at the new Catholic university in Dublin—jottings of observations about and extracts from ancient and contemporary scholars transcribed in an intimidating variety of languages: Greek, Latin, Italian, French and German as well as English. These two documents were the foundation of a research project that has revealed a formidable controversialist, who, on becoming convinced that the true Church must possess valid jurisdiction as well as valid orders, became one of the doughtiest defenders of the papacy writing in English in the nineteenth century.

I owe a great debt to Professor Alan McClelland, who encouraged me to set out on this path and to continue to the end. His willingness to share his knowledge of the Victorian Church, especially the impact upon it of Cardinal Manning, as well as his expertise on the development of Catholic education have been an invaluable and unfailing resource. I am also most grateful to Mrs Pat Cook of the Launton Historical Association, who shared with me her invaluable archive and took me on a tour of the parish church where Allies laboured with no outward success. Amongst others who provided insights were the descendants of Allies's dear friend John Hungerford Pollen, especially Peregrine Pollen. Daniel Joyce at the Birmingham Oratory was kind and patient in letting me consult the Newman correspondence; but now there is no need to travel there, the magnificent digitisation of so much Newman material having made his correspondence instantly available. And in this way also I have been able to look at a book of poetry that Allies had printed in 1837, which has just come to light in Eton College Library; I should like to express my thanks to Dr Coane for turning its pages for me remotely.

I found it difficult to form a judgment on Allies, a rather prickly and unsympathetic character, whose disagreement with Newman perhaps put him on the wrong side of later developments in the Church. But he was firm and undeviating in his beliefs and I stand in awe at the clarity and forcefulness of his writings.

✣ 1 ✣

THE MAKING OF A CONTROVERSIALIST

A merchant family

In his history of the Bristol pottery[1] William Pountney makes a minor error. He asserts that Edwin Allies—joint owner of the business between 1816 and 1835—was the son of Sir John Allies, a sugar planter in Barbados.[2] This mistake as to parentage, stemming perhaps from a half-remembered conversation, is excusable: Edwin Allies was wealthy, and in eighteenth-century Bristol most fortunes came from slavery; the profits of the trade and of the plantations. The truth, however, was less problematic. Edwin, born in 1782, was one of the nine children of James and Hannah Allies. His father was a successful businessman in Worcester, who on his death in 1832 owned estates in three counties. Along with these substantial possessions he seems to have bequeathed to his children a shrewd business sense. Two of his sons were established as prosperous leather dealers in Worcester, George Allies becoming the city's mayor in 1838. Another who joined Edwin in Bristol also dealt in leather and a fifth moved to Wiltshire, where he traded in ironware.

'In trade' they surely were, yet in a society acutely aware of birth and matters of status, the Allies were proud of their lineage. The family was ancient, had once borne arms, and had pretensions to gentility. In recognition of this one of James's sons was encouraged to forsake the world of commerce. In December 1805, at the age of twenty, Thomas Allies entered St Edmund's Hall, Oxford. The choice of college was significant. St Edmund's had long been at the centre of Evangelicalism at the university and Bible religion was the atmosphere in which the young man grew up. His mother's family, the Somersetshire Duddons, were steeped in Independency. She, however, felt able to join her husband in an Established Church increasingly alive to its Reformation heritage, and their son was to become, in the words of his granddaughter, a 'mild and pious minister of religion.'[3]

In 1809 Thomas was ordained as curate of Wraxall on the outskirts of Bristol. The rector, James Vaughan, had himself graduated from St Edmund's and was a disciple of Thomas Tregenna Biddulph, the vicar of St James's in the city and the acknowledged leader of Evangelical Anglicanism in the West of England. In 1816, Biddulph's eldest son began his clerical career by also becoming Vaughan's curate. Unsurprisingly, Thomas was drawn into friendship with the Biddulph family and other members of the pious congregation at St James's, among whom most prominent were the Fripps, a family at the centre of Bristol's commercial, religious and cultural life. Thomas was soon romantically linked with Frances Elizabeth Fripp and the couple married in April 1812. She was six years his junior and even wealthier, having inherited estates in Dorset following her father Samuel's death some two years before. He had been a stern Moravian, and whilst his children disowned his dissent, the substantial soap works he established was the source of their fortune. It continued to flourish under the ownership of Frances's brother, Edward Bowles Fripp, a church warden at St James's and stalwart of the local Church Missionary Society.

Like Thomas Allies, Edward Fripp's elder brother Samuel had also forsworn trade. After studying at Queens' College, Cambridge, he had been ordained into the ministry of the established Church and served for a short time as a curate in Kent. In 1811 he married—at St Margaret's, Westminster—a daughter of the celebrated marine artist, Nicholas Pocock. The couple moved to Bristol, where the Pocock family had its roots, and there brought up a large family. Two of their sons, Alfred Downing and George Arthur, inherited their grandfather's artistic talent and became artists much admired by their contemporaries; the former was to marry a daughter of the Bristol pottery owner Edwin Allies, further linking the two families. After his marriage, Samuel Fripp resigned his curacy and abandoned the ministry. With his substantial private means he was able in quiet retirement to indulge his taste for musical composition. He also studied theology and became so dissatisfied with the teachings of the Established Church that in 1819 he declined a desirable Bristol living offered to him by the mayor and corporation. At length, by now convinced that 'the creeds and articles of the Church of England were not in accordance with Holy Scripture'[4] and having consulted at length with Lant Carpenter, minister of the Unitarian Chapel at Lewin's Mead Bristol, he reached the end of his pilgrimage on 6 January 1822. On that Sunday evening he delivered 'to a very crowded' chapel congregation a discourse on the leading doctrines of Unitarianism, explicitly avowing his adoption of them and consequent secession from the Church of England.[5]

His brother-in-law was, however, secure in his Anglicanism, and two months after his marriage Thomas moved to a curacy at Midsomer Norton, an area well populated with his mother's family. It was here on 12 February 1813 that Thomas William Allies was born. Tragically, Frances died just one week after giving birth. Her family rallied round the grieving widower and the baby was taken to Bristol, where he was christened at St James's, and here a few days later his mother was interred. Before long Thomas had returned to the city as curate of Henbury, where the Fripps lived and where he could be close to his infant son. Over the following years the links between the Allies family, the Fripps and the Biddulphs became ever closer. Thus in 1815 Thomas, along with his brother John, became trustees for another brother, Edwin, in respect of his house at 24 Pritchard Street; the other trustees were Edward Fripp and Thomas Shrapnel Biddulph—T. T. Biddulph's eldest son.

A young curate, a widower with an infant son, needed a wife. Thomas's choice fell on Caroline Hilhouse. They were married in May 1815, and at the age of twenty-four she happily took on responsibility for a two-year-old stepson. Caroline was a young lady of decided and forceful views, but as these were strongly Evangelical her husband could not object. Besides, she had the most desirable quality of being the daughter of an extremely wealthy Bristol shipbuilder, James Martin Hilhouse, who in 1772 had established his company in Hotwells using as capital part of the fortune that his father had made as a privateer during the Seven Years' War. With the boom in shipbuilding as Britain expanded its fleet in the forlorn attempt to subdue its American colonies and their French allies, Hilhouse's business flourished. The war with France resumed a decade later, and by the turn of the century he owned one of the city's largest industrial concerns. In 1814 his yard launched the first steam ship to be built in Bristol, the *Charlotte and Hope*.

There was another side to Hilhouse. He was a proficient amateur artist, a serious collector of paintings and a patron of artists, who along with other eminent Bristolians commissioned their townsman Nicholas Pocock to depict a series of naval engagements in the Revolutionary War. In his latter years—he died in 1822—and after handing responsibility for the shipyard to his son George, he turned his attention to oil painting, and not without success: his name occasionally appears in the catalogues of the auction houses.

Thomas would have been comfortable with the artistic ambience of his father-in-law's home, for he too shared a taste for the fine arts. How long this interest had existed and what inspired it cannot now be established, although it is unlikely that it originated with his courtship of Caroline, for it seems that his childhood home in Worcester was a cultured place that welcomed artists. One of his sisters married Richard Dighton, who was a talented artist, well established in Worcester as a portraitist. In the 1820s he painted Thomas's parents, James and Hannah, who are depicted as a conventionally respectable middle-class couple, albeit Sarah is holding a book rather than her sewing.[6] And whilst her husband's firm grasp of a stout stick does not mark him out as a man of ostensible aesthetic sensibility, his long and detailed will made particular mention of 'my ... books, prints, pictures'. His son, the Reverend Thomas Allies, also accumulated a significant art collection, including some important old masters; it would be interesting to know what pictures adorned the walls of the home at Charlotte Street in the elegant Bristol suburb of Clifton, where in the 1820s he lived with his second wife and young son, who was later joined by two half-sisters, Mary Anne and Caroline, who was born with a serious disability. His collection of artworks continued to grow, helped by the will of his father-in-law, which stipulated that all his oil paintings 'not painted by myself' were to be shared among his seven children, with each 'chusing successively according to seniority of age'.

At first blush it is perhaps hard to reconcile the world of trade and Evangelical beliefs with high art and connoisseurship. Yet there is no contradiction. Painting in the early nineteenth century was for most of its practitioners a trade, with profit as its objective. Occasional sharp dealing was not unknown. Robert Dighton, father of Richard and the more celebrated artist, was notorious for having stolen and sold numerous works from the British Museum Print Room. When the scandal came to light in 1806 a veil was drawn over the matter and his only punishment was exile from London.[7] Moreover, aestheticism and puritan beliefs could happily co-exist, despite the later scepticism of Thomas William Allies's daughter Mary, his first biographer, who thought an appreciation of sacramental Christianity essential for good taste.[8] Yet Ruskin, for example, was to combine an all-absorbing biblicism with the most refined appreciation of the glories of mediaeval art and architecture, as well as championing the innovative genius of J. M. W. Turner. The celebrated artist John Linnell, with whom Thomas Allies was to have a complicated relationship, was himself deeply religious. In her notes for the Linnell Centennial Exhibition at Cambridge in 1982, Katharine Crouan pointed to an Evangelical conversion in 1811 as most significant for his artistic development, claiming that reading Paley's natural theology with the eyes of faith 'led him to understand landscape and the meticulous organisation of its design as direct proof of God's existence … Accuracy became a moral obligation. The immediate effect of this spiritual revolution heightened the realism and consequently the intensity of his landscape drawings.'[9]

If there was any contradiction between aestheticism and serious religion it may have had more to do with the underhand practices sometimes associated with art dealing than with any theological considerations. And it was for this reason that the relationship between Allies and Linnell became notorious. The two men first became acquainted when Thomas and Caroline were in Southampton for the birth of their first child, a son named George after uncles on both sides, who was baptised at All Saints' Church in June 1819.[10] Unhappily the little boy failed to thrive and died within a few weeks. His grieving parents lingered in the town, with Allies spending time in the company of the engraver D. C. Read, an old friend, who in the autumn introduced him to John Linnell, who had come to paint in the area. Some years later Linnell recalled the encounter:

> During my stay in Southampton Mr. Allies, a friend of Read and who was very fond of the arts, wished me to paint a life size portrait of Mrs. Allies, but as he said he was not rich he would pay me partly in money and give me a picture from his collection, for he had some genuine pictures, and I was glad to accept the offer. To obtain one picture by Poussin,[11] I painted a copy of it besides my portrait, I got one more by Everdingen[12] both of which are still in my possession.[13]

As well as the oil painting of Caroline, Linnell also made a sketch of Thomas. When A. T. Story wrote his four-volume biography of the painter in 1892, both of the pictures he obtained from Allies, works of major importance, were still in the possession of the Linnell family. In retrospect the bargain seems unequal; yet Allies cannot be dismissed as simply naïve; some indication of his shrewdness is apparent from his correspondence with Linnell, now returned to London:

> Knowing your partiality for good apples I have sent you a few of which I beg your acceptance. I am much obliged by the trouble you have taken in endeavouring to obtain a cartoon to complete my set, but the price you mention is more than I should chose to give. I must therefore decline the offer unless the person possessed of it would consent to take three guineas, and also provided you think it a very fine impression, in which case you will have the goodness to enclose it with my pictures and I will settle with you for it when we have the pleasure of meeting, which I hope will be in the Spring. Your picture has been much approved and admired by those who have seen it. Mrs. Allies unites in compliments to Mrs. Linnell and yourself.[14]

On 16 November Allies wrote again: 'The pictures arrived safe and in good condition and fully assured my expectation except a little dullness and roughness in one part of the Gainsborough which I suppose must have been caused by the varnish being chilled'.[15] At this stage Allies was apparently quite happy with their arrangement and told Linnell:

The Making of a Controversialist

'Captain Rainier called upon me last week and admired your pictures exceedingly, he took your copy for the original picture and thought the painting displayed not only fine painting but good taste.'[16] It might be that in 1819 Allies was short of money yet anxious to have such an eminent artist paint his wife's portrait. Whatever his reason for agreeing to the proposal, he appears eventually to have regretted it, and after making his feelings known to Read, he unsuccessfully requested Linnell to return his pictures in exchange for cash. The latter's reputation was damaged by the incident. Read, seeking to ingratiate himself with John Constable—a notorious gossip—unwisely told him about the bargain. In 1821 Linnell failed in his attempt to become an associate of the Royal Academy, and two years later learnt that this was probably because Constable told some academicians just before the election 'that Linnell had cheated D. C. Read and Mr. Allies during his visit to Southampton in 1819.'[17] Linnell's modern biographer, a descendant of the artist, attributed Constable's actions to his fear of a potential rival for election to the Academy,[18] adding, as regards Allies, that 'he seems to come out of the affair as a rather slippery character ... Mr. Allies was probably the cause of much of the trouble ... he wanted a portrait of his wife but did not want to pay for it ... though later perhaps, he wanted to change his mind and pay cash, but by that time it was too late.'[19]

In 1823 Linnell, wishing to repair any damage to his reputation, asked Read to 'state that you know nothing to my dishonour in my dealings with the Revd Thos Allies.' Read was unable to reassure him, averring that Allies 'often said to me—that he disliked your conduct very much, for he wished to pay you in money for the portrait of Mrs A. and was very angry with me for taking your part ... and that he should never call upon you or take the least notice of you.'[20] Linnell then approached the offended party directly; in April Allies replied in conciliatory fashion:

> I have no hesitation to state that in your transactions with me at Southampton there was nothing which involved your character as an Artist or a Gentleman; I always thought, and still think that there is considerable merit in your pictures and which is the opinion of many of my friends who are much better judges than myself ...

> It is to be regretted that after a lapse of nearly four years, any altercation should arise between friends respecting transactions with a stranger, which were unimportant in their nature; exchanges of pictures are seldom satisfactory, especially when an artist values his own productions, and there certainly were some trivial circumstances attending ours which has made me somewhat dissatisfied, and I have a recollection of having expressed myself to this effect with Mr Read.[21]

Linnell explained his case to Constable and asked him to sign a document stating that he had 'completely confuted Mr Read's assertions respecting the transactions between Revd Thos Allies & myself by two letters to me from that gentleman soon after, altogether satisfactorily proving the falsehood of representations made by Mr. Read to Mr. Constable concerning my conduct at Southampton in September 1819.'[22] Constable would not sign but agreed—somewhat vaguely—to take steps to correct any damage done to Linnell's reputation. Thus the Reverend Thomas Allies's brief incursion into the annals of art history. What happened to his art collection is not known, nor is the fate of the 'life-size' portrait of Mrs Allies.[23] However, the relative financial security of his widow might have been linked to the sale of these valuable paintings.[24]

The young scholar

Born into a home that combined high art, romanticism and Evangelical religion, Thomas William grew up a rather solitary child. He was almost five when his first sister, Mary Anne, was born, followed three years later by Caroline, a lifelong invalid. Their mother presided over the home with firmness and loving affection. Her husband was not a forceful personality but she certainly was and not loath to express her views, especially on matters of religion, and would undoubtedly have censured the apostasy of Samuel Fripp in 1822. 'With her it was a proof of affection to disagree.'[25] As the only son in a household of adult debate, discussion and sometimes lively disagreement, Thomas William grew up introspective, opinionated, and with a high view of his own intellect and destiny in the world. He loved books and was a ready scholar able to thrive even in the somewhat uncongenial atmosphere of Bristol Grammar School, where he began to absorb a classical education from its notorious headmaster, John Joseph Goodenough.

He was one of fifty or so paying scholars in a school established to provide free education 'to all the sons of freemen within a mile of the liberties of Bristol'. The institution was visited by the Charity Commissioners in 1821, when there were only four or five free scholars on the foundation. Largely for pecuniary reasons the headmaster was anxious to limit their numbers. Moreover, free education had its limits, Goodenough informed those who wished to educate their children for trade that he considered himself 'bound only to teach the learned languages', making it clear that additional instruction in 'useful subjects' would be charged for: 'It was stated by Dr Goodenough that when a shop-keeper applies to have his son received on the foundation, the classical nature of the school is made known to him, that he may judge whether it be consistent with his object to send his child'.[26] Very few citizens elected to pay the additional sixteen guineas that the doctor required to put the foundation-boys on a footing with his private pupils as to all branches of education. The school's historian describes Goodenough's outlook as the 'quintessence of snobbery'.[27] John Wade, the author of *An Account of Public Charities*, published in 1828, was inclined to suspect collusion:

> There is something of a tragi-comic character in the history and management of this foundation ... we cannot imagine with what kind of faces the members of the Corporation, and more especially Dr. Goodenough can daily meet the citizens of Bristol ... the youth on the foundation now amount to the prodigious number of FIVE, for whose ample accommodation there is a school-room *one hundred feet* long and a dormitory of equal dimensions, and for the 'better education and bringing up' of this immense multitude of children, there are 590 acres of arable, meadow, pasture, and wood land besides messuages.

The writer asserts that this scandalous misuse of the endowment began when the son-in-law of an alderman was appointed master. 'Doubtless the *Magnates* of the city do not think *sixteen guineas* too much for the education of their children by a D.D.'[28]

Thomas Allies, still a curate, took his place among the subscribers to Samuel Seyer's *Memoirs Historical and Topographical of Bristol*, published in 1821, numbering him among the city's leading citizens, well able to meet Goodenough's terms. His son took instinctively to Latin and was soon noted as precociously talented. In September 1825 the young Thomas was feted for delivering a prize essay before the mayor and corporation of Bristol. The prize had been established by the Whig politician, Sir John Cox Hippisley, who had recently died at his seat of Ston Easton in Somerset, not far from the birthplace of Allies's mother.[29] Hippisley had himself been a pupil at Bristol Grammar School and lamented the decay into which the school had fallen under Goodenough's predecessor. At a dinner in the city in April 1802, in order to encourage a revival of the school, he declared his intention of establishing an annual prize of a gold medal to be given to the boy producing the best composition on a given subject, but it was only to be awarded when sufficient competition might be expected.[30] Up to the arrival of the new headmaster in 1812, no award had been made and it was hoped that standards would rise enabling the prize to be awarded. But if any revival occurred it was short lived and after Allies's success the prize lapsed and the Grammar School sunk into progressive decline. By 1820 Goodenough had secured a comfortable living in Buckinghamshire; his interest in the school slowly declined and he ceased taking new private pupils. The school's plight elicited no response from the unreformed Corporation and by 1829 there were no pupils remaining.

Thomas quit the school in 1826 and in April the following year was enrolled as an oppidan of Eton College in the house of the Reverend Edward Coleridge. His path to England's premier school was eased because his father had recently been presented to the living of Wormington in Gloucestershire. This was a valuable prize and came to him rather fortuitously as the fruit of a network of Bristol contacts and friendships linking this inoffensive cleric with the profits of slavery. Samuel Gist was a Bristol adventurer who in the middle years of the eighteenth century managed a tobacco estate in Virginia. When its owner died Gist married his widow and as a result came into immense wealth in land and slaves. With the outbreak of the Revolutionary War he returned to England and purchased estates including that at Wormington. He died in 1815 leaving a complicated legacy. In the United States his will provided for the freeing and re-settlement of some 300 slaves. As regards his English possessions he named an heir who could not be traced and there was a wait of several years to see whether a claimant would come forward. No one did and after wearisome proceedings in Chancery, a cousin, Josiah Sellick of Bristol, was named as beneficiary and assumed the name of Gist. He was the business associate of George Hilhouse, who had been appointed administrator of the Gist estates until the inheritance was settled. In 1826 the vacancy of the living of Wormington gave the new patron opportunity of expressing his gratitude by offering the rectory to Hilhouse's brother-in-law. Thus did the Allies family come to share in the taint of slavery. In Bristol this was hard to avoid. For example, when Walter Trevelyan, rector of Henbury (Allies had been his curate), died in 1830 he left to his two sons 'several estates in the island of Grenada with negroes, rights and appurtenances'.[31] And in the graveyard of his church of St Mary the Virgin can still be seen the tomb of Scipio Africanus, who died in 1720 aged eighteen, one of the few memorials to a slave living in England.[32]

The Reverend Thomas Allies spent the remainder of his life as rector of Wormington, but he was not in good health and was frequently away from the parish at his house in Bristol. He died at Malvern in 1838 at the age of 53, living just long enough to see his son ordained as a deacon in the Church of England: a somewhat surprising outcome, perhaps the answer to his father's anxious prayers. For on arrival at Eton, Thomas William Allies had in mind a very different future for himself. He wanted to be a great poet. An only son, growing up in an artistic home, much smaller than other boys of the same age, rather self-conscious and isolated, he lived very much in his own world of books. He was sure that Eton would be the making of him and that the deep study of the classics could become the wellspring of his muse. As he later explained, his years at Eton had been dominated by one thing alone—'a desire for excellence':

> Early study and very deep enthusiasm have fixed this desire on one particular point of intellect—Poesy... I should never have embraced the study of Greek and Latin with such ardour had I not with a pardonable infatuation arising from the perversion of education in England, believed that the springs of inspiration rose in the mountains of Hellas.[33]

He was a diligent and a brilliant scholar, and his talent was soon recognised. Notwithstanding that to his detractors the Master of Bristol Grammar School stood as representative of a dying breed of indolent eighteenth-century clerics, Goodenough the classicist had done his work well. By contrast his successor as Allies's mentor, Edward Coleridge, the poet's nephew, was very much the prototype of the earnest Victorian. Appointed to Eton in 1823 he strove, in the face of opposition, to introduce a more overtly religious tone into college life and became the first assistant master to have family prayers, an innovation that was at first reprobated by the headmaster, the redoubtable Keate.[34] However, his position received a significant boost when in August 1826 he married the headmaster's daughter. Their home became a model of domestic piety. His reforming efforts were considerably encouraged by the establishment by the 4th Duke of Newcastle of a scholarship, which proved to be a landmark on the road to a more religious ambience in the school.

> His Grace's main wish and intention in endowing these Scholarships was to encourage religious learning, a competent knowledge of which is a necessary preliminary qualification. This branch of the examination consequently precedes all others, and any candidate failing in it is at once disqualified.[35]

The need to prepare the upper scholars for this annual challenge enabled Coleridge and two of his colleagues 'to substitute a lesson in the Greek Testament for a repetition of Virgil or Juvenal on Sunday mornings.'[36] In his house the scholars found security, pious influences and—for those willing to receive it—academic stimulation. Under this tutelage

Allies became in 1829 the first winner of the Newcastle Scholarship; Coleridge's pedagogical reputation was thereby secured and he went on to produce a succession of Newcastle Scholars.[37] The prize was worth £250, a considerable sum for a young man.[38]

Arthur Henry Hallam, who left Eton in July 1827, soon after Allies arrived, provides testimony to the latter's reputation for scholastic excellence. In March 1829 he wrote to his father from Trinity College, Cambridge, referring to the contenders for the Newcastle:

> I understand the Eton scholarship is soon coming on, and that Brown is likely to succeed. However, when my tutor was there, he told me Allies & Herbert were the most promising candidates, the former being extraordinarily clever, and the latter having beaten 40 candidates for a Balliol Scholarship at Oxford.[39]

In 1829 Richard Lewis Brown was the college's senior scholar and thus had received a monetary benefit from the already archaic *montem* ceremony of that year.[40] He did not win the Newcastle; Henry Herbert was ranked second to Allies and was awarded a gold medal valued at six guineas.

Coleridge was a connoisseur. When the German art historian, Gustav Waagen visited the college he described the walls of the master's house as 'richly adorned' with 'water-colour drawings by the first masters of the modern English school', adding, 'Mr Coleridge is one of Turner's warmest votaries, and possesses drawings by him which fully justify his admiration'.[41] Coleridge regularly commissioned the eminent portraitist Mary Carpenter to produce small oil panels of his scholars that he bequeathed to the families of the sitters.[42] One such study forms the frontispiece to Mary Allies's biography of her father. Among Allies's contemporaries in Coleridge's house was one who would eventually join him in the Church of Rome, the artist and Wiltshire magistrate, Richard Hungerford Pollen. But it was the latter's brother, John Hungerford Pollen, who arrived at the house in November 1832, and another Etonian, John Wynne, who were to be numbered among Allies's closest friends and fellow-travellers on the same spiritual pilgrimage.[43]

The young romantic

In June 1828, the fifteen-year-old Allies was elected scholar of Wadham College, Oxford, and according to the college registers had the unique honour in not first being a Commoner.[44] He was admitted in November before sitting for the Newcastle. Under the wardenship of William Tournay (1806–31) the college had acquired a reputation for scholarship, and between 1828 and 1834 provided three winners each of the Newdigate English Prize and Dean Ireland's scholarship in the classics. Allies, still a schoolboy, won neither, but his academic prowess did secure him college prizes. He was from 1830 to 1833 Hody Exhibitioner in Greek (value £15) and in 1832 was selected as Goodridge Exhibitioner (value £9). Yet despite this success, perhaps in measure because of it, at Wadham Thomas became disillusioned, concluding that the Classics were irrelevant to his long cherished desire for literary fame. These studies became increasingly wearisome to him; swept along by the Romantic revival he no longer believed that 'the springs of inspiration rose in the mountains of Hellas'.

> One book undeceived me; I remember its effect on me, when just seventeen, in April 1830—Moore's *Byron* disenchanted me: after that I loathed Oxford and its studies more and more; melancholy, lowness of spirits, dissatisfaction, all springing from the notion that I was forced to exertions which would work the very opposite effect on me to that for which I panted, made me so continually wretched that I am satisfied I could not have endured that life much longer.[45]

Among his Oxford contemporaries he was particularly drawn to a fellow collegian, a Commoner, Thomas Harding Newman, who was admitted to Wadham in May 1829. He came from a wealthy family of Nelmes in Essex, whose wealth was accumulated, at least in part, from the proceeds of slavery. In 1783, this young man's grandfather, Richard Harding, had taken the name of Newman on inheriting property from his mother's family. For his descendants a new name had the advantage of disassociating them from the Hardings, who had owned Jamaican plantations for several generations. However, the second marriage of Thomas Newman's father to Elizabeth Hall had united him to another substantial slave-holding family and in 1831 he inherited a one-third share in Blue Hole estate in Hanover, Jamaica, from his aunt Eliza Mary Tharp.[46] This was the time when the abolitionish campaign was reaching its climax, and knowing that his own father had indirectly benefited from it, Allies must surely have discussed with his college friend the moral considerations involved. If Newman had any sensitivity on the matter it did not inhibit him from pursuing, as late as 1863, a case in Chancery for an increased share of the compensation of £2272 given to Mrs Tharp's estate on the emancipation of its slaves in 1833.

As young men both Allies and Newman regarded themselves as gifted with artistic sensibility and indeed the latter could claim some connexion to the literary world through his step-mother. Born in 1789, Elizabeth Hall lost her mother when still a child and was cared for by various relatives and friends, some of whom were intimate with members of Jane Austen's extended family. It is likely that Elizabeth stayed at the home of Colonel Thomas Austen, the author's cousin, and probably met Jane herself, becoming a lifelong admirer of the novelist and her works. On her marriage to Harding Newman in December 1817 Colonel Austen presented her with an oil painting which he claimed was a portrait of Jane, and which later come into the possession of the Allies's college friend. Whether it is a genuine likeness of the novelist or a portrait of another young lady is still a matter of enormous controversy, Thomas Harding Newman himself was convinced of its authenticity.[47]

Newman was awarded a Goodridge Exhibition and in July 1832 elected a demy of Magdalen College.[48] Such early promise proved deceptive; he remained in Oxford, became a doctor of divinity and lived a gentle and undemanding life as a fellow of Magdalen: a noted eccentric, the doyen of a rather undistinguished company 'born to eat their founder's venison and drink his wine.'[49] Theologically, this Newman and Allies trod very different paths; only nominally was he ever confused with his more famous contemporary of Oriel. Indeed, he actively opposed Tractarianism and in 1847 joined with A. C. Tait,

A. P. Stanley and many others in protesting against this party's 'throwing obstacles in the way of the elevation of the present Regius Professor of Divinity at Oxford to the Bishopric of Hereford', stigmatising this as 'unjust to Dr. Hampden, disrespectful to her Majesty, and likely to prove highly prejudicial to the best interests of the church.'[50]

All this was in the future, as young men neither Allies nor Newman were much interested in religion. With the High Church revival still embryonic the focus of religious interest in the university was the secession of Anglican Evangelicals into dissent. Gladstone, a student of Christ Church, took a particular interest in these things, although when in May 1830 he took wine with Allies—they had briefly been contemporaries at Eton—it is unlikely that the latter was much interested in discussing Mr Bulteel's recent sermon.[51] The puritan curate of St Ebbe's had launched a furious attack on the Oxford establishment, eliciting some sympathy from the future prime minister. Allies's absorbing interest was rather the poetic and artistic sensibility. A taste fully shared by Harding Newman, who according to his brief but widely re-published obituary was a 'man of very high attainments in art and a very popular member of the Athenaeum Club.'[52] On his death in 1882, his extensive collection of etchings and engravings including many by Girton and Turner was auctioned at Christie's. The young Thomas William Allies did not collect paintings but he believed in poetry and idolised Byron and in August 1831 undertook a solitary pilgrimage to Hucknall in Nottinghamshire to kneel before the poet's tomb. His wistful inscription in the Visitors' Book stands as testimony to his devotion.[53]

Despite a growing distaste for classical studies Allies embraced the intellectual life of the university and like many Etonians played an active part in the Oxford Union, then entering in its golden age, and along with future friends like W. G. Ward and Charles Marriott contributed to its debates. In later years he claimed that as a young man he was a radical and freethinker; a claim substantially disproved by the fact that on 27 January 1831 he moved in the Union the following resolution: 'That it behoves all lovers of their country to unite against the Spirit of Democracy which is tending to destroy the Constitution in Church and State'. He was supported by Marriott and opposed by A. C. Tait.

Acland, in the chair, proposed a compromise amendment: 'that evil principles are gaining ground which can only be resisted by the adequate discharge of private duties', which was voted on and carried by a small majority.[54] The following year, however, Allies was recorded as speaking against the motion 'that the revolt of the American colonies was not justifiable'. Despite these diversions and his disenchantment with the classics, in 1832 he crowned his academic career by gaining a first in Literae Humaniores, returning to college in October to continue his studies in order to obtain a fellowship.

Anxious to follow his poetic star he thought of this as wasted time, merely toiling 'at a course of studies I detest'.[55] He and two other scholars (both much older than him) were elected probationary fellows in July 1833. He, however, redeemed the time by serving on the Union Committee, and for the Lent term 1833 was appointed its librarian. It was a time of political turbulence following the struggles of the Whig Administration to enact parliamentary reform, and divisions in society were mirrored in the Union. One sign of this was the election of Edward Massie as its president at the end of 1833, which was significant because he was from Wadham not a college much associated with the Union; not from a major public school he was branded a 'liberal and a reformer'.[56] His opponents believed—correctly—that he would seek to reorganise the committee in his own political image and in this was being assisted by another Wadham student, Thomas Brancker. In protest his conservative opponents, formed an alternative debating society: the 'Ramblers'. Besides Ward and Marriott, other members included Roundell Palmer and Mark Pattison; its president was Edwardes Lyall, who became a distinguished judge, and Allies was its secretary. A critic remarked that 'little could be expected of a club of which the president was Lie-all and the secretary All-lies'.[57] From his involvement with the Union Allies made lifelong friends, but perhaps also some enemies and his relationships with the other fellows of Wadham came to be marked by mutual animosity. Prominent among his political adversaries in the Union was Robert Lowe of University College, whose political career was to impact significantly on the interests of Catholic education, for which Allies became a chief spokesman when in 1853 he was appointed secretary of the Catholic Poor-School Committee.

Still not twenty-one, by 1833 Allies knew that his calling was not to academia nor to politics, but to poetry. He and Harding Newman were convinced that their artistic sensibilities would only flourish in the atmosphere of European romanticism, and they were particularly drawn to Italy. After graduating Allies announced that the time had come for him to 'embrace a life of action', that only travel would help him attain 'the power of interpreting man and nature for myself without the medium of books' because 'continued study vitiates the mirror of our vision'.[58] Appropriately for the fledgling poet the final spur for him to quit the security of Oxford was an emotional crisis. He recalled the exact date: on the 18 June 1833 his 'feelings received a real shock'. Unfortunately, he is less explicit on the circumstances, but for a young man of an ardent and romantic nature it was surely disappointment in love. 'I should never have had the resolution to become a traveller, but for the strong reaction and desire of independence of heart produced on me by S. C.'s perfidy and concealment'. Introspective and deeply self-conscious Allies found it hard to cope with the pain of rejection: 'I despair *almost* (and yet I should be wrong if I said *entirely*) of inspiring such an affection, as I know I could feel, full, unwearied, eternal, and which alone I would accept'. He was unsure whether he could ever trust the protestations of any future sweetheart: 'I am not quite decided what she is but should look twice now before I trusted her'. All of these musings come from a long review of his life that Allies wrote, far from home, on his twenty-first birthday, 12 February 1834.[59]

Before leaving for the Continent he returned to Oxford for the Michaelmas term, which began on 10 October, soon becoming one of the disaffected 'Ramblers' who expressed their distaste for the new president, Massie, and his liberal acolytes, by boycotting the official debates in Wyatts's rooms. Allies and Newman, however, had probably already left the country when at an overflowing meeting Massie tried and failed to secure the expulsion of the dissidents.[60] Their date of departure is not recorded but it may be assumed they left not long after the end of term on 17 December.

They were in Paris for Christmas, and it seems they stayed in France, travelling to Normandy, before crossing to Jersey, and returning home in the early summer of 1834, shortly before Thomas's election as a full

The Making of a Controversialist

fellow of Wadham College. In Paris he wrote several poems, but back in Oxford he was unsettled and unsure about the future; he wondered whether a sojourn in Italy would serve to prove his gift. He had fallen out of love with Byronism and in his twenty-first birthday reflections claimed to have shaken off its evil influence: 'Byron almost made me both misanthrope and mysatheist; but the tide has now turned entirely the other way. I believe fully in my God.' It was Ash Wednesday, perhaps explaining why his thoughts turned to his own mortality:

> One of the deceits man seems determined to impose forever on himself is, to consider death an evil, something to be fled from and never welcomed. It is a deceit in which I will not participate. Not in a presumptuous spirit, but with the deepest hope and faith, I bless ten times more the day of my death than that of my birth.

He may have been disillusioned with Byron but was still consumed with artistic ambition. Indeed a sense that he could never achieve in life all that his soul longed for was to his mind a pointer towards the reality of personal immortality:

> So far do my wishes outstrip my power of enjoyment, so far does this capacity exceed the means of supplying it, that I feel with the whole truth of my being that earth cannot be intended to be a permanent home... [W]ho can fly the void of his own soul? Who would fly it, for it proves our immortality?

An innate religious nature was reasserting itself, but Christian humility eluded him; he could not dispel the belief that he had it in him to become a great poet.

> Some wise man has said that every one has a secret belief of something extraordinary in his destiny; I, at least, acknowledge the innocent vanity. I was long before I discovered its existence; and though I am often in the state Sydenham who describes of poor Auriol, when, introduced

into the most talented society begins to suspect in himself a want of the adored genius which had been the dream of his life;[61] yet, were this lurking hope taken away, I am sure I should sink into utter listlessness.

Of one thing he was sure; he did not wish to enter a profession, all of which were 'leagued in array against the cultivation of the mind'. 'The law eats up the time and, worse still corrodes the heart; the scalpel cuts off very summarily the finer perceptions of our nature; the lowly though invaluable labours of the Church do not permit the neophyte to indulge even a wish for his own intellectual promotion, and besides cut off the means of attaining it from the solitary life they impose'. He wondered if he could 'evade all these till my thirtieth year'; though perhaps not even then would he really 'know himself'. These yearnings for personal fulfilment have a rather contemporary tone, but his closing thought belongs to an age of unquestioning faith:

> Ah! whatever comes, here on the threshold of manhood, I beseech of Him, who giveth upbraiding not, that His light in my heart become not dim, and His love be unforgot! That I may hallow whatever and however little the gifts He has given by the end I seek for: oh, not my own glory, but I must have the power to cast away self![62]

Allies was now clear that to pursue his gift he must first 'purify his vision' from the contamination of classical scholarship, an objective requiring an openness to new experiences, to different cultures and languages. It seems, however, that his parents wished him to settle to a profession, so that when he did leave again for the Continent, accompanied by Harding Newman, it was in defiance of their wishes. Information on this period of his life is scanty, one clue is an entry in his diary for 11 July 1839: 'Determined to keep this day as day of penitence, in remembrance that five years ago I began a course of deliberate disobedience'. And on 26 July: 'Five years ago (how like a dream does it seem!) I left England a second time—How painful and sad to me is this portion of my life! How can I be sure that I have really repented of it'.

Their expedition was in the tradition of the Grand Tour, a not uncommon rite of passage for young men of means. The usual route through France and Switzerland and into Italy remained challenging, not least in crossing the Alps, and it was to be a decade at least before the coming the steam train alleviated the rigours of the journey. However, among Allies's circle of friends and connections at Bristol, Eton and Oxford, there was a tradition of European travel, and he would have been provided with background information and letters of introduction to Anglophile families known to welcome visitors. For example, Edward Willes of Newbold Comyn near Warwick, who was well acquainted with Thomas's father, had spent many years on the Continent in the 1820s, and had been in Rome the previous year.

Allies left no account of his youthful travels. One source of information is a collection of his poems that he had privately printed in 1837; in many cases the date and place of composition is given. From this it seems that the travellers journeyed to Italy and spent much of 1835 in Rome. Where they lived or how they spent their days cannot now be discovered; presumably the letters of introduction they carried led them to be welcomed into the higher ranks of Italian society—although perhaps not the highest? The first Italian poem, dated 11 May 1835, is entitled 'On seeing the Prince Borghese and the Lady Gwendoline Talbot, render thanks at St. Peter's on the morning of their marriage'. It is unlikely that either he or Newman were among the wedding guests. Allies may have found a home as a tutor, possibly with an Anglophile Italian family called Gaggiotti. In 1839, and now an Anglican clergyman living in London, he became a trustee in the marriage settlement between Gustavo Gaggiotti and Mary Barham the wealthy niece of the Earl of Thanet. Gaggiotti's address was given as 'the Palazza Nuovo Borghese'. His wife was also related to the Earl of Clarendon—Foreign Secretary under successive Whig administrations in the 1850s—who appointed Gaggiotti as British Vice-Consul in Ancona.[63]

Towards the end of 1835, Thomas travelled south, staying in Sicily, and visiting the ruins at Tauromina and Syracuse, where at the fountain of Arethusa he was accosted by washerwomen demanding a *grano* (halfpenny). Thereafter he stayed at Naples and Sorrento, and probably on Capri, before returning to Rome and later Florence. In August 1836 he was again in Naples. In view of his subsequent life the fact that he casts a veil over this period is unsurprising, although there are hints of romantic entanglements and involvement with Italian radicals: the Carbonari were particularly associated with Naples, although by the later 1830s they were declining as an active political force. After his conversion he deplored these years of self-imposed exile, writing in his diary on 10 July 1839, 'Looking at the anniversary of this day three years back I am shocked at the state of my life my journal betrays—how can I be sufficiently thankful for having been awakened from it'. Later, when he came to write *A Life's Decision*, the account of his journey to Roman Catholicism, his judgment on this period is entirely negative: 'I came back from several years travelling, quite unsettled, perfectly irreligious, desirous of distinction, but with self for my sole idol'.[64] He ceased attending any church and the poetry from 1836 is uncompromisingly anticlerical. Thus, reflecting on St Peter's and the Vatican, he writes of a monument

> of slavery past and misbestow'd obedience—
> Throne of the false Chief-Priest, Thought's sternest Despot
> Who guards the key of knowledge as the fruit
> Erst of the dragon-watched Hesperides.

In 'Farewell to Rome', he castigates the 'Man of hypocrisy and sin' for seeking 'to forge for earth that impious chain binding and crushing heart and brain'. Although there are no overtly political statements, his sympathies can be inferred. For example, at Syracuse, standing 'within the caverns of despair', he reflected on

> The last scorn'd province of a realm enslav'd
> Cloister, and convent grated from the day
> Attest the slumb'ring city's last decay,
> This of blind idleness the favorite sty,
> That, refuge of the nobles' poverty;
> Mothworms alike that feed on humble toil,
> The brand of state's and church's double spoil.
> Two plagues together still have rag'd and cess'd
> The despot monarch, and more despot priest.

The Making of a Controversialist

Allies labelled his time in France and Italy 'the apostasy'.[65] Yet, in retrospect it was to prove most valuable, making him one of the few English Church historians who could engage with the untranslated works of European scholars and communicate with them in their own tongues. As a Catholic writer his proficiency in Italian would be particularly valuable.

The circumstances that brought his *Wanderjahre* to an end remain mysterious. He recalled Tuesday 4 October 1836 as a day of crisis, 'the most terrible in my existence', and of being 'preserved throughout those frightful scenes, and brought out after much trial into open ground'.[66] As a young man who could view quite commonplace circumstances as episodes in a personal drama it is likely that the reality was less lurid than he remembered, but he nevertheless considered it no longer safe to remain in Naples, where it seems he was. By the end of November he was in Paris and probably with his family for Christmas. The sense of crisis that marked his return to England was compounded by a bad conscience, the troubling knowledge that his father was in declining health and did not have long to live. And at a deeper level, an as yet inchoate sense that it would take more than the inspiration of the South to turn him into a great poet.

A conversion of the heart

The young poet arrived back in England listless and unsure about the future. His dreams of finding fame had not been realised. Perhaps they never would? Yet he still harboured ambition and was soon beginning to wonder whether he should now go north; perhaps travelling in the German lands would fire his creativity? But first there were domestic duties to be attended to, especially the need to spend time with his mother and ailing father at Malvern. Visiting Cheltenham, he again met Harding Newman, who had returned to England before him, who was there with his family.[67] Cheltenham's churchmanship was dominated by the ministry of Francis Close, a leading Evangelical, the rector of St Mary's; Allies's stepmother would have been a strong supporter, encouraging Thomas to join his large congregation.

In the new year Allies returned to Oxford, remaining there as a fellow of Wadham College. On 4 February 1837, just a few days before his twenty-fourth birthday, he was awarded his MA and was now of age to minister in the Church of England, with his parents perhaps suggesting that he should become one of Close's curates.[68] But now he had no thought of this, nor any apparent interest in religion: 'At Oxford and in my wander-years it was the one subject for which, among moral and intellectual subjects, I not only had no taste, but the most marked repugnance.'[69] His dreams of poetic greatness were not extinguished and he had a number of poems he thought worthy of publication. This was not to be, although later that year some were privately printed without an author's name, as if to mark the end of one life and the beginning of another. Because his life was now to be turned upside-down. Not only did he did not go to Germany but before the year was out he had been ordained to the ministry of the Church of England. Allies was to become not a celebrated romantic poet but rather one of the nineteenth century's most powerful advocates of dogmatic Christianity.

It might have been far different. He might have gone to Germany, and, lacking the artistic genius to achieve his consuming desire, returned to spend the rest of his days in scholarly detachment, perhaps with a wife and a good Living. His bachelor friend T. H Newman, who experienced no religious awakening, nevertheless took orders and became notorious among the idle dons of Magdalen: well fed, a little cynical, travelling between Oxford and his London club, filling his hours with connoisseurship and literary criticism. But Allies was to walk a different path, for in the summer of 1837 he experienced a profound religious conversion in which he became by his own account 'a new moral being'. What actually happened, the precise circumstances of this tempest, are shrouded in mystery and Allies himself throws very little light on it: 'I had intended to go abroad again, to Germany. Instead of this I fell into a great sorrow, in consequence of which for some time I hovered between life and death, so keen was the stroke. In the meantime I was determined by this to take Anglican orders, and to give up a roving life.'[70]

What remains is a diary written when the events relating to his conversion crisis remained fresh in his mind and still rankled. On 16 June 1839 he wrote: 'I have not forgotten today as the second anniversary of my meeting C—how strangely was I led to that place—it seems this was to be the crisis of my life—I know and acknowledge the real view that I should take of that fiery trial, yet am I ever tempted to repine, to desire the fruits without the discipline'. The diary provides a clue as to C.'s identity by linking this name with another. On 31 May 1839 he wrote: 'The prevailing cause of my low spirits is certainly the conduct of C. R. S. and Willes—I never can get it off my mind'. He admitted to being 'constantly tempted to anger against Willes'.[71] Just a few days before he had written, 'At various times lately I have been grievously agitated by the thought of Willes's treachery—it seizes on me especially when I rise in the morning—it is quite beyond my power to banish the thought which impedes my prayers'.[72]

In October 1839 he accidentally encountered C. R. S. on a visit to Bristol and said 'she looked as pale as death', adding 'how very strange this coincidence and her and my sudden coming here are'.[73] Although not capable of final proof it is likely that, returning from Italy, Allies became romantically involved with, and humiliatingly rejected by, Clara Rosalie Stonhouse, the youngest child (one of seven daughters and five sons) of Timothy Stonhouse-Vigor, archdeacon of Gloucester. She was born in 1819 when her mother was in her mid-forties; her family and the Allies lived in close proximity at Clifton and moved in the same social circles. When Allies met her on returning from Italy she was eighteen years of age;[74] the drama of her involvement with him was played out at the home of her sister Emily, who lived at Goodrest Lodge, a gothicised country house in the village of Shinfield, near Reading.[75] Emily Stonhouse had moved here on her marriage to Edward Willes in December 1819. The Willes family estates were at Newbold Comyn near Warwick; after the death of his father in 1820 Edward had implemented plans for the development of this property and adjacent land at Leamington Priors, which by the end of the next decade were being transformed into the thriving Victorian resort town of Royal Leamington Spa. He and Allies's father had a shared interest in art, both considered themselves to be patrons, and were enthusiastic collectors meeting at galleries and auctions in the West of England. Clara's elder brother, Charles Stonhouse was a competent draughtsman, who achieved some success as a book engraver.[76] In 1826 Willes had arranged that he should become a pupil of the celebrated artist, Sir David Wilkie, who took him on a painting tour of Spain.[77]

Clara was a frequent visitor to her sister's house and Emily's involvement in caring for her younger siblings was presumably taken for granted. On his return from the Continent Allies divided his time between his parents' house and Oxford. From May 1837 he lived at Goodrest Lodge, where it is likely that he tutored Willes's son (also called Edward), who was due to go up to Eton. It was here that he suffered the terrible shock, precipitating the crisis that led to his conversion. Two years later, after hearing a sermon on the divine grace that led Onesimus to Rome, he mused on 'the Providence which conducted me to Goodrest'.[78] The precise events that affected him so deeply are not recorded and what follows can be only surmise, but it is likely that they had to do with a romantic entaglement with Clara. Some poems that seem to speak of her were among those he had printed. For example, 'As on thy radiant brow and eyes I gaze; The ashes I deem'd dead yet seem to burn'.[79] The poetic mood is not exultant; there is a sense of foreboding, illustrated by a poem dated 'Eton 13 July 1837', which he entitled 'On seeing a lady repeatedly smell some roses which were afterwards found to be artificial'.

> By me, too, all the rich heart's store
> For one fair rose was given;
> I deem'd its leaves unstirred before,
> Its fragrance full of heaven.
>
> But when in passion's erring hour
> With heart that vainly bled
> I sought to touch that worshipp'd flower,
> I found its leaves were dead.

When Clara's father died in 1831 it is likely that Edward Willes, her brother-in-law, assumed some responsibility for her, and this might explain the perceived 'treachery': his part in thwarting the dream that had now conquered Thomas's heart. Receiving news that his father's health had deteriorated he returned home, but on 25 July 1837 was again at Goodrest. Now came the crisis. It is likely that in a confrontation with Willes, Thomas was rebuffed and dismissed out of hand as an unsettled young man tainted with radicalism with no secure future; and, what was far worse, well-known as having uncles and cousins who were 'in trade'. Months later Willes would write to his son, by then a scholar at Eton, warning him to stay away from Allies and describing his conduct as 'unfriendly.'[80] Perhaps Willes—seeking to protect his charge—expressed himself too freely, belittling her suitor's supposed poetic abilities. Such candour, laced with animosity, would have been humiliating, bringing into focus what Allies had struggled to suppress: the fear that his dream of achieving literary greatness, even domestic happiness, was simple self-delusion.[81]

The background to this crisis was the long self-imposed exile that Allies believed his quest for poetic inspiration required. Absence from home had become increasingly painful, and when he returned, he may well have been physically weakened, certainly he was fragile emotionally. Years of living among strangers had taken their toll; Allies had a deep yearning for close companionship and the security and the sense of belonging that a wife and family would bring. These hopes, along with the vision of himself as a great poet, were suddenly crushed. Hitherto he had revelled in academic success and admiration; perceived betrayal and rejection were new experiences and almost impossible to cope with. Contemporary literature was replete with examples of heartbreak leading to serious illness even death. And Thomas was enough of a romantic to be deluged by a flood of grief and self-pity, a sorrow so great that in his recollection he 'hovered between life and death.'[82] Yet, something more was involved in these events than simply spurned affection or thwarted ambition. Allies had never been completely at ease in the guise of a free thinking romantic. The religious influences that shaped his childhood were too strong for him. But it took a deep wound to his self esteem and the physical illness it precipitated to seal his religious conversion.

Some clue as to Allies's state of heart as he emerged from illness can be glimpsed from the poetry he continued to write, especially the verses occasioned by the death in August 1837 of Henry Herbert, his competitor for the Newcastle, who had drowned whilst on a walking tour of Switzerland.[83] A tragedy that elicited an elegy written in Thomas's best sub-Byronic style.

> Perish'd so soon, in all thy pride of youth,
> With breast so full of love to God and man,
> And yearning after all immortal truth?
> Is this the limit of thine earthly span?
>
> I would rejoice that thou art callèd hence
> In youth, in Hope, in Faith, in Innocence.[84]

The poem speaks of the author's sense of failure and disappointment

> Oh! Joy that thou hast left the worst behind;
> The blight of heart, the fever of the mind.
> For bless'd are they who early find that goal,
> And need no suff'ring to make pure the soul.

A month before this poem was written, on 29 September, Allies had taken Communion 'for the first time since my apostasy'. This marked the beginning of his new life. But he was not quite ready to bury completely all traces of poetic ambition, and arranged to have a number of his poems printed by the Oxford publisher D. A. Tallboys. Only one other dates from after his conversion, it is called 'Holy Ground', and speaks of a location hallowed by its association with Clara:

> For *there*, upon a day more blest,
> Her heart to mine in answer beat
> Her form to mine in rapture prest,
> Had earth been thrown beneath my feet
> I had seen nought therein to prize
> By that dear face, those gentle eyes.
>
> And that one memory, dearest *now*
> By sorrow consecrated most—
> Whatever pain my heart may bow
> Though life's best hope were whelm'd and lost—
> Nor time nor change shall rend away
> While soul yet warms this frame of clay.

A copy of the book is preserved in Eton College Library, presented to Edward Coleridge, with a manuscript inscription dated 7 December 1837, which reads: 'These poems (which he would not venture to place in the hands of any but a Friend) are presented with feelings of Filial gratitude by his old Pupil'. The introduction to the collection is a lament for a 'dropped lyre'.

> Records of secret thought, of high desire,
> Of the heart's yearning, passionate, but vain,
> For something earth may image, not contain;
> I send you forth, faint sparks of a quenched fire,
> Which glimmers yet within me, but the lyre
> Drops from my hand: its chords are jarred and wrung;
> The soul of harmony is gone; unstrung
> Must be the chords that breath'd it. I aspire
> No more to heaven, no more enchantment seek
> From nature or the human soul.

Some of the poems, written before his sixteenth birthday, exhibit precocious ability,[85] and the poetic standard is high throughout. Yet this book was never published. Its printing marks an end. A new life had begun; the introductory poem concludes, 'Vow'd to stern duty since it lost the smile which made of this dark earth a heaven erewhile'.

'Stern duty' was the path to priesthood. Having secured the necessary approvals on 17 December Allies was ordained deacon at Christ Church Cathedral, Oxford: the rapidity of all this underlining the shallowness of his previous rationalism and anti-clerical posturing. Like St Paul he had been 'kicking against the goads'; the shock of rejection gave him permission to re-embrace the innate religiosity revealed in his twenty-first birthday musings. It was a new beginning and the start of a religious journey to be consummated by a second conversion thirteen years later: 'I begin this sketch in 1837, because my life then encountered a great change. God took me and cast me into a furnace seven times heated, and I came out a fresh creature ... I began to make him my object; whereas the world had occupied me before.'[86]

As he convalesced Allies undertook a profound reappraisal of the direction of his life. The long-held perception of himself as poetic genius or failing this, eminent man of letters, was quite shattered and it took him several years to recover from the blow. He said that he emerged from the crisis 'a new moral being... God, not self, became the motive of action'. The volume of poems remained as a warning:

> The bubble of the world had broken to me. An early, and till then cherished, desire seemed scattered away for ever before that tempest, and became a *vanitas vanitatum*. It has never resumed any power over me ... But more than this. The effect of that terrible blow was such that even the desire for intellectual distinction did not reappear with any force for several years. I recovered from it at length upon my marriage in 1840.[87]

Seeking direction

Newly ordained, Allies spent Christmas at Malvern with his family. There, asked to conduct a funeral he reluctantly acceded, it was his first 'ministerial act' in the Church of England.[88] As a neophyte himself he felt no call to preach to others; rather, seeking time to consider the direction his life should take, he returned to his fellowship, also visiting Eton, where he helped to tutor boys preparing for the Newcastle scholarship.[89] His election as Wadham's humanity lecturer might have been the beginning of a scholarly career as it had been for the celebrated Humphrey Hody, elected to this same post in 1685, but Allies was uncommitted to academia and arranged for a deputy to give the lectures. He remembered being alone in Oxford at this time, and although there is no record of his attending St Mary's, where John Henry Newman was awakening hearts, he must surely have been stirred by the new spirit that was abroad in the city. For the present, however, his theological studies were focused on gathering material to compete for the Denyer theological prize, which he won with an essay on a set theme: 'the influence of practical piety in promoting the temporal and eternal interests of mankind'. The field—restricted to those in deacon's orders having matriculated between eight and ten years before submission—could not have been large and two prizes of £30 were awarded each year. Nevertheless, success ushered him into distinguished company. The other winner in 1838 was the distinguished scholar Robert Scott, while a previous prizeman was Henry Wilberforce (1836), and Mark Pattison was to win twice (in 1841 and 1842). He read his essay in the Divinity School on 12 June and it was published immediately; Gladstone was reading it a fortnight later.[90] Allies perhaps wrote from personal experience when he concluded that only the severest trial can induce 'constant reference to that Being who alone can recompense sorrow, can satisfy desire, can fill up the aching void which dwells in the human soul.'[91] Yet he had experienced enough of the sensual life not to dismiss entirely its attractions:

> The voluptuary ... enjoys some pleasures from which the virtuous man must certainly refrain, but besides the expense of time and fortune, the obloquy and probable injury to health, which are the natural consequences of a life of dissipation, does not the habit in which he indulges deprive him of more gratification than it confers?[92]

Allies sincerely shared the opinions of his academic judges and was quite happy to make the case they would have expected to hear. Piety, which he defined as 'the conformation of the whole mind and will ... to the will of God', was a universal need and the only basis of a sound society; and as it was the only path to personal fulfilment the poor were especially privileged! 'The doom of so large a portion of our race to physical evils and manual labour is favourable rather than otherwise to the moral being. Every circumstance of difficulty, every link of dependence, every suffering and every want, tears from the mind the deeply-cherished notions of self-sufficiency.'[93] Willing acceptance life's trials as ordained by God 'for a season only and noted down by one who never forgets' and rewarded by him—also brings with it inestimable benefits for society as 'a preservative from anarchy'. Indeed, considering the threat now posed to ordered society by the steady advance of democratic principles, practical piety represented a vital safeguard:

And now that the reign of force, of authority, and of prescription is passing away from the minds of men; now that government must depend on the power of persuasion over the wills of the multitude, woe to that country where the multitude is an ignorant and irreligious mass, subject to no supreme internal guidance ... Were religion but the poor man's consolation it would still be of universal importance to the temporal happiness of the world since the world lives by the poor. But if the poor man becomes a *legislator*, how will they fare who are raised to an artificial superiority by the industry or force of their ancestors, or by intellectual or social pre-eminence? ... Religion is the only immovable principle of order ... There was wisdom in those ancient kings, who joined the priestly to the royal office. Where extremes of wealth and poverty are seen side by side, and all that can tempt rapacity is in the very grasp of hunger and ignorance ... if such a country has any hope of peace, good order and prosperity ... it must be in the far wider dissemination of the religious principle accompanied by a far deeper operation of the divine influence, than the world has ever yet witnessed.[94]

This was not deep theology, nor was it expected to be; religion as social control was what Oxford expected to hear. But Allies as a sincere believer was sure that 'the attainment of piety ... is not one object with many others of our earthly studies, but it is the single end which we are to pursue ... The only right employment of time is to gain eternity.'[95] Having so recently experienced rejection and humiliation he could speak with authority. 'If the goodliest fruits of earth turn to ashes on our lips, shall we therefore mourn as those who have no hope; or shall we acknowledge that our abiding place is not here; and that we look for better things to come?'[96] His vision of piety was coherent but perhaps not attractive. Later as a country clergyman he was never able to communicate the warmth of the Christian message: of a community bound together by the deep bond of shared beliefs. From the pulpit and in person he presented religion as a rigid code, a cold morality to be enforced by fear of the eternal consequences of disobedience and error. In England at least, it was becoming an untenable position: authoritatively given religious standards were no longer sufficient to underpin the existing order of society, individualism and the popularisation of the scientific viewpoint formed a powerful corrosive. Religion was being privatised and the role now ascribed to the state was to protect liberty of conscience. The remainder of Allies's long life can be seen as his struggle to secure firm ground from which the objectivity, relevance and importance of practical piety could be proclaimed.

At the centre

A week or so before delivering his thoughts on piety Allies had moved to London, taking rooms in Duke Street, off Portland Place. He wanted a breathing space, time to deepen his theological awareness and to seek illumination as to his future direction. He was also anxious to supplement his income and through the good offices of his friend Edward Coleridge at Eton, he recruited pupils. This offered benefits besides the financial, giving a structure to his days and potentially providing an entrée into influential society. Coleridge's help was invaluable because parents with sons destined for Eton often ask him to recommend a suitable tutor to prepare them. He bore an influential name, and as the younger brother of Sir John Taylor Coleridge, a judge of the Queen's Bench, was on social terms with senior members of the judiciary, some of whose sons were his scholars at Eton. He and his brother were at the centre of High Church Anglicanism and were strong supporters of the Oxford Tractarians; Sir John had known and respected John Keble since their undergraduate days at Corpus Christi College. As a scholar at Eton Allies had been introduced to members of the Coleridge family, and in old age reminisced about visiting the Tower of London as an undergraduate accompanied by the ten-year-old John Duke, the son of Judge Coleridge.[97]

So it was not hard for Allies to find pupils. Frederick William Coleridge,[98] the judge's youngest child, who would be nine in August 1838, needed a tutor, as did the son of the equity judge, Baron Alderson, Edward Packenham ('Packy').[99] Both boys began at Eton in the early part of 1840. Alderson too was an acknowledged High Churchman and he and Sir John Coleridge were among the many influential members of William Dodsworth's congregation at Christ Church, Albany Street. Edward Coleridge recommended the church to Allies, who was becoming increasingly sympathetic to Tractarian views, and after sampling other ministries, he became a regular attender, valuing above all, the weekly communion at which he often assisted. Dodsworth had begun his metropolitan ministry as an Evangelical occupying the pulpit of a proprietary chapel in nearby Margaret Street, where he was a forceful preacher strongly influenced by the incarnational and apocalyptic theology of Edward Irving and perhaps for this reason had become increasingly attracted to High Church sacramentalism. By the mid-1830s he was a committed Tractarian and a leading representative of the Oxford Movement in the capital.[100]

Among Allies's other pupils were Thomas Erskine,[101] whose father had just been appointed judge of the common pleas and also a son of Lord Cottenham, the newly ennobled Lord Chancellor in the Whig government.[102] Judge Erskine was an Evangelical, who had served on the national committee of the Church Missionary Society. In 1840 he was appointed president of the Trinitarian Bible Society but in retirement at Eversley in Hampshire became the close friend of an Anglican of a different theological outlook, the rector, Charles Kingsley. Allies got on well with Erskine but had less to do with Cottenham, who was a rather forbidding character.[103] Most of the judiciary lived close together in an area around Bedford Square not far from where Allies lived and from time to time the boys' parents invited him to dinner. His closest links were to the Aldersons, at whose home he was always welcome, and where he came to be regarded almost as a member of the family.

The young Queen Victoria's judges were a most cultured company. In the opinion of Charlotte Yonge,

> it is probable that there never was a period when the Judicial Bench could reckon a larger number of men distinguished not only for legal ability but for the highest culture and for the substantial qualities that command confidence and respect. Those who can recollect the regard in which were held the

names of Parke, Denman, Alderson, as well as Patteson and Coleridge, and somewhat later though still contemporary, Erskine, Wightman, Erle and Talfourd, will feel that the middle of the nineteenth century was a time when England might well be proud of her judges.[104]

Not long after moving to London, Allies was required to go to Malvern, where his father's health was rapidly declining and was with him when he died on 25 July 1838, leaving a widow and two unmarried daughters. Thomas stayed with them for several weeks, but by the autumn had returned to London and to his pupils. He found the daily routine—filling the heads of young boys with Latin grammar—somewhat irksome, but it provided a useful source of funds whilst he pursued his two great interests: the search for a wife and the study of theology.

Will you marry me?

Allies's deep wish for a wife and the comfort of domestic life had if anything been intensified by his emotional crisis, and in this regard a visit to Cheltenham during his recovery, in October 1837 was charged with significance because it was there that he first met Eliza Hall Newman, his college friend's half-sister. She was not yet 16 years old,[105] but it seems Allies almost immediately began to ponder whether she might one day become his wife and give him the connubial security for which he yearned. After a year he began his suit, seeking invitations to visit Newman's family, and spent a few days there in the autumn of 1838. Although Eliza seemed completely unaware of the purpose of his visits, Allies felt that her father should be aware of his motivation. His response was understandably guarded, but the suitor was undeterred: prospects of married happiness dominated his thoughts. On 5 May 1839 he wrote in his diary: '*one longing* accompanied me everywhere, most often in crowded assemblies'. He felt he could not be happy without 'a companion … all my longing is for domestic society'.[106]

The opportunity for him to declare himself to Eliza came when he was invited for an extended stay at her home in the summer vacation of 1839. After some days of rather tentative wooing he was advised by

Miss Pickering,[107] who shared the young girl's confidences, to be 'more direct'. So when they were alone together he told her that 'she had not understood the drift of my visit' and asked permission to 'see more of her'. The outcome was wholly satisfactory: 'she assented to my request... and received my kisses.'[108] Thereafter, matters progressed rapidly in the desired direction. Allies wrote that the harmony they enjoyed was 'too blessed to believe'[109] and it was not long before he asked her to marry him. This was too precipitate, not yet eighteen and happy and secure in her family circle, she said that she had no thought of marriage. When Thomas pressed she finally conceded that if ever she did marry anyone it would be him. For Allies this was enough, and when her father, who had been away on business, arrived home he immediately asked for his approval and wrote in his diary on 2 September, 'After dinner got Mr. N's consent to our seeing and corresponding: he was disposed to be restive at first but at last came round, only stipulating that marriage should be put off two years and that the minimum income should be £600 per year'.[110]

Eliza with her brother Thomas then travelled with him to Cheltenham, via London and Oxford. Here Allies left them to join his step-mother and sisters in Clifton and with them visited Clevedon, where he reflected on the changes in his life since he had last been there twelve years before. Returning to London he anxiously awaited a letter inviting him back to Nelmes. It never came. He suspected that some of the Newman family, especially Eliza's brother John, opposed the match. When at last a letter did come at the end of October, his fears were confirmed: it was from her father, informing him that Eliza 'wished to break off all intimacy thro' disapprobation of relations'.[111] Extremely agitated, he at once travelled to Essex, where Mr Newman agreed that he might speak to Eliza, who was staying at Bristol. Allies wasted no time in going there and conferring first with the friends she was visiting. He was assured 'that her affection was unchanged—but the grand obstacle is that they have found I have connections in trade'. After some hesitation Eliza agreed to talk to him but was torn between his protestations and her family's wishes; on parting she said she would be guided by her father's advice. Thomas waited some days and on the last day of the month received a letter from her confirming that she did not wish an engagement, but saying that if he waited for two years until her twentieth birthday then he might write to her again. 'I was paralysed at this, but consented, and with difficulty forbore reproach ... [she] would not see me. I could do nothing ... Left Bristol at seven with a heavy heavy heart.'[112] Back in London he consoled himself that his position was not without hope. On 1 November he wrote in his diary, 'God give me strength to bear my great trial and bless and keep her—my fervent and constant prayer.'[113] It was All Saints' Day, but Allies did not record attending any church.

The making of a Tractarian

Ordination was a statement of intention, it announced a change of direction; but Allies was unsure of his churchmanship even of the philosophical foundations of his belief and quite unclear about what sort of minister he wished to be. He remembered that following his conversion he 'had some thoughts of trying to be curate to Mr. Close', the celebrated Evangelical;[114] but as 1838 closed the influences being exerted upon him came from another direction. On 20 December he dined with his old Oxford friend, now Fellow of Balliol, W. G. Ward and wrote in his diary that he was 'shocked at what he told me of the Newmanites. He is become one himself from being greatly opposed.' He had read 'some of Newman's lectures on Church doctrines' and confessed to 'thinking them Jesuitical now and then.' On Christmas Eve he was with Edward Coleridge, who assured him that 'every reasonable man' agreed with the Oxford School. 'I have since been reading Newman's lectures again, and they seem to me just the truth. Is this an accession of light, or is it mere weakness of judgment? How wonderfully one's own state of mind influences one's intellectual judgment!'[115]

During the following year Allies's theological musings took second place to his pursuit of Eliza, although he regularly read Newman's sermons and with increasing appreciation. But with the autumn and condemned to wait two years before his courtship could be resumed he was free to devote more time to systematic study. An emotional crisis had re-awakened a latent faith, and although he had once called himself a rationalist, at the deepest level he had never really been a sceptic. The whole bent of his mind was a distrust of the Enlightenment, a position from which he never wavered, and this drew him to the same distrust of liberalism that characterised the Oxford School. In August 1839 he read a metaphysical essay by the American scholar, James Marsh, prefixed to a new edition of Coleridge's *Aids to Reflection*,[116] and observed, 'I have always by a sort of instinct hated Locke's Philosophy'.[117] He now sought to put his instinctive beliefs on firmer intellectual foundations and his reading became increasingly cerebral, focusing largely on the work of Anglican scholars. In November he began to study Van Mildert's Boyle Lectures[118] (delivered at his own church of St Mary's Marylebone between 1802 and 1805 and published as *An Historical View of Infidelity, with a Refutation*) in which the future bishop of Durham castigated the opinion that unaided reason could establish a satisfactory basis for belief. He denounced those continental theologians 'who, professing a desire to make Christianity more acceptable to men of a philosophical and sceptical turn of mind, have manifested a disposition to abandon almost all its distinguishing and essential doctrines … treating its sacred records as works of merely human composition'.[119] Allies was particularly struck by Van Mildert's conclusion, which he summarised in his diary:

> the same arguments, which shew the incapability of man by the light of nature to *discover* religious Truth, will serve likewise to show that when it is *revealed* to him he is not warranted in *judging* of it merely by the notions he had previously formed … These two capital errors have misled me since my 16th year—practically I have endeavoured to discard them the last two years: but I never before saw their falsehood *in fact*. I think I have now ascertained it, and it delivers one from a world of perplexity. I have been wont to suppose the human intellect *naturally discovering* God, and in the mind an ultimate standard of right and wrong. The discordance of revealed truth with this self-made standard has been one of my several trials: now I reject it altogether and trust in religion to nothing but faith.[120]

But his vision was not completely unclouded. On 13 December he wrote of the 'longing for clearer ideas about first principles' that had led him to study Ellis's *The Knowledge of Divine Things from Revelation not from Reason or Nature*.[121] He also perused Norris's *Essay towards the Theory of an Ideal or Intelligible World*,[122] which at first he found hard-going: 'I never read metaphysical works without doubting whether one gets any real knowledge—everything seems so intangible.' But his perseverance was rewarded and by the time he had reached the fourth chapter he was led to exclaim: 'I have nearly given up innate ideas.'[123] As 1839 ended Allies was becoming surer of the intellectual foundations of his faith. His spiritual temperature remained, however, highly variable.

The search for employment

Taking pupils provided time for study, but was not the high-status, well-paying employment that might convince Eliza's father that he would make a suitable husband. By the summer of 1839 he was preaching wherever opportunity arose, and was open to accepting a living should a suitable position be offered. But nothing came and the need to find employment loomed ever larger. On Friday 20 September 1839, at Eton for the weekend, he discussed the matter with Edward Coleridge, who advised him to write to his brother the judge and to Baron Alderson for their advice. He returned to town feeling a little sorry for himself, 'there is not a soul for me to speak to among its 1,600,000 inhabitants'.[124] His mood was not improved when Judge Coleridge's reply to his letter was 'less sanguine' than he had hoped. Alderson did not respond for several weeks, but when he did it was with the encouraging news that the living of Ipswich held by his brother might soon become available and that he would support Thomas's application. In the event this opening did not materialise and Allies turned his attention to a different sphere of service: the teachers' training school that the Church of England's National Society for the Education of the Poor hoped to establish. Under the leadership of Gilbert Mathison, T. D. Acland and W. E. Gladstone, a small ginger group on the Society's Committee of Management was seeking to revitalise its work, and chief among its aims was the improved training of schoolmasters. By the beginning of 1839 premises for a new central college were being sought in London and at the Society's annual meeting on 29 May (which Allies did not attend) the new vision was announced to the public. Soon thereafter the Society began to look for a principal; this was seen as a prestigious appointment, and Frederick Denison Maurice was among those expressing interest.

The decision was delayed and it was some months later when Allies began to wonder whether this might be a suitable position for himself. Visiting Eton on Saturday 2 November (he frequently went at the weekend, the train from Paddington to Slough took just 30 minutes) he discussed the matter with Coleridge and with the bishop of London, who was also visiting. He was Charles James Blomfield and a key member of the National Society Committee that had agreed to defer the appointment of a principal. To obtain his confidence was critical and when Allies discussed the position with him he was encouraged to believe his application would be well received. With the active support of Justices Coleridge and Alderson and after canvassing committee-men such as Gladstone and William Cotton,[125] Allies became quite optimistic about his prospects. But then came a letter from Cotton, saying that he could not give him much hope. He was the Deputy Governor of the Bank of England, and Allies went there immediately to see him: 'he was very kind, and said the Bp. was very favourably inclined to me—but there are many to be here consulted, and so far as I can gather the chief objection to me is "that my bodily presence is weak" he did not state this but I inferred it'. This was a reference to Allies's height: he was unusually short. It was something he was very sensitive about: 'This the great trial of my life has now been of serious prejudice to me'.[126] He may have been over-sensitive and too hasty in interpreting a rather guarded reply. Reflecting more coolly on what Cotton said he decided to ask his friends to write to the members of the Committee assuring them of his orthodox churchmanship.

In fact, because of his comparative youth Allies was never in serious contention. After a church service on 22 December, Dodsworth told him that he had been speaking to the bishop of London, who considered Allies's age and inexperience insuperable objections. Any lingering hopes were dashed when Alderson showed him a letter from Blomfield, in which the bishop, whilst expressing a good opinion of him, said 'that he did not possess in sufficient measure, the personal qualities required for the appointment'.[127] By the spring of the following year the Committee had decided that George Augustus Selwyn should be offered the position. He did have the necessary qualities, whilst a curate at Windsor he had won a favourable reputation as an effective organiser and a promoter of cathedral reform. He was a convinced Tractarian and for this reason eventually refused the appointment believing that a clergyman should be under direct episcopal control, not accountable to a committee. The man eventually chosen at the end of 1840, Derwent Coleridge—third child of the poet—was thirteen years Allies's senior and as vicar of Helston had already built up a school with an excellent reputation. He was to remain as the head of what became St Mark's College until 1864 and was undoubtedly a wise choice.[128]

For Allies this failure was another disappointment; he greatly enjoyed the social and intellectual stimulus of metropolitan life and disliked the thought of accepting a living that would take him away from it. On 4 December he noted in his diary: 'At Alderson's in evening—He talked to me most kindly about the mastership. Offered to apply to the Chancellor: declined at present, as I dread being banished into the country.' He resolved to take more pupils of which there was a ready supply. As regards his ministry, he wondered whether he might become a licensed curate to Dodsworth or perhaps apply for one of the new district churches that were being erected under the aegis of the Metropolitan Churches Fund that the bishop of London had established in April 1836.[129] However, thanks largely to Alderson's representations, Blomfield had other plans for him and early in 1840 invited him to call. Allies noted in his diary that he was not expecting much. He was wrong; the bishop asked him to become his Examining Chaplain.[130] It was a significant diocesan appointment and he accepted with gratitude.

He took up the appointment on 1 May 1840. With his stipend and his feet placed on the first rung of the ladder of ecclesiastical preferment he felt he could resume his courtship. Although the stipulated two years had not passed, Eliza was prepared, with the consent of her father, to contemplate the prospect of life as Mrs Allies. On 1 October 1840 the marriage was solemnised at Marylebone parish church by Blomfield himself. She was aged eighteen and he was twenty-seven. Within a year their first child was born, a son whom they named Edward.

At the heart of a great system

Allies had made a good impression on Bishop Blomfield. He had waited on him formally in pursuit of his career and they had met on social occasions, particularly at Baron Alderson's table and at Eton. He seems particularly to have charmed Mrs Blomfield, who twenty years before as Mrs Kent, a young widow, had married the widower bishop. For example, on 10 May 1839 Allies noted in his diary:

> Evening at Alderson's—Bp. of London, Durham and Norwich—Mrs Blomfield an exceedingly pretty woman—Talked to me for some time—her son, Mr Kent at Oxford, just going up—She was very free spoken about the Bishop's rise, and the necessity of his family exerting themselves.[131]

Undoubtedly his London friends had sought to influence the bishop on his behalf. But Blomfield needed an effective chaplain. He already had several but they were of limited usefulness having other important duties. William Hale, for example, was archdeacon of Middlesex, and Augustus Campbell, rector of Liverpool. Two of the bishop's brothers, George and James, had also been appointed. The former was rector of Stevenage and a rural dean and the latter had recently been presented to the living of Launton, in the diocese of Oxford, but in the patronage of the bishop of London. John Sinclair was an examining chaplain, however, the position was a sinecure, awarded at the instigation of Joshua Watson, so that he could work full-time as secretary of the National Society. Someone was needed therefore to take responsibility for the numerous candidates for ordination within the London diocese and Allies soon discovered that he would be kept fully occupied, dividing his time between Fulham Palace, the bishop's residence and the diocesan place of business, London House in Aldersgate.

There was little spiritual or emotional *rapport* between the bishop and his new chaplain. Blomfield has been described as 'sarcastic' and 'overbearing', too conscious of his own dignity ('even when he smiled, he smiled episcopally'[132]). He was supremely a man of business, motivated by a sincere conviction that the Church of England had to be remoulded to minister effectively to a nation undergoing profound change. Appointed to the capital in 1828, he was just the man to work in harness with the reforming Whig governments of the 1830s. His 1834 Charge to the Clergy was unequivocal: 'The people are not adequately supplied with the means and opportunities of Christian instruction and Christian worship. We want more churches, and more clergymen.' In illustration he cited the north and eastern parts of the metropolis with one church or chapel for every 19,000 souls and one clergyman for every 14,000.[133] He responded to the need by establishing funds for the building of metropolitan churches, and became an enthusiastic participant in the work of the Ecclesiastical Commission, established in 1832, but given clearer shape by Sir Robert Peel three years later. In essence, its task was to secure the more efficient use of the Church's income.

One of the bishop's concerns was to elevate the educational and social standing of his clergy, demanding that, 'clerical accomplishments should be raised with the rising standards of every other profession.'[134] With his background as an eminent classicist he saw competence in the ancient languages both as a mark of respectability and a measure of intellectual ability and was reluctant to ordain men who without a good reason did not have a university degree. To those who stressed their piety as compensation for a lack of academic qualifications he answered that 'if a young man, with all the advantages of a good education, and knowing himself to be destined to this sacred and arduous calling, is unable to write Latin correctly, and to construe the Greek Testament, at the age of three and twenty, he is either greatly deficient in diligence and seriousness, or he is not qualified by natural endowments for the office of an expositor of God's word.'[135] Given this, it was understandable that Blomfield should consider Allies's scholarly achievements as ideally qualifying him to act as an examining chaplain, judging that these more than compensated for any pastoral inexperience.

Towards the end of the nineteenth century Benjamin Armstrong, the vicar of East Dereham, remembered the start of his clerical career. In November 1840, as a graduate of Caius College, Cambridge, aged twenty-three and resident in the capital, he wrote to the bishop of London requesting ordination. The matter would have been delegated to

Allies, who asked that the candidate should study seventeen substantial volumes before attending for examination in June the following year. The Greek Testament (with Elsey and Slade's notes) was stipulated along with a selection of standard Anglican texts (such as Burnett on the Articles, Wheatley on the Prayer Book and Hooker's *Ecclesiastical Polity*). Somewhat old-fashioned theological works such as Prideaux's *Connection*, Butler's *Analogy*, Paley's *Evidences* and Newton on the *Prophecies* featured on the list along with the *Ecclesiastical Histories* of Mosheim and Burton. In addition, knowledge of more recent scholarship was required, for example Bishop Sumner's work on the *Evidence for Christianity* (1824). Candidates were also expected to be familiar with Palmer's *Origines Liturgicae* (1832) and MacBride's recent lectures on the *Diatesseron* of Tatian (1836).[136]

Armstrong recalled that the examination took place at Charterhouse and lasted four days. Thereafter he proceeded immediately to ordination on Sunday 6 June 1841. At the service the bishop addressed the candidates on doctrine and the standards he expected from them.[137] Allies was present at this and four other half-yearly ordinations: the first in June 1840 and the last on Trinity Sunday 1842 (22 May). The candidates he examined reflected the changing nature of Anglicanism. Despite Blomfield's dislike of *literates* (non-graduates) increasingly the ministerial needs of a Church with an expanding global mission was being supplemented from this source. Numbers of such men came from the Church Missionary Society, whose college was at Islington, from the Society for the Propagation of the Gospel and from the London Society for Promoting Christianity among the Jews. The Evangelical candidates soon sensed that the examining chaplain did not approve of their theology, though none were rejected on theological grounds.[138]

The Church Missionary Society men were soon on ships bound mainly for India and West Africa; but there were exceptions, such as George Percy Badger, who was to become a distinguished scholar of the Nestorian Church.[139] Ordained deacon in December 1841, he set out four months later on an expedition to Mesopotamia. Among the S. P. G. candidates examined by Allies was Vincent Stanton, who would travel to the new colony of Hong Kong. Some of his graduate ordinands had already distinguished themselves academically. Daniel

Moore, ordained as priest in June 1841, had won the Hulsean Prize in 1838 for an essay in defence of the Apocalypse ('The mysteries of Revelation no solid argument against its truth') a work lauded by the *Eclectic Review* as 'a masterly production'. Frederick Poynder of Wadham College, who entered the diaconate six months before, was in 1843 to follow in Allies's footsteps when his essay on practical piety won the Denyer Theological Prize. Increasingly these university men were being shaped by Tractarianism.

Blomfield declined to define his own churchmanship, and although leaning towards High Church views he adopted a pragmatic approach to doctrine and was quite happy to ordain strong Evangelicals such as R. S. Tabor (for many years a distinguished headmaster of Cheam School), and James Cohen, who became active in the Evangelical Alliance (both admitted deacon in May 1842). Allies maintained contact with a number of the men he examined, those with whose theological views he sympathised. C. C. Spencer, for example, who went on to serve as curate to W. J. E. Bennett at St Paul's Knightsbridge,[140] and the poet Robert Eldridge Aris Willmott, who became a minor literary celebrity. Of all the young men who passed through his hands it was Nathaniel Woodard who achieved the greatest fame. Like his examiner, Woodard's outspokenness was capable of upsetting his colleagues and he was dismissed from his first London curacy after preaching on confession as necessarily linked to absolution. Another Tractarian, William Wheeler invited Woodard to his parish of New Shoreham and it was here that he began his first school for the sons of the middle class. In 1849 Allies was to send his eldest child, Edward, to him as one of the first boarders.

One of the early candidates to appear before him was Henry Holden, ordained in 1840. In September 1845 W. E. Gladstone wrote to Allies asking his opinion as to Holden's suitability to become Warden of the college that he and James Robert Hope planned to establish to train young men in the faith and traditions of the Scottish Episcopal Church. Allies had no hesitation in recommending him and mentioned that when Holden was examined for deacon's orders in December 1839 Archdeacon Sinclair had been so impressed that he had thought of proposing him for the principalship of the National Society's Training College.[141] Did Sinclair tell Allies this and if so did he know that Allies himself had been rejected as unsuitable for the position? Holden did not go to Gladstone's foundation but in January 1846 became headmaster of Uppingham School, where he remained until 1853, to be succeeded by Edward Thring.

Although his duties in respect of ordinands occupied much of his time, Allies was also involved in many other aspects of the work of the diocese and the wider Church. The bishop of London was traditionally responsible for all overseas Anglicans without a diocesan bishop, and Blomfield was an enthusiastic supporter of colonial bishoprics. This interest was shared by Edward Coleridge and some other friends of Allies at Eton, a group that was closely associated with the consecration of Selwyn as bishop of New Zealand in 1841. The following year Allies was appointed secretary of a special committee on which Edward Coleridge also served, established to raise subscriptions for the endowment of a bishopric of Van Diemen's Land.

Theological certainties

Allies, who waited on Blomfield every morning, commented that he was worked so hard that on returning home in the afternoon was frequently too tired to pursue serious theological studies.[142] Yet study he did, and in seeking secure foundations found the writings of the Tractarians increasingly congenial. In the previous year he had judged Pusey's tract on baptism 'admirable' and Newman's sermons were meat and drink to him: 'I find in these men a far higher strain of piety than in the opposite school. Newman's sermon on Saul and Jeroboam is admirable.'[143] He was persuaded by Newman's vision of the *via media*, and became one of the growing band of clergy marked out as representing the Oxford teachings in the capital. In addition to Dodsworth, Allies sought out the friendship of W. J. E. Bennett, minister of Portman Chapel, often assisting him on Sundays. When Bennett was first appointed in 1836 his theological views were not particularly High Church, so that in a work on the Eucharist that appeared in 1837 he advocated a receptionist theology and denied the Real Presence. Yet the Oxford theology had real potency and by the time Allies became associated with him his views had changed profoundly. Revisiting the subject of the Eucharist in 1842, he advocated sacramental confession and as noted by his biographer, a contemporary, he 'speaks of the Sacraments as channels of Grace; advocates the mixed Chalice... and wishes the Prayer of offering the Sacrifice were joined to the Prayer of Consecration as of old.'[144] Bennett was interested in Roman Catholic doctrines and introduced Allies to the Missal, but never himself succumbed to that Church and in 1842, preached a series of sermons on 'The Distinctive Errors of Romanism', though his measured critique of Roman 'additions' was deemed inadequate by his Evangelical brethren.

Although not published until April 1844, Allies's first substantial work, *Sermons on the Epistle to the Romans and Others*, comprised twenty-one discourses mainly prepared during his time in London and most probably delivered to Bennett's theologically sophisticated congregation. They mark the writer's coming to grips with Tractarian doctrine and in particular the eight sermons on Romans are indebted to Newman's *Lectures on Justification* published six years before.[145] The tone throughout is strongly opposed to Evangelical theology. For the young chaplain so recently returned to faith from rationalism and intellectualism the security of Holy Church represented the only sure path to salvation: 'the mind of the whole church alone is able to read the Book and declare the interpretation thereof.'[146] The true Church system, he affirmed, must stand between the extremes of a theology that 'so priced and measured out every act of mortification and penance, that heaven might seem to be bought by human works', and the view, widely held 'in our own time and nation', in which the Gospel is seen '*exclusively* as an offer of mercy, as a free gift, extending not only to the pardon of sins committed *before*, but of those incurred after, its reception.'[147]

Allies was quite sure that Anglicanism purged of its puritanism constituted this true Church of which it was 'of infinite importance to be members'. 'All the blessings of Christ's atonement are restricted to the body of Christ, His Church.'[148] Salvation came only through adherence to the Church's teachings and participation in her sacraments. Regeneration was through baptism, indeed,

> any minister of hers that does not hold forth that teaching must knowingly pervert her meaning. Anyone who attributes spiritual regeneration to anything else but the act of God in

holy Baptism is giving a direct contradiction to his Church, and to the formularies which he has sworn to uphold, not to mention the whole authority of scripture, and the overwhelming voice of all Christian antiquity.[149]

He relentlessly assailed Evangelical doctrine, stressing that justification is the fruit of obedience, springing from a life renewed in baptism. Justification is by faith, but faith properly understood:

let faith be considered the bare act of belief apart from holiness, obedience and love, which are its proper works and operations, and let a justifying power be attributed to such a faith, and we have the most destructive of all heresies. Let the essence of justification be placed rather in the apprehending of Christ by belief in his atonement, than in cordial obedience to his will; rather in contemplating Him without us, than receiving Him within us; then talk as we may of the corruptions of other branches of the Church, let us be assured no more flattering unction was ever laid to the sinner's soul than this, the most profligate of Indulgences, the most deceptive of Pardons.[150]

Thus Allies echoed Newman's great theme, that the faith that justifies stands for all the graces infused into the Christian heart. There could be no compromise with the Reformers. On Easter Day, 1842, preaching on the text 'Jesus ... delivered for our offences ... raised again for our justification (Romans iv 25); Allies warned his congregation against Lutheranism: 'the unscriptural and unreal notion of a nominal righteousness and external justification is the secret source to which must be traced most of the spiritual evils which afflict us as a Church.'[151] Before publication, Allies referred the sermons to Newman, who approved of the theology as echoing his own. Much later, in September 1845 John Keble reviewed the work in the *Christian Remembrancer*:

Taking Mr. Newman on Justification for his guide, but availing himself also largely of the remarks of S. Chrysostom,

of Calmet, and of other orthodox commentators, the author
has thrown himself with a sort of youthful enthusiasm, which
seems to us very engaging, into that view of the doctrines of
grace, which is generally allowed to have been the view of the
whole early Church, at least down to the time of S. Augustine.

The review concluded that 'amidst all that is now humbling us to the dust, both from within and from without, it is a great and real support, to hope that this ancient and true doctrine has been effectually revived in our Church.'[152] Allies's convinced churchmanship was for Keble some consolation in the face of the dread filling so many Anglican hearts of Newman's imminent submission to the Church of Rome. It was the great crisis of Tractarianism, but Allies's book betrayed no unease at all as to the future of Anglicanism. The last sermon ('The dispersion of Babel and the Unity of Pentecost') sought to establish the spiritual foundations of the Church's oneness in the 'unity of Pentecost' and its last page is a plea that 'heavenly citizenship' be once again 'put forth as the most precious gift of God to man'. Then might 'the city of God yet raise her bulwarks impregnable in the midst of the world, no longer the mock of the scorner, but the refuge of the lonely, the chosen home of the sanctified, the consolation of the mourner.'[153]

Confident that he had found the truth Allies was insensitive to the doubts and concerns of others, quite unable to enter into the minds of those who disagreed with him. Indeed, his appointment at the ecclesiastical centre seems to have re-awakened an innate sense of intellectual superiority that had been temporarily quietened in the aftermath of his conversion crisis. In particular, he regarded his bishop as sadly lacking in theological understanding: 'I felt myself stronger and more advanced in Church views than he was'. The difficulties Blomfield faced in maintaining concord among his clergy meant little to him and he completely rejected the thesis that accommodation and pragmatism were necessary sacrifices if the Church was to minister to a rapidly growing urban population. The political skills required of his superiors he held in particular contempt. Writing of Blomfield's 'truckling to expediency, and continuously attempting to sit between two stools', he proclaimed himself free 'from all danger of being Lambethised'[154] and was quite unwilling to exercise any moderation in expressing his views. He must surely have been aware that even a tolerant master like Blomfield required a certain restraint among his staff.

> Instead of keeping my counsel and holding my tongue when Dr. B produced at his own table, or elsewhere, some sentiment extremely uncatholic or perhaps I should say unchurchmanlike I not seldom ventured to oppose it. I believe one great admirer of the Bishop, Mr. W. Cotton, called me for this a little bantamcock.[155]

The inevitable collision did not come immediately. The bishop was quite sympathetic to 'moderate Oxford'. In 1839 he wrote to Daniel Wilson, bishop of Calcutta, that by placing 'the Church's authority and office in a striking point of view' the Tractarians had 'done much to counteract the evil effects of that low Church spirit which has of late years weakened the Church and encouraged the Dissenters.' He believed that the rediscovery of Church principles posed no essential threat: 'God be praised, we have our Articles and Liturgy, which those writers can never torture into speaking their own language!'[156] He did not allow for Newman's verbal ingenuity. Yet even when Tract 90 appeared in February 1841 Blomfield was determined to find some consolation, telling Golightly that it would 'do good ... by opening the eyes of some of the young men who have taken up the opinions of the Tractarians.'[157] He thought it inexpedient that the university authorities should take any official action.

If Blomfield expected that Newman's apparent endorsement of the Articles as essentially compatible with Tridentine doctrine would cause his chaplain to reconsider his unqualified admiration of him he was to be disappointed. It was a turning point in their relationship; Allies recalled 'I was disgusted with Bishop Blomfield', adding 'and he, I believe, with me, because I would never disavow or censure Tract 90.'[158] The unbridgeable gap in their understanding of the nature of the Church of England and its mission was becoming ever more apparent, as Allies later explained to W. E. Gladstone: 'there was considerable difference as to our views on certain high points e.g. Eucharistic Presence & Sacrifice and others which I both seemed to read in the Ancient Fathers and accepted from the yearning of my heart—whereas he appeared to think the Reformation had eliminated such doctrines from the English Church.'[159] This daily irritation undoubtedly exacerbated the bishop's increasingly adverse opinion of the Tractarians. Towards the end of 1841 he confided in Walter Hook, the vicar of Leeds that, despite their professed exalting of episcopal authority, for the advanced Tractarians,

> there is only *one* bishop to whom they are disposed to pay implicit submission ... the moment any of their own bishops ... say anything in opposition ... an outcry is raised against them and they are charged with schismatical irregularity, anti-catholic latitudinarianism, and even 'flat heresy.'[160]

Many of Blomfield's episcopal colleagues feared that the Reformation settlement itself was under threat. In Oxford the anti-Tractarian forces began to organise and towards the end of 1841 the balance of theological power was put to the test with the election of a new professor of poetry in succession to John Keble. The candidate supported by the outgoing professor and his sympathisers was the gentle priest and acknowledged poet, Isaac Williams. But as the author of two tracts on 'reserve in the communication of religious knowledge', the Evangelicals had marked him down as a dangerous enemy of 'full gospel' preaching. They brought forward their own candidate, James Garbett, a graduate of Brasenose, not a poet at all, but a clergyman who had written on literary matters. It was always likely that theological rather than academic or poetic considerations would sway the issue, but this became inevitable when E. B. Pusey published a circular urging members of Convocation to vote for the candidate whose 'aim it has, for many years, been to promote the sound principles of our Church, according to the teaching of her liturgy.'[161]

Pusey's advocacy stirred his opponents into action; a committee was formed at Wadham—by tradition a home for Evangelicals—and all members of the college were contacted and asked to pledge their support for Garbett. Upon receiving the letter Allies wrote to the Trinity Committee, which had been formed to support Williams, pledging his vote to their candidate. According to J. H. Newman, who does not mention his source, Allies was offended by his College Committee's threatening tone: 'the Wadham people that canvassed him had mentioned ulterior measure'.[162] In the outcome the Tractarians were defeated—Williams withdrew after a comparison of promises—yet they did manage to garner a very large body of support which did nothing to allay episcopal concerns.

Whether the Wadham Committee took any action against the recalcitrant Allies is not recorded, but he would soon pay a heavy price for his outspokenness, although nemesis arose out of another theological controversy that occurred around the same time as the poetry professorship contest. It concerned the christening of the Prince of Wales on 25 January 1842. Among the sponsors was the King of Prussia, a Lutheran, making him, in the eyes of the advanced Tractarians, little better than a heretic.[163] Just days before the ceremony Allies was in the company when Blomfield criticised 'some of the Oxford party', who were protesting at the King's involvement. At this his chaplain rushed to support his Catholic friends. The bishop's brother, the rector of Launton in Oxfordshire, was present at the exchange and witnessed Blomfield's exasperation. It was the final straw and two days later he told Allies that he could have the living of Launton but that if he refused it no better offer would be forthcoming. Within three weeks he was inducted into the Living.[164] 'It was undoubtedly for my Church principles, and the dread to what they might lead, that the Bishop discarded me, and sent me to Launton, where he thought I could do little harm'.[165]

Allies saw it as a sentence of internal exile, the death-blow to his dream of becoming a powerful influence for Tractarianism in the capital.

> Being sent to Launton was a disgrace which I had incurred for following *bona fide* my principles, and not being *Lambethised*. It seemed to destroy my prospects, remove me out of the way of distinction, from friends and connections, and the power of influencing others, especially the young. For many years I keenly felt it as all this. My heart sank within me at the prospect of going there; sank within me during all the interval between accepting the living and going to reside on it; sank within me on the evening of arriving there; and

> my wife shared in these feelings. We felt ourselves tossed into a desert ... I was burning to have a large and influential congregation, such as Dodsworth's which I think had always been before my eyes as a sort of model. I longed to carry out my Puseyism on a large field. Without, I think, any bent to the pastoral office, I had considerable love of preaching, and very great feeling and love of theology as an organic structure of divine doctrines. I was yearning after the Catholic system in its fullness, without the least suspicion where it was to be found. As to all this, Launton was the most thorough damper which I could have received. Dr. Blomfield intended it for such. It was his mode of punishing me for having entrapped him into the discredit of having a Puseyite *prononcè* for his examining chaplain.[166]

He knew he had no choice; Blomfield had said: 'I advise you to take it because I can give it to you now, whereas later on I may feel unable to offer you a living.'[167] Yet Allies's assumption that something sinister was going on is surely unfounded. How could Blomfield continue to employ as a confidential assistant someone who did not sympathise with him, did not even respect him? And far from inflicting a punishment, the bishop was being very generous. His brother, the rector, was unwell and wished to lay down the responsibility and remove to the parish of Orsett in Essex, which had become vacant through the death of its incumbent, J. F. Usko.[168] This living had so few parishioners as to be almost sinecure yet was worth in excess of £850 p.a. The bishop was patron and wanted his ailing brother to have it. The Oxford parish with a population of 619 souls was itself a desirable appointment yielding a net income of £618.[169] There was a large and comfortable rectory and the village's closeness to Bicester, where the railway would arrive in 1844, and to Oxford meant that it was far from isolated. Just a few miles to the north was Mixbury with its long serving rector, William Jocelyn Palmer, father of William Palmer of Magdalen, a leading Tractarian protagonist, who became Allies's close friend and fellow traveller on the road to Rome.

✢ 2 ✢

The Tractarian Whirlwind

A country parish

According to Bishop Blomfield, in the fifty years before his brother was appointed to it in 1837 the parish of Launton had been sadly neglected. William Frederick Browne, the previous incumbent, was a caricature eighteenth-century clergyman: magistrate, sportsman, farmer and incidentally, pastor. Instituted in 1780, he started as he meant to continue, after two years of his ministry the churchwardens noted: 'The Church is greatly neglected. Servis on Sundays sometimes once, sometimes twice, very seldom on holy days. Catecking very little, very much quarilling with neighbours.'[1] The rector greatly annoyed the parishioners by keeping the churchyard gate locked on Sundays. This seems to have been because he wished to delay Morning Prayer until his business affairs had been attended to. J. C. Blomfield, the son of Browne's successor, who replaced Allies as rector in 1850, noted in his history of the parish: 'The hour of service on Sunday mornings was very irregular, depending on the time the wagon from London reached home and brought the weekly account of the sale of butter, eggs and other farm produce which had been sent in the previous week to the London market.'[2]

Browne preached on alternate Sundays and at the time of his parish return in 1811 was administering communion four times a year to between six and twenty people.[3] He steadfastly ignored the growth of dissent as it expanded to fill the religious void. In August 1807 the *Evangelical Magazine* reported: 'A very general spirit of enquiry having appeared for some time in the village of Launton, near Bicester, some serious persons were excited to communicate to them the word of life. For some months the services were carried on in a private house, which being found insufficient, a chapel was erected, which was opened June 3.'[4] The following year Browne reported to his bishop: 'a Presbyterian meeting house was built last summer and I am informed that the greater part of my Parishioners attend it.' However, he was sure that they went 'more from curiosity than any religious motive as my parishioners in general have attended the church quite as regularly as before.'[5]

The rector remained in office until he died in 1837 at the age of 82. It was said in the village that having been so long in the parish he was reluctant to depart and his ghost haunted the rectory, a supposition to which Eliza Allies was able to attest.[6] Nevertheless, under his successor 'a new order of things was at once begun.' James Blomfield and his large family including four resident scholars stayed just long enough to give the inhabitants of Launton a taste of his brother's zeal for the revitalization of parish life. Reform began with the re-ordering of the church. During Browne's incumbency the medieval screen had been covered with lath and plaster and a doorway inserted; this covering was removed and the chancel cleared of box pews. As regards parish life, 'Sunday schools were opened; the schoolroom was built, the church was repaired, and a decent order introduced; church services were increased; a coal and clothing club and a lending library were started; allotments of land were made to the villagers; pastoral visiting became customary.'[7]

There were other changes, but Blomfield stayed only four years and with Allies's arrival five months after being inducted the parishioners encountered a new and more problematical sort of zeal. Called to minister in an ancient building originally named in honour of the Assumption of the Blessed Virgin Mary, the new rector believed that the Church's ancient glory could once again capture the hearts of the common people: 'In July 1842 I went there with the firmest confidence in the Church of England, grieved at the conduct of her bishops, but convinced that a great future was open to her if the Puseyite movement was not stifled.'[8] There was no doubting his enthusiasm and sincerity. In the words of Blomfield, his successor, the son of his predecessor, who wrote a history of the parish, 'No clergyman ever entered on his duties as a parish priest with a more earnest desire to be faithful than Mr. Allies ... he was happy in his new charge and in his earnest zeal for the care of his parish there seemed a promise of much coming good.'[9]

Perhaps more zealous than happy, but now committed, so that on his induction as rector he presented the church with an inscribed flagon and also—with his wife—an alms dish in thanksgiving for their first-born son. Another silver plate was presented in the autumn of 1842 to mark Eliza's survival after the birth of their second son, Henry Edward, who lived for only a few days. As regards the fabric of the church, Allies continued his predecessor's good work and the box pews in the nave were taken out. It was his intention to build a new chancel, but for reasons to be explained the plans he developed were never executed. He did, however, early in his ministry, install a new altar. In accordance with his Catholic principles it was a stone slab, supported by two stone uprights fixed to the wall. This was 'stigmatized as the first stone altar since the Reformation' and drew a great deal of adverse comment, particularly from the vicar of nearby Yarnton, Peter Maurice.[10]

The altar was an outward sign of the new rector's confidence that the English Church 'had inherited the full mediaeval rights of the Catholic Church.'[11] That he failed completely to understand that this world could never be recovered was the undoing of his ministry; inept and insensitive attempts to impose on his people a sort of pre-Reformation clericalism proved disastrous. In Blomfield's restrained opinion, 'he without doubt lacked wise judgement. Having never had previously any parochial experience he was little fitted to bear the evil will and opposition which his zeal provoked and his treatment of the Dissenters, many of whom had separated themselves only on account of the Church's neglect, was ill-advised.'[12] Soon after his installation in July Allies sent a printed letter to all parishioners. It caused deep offence. The document has not survived but some impression of its tone may be obtained from the letter the bishop of London wrote to him in November 1842 when complaint was made to him. He said of its concluding sentence, it 'is one which ought never to have been penned by a clergyman. There is a vehemence and want of temper in it, which I think wholly inconsistent both with the wisdom of the serpent and the gentleness of the dove. You will be taught by experience that the modes which you have adopted for reclaiming poor and ignorant people into the error into which they have been driven by the Church's neglect are not the most consistent with the Church's spirit.'[13]

Allies never did learn to conciliate his parishioners. A few months after his arrival one of them in conversation accused him of being a 'Roman &c.' His response was reported in a newspaper: 'Mr Allies sent the parish constable after the man, and thus Mr. Freeman, of Launton, farmer, was deprived of his freedom, and confined and handcuffed in the village public house for seventeen hours!'[14] A year later there was another confrontation with the same man:

> The worthy Rector of Launton refused to allow Mr James Freeman, a parishioner, to have a grave prepared for the remains of his child by the remains of Mr Freeman's own mother. The truth is, Sir, Mr Allies had that part of the churchyard, through which he and his family pass from their mansion to the church, levelled last winter without the consent of the parishioners ... and therefore he is unwilling that the parishioners should bury their dead in the spot which has felt the power of his levelling. But Mr Freeman would not be put off ... and therefore he sent to Bicester for Mr Maley a solicitor, who in company with himself, paid a morning visit to the churchyard and the Rev. gentleman's obstinacy was overcome.[15]

These newspaper reports should be read with some caution, the copy presumably being supplied by the aggrieved parties. Freeman was an eccentric and notably litigious and was eventually imprisoned for debts owed to various lawyers. For his part Allies never thought it necessary to respond to allegations in the press, let alone make any apology.

The war on dissent

Allies wrote that he went to Launton with an 'almost overweening confidence' in the position of the Church of England, evidenced 'in that autumn of 1842 by my conduct towards the Dissenters.'[16] He wasted no time in deploying all available means. His letter to all parishioners had contained a threat: those who did not attend the parish church would be required to quit their tenancy of church allotments. He was as good as his word; a new lease condition was imposed requiring that tenants should undertake never to enter a dissenting chapel. Many refused to comply, as was widely reported:

> Launton is a village and its population is about 660 persons. The living, including fees, offerings &c. is about £800 per year. A part of the church lands was let about forty [sic] years ago by the Rev. James Blomfield, late of Launton, into small allotments to field labourers of the said village, including several Methodists and Independents. The present Rector, the Rev. Mr. Alies [sic], had his rent day on 25th of August 1842 … It is now our painful duty to inform the public, that on the rent-day Dissenters and Churchmen were requested to sign a written document, promising never to enter a Dissenting chapel; … about twenty families, the weekly earnings of each are about nine shillings, have been deprived … of a part of their poor living.[17]

Another newspaper described the reaction of the excluded, concluding that the rector's behaviour was a moral outrage:

> In vain did they represent that they had consciences; in vain did the widow plead and the fatherless petition … In spite of tears, and entreaties that would have moved a common pickpocket, and regardless of the execrations of mankind, he thought of his duty, and himself alone: he stuck to his 'principle' without flinching.[18]

The Congregational minister at Bicester, William Ferguson wrote to the *True Tablet* newspaper:

> Protestant Dissenters have during the last thirteen months past, circulated some hundred copies of the sacred book among the labouring poor … and nineteen neat pocket Bibles were presented by us, on the 19 September 1842, to eighteen

field labourers and one widow, who have been deprived, within the last five weeks, of their potato land by the Catholic Rector of the parish of Launton, Oxon., because they refused to sign a paper promising that they would never enter a meeting house again![19]

The *Tablet*, being a Roman Catholic organ, was intrigued by Ferguson's reference to the 'Catholic Rector', but the solution was supplied in the *Cork Examiner* of 30 September, which identified him as 'the Reverend Rector Allies in England', castigating him as 'a haughty Churchman'.

Those deprived appealed to the patron of the living, whereupon Blomfield chided the new rector for 'the harsh and hasty manner of their ejection':

> I am far from disputing the position that dissenters can have no claim to any benefit from that which is the property of the Church, nor do I question the propriety of withholding from them the favour which you grant to members of the Church: but that which is in principle right may be so done as to become wrong, and this seems to me to have been the case with your proceedings respecting the allotments at Launton. You appear not to have made any allowance for the peculiar circumstances of the parish, the inhabitants of which have been for forty years so grievously neglected that it is a wonder they were not *all* confirmed dissenters. Looking to this and their want of knowledge it was obviously a case which required to be treated with a gentle hand, one in which the people were to be led, rather than driven back into their pasture which they had quitted for lack of food: nor do I doubt from what had been effected in that way, during my Brother's short incumbency, that in the course of a few years, dissent would have been nearly, if not quite extinguished in that parish. I am very much mistaken (I hope, I may be) if you have not given it vigour and perpetuity.'[20]

Blomfield said that his brother had adopted a very different policy:

There would have been little or no objection, to your gradually eliminating obstinate nonconformity from the list of your tenants, what is complained of, and I think justly, is the harsh and hasty manner of their ejection. By a kind and careful expression of sound Church doctrine my Brother had brought many from the Meeting House to the Church; those who still remained dissenters also half churchmen, sent *their children* to his school and to Church: and so where the parents were still in error, their offspring were being brought to a true profession; and as those parents were the amongst the most steady and serious of the parishioners, this was a great point to gain ...

My conviction is the effect of your requiring written promise of never again entering a meeting house (which I, if I had been one of them would never have signed) has been to take from 19 or 20 families many of them good church people, a great part of their means of subsistence in a relatively poor district, is to deprive yourself of a powerful means of converting evil-doers and rewarding honest industry. The dissenting Sunday School had entirely ceased it is now revived and flourishing. Your requiring a written promise was plainly an affront to conscientious churchmen and a sop to the thoughtless and ignorant. What you should aim at is not to make men *promise* to come to Church but to convince them of the duty of doing so.[21]

The bishop showed his exasperation by removing Allies's name from his list of chaplains.[22]

The war on dissent raged throughout Allies's incumbency. His principal foes, the Launton Congregationalists, were well organised, and in their minister William Ferguson had an able commander. He had been recognised as pastor of the Bicester Congregational Church in 1840 and shepherded the Launton flock as well. From his pen came a stream of pamphlets and letters to the newspapers, castigating Anglicanism in general and the rector of Launton in particular. The newspapers in reporting an encounter in which Allies, drawing upon the account in

Numbers 16:1–40 of Korah's rebellion, warned a dissenting family of the dangers to their eternal welfare of remaining outside the Catholic Church, were probably informed by Ferguson, who was present at the time. The article concluded by noting the arrival of Mr Rolls, one of his deacons, who said:

> 'Mr. Allies, I have heard that you have said that Dissent is as bad as drunkenness.' 'I will tell you what I have said' replied Mr. Allies; 'I said that neither drunkards, nor whoremongers, nor adulterers shall inherit the kingdom of God, and that schismatics are as bad as whoremongers &c.; or, if you will have it in plain English, that Dissenters are as bad, and therefore they cannot enter the kingdom of heaven. I will do all I can to put down Dissent, and your meeting-house in my parish.'[23]

Allies suffered much for the cause: paying a high price emotionally and financially as he implemented a strategy of excluding all non-church families from the tenancy of glebe lands, and seeking to persuade his tenants not to buy from dissenters. According to newspaper reports, Eliza, in her parish visiting, reinforced the message, telling one family: 'I pity you very much, you are led captive by the old one. The true light is come into the parish, and you will not follow it, but you will follow that Ferguson—what a pity—I do hope you will consider of it and come to Church.'[24]

Despite Blomfield's wise words, Allies continued to use all available means to enforce conformity and was prepared to deploy spiritual as well as economic weapons. According to an anonymous correspondent to the *Oxford Chronicle*, on Sunday 15 October 1843 he refused to baptise an infant 'because one of the godfathers, though a churchman, is guilty of that great and condemning sin of attending occasionally at the Independent Chapel in Launton.'[25] Under Blomfield a Church school was established and in 1846 it was enlarged, but only for the children of Church-goers. This was in response to the Congregationalist school opened under the aegis of the British and Foreign School Society in 1845. Allies was prepared to use bribery; with church land becoming available he offered to the villagers the tenancy of about twenty two one acre plots. As reported in *The Oxford Chronicle*, his aim was 'to increase his real income, and to do away with the British School in the village. Before he would let the poor men have the land, he made all those who have children in the British School promise to take them away and send them to the National School.'[26]

The war on dissent was waged even over the bodies of the dead. The Launton churchyard, in common with other parishes, was the community's burial place and under common law Nonconformists had a right to be buried there; moreover it had long been accepted that the incumbent could not refuse to read the burial service over their graves.[27] But for clergymen caught up in the flood tide of High Church movement, these requirements rankled. They pointed to a higher authority: the Prayer Book rubric requiring that 'such office (the burial service) is not to be used for any that die unbaptized, or excommunicate, or have laid violent hands on themselves'. Surely, they argued, if dissenters were not *ipso facto* excommunicate, they were certainly unbaptized if christened by anyone other than a validly ordained priest of the Church of England. On these grounds, in 1839, the vicar of Gedney in Lincolnshire, T. S. Escott, had refused to bury a child baptized by a Wesleyan. The case went to the Court of Arches where the dean, Sir Herbert Jenner, ruled that 'the law of the Church is beyond all doubt that a child baptized by a layman is validly baptized'. On appeal the Judicial Committee of the Privy Council upheld the decision. In defeat Escott wrote to *The Times*:

> The Privy Council have given a decision by which a clergyman is to be suspended for three months for doing his duty—for refusing to use the burial service at the interment of one who had died 'unbaptized' and in order to put a face on this decision the Council has asserted that every human being, whether schismatic or otherwise, may validly perform the holiest office of the priesthood of God ... And will you reverend brethren, sit down quietly under such mockery as this? No, surely you will not! But you will unite in petitioning your respective diocesans to oppose, in the proper place, the wicked insult which the Privy Council has thrown on

the Word of God and His Church, and to memorialise the Queen of the realm respecting that religion, which the Queen as well as the Council, is sworn to defend.[28]

The letter was dated 20 July 1842. Allies, who had just taken up the living of Launton, sympathised wholeheartedly with Escott's appeal. He wrote to other like-minded clergymen and with some of them formed a committee, which drew up a petition addressed to diocesan bishops and to the archbishop of Canterbury. Committee members invited clergy in their respective deaneries to sign. They were not successful. According to one of the organising clergy, Edward Browne, the curate of Bawdsey in Suffolk, who later followed Newman to Rome, it attracted only 126 signatures and was never sent. A similar petition addressed to the House of Lords demanding liberty of conscience for the Anglican clergy was also was quietly abandoned.[29]

Subsequently a number of Anglican clergy were prosecuted for refusing to bury dissenters. All were convicted. Allies, however, was not to be intimidated. His views were well known locally. In October 1843 a letter in the local newspaper contained the information that 'rather than give him any trouble' the child of a parishioner was 'buried among the ashes of the Non-conformists at Bicester, in the ground attached to the Congregational chapel in that town'.[30] The issue came to the fore the following summer. *Jackson's Oxford Journal* reported a young woman's dying wish that she should

> be laid by the side of her friends in a certain part of the [Launton] churchyard. She was a Wesleyan, although baptised in church, and the Rev Mr. Allies in consequence, not only refused to let her lie where she had desired, but refused to bury her at all. The village was a scene of horrible confusion. Hundreds of persons were present while the corpse was at the churchyard for interment. Eventually the Rev Incumbent ordered a grave to be dug at the entry of the churchyard to bury the corpse in. The deceased's friends paid the clerk his fee and dug a grave in the spot where the deceased had wished to lie, in spite of the clergyman, who performed the burial

service over the empty grave, while the friends interred the deceased in the grave they had dug, and sung a hymn over the body.[31]

The burial took place on 4 July 1844. Rather disconcerted by the fury he had aroused Allies asked J. H. Newman, now his principal spiritual guide, his opinion on segregating the graves of dissenters; his friend counselled caution:

> The commotion it might excite would be so great as to render your rule of burying them in a particular spot inexpedient... I think it is inexpedient to seem to be attacking good people, or those who seem such. Your having *begun* the rule, is a reason for continuing it; else you might seem capricious. On the whole I think I should have been afraid of so decided a step, had it been a question of myself but this does not prove it is not right.[32]

Accounts of the proceedings appeared in newspapers far beyond Oxfordshire, with titles such as 'Puseyite persecution'.[33] Allies and the other younger Tractarians embraced this hostility as the cost of discipleship. Much of the press saw their programme as a new clericalism that threatened Reformation freedoms and urged the bishops to act. Some years later Ferguson recalled the incident in a polemical pamphlet:

> In a certain church-yard in the county of Oxford stands a grave, which was dug at the clergyman's request, and at a considerable distance from the other graves. The rector had this grave dug for the reception of the corpse of a Wesleyan Methodist. The priest, as he calls himself resolved that the remains of Methodists and Dissenters should not be buried in that part of the yard occupied by the *dead* of the Church. The precious ashes of the members of the Established Church were to be kept separate from the vile ashes of all schismatics. But the friends of the deceased refused to act as a jury for the earthly judge, and therefore buried the corpse close by

the other graves. The clergyman, however, nothing daunted, read the funeral service over the empty grave!!![34]

Unwilling to bury dissenters, Allies, despite his position as a minister of the national Church, refused altogether to solemnise their marriages. When in April 1846 he declined to read the banns of a Wesleyan couple, the matter was widely reported[35] and appeal was made to his diocesan, the newly consecrated bishop of Oxford, Samuel Wilberforce.[36] If Allies's relationship with Blomfield had been fraught, that with Wilberforce was to be one of ongoing cold war. Both bishops were ambitious, sure they could reform their dioceses and equip the Church of England to meet the challenges of the 'Steam Age'. Unlike his episcopal brother Wilberforce sought to gain his objectives through charm. It proved his undoing, for he is remembered, unfairly, as a model of insincerity, seeking to be all things to all men. And it was a strategy that made no impact at all on Allies. The men had met the year before when, as dean of Westminster, Wilberforce visited the Abbey's manor of Launton. Allies had noted in his diary that the dean knew about his friendship with Newman[37] and so he may not have been surprised to receive such a complaint. The bishop asked his rector to explain himself. Deeming Allies's attempted justification unsatisfactory, he referred it to the bishop of London and to lawyers, ecclesiastical and civil. Based on their advice his censure was unequivocal:

> They all agree: (1) that you are absolutely bound to publish the banns and perform the marriage of all persons ... *not being excommunicated by sentence of the Court*. (2) That you may be compelled to do so by process of the court; and (3) punished probably at the Common Law and certainly in the Ecclesiastical Courts for your refusal.

He patiently explained that ministers of the Catholic Church are also 'ministers of a church which *has been truly* a national Church; and so they have succeeded to public national offices'. 'Holding preferment by law' no Anglican minister could refuse to obey the law 'in virtue of which we retain our benefices'. He urged Allies 'to re-consider the position you are assuming', stressing that the Church herself was largely responsible for the dissatisfaction of those who sought to leave the fold. Clergy should value the 'permissive power' that remained by which they were enabled 'to retain any hold on those who will be so greatly injured by departing and who can be retained only by a very large admixture of a gentle and loving forbearance with any attempt after revived discipline.'[38]

It may be inferred that the rector submitted to what he was told was the law of the land. Ferguson, however, continued his onslaught. In 1848 he addressed a pamphlet to the bishop of Oxford highly critical of his practice and policies as regards High Church clergy.[39] *The Wesleyan Methodist Magazine* considered the strictures well deserved:

> The exposure of the papistical sentiments of Mr. Allies, rector of Launton, in the diocese of Oxford, demonstrates, that a man who teaches the vile mummeries of popery may, under the Bishop of Oxford, be recognised as a minister of the Establishment. The rebuke which Mr. Ferguson has given to the Bishop is well, and deservedly, administered; it is gentlemanly, caustic, and forcible. We wish for the pamphlet a wide circulation.[40]

In his mission to re-establish the rights and ancient teachings of the Church Allies faced a more formidable challenge than nonconformity. This was the open enemy; more insidious were those of her own authorised teachers whose theology he considered little better than dissent. Among these was the man appointed vicar of Bicester in 1843, John William Watts, a convinced Evangelical 'whose highest happiness was in the work of striving to win souls.'[41] Just a few miles apart geographically the two men were separated by a vast theological chasm. In 1847 Watts circulated a document impugning the doctrine of baptismal regeneration, which Allies, took delight in delating to his bishop. Wilberforce tried to mollify him, pointing out that as Watts had not categorically denied a Church teaching he could not be punished, moreover that men of his persuasion 'with all their errors of opinion, were in the main matter sound, and amongst the most devout men we had.'[42] Allies was outraged that Wilberforce apparently viewed the doctrine of baptism as a matter of opinion and demanded that action be taken. The bishop's reply was a stinging rebuke:

> Your letter has given me great pain, from the insight which it gives me into your mind. It is in almost every respect what a letter from a Presbyter to his bishop ought not to be: and this especially worthy of [rebuke] from one who professes to hold the office of a Bishop in reverence as the appointment of Christ ... You are very little aware of the Spirit which is in you. There is a self-sufficient bitterness running through your former and your present letter. In that you undertook to excommunicate a brother presbyter, your elder [in] the ministry; in this you insult your Bishop; insinuate that he has been guilty of dereliction of duty, and threaten, as the consequence of your opinion not being adopted, separation from the Church of your Baptism.
>
> For the sake of your own soul, I beg you to see the state to which self-confidence is lifting you up: for in truth such conduct does bespeak one, who is not far from being taken in the 'snare of the Devil'.[43]

Allies, although acknowledging that his letters may have given 'needless offence', was unrepentant, remaining gravely offended that 'certain great doctrines of the Gospel may with perfect impunity be denied' in Wilberforce's diocese. The bishop brought the correspondence to a close:

> You do not know what may have passed between me and Mr. Watts. The mode and spirit of your complaint make it impossible to speak to you on that head. The only inference you ought to draw is this, that a presbyter in this diocese who assumes to himself the office of judging his brother, and proceeds publicly to anathematize him uncondemned, will draw down upon himself my grave rebuke.

He denied that the doctrines of the Church in her liturgy and Articles could be called 'opinions'.

Why do I thus, as it were, exculpate myself to you? ... I do it perchance I may, through God's grace, win you to see something of that judging self-assuming spirit which is so strong within you, and which must, if it be not cast out, mar your ministry if it does not slay your soul.[44]

Wilberforce had indeed informed Watts of Allies's complaint of 'great scandal caused ... by the avowed subscription by you of a declaration by which the Articles and Liturgy of the Church of England are depraved.' And proceeded—gently—to point out how the document's assertion that 'Ungodly persons have neither been born again of the Spirit nor justified, although they were baptized in infancy', conflicted with the Articles and the words of the baptismal service. He concluded his letter by asking for Watts's understanding, 'I cannot effectually guard the purity of the faith in that portion of the Church committed to me, from dishonesty of subscription on the part of the Romanizers, if I wink at a like sin on the side of the Puritanizers.'[45]

Controversy at Oxford

Allies owed his theology to J. H. Newman and also valued, but often ignored, his practical counsel. Their intimacy dated from 1842, when, a few weeks before being inducted as rector, Allies was in Oxford for the bishop's visitation, and on 25 May both of them heard Bagot deliver his charge. Over a year had passed since the publication of Tract 90 and the cessation of the Tracts at the bishop's request. The controversy, however, rumbled on and Bagot felt he had to deliver an opinion on 'the most remarkable movement, which for three centuries at least, has taken place among us'. His adverse judgment marked a turning point. Of all the bishops one of the most irenic, he was sure that the Church had benefited considerably from Tractarian teachings, but of Newman's attempt to convince his more radical followers that the Thirty-Nine Articles were not Protestant in intent, he found little positive to say: 'I cannot persuade myself, that any but the plain obvious meaning is the meaning which as members of the Church we are bound to receive; and I cannot reconcile myself to a system of interpretation, which is so subtle, that by it the Articles may be made to mean anything or nothing'. For Newman—whose chosen battle was with liberalism and theological relativism—seemingly to be accused of slipperiness was wounding. And Bagot's attempted conciliation was unconsoling: 'I think few living men have written more ably upon the errors of the Romish Church, and the sin of leaving our own Church for her communion, than the author of the Tract'.[46]

By now, however, Newman no longer regarded Rome as the enemy, but rather the focus of unity. Within a year would formally retract all his polemical writings against her, but for the present kept his doubts to a small circle of trusted friends. Thus in May 1842 Allies having no idea that the vicar of the University Church might be troubled about the position of the Church of England, was delighted to find himself sitting next to him at the visitation dinner. He looked forward to having more frequent contact with the person whose writings had done most to shape his understanding of what it meant to be a Catholic Christian. Mary Allies was to say that as Byron had so strongly influenced his youth, in the years of her father's 'ripe manhood' he 'lived more and more upon Newman's mind'.[47] He said of himself that as a young priest the view he formed of Anglicanism was really 'Newmanism'.[48] In September he visited him at Oriel and a few days later wrote seeking guidance on how best to read the Church Fathers, whose works he had purchased now that he had the peace and seclusion for study. On his mentor's recommendation he did not begin a systematic study but rather 'dipped' into them as he prepared sermons or studied some theological controversy.

Unhappy in his parish, Allies was often at Oxford and was fully engaged with its religious controversies. He was of the same age as the younger generation of Tractarians and set about establishing contact with them. W. G. Ward, Fellow of Balliol, who had first stirred his interest in the *via media*, was one example. He was now in the vanguard of the Movement; with an analytical mind 'unafraid of inferences'[49] he could discover no good reason why the Church of England should be hobbled by its Reformation Articles, and the collective episcopal censure of Tract 90 had not restrained him at all. Two decades before, Newman as a young curate had rejected Protestant theology as ill-suited to the realities of human life and for a while had rested in Anglicanism's Catholic inheritance. But now, unable to answer Ward's persuasive logic, he too was being drawn inexorably towards Rome. Of these disturbing currents Allies seemed largely unaware, still confident that the English Church retained an inherent life and would again wear her pre-Reformation dress.[50]

In this cause he was willing to sacrifice, defying those in authority over him and spurning friendly advice. And as the tide began to turn against the Tractarians so there was a price to pay. When the university censured Pusey's sermon on the Eucharist, delivered on 14 May 1843, he joined with other non-resident members in writing to Dr Wynter, the Vice-Chancellor, to express their 'serious regret'. Wynter dismissed the protest as 'deserving of the strongest censure' and refused to receive any communication. Edward Badeley, the ecclesiastical lawyer, published the correspondence in *The Times* of 19 August 1843 where Allies's name was numbered among the great and the good of the 'Puseyites' including Gladstone, W. F. Hook the vicar of Leeds, John Keble, H. E. Manning the archdeacon of Chichester, and his close friends John and Edward Coleridge.

At Launton, in consultation with Oxford friends, Allies prepared his *Sermons on Romans* for publication. Despite once having been admonished by the celebrated Sydney Smith for an infelicitous turn of phrase,[51] he was confident enough to send the manuscript to Newman in December 1843. He replied, endorsing Allies's understanding of the 'justifying principle' and expressing his confidence that the sermons would do good. However, when asked that the work might be dedicated to him, Newman demurred. He no longer shared the author's exuberant confidence in the Catholicity of the Church of England as expressed, for example, in the sermon entitled 'The Visible Unity of the Church', which asserted that the state in establishing the National Church

> says to you, as a parent to children; I have tested her claims, I have enquired into her pretensions, and because I acknowledge her to be a true branch of the Church Catholic of God, to whom alone the promises of salvation are made over, therefore I have established her in great honour, I have sanctified my laws by her awful name, and anointed the Defender of them by her Ministers ...

> She then, is that one divine society, to whom in this land, the message of salvation and the means of grace are entrusted. She is, and for seventeen hundred years she has been among us, that one Body dwelt in by one Spirit, preaching one Lord, declaring one Faith, offering one Baptism, commissioned by one God and Father of all. She, and none other, is in this nation, the fold of Christ. *She, and none other*, because two Folds there cannot be, two Churches, two Bodies, two Kingdoms, two Cities, two Brides of Christ, God has not made. One Church united in profession of faith, in prayers, in ministers, in sacraments, God has set up. She claims in this realm to be such. She is either such, or there is another. But where is that other? By your presence here you acknowledge her to be that one true Church; for otherwise to partake in her prayers were a sin.'[52]

Newman, who had now resigned as vicar of the university church of St Mary's and was living in monastic retirement at Littlemore, replied as follows to Allies's request: 'I have a very great dread of committing others to any association, however faint or vague, with myself. I will say to you what the occasion makes me say, but which I should not like repeated as from me, that I am not to be trusted. Others say this freely; though it is not well openly to profess it.'[53] With characteristic insensitivity Allies pressed him about the dedication and at length secured his consent: it is dated Easter 1844, from 'one thankful for his teaching, and still more thankful for his example'.

Allies sent his book to a wide circle of friends and former colleagues, among them the warden of his own college, Wadham, notwithstanding the fact that Benjamin Parsons Symons was an Evangelical and had been one of the six doctors who with the Vice-Chancellor had condemned Pusey's sermon. Symons expressed gratitude but felt moved also to write:

> The dedication, however, has caught my eye, and it would be uncandid not to acknowledge that it has awakened some painful apprehensions. For I cannot but deplore 'the teaching' for which you express yourself thankful, and I believe it to be

really obnoxious to the grave charges which three-fourths of our Spiritual Governors have pronounced upon it. Of 'the example' I will not trust myself to speak, as I have no wish to give you pain, or to exercise uncalled-for judgement on a fellow-Christian, however erring he may appear to me.[54]

This insulting letter must have been painful to receive, but Allies did not have long to wait before an opportunity to retaliate presented itself. In October it would be Symons's turn by rotation to be appointed university Vice-Chancellor; ratification by the Convocation was needed but this was a formality. The Tractarians, however, saw both Symons, and Wynter the retiring Vice-Chancellor, as theologically tainted, unfit guides for a Christian university, and during the Long Vacation a number of letters appeared in the *English Churchman* opposing the former's appointment. J. B. Morris of Exeter and Henry Wall of Balliol took the lead in garnering support, the latter, although never an avowed Tractarian, was a good friend of Allies; a man of acute intellect, who in 1859 became the first Wykeham professor of logic.[55] *The Times* sided with the dissidents:

> Most members of Convocation, especially those who live at a great distance from Oxford are disgusted by the perfect turmoil in which the University has been kept by the factious and unjustifiable proceedings of the present vice-chancellor, and as Dr. Symons is well known to have similar propensities it is probably thought desirable to nip them in the bud.[56]

To underline his position, the editor required the supporters of Dr Symons to pay for a classified advertisement, which appeared on 1 October:

> It being now known that it is intended to oppose the nomination of Dr Symons as Vice-Chancellor for the ensuing year a committee of members of different Colleges has been formed in Oxford for the purpose of supporting his nomination. All members of convocation who may be desirous of co-operating with the Committee are requested

to send their communications under cover to the sub-Warden of Wadham College. (Oxford, 26 September 1844)

The Committee distributed a circular letter, soliciting support for their cause and Wadham men, led by John Griffiths, the subwarden, stood united in their anti-Tractarianism. Allies was the sole exception. His loyalties now lay elsewhere, and having seen the advertisement he immediately wrote to the Newspaper to express his indignation, his letter appeared under the pseudonym 'A Late Fellow of Wadham College'.

> You who are not accustomed to the indirect mode of proceeding practised by a certain party here, will perhaps be surprised to learn that the friends of Dr Symons are now recommending him to the office of Vice-Chancellor by stating that he is of a most mild and innocuous disposition, that he has always regarded Dr Pusey personally, with a very high esteem, and that he has never used any expression whatever which could lead me to suppose that he would exert his official irresponsible authority as Vice-Chancellor 'to put down the Puseyites'.
>
> Now, I say that this is neither more nor less than unfair and disingenuous. Dr. Symons's true recommendation to Convocation is this—'I have cordially approved and advised every measure of Dr. Wynter. I have ever been one of his secret conclave. I was one of the seven who judge without hearing, and punish without stating the crime. I counselled Dr. Wynter to veto Mr. M'Mullen's degree as a Puseyite,[57] and I will do the like in my own person when an enemy of sufficient importance is to be crushed' ... I affirm positively that Dr. Symons, where he was not at all called upon to express an opinion, has been known to apply terms to the belief and practice of the most eminent living name in English theology, and Dr. Pusey's most intimate friend, such as, after reflection, I think could only be applied with propriety to a convicted heretic. If he speaks thus out of office, what will he do in office?[58]

Giffiths responded with his own letter, copies of which were widely circulated among members of Convocation, affirming that it was 'morally impossible' that the writer could have 'any personal knowledge' of Symons's involvement with Wynter. He then disclosed that it was in a letter to 'the Rev. Thomas William Allies, Rector of Launton, near Bicester, Oxon.' that the Warden had given his adverse opinion regarding 'Dr. Pusey's most intimate friend'. The circular concluded rather ominously: 'Though I [have] been engaged for some time tracing to their origin a number of rumours of a similar kind, which have been circulated to the Warden's disadvantage, the only authority which I have found to be alleged for any of them, is this letter.'[59] Convocation voted on 8 October. For Allies and his friends it was a disaster. Symons was confirmed in office by 882 votes to 183.[60] The Protestant press noted with glee that the subwarden's appeal was 'answered by the personal attendance of ninety members of the college, which has only 108 Masters on its books; and only one man voted against the Warden.'[61] In the glow of victory Griffiths wrote to *The Times* demanding that the identity of its correspondent calling himself 'A Late Fellow' be disclosed. 'I do not seek this information for the sake of gratifying curiosity, but because we feel it to be our duty to mark by some further proceedings, our sense of the charges and insinuations which the letter contained against the head of our college.'[62] Despite the editor declining to oblige, the Fellows found Allies guilty *in absentia* and wrote informing him that he was no longer a member of their common room. 'A mean act of impotent revenge' in the words of another correspondent to the paper.[63]

One possible reason for the small number of *non placets* was a sense among previously sympathetic clergy that an extreme element was exercising a worrying power within the Tractarian party. The influential vicar of Leeds, W. F. Hook, spoke for these concerns in a circular dated 4 October. Alarmed by W. G. Ward's recently published *Ideal of a Christian Church* he said he could not join the protest against Symons for fear of being identified with those 'who advocate the extreme opinions of Mr Ward, and who form what is called the Romanizing party in the church.'[64]

Christianity at home and abroad

Allies regarded his incumbency at Launton as being sent into exile. Neither he nor Eliza were ever truly happy there. The opposition they so soon encountered was a rude awakening to the realities of parish life. Their sense of isolation was, however, occasionally lifted by visits from Oxford friends and the ebullient William George Ward was particularly welcome, especially by the youthful and high-spirited Eliza, who celebrated her twenty-first birthday on 17 December 1842. Ward was in the Tractarian vanguard, increasingly feeling that his communion was adrift and must somehow be re-incorporated into Catholic unity as represented by the Church of Rome. He and Allies often discussed such matters and it was during a visit early in 1843 that he had mentioned that Roman Catholic priests celebrated the Eucharist daily. Allies confessed that he was astounded by this; it 'went far to overthrow all my anti-Catholic prejudices...From this time forth I began to use the Anglican communion service by myself in the chancel of my church... It quite took my breath away'.[65] In her biography Mary noted that 'he began a daily celebration with closed doors, locking himself for greater reverence in the chancel'. Thomas's evolving sympathies with Roman Catholic practices created domestic tensions; Mary observed that at the daily Eucharist

> My mother herself was not allowed access to the church, nor indeed, possibly did she desire it. No one was ever a greater enemy of shams, and she seems to have known intuitively what love for the Mass means. My father also set up daily Matins and Evensong, a very unusual practice in those days, and he insisted on my mother's presence at Evensong, even though it obliged her to shorten her drive in the afternoon. My mother obeyed under protest; she did not like it, and she said so, but always strove to please him.[66]

Eliza must have wondered at her husband and the circumstances she now found herself in. She was obedient but not submissive, valuing highly her own judgment, and unafraid of voicing her opinion no matter how exalted the company. She has been described as 'sprightly',[67] a judgment supported by the use she made of the rectory's reputation for being haunted by a previous incumbent, 'She used to dress in a sheet at dusk when she thought "walking" was expected of Dr. Browne, and with a lantern in her hand would sally forth. She thus scared away those who were attracted by her fruit trees, especially her wall fruit. Oxfordshire is celebrated for its apricots, and so was Launton.'[68]

Eliza dutifully took her religion from Thomas and took it seriously, sympathising with him as he battled recalcitrant parishioners. As 1843 unfolded the young couple became increasingly unhappy, frustrated with their lot. Allies wrote to the bishop of London, requesting a new living. There was no reply. Eliza was pregnant and they agreed that a change of air was essential. A curate was engaged and in July they went to Ramsgate. The sea air did not much help and after a few weeks they returned to Launton, where a son was born. Named Henry Edward, he lived 'only long enough to be baptised.'[69]

Yet for Thomas this brief time away marked an epoch in his spiritual journey. At the resort itself he 'found no stimulation' and so decided to leave his wife and child behind and cross the Channel for a brief architectural tour in Normandy. He later said it was a spur of the moment decision, but his interest in gothic architecture was real enough. On returning to his parish, he joined the Oxford Society for Promoting the Study of Gothic Architecture, and corresponded on architectural matters, contributing to a study of monumental brasses.[70] But the impact of France extended beyond architecture. He had been intrigued by what Ward had told him about the continental Church, and may well have read Frederick Faber's new book, *Sights and Thoughts from Foreign Churches*, which had caused a furore, not least in Oxford. Despite being rector of Elton in Huntingdonshire Faber was unashamedly admiring of the Roman Church in comparison with his own and through the mouth of an imaginary travelling companion, a medieval monk, he belaboured the Church of England.

> You are not a fasting Church; yet every other Church in the world has been so from the earliest times. Your clergy, as a body, do not own their apostolical lineage as essential

to the construction of a church and the administration of the Sacraments. Your Church cannot excommunicate and shrinks, very uncharitably, from anathematizing heresy. Your people do not believe that infants are actually regenerated by Baptism. The commemorations of the departed are disused ... You do not elect your own bishops. Your clergy venture upon the liberty of marriage ... The glory of the Sacrifice of the Altar is clouded among you, which must lead in the end, to a clouding of the Sacrifice of the Cross. You do not honor tradition, which must in the end, lead to a dishonoring of Scripture.[71]

Faber's ghostly *alter ego* concluded that these were 'suspicious characteristics which lead foreigners to think, that your Church is only a Church upon paper'.[72] It was for Tractarians an unsettling conclusion and encouraged some to follow Faber's path to reconciliation with Rome.

Allies was a seasoned traveller; it was only six years since his humbling retreat from Italy. Now in 1843 he was returning to the Continent a different person: a priest, he believed, of the Catholic Church. This visit, the result he said, of 'the lassitude of mind and thirst for stimulus which the solitude of Launton had created', left on him an indelible impression. Repeated visits to France and then to Italy were to create and reinforce a disgust with the Church of England similar to that expressed in Faber's book. With improved transport—steamships and railways—increasing numbers of English people were visiting the Continent. Guidebooks proliferated. When, on 8 August 1843 Allies and his sister-in-law, accompanied by 'Mr Richardson' (probably her husband), crossed the Channel they would have had Murray's *Handbook of France* or something similar, perhaps the new English translation of Licquet's introduction to Rouen. Their tour lasted a fortnight and included visits to Le Havre, Rouen, Amiens, Beauvais, Mantes,[73] Chartres and Evreux. Allies made extensive notes on church architecture, writing up his journal on return. But in it his reflections went beyond the relative merits of gothic buildings. An astounding and most troubling revelation was the apparent centrality of religion in the lives of the French peasantry, so different from the dismissive attitude of his own parishioners.

> What would I give to be able to keep the doors of my church open from morning to night, and to see my parishioners come there not only to join in public, but to offer private, devotions and to confess to their priest, as I witnessed on Monday, August 14, at the village of Poix! Such a thing in England seems beyond the reach of the wildest imagination.[74]

Such was the tenor of his journal, which, in all simplicity, he sent off for his friend Edward Coleridge's perusal and comment. The Eton master was troubled by its naiveté concerning 'Roman error' and alarmed enough to forward it to Charles Dyson, rector of Dogmersfield in Hampshire, a friend since their time at Corpus together. He was alarmed. And there was reason to be concerned; within the past month William Lockhart, despite having promised Newman that he would wait for three years, had left the Littlemore community to visit Father Gentili at Loughborough and had become a Roman Catholic, the first of the inner group of Tractarians to convert. Allies's friends discerned in him a similar attraction that unless checked could issue in the same disaster. They misjudged him; the returned traveller was untroubled: 'I thought the caution then very unnecessary ... I was simply striking an equitable balance between two communions, as an observer from a rock discerns two contrasted landscapes.'[75] It was true; so deeply imbued with cultural anti-Catholicism, he was conscious of no temptation at all and had commented in his *Journal* that the 'mariolatry' he encountered in France was as bad as he had expected: 'It certainly seems to me the *black spot* of the Roman Church.' Yet Dyson's suspicions were not allayed when Allies went on to speculate that perhaps this exaltation of the Virgin had helped to safeguard the orthodox understanding of the Incarnation. 'There must' he surmised 'be some far deeper principle in the universal reverence paid to the Virgin than we are accustomed to allow' whereas 'the Protestant tone of thought seldom ... considers the part she had in the mystery.'[76]

Returning to his rectory, although undisturbed in his Anglicanism Allies had been deeply affected by what he saw of religion in France, sensing a Church revitalized, redeeming the poor from the humiliation of the Revolution. He concluded that its effectiveness sprang from beliefs and practices that most of his fellow Anglicans would have condemned as heretical:

> The spectacle of 40,000 curés, working in poverty and self-denial, and wholly devoted, day after day, to their sacred functions, cannot but make a great impression upon infidel France. Surely this is the salt that preserves her from thorough corruption, and by their daily intercessions, united with those of the Saints who built her churches, or whose relics lie deep beneath their foundations, the spirit of lawlessness is kept in check.'[77]

By contrast he found his own communion sadly deficient:

> I am with shame obliged to feel and confess that a pious Roman Catholic coming to England, so far from being touched by the purity of our faith or the warmth of our love, would probably be shocked at every step by a subtle irreverence which has infected our whole tone of thought and mode of action in holy things. It has become the atmosphere in which we breathe—by which even the instinct of the true Christian mind is so deadened that it cannot be aware, without going out of it, how much we have lost.[78]

His journal ended with a lament that having escaped 'the fearful taint of idolatry' the Church of his baptism had become 'so heathenised, so infected with indifference, and perverted by anti-Catholic prejudice, that *even the actual Church of Rome* can set her finger upon our defects and degeneracy'.[79] Unmoved in his conviction that Anglicanism was the reformed and purified faith of the primitive Church, for Allies the 'dim religious light' of Chartres had illuminated another world; this brief memory of Normandy became a recurring image, the touchstone of all that rankled with his daily lot as an English parish priest:

> How often when unable to get at the conscience of some hardened old sinner, when sighing over the closed breasts,

to me, of my school-children, did that hurried visit, while the horses were changing, to the Church of Poix, on the eve of the Assumption, and the people waiting at the confessional, recur to my thoughts!'[80]

The cost of discipleship

Allies returned to ponder another challenge that he could not dismiss: the revelation that in the French parishes the confessional was central to religious life. The more he studied the subject the more he became convinced that 'post-baptismal sin required sacramental confession and absolution.'[81] He asked a most reluctant Newman to become his confessor and by persistence wore down his objections to assuming this spiritual office. Allies made his first confession at Littlemore on 30 April 1844 and the two men agreed to meet quarterly thereafter. As Thomas examined his conscience and talked with his celibate friend about the sacerdotal ministry and as he studied the idea of priesthood in the history of the Church, a new and disturbing line of thought opened up for him with profound implications for his domestic life. He found himself being driven towards an opinion that caused him 'considerable disquietude': that the married state was incompatible with the priestly office:

> I was now arrived at the true notion of the presbyterate, as a real *sacerdotium*, as an office the main function of which was to offer the tremendous and unbloody Sacrifice for the living and the dead. Instinct itself whispered to me that such a function and the use at least of marriage did not go well together.[82]

This view gradually took possession of him in the months after the birth of his third son, Henry Basil, in May 1844. A visit later that year to the Catholic seminary at Prior Park, where he was shown around by Dr Fergusson, a young priest, who had in April arrived from Rome, did nothing to calm his anxious introspection: 'I gathered from him that a priest should celebrate daily and confess every fortnight.'[83]

In June 1845 he travelled to France again, this time accompanied by Charles Marriott. Before sailing from Southampton they stayed for a few days with John Keble and his wife at Hursley parsonage. For some this rural ministry was the Tractarian ideal exemplified. Not so for Allies. Such quiet Anglican domesticity seemed profoundly at odds with what he now believed priesthood to require. He later wrote of Keble:

> Confessor or martyr he was not made to be, but an ecclesiastical Walton, fishing by the side of quiet streams, and enjoying the lights and shadows as he dangled his trout at the end of his rod: no Athanasius, as I had dreamed, but an Anglican parson.[84]

He blamed such easy-going Anglican mentors for having misled him about the true nature of the priestly office. It was a discovery that must have caused unhappiness and tensions in the rectory, only hinted at in Allies's spiritual journal. The new baby was, however, a comfort as was the blessing of his having Newman for a godparent; the prayers and the counsel of a saint counted for much and early in life Basil discovered a vocation to the priesthood. The extent to which Thomas talked with his wife about the connexion between priestly celibacy and the efficacy of sacramental ministry must remain veiled; but for Eliza the knowledge that her husband felt able to continue administering the sacraments was surely of little comfort. In July 1846 she gave birth to their fourth son, Cyril, but there were to be no more children until Mary Helen in February 1852, when Allies had been a Roman Catholic and a layman for eighteen months. As a Catholic thinker, questions concerning the married state and virginity continued to occupy his mind, and his studies. He was particularly interested in the writings of the Fathers on the subject. In 1863 he read Augustine *On Continence* and commented:

> That the *contest* with concupiscence lasts all through this life, and it is the reward of the future to be without it, he lays down repeatedly, and that *continentia* is not a result of mere human purpose but a divine gift.[85]

Among the other Fathers that he studied on the same subject he noted a line from a poem by St Gregory Nazianzen, 'where he likens married life to a snail or a tortoise painfully dragging his shell.'[86] We cannot know how his evolving theological views impacted upon his marriage, but when in September 1850 he became a Roman Catholic and accepted that he was—and had always been—a layman there must have been a release of tensions, especially for poor Eliza. After Mary Helen there were to be two more children, Mary Frances in September 1853, and in February 1855, Bernard Joseph, who lived for a month.

A shock to faith

From the time of his arrival in Launton through studying the Fathers and conferring with Newman Allies was comforted by the sense that his understanding of the Catholic faith was being ever deepened, although this did little to ease the daily frustrations of parish life, and his sense of spiritual impotence. His long-suffering wife must have been perplexed by her husband's developing creed and its impact on his behaviour. She was compelled to share his martyrdom: the hostility of parishioners, estrangement from other local clergy and ridicule in the newspapers. And there was an underlying fear: of the lure of Rome and the ostracism and financial hardship that conversion would involve, practical considerations which seemed hardly to weigh with Thomas. But he was aware of Eliza's restiveness, and reflecting on their first year at Launton he recalled her complaints about the time he spent examining local churches for architectural survivals of pre-Reformation worship, speculating that she 'instinctively drew back from it as tending towards Rome.'[87]

This architectural interest had consequences for his own church. In December 1843 he decided, without any consultation, to remove 'a hideous gallery... the chosen resort for young men and women... being equally convenient for nut-cracking and love-making.'[88] Village reaction was predictable: 'Dire was the anger which its removal occasioned in many such breasts.' He found the opposition bewildering and irritating. Eliza began to doubt his stability. She was, he reported, 'seriously out of temper' at him. 'The truth was, she looked with suspicion on everything

I was doing.'[89] Then in the spring of 1844 he made another unpopular decision to re-pew the church with open oak benches. 'If a word were required to be said on the detestable system of pews, it would be sufficient to refer to the testimony still borne by foreign churches to a better arrangement.'[90]

That he personally bore the cost of this work confirms his complete commitment to his parish church and its worship. Yet in just a few months, by the time the work was completed in September,[91] his confidence in Anglicanism had received a heavy blow, causing him to reconsider his plans for the structure of the church. The reason was that he had read Ward's *Ideal of a Christian Church*. The book that alarmed so many, so unsettled him that from December 1844 in the Launton baptismal register he ceased to style himself presbyter 'of the Holy Catholic Church' and substituted 'of the Church of England'. The *Ideal* was excoriating. Ward maintained that the Reformation had wounded the universal Church in much the same way as the Arian heresy and was 'wholly destitute of all claims on our sympathy and regard'. Healing could come only through reunion with Rome—the ideal Church. And here he saw encouraging signs. That 'the whole cycle' of Roman doctrine was 'gradually possessing numbers of English Churchmen' was a cause of 'joy and wonder'. The author issued a challenge to the university authorities that they could not ignore: 'Three years have passed since I said plainly that in subscribing to the articles I renounce no one Roman doctrine.'[92] Thus it was that on 13 February 1845, Allies attended Convocation to vote with the minority against the resolution that because Ward had subscribed to his communion's Articles of Religion in obvious bad faith he should be censured and stripped of his degrees.

The day before the vote in Convocation was Allies's thirty-second birthday and he marked the occasion, as was his custom, with an assessment of the changes that the year had wrought in him. On reflection, Ward's book had only brought to the surface a growing sense of unease:

> Since my last birthday one very important change of view has developed itself—a secret and yet undefined dread that we are in a state of schism. All that I see around me seems

so little like the Church, as either revealed in the Bible, or realised in the early ages. Confusion of face meets us on every side. In this respect Ward's book gave but an articulate voice to the conclusion to which I had been for some time more and more inclining.[93]

Allies later identified the *Ideal* as a milestone on his path from considering 'Anglicanism as a *machine out of order* but *restorable*, to considering her a monster with two heads and no feet.'[94] But that point had not yet been reached, and discontent with a relationship does not necessarily mean divorce. Before such a great issue could be decided he needed to grow spiritually:

God's providence in sending me to this place, hitherto so dark and discouraging to me, has been greatly unfolded. Surely it is a place of refuge for me. An Egypt or a Nazareth in one point of view, but a Zoar in another ... I was in great danger of perishing through vain-glory; therefore I am corrected by a place the whole tendency of which is to lead me to work unto God, and not as unto man, as well as to humble and sadden me.[95]

And maybe Ward's logical penetration was an inadequate guide; if his spiritual understanding was deficient, his counsel might be tainted. On the evening of the vote in Convocation Allies had dined with William Palmer at Magdalen College and then went with him to Balliol to visit Palmer's brother, Edwin.[96] He noted, rather disapprovingly, that whilst he was there Ward came in, 'in very high spirits, evidently from the weight taken of his mind.'[97] That night Allies, who was *persona non grata* at his own college, slept on a sofa at Magdalen College, in the rooms of Thomas Harding Newman, who was a fellow, for although their theological paths had diverged, their friendship remained. The following day, as Allies strolled with Ward in the Parks, he accused him of

imitating the conduct of the reformers which he so censures— i.e. dissenting on his private judgment from the Church in which he was educated, and preferring the Roman Church, without having the means of truly knowing her *indoles*.[98] He denies this; but there is considerable truth in it.[99]

Afterwards they went together to Pusey's rooms in Christ Church, and found him in low spirits about the Church. Just before quitting Oxford Allies learnt from T. H. Newman of Ward's intention to marry. He no doubt felt that it confirmed his suspicions regarding the latter's judgment and all the more so because he had not been told directly.[100] Given all his soul-searching about celibacy he was amazed, and his shock would not have been lessened when he heard Ward's explanation, which he noted in his journal:

> Doubtless in a pure Church priests should not marry; but I am a priest in the Church of England, which is impure, so I shall.[101]

Confused and uncertain, Allies drew 'comfort and support' from J. H. Newman, simply from 'seeing him where he was,'[102] meaning still an Anglican. Soon even this solace was to be withdrawn. In May he and William Dodsworth, anxious to know more of their leader's state of mind, visited Littlemore and were disturbed by the tenor of his remarks on the separation of the English Church from the rest of Christendom. As they left Dodsworth asked Newman directly if they could deny the rumours of an imminent secession. His response left them in no doubt: his departure was inevitable.

Allies certainly agreed that his Church was isolated from the rest of Christendom. But a nagging unease is far from intellectual conviction and he felt no calling to follow his mentor. There were indeed inconvenient facts that needed to be confronted, but these could be left for a more convenient time; perhaps one day they would be seen as temptations to leave the path of duty. Encouraged in this by Dodsworth and other 'old-fashioned' Tractarians like Pusey and William Palmer,[103] as a young man with a growing family Allies could not visualise himself as anything other than an Anglican clergyman. Launton might be hard, but it was the call of duty, and he continued to spend largely from his income to preserve and enhance the fabric of the church. So much so that in the summer of 1846 financial need caused him to write to W. E. Gladstone:

> Should you hear of anyone wishing to have a boy prepared for Eton, and to be put up with one or two others, I should be much obliged to you to recommend me. The work of restoring my Church has compelled me to take pupils.[104]

That the pains his parish brought him could be a means of sanctification was a recurring thought and consolation. For outwardly he was ineffective: dissent was going from strength to strength, whereas—beyond the walls of the rectory—Catholicism had made no headway at all.

> My people obstinately refused to discern the difference between the Church and the meeting-house, unless, indeed, by the unacceptable way of preferring the latter. I preached to them over and over again what schism and heresy were, and they never would understand that there was any sin in them, or cease from the unlimited practice of them. I strove to make them frequent the Sacrament, in vain. Low, disunited, immoral, conceited, brutally ignorant and brutally obstinate, they were and they would be. Reverence for my office they had none; consideration for me as a gentleman and landlord, and occupant of a large glebe, they had. I tried to make myself their friend in every conceivable manner, and with profuse expenditure; but with little success. And then, whenever I tried to rest on the Church's regulations and means of grace, they seemed to produce no effect.[105]

According to Mary Allies—of all his children closest to him in thought and feeling—her father 'took possession of his parsonage, a ripe scholar, longing for intercourse with intellectual minds and also to win souls.' Unfortunately the two aims implied a contradiction. His parishioners could not enter into his scholarly musings but neither could he, unlike his Divine Master, enter into their everyday concerns, and by using these things illuminate the spiritual realm. 'He did not freely unlock the treasures of his mind, for he knew by a long experience that few stop to grapple with intellectual subjects. The rector of Launton very soon discovered that he could not reach his farmers' souls.' She further analysed the problem:

> He was not exactly the man to deal with the British farmer, for his thoughts never ran on crops, turnips, or the price of wheat. The entries in his diary show that he took the shortcomings and ignorance of his parishioners sorely to heart. 'The state of the people here is frightful,' he wrote after a two years' experience. At no period of his life can I fancy him having a brisk talk with a poor man. He could not enter into the small things which a farmer loves.[106]

Allies found his solace in the works of the Fathers that lined the shelves of his study, but what he discovered in these pages accentuated his sense of separateness, perhaps even superiority:

> As I saw their mighty folios ranged round my room, I felt that I was not alone, that I had a ground for what I believed, that I stood on a higher footing than the system in which I lived, and was acquainted with those who enabled me to *judge* that system.[107]

Thus study of the early Church helped to reconcile him to pastoral failure. Rather than arising from any deficiency within himself the problem was the system within which he was called to work:

> Of course, as a beneficed clergyman I had practical work to do, a weekly office of teaching and worship, sick and dying calls. The whole practical working of the Anglican system was thus brought before me. And I found daily and weekly that *it would not go. Cela ne marchait pas.* Theoretical difficulties had a new edge given to them by practical daily disappointments.[108]

Yet other Tractarian pastors laboured in country parishes and earned the love and devotion of their flocks; at Lavington, for example, where H. E. Manning ministered and of which he wrote, 'I loved the little church under the green hillside, where the Morning and Evening Prayer and the music of the English Bible for seventeen years, became part of my soul';[109] at Hursley, too, where John Keble was revered. For this humbling daily ministry Allies was tragically unsuited.

The lessons of continental Christianity

Such daily toil and anxiety could be borne only so long, and during 1845 Allies became increasingly restless, convinced that he could not stay 'the whole summer without suffering to such a degree as to incapacitate me for work... [T]he extreme mental solitude of Launton made me feel that I needed such a change of scene as perhaps foreign travel alone supplies'.[110] Images of Catholic devotion haunted his thoughts fuelling a desire to return to France. When he learnt that Charles Marriott, whom he had known since undergraduate days when both were members of the 'Ramblers',[111] also planned to go there, his mind was decided. Marriott was a fellow of Oriel, and an early friend of J. H. Newman, although not an advanced Tractarian and not a member of the Littlemore community. As the summer progressed and Newman's conversion was expected daily, Marriott welcomed the opportunity to escape the fraught Oxford environment. Allies, however, who later said that his purpose in going to France was 'to find the truth at all costs' may not have been the best travelling companion for his peace of mind.

Reporting on French ecclesiastical affairs was becoming a popular recreation for English divines.[112] For example, Christopher Wordsworth, canon of Westminster and former headmaster of Harrow School, had spent August 1844 in and around Paris talking with prominent clerics and educationalists. Among them were Augustin Bonnetty, an Anglophile writer and journalist, the Abbé Guéranger, restorer of the Benedictine order, and Jules Gondon, editor of the influential newspaper, *Univers*. The last named was well informed on English Church matters, having written a book on the Catholic movement.[113] He also consulted Lamennais, the celebrated editor of *L'Avenir*, whose attempts 'to unite popular with papal principles' had been rebuffed by Rome. He, according to Wordsworth had by now 'removed himself out of the sphere of revealed religion.'[114] Allies and Marriott were to meet all these except Lamennais, although they did call on his one-time collaborator, Lacordaire, who remained an active force in religious circles.

On return Wordsworth quickly published a book entitled *Diary in France Mainly on Topics concerning Education and the Church*. He found things to praise, particularly aspects of Catholic worship such as congregational chanting, and opined that such 'heart religion' was the outpouring of the ancient Catholic faith of which the English and Gallican Churches were national branches. But he judged 'papal religion' a baleful and oppressive influence and filled his pages with invective against Ultramontanism, the steady advance of Roman influence. Indeed, the severity of his anti-Roman polemic was such that when Lord John Manners complimented the book in a parliamentary debate on the Maynooth Grant (April 1845), the arch-Protestant member for Lincoln, Colonel Sibthorp responded with a loud 'hear, hear'.[115] Wordsworth was an Establishment figure and the lesson he drew from his time in France was that Louis Philippe's 1830 settlement severing the link between Church and state had been a historic error. 'The Crown has suffered irreparable injury from the annihilation of the Church as an *Establishment*. The Church being left to itself has become *un-national* indeed *anti-national*.'[116]

The book contained a good number of gratuitous sideswipes. It joined, for example, in the national sport of lamenting the moral tone of French society:

> authenticated records of flagrant iniquities meet the eye and ear in this place with a degree of frequency and publicity which is a melancholy proof of the inefficacy of the religious teaching and worship of the Roman Catholic Church as it exists in France.[117]

The apparent disconnection between morality and religion in Catholic countries was a problem for many advanced Tractarians, who otherwise longed for re-union with the see of Rome. Indeed Allies himself, for all his admiration of the French Church, could not help but conclude that the Revolution had seemingly turned France into an 'infidel country' in which only the 'the *lowest classes* and women' were Christianised. In marked contrast to England it was 'rare to see a man—very rare indeed a *gentleman*—attending a service.'[118] Among those who were challenged by a perception that in Britain there was a higher moral tone and that Protestantism was associated with greater social stability and coherence was Henry Edward Manning, the rector of Lavington in Sussex. He was already a close friend of Dodsworth when Allies began to correspond with him: seeking the spiritual help that Newman had once given him. Manning wrote to Allies about the issue of 'moral tone' in December 1848:

> One thing is a difficulty to me. How do you explain the fact that England is in a higher state, social and political, firmer and more united than France or Italy? This sometimes tempts me to think I hardly know what.[119]

Allies essayed a solution illustrating his dislike and distrust of 'Church of Englandism', surmising that as a nation of shopkeepers the English knew well the value of probity and how to accommodate and compromise, because any disturbances would interfere with the process of making money. 'Tyre, Sidon, and Carthage were very quiet and well-behaved places, when they deserved the bitterest condemnation of Isaiah.'[120] Allies visited Manning in London a week after this letter and the topic was again discussed:

> M. set forth as a problem to be discussed how it was that the countries which had received the Reformation had so increased in civilisation, wealth, outward prosperity, and good government, whilst those that had remained faithful to the Holy See, had as much declined.

Henry Wilberforce was also present and all three agreed 'that it was a great difficulty, telling not for the Church of England, but against any Church system, and in favour of Arnoldism.'[121]

Where the religion of Launton was not dissent it could perhaps be classified as 'Arnoldism', which Allies defined as 'a belief in one God, a Redeemer and a Sanctifying Spirit disengaged from any ecclesiastical and sacerdotal system.'[122] It was largely an orderly place, whose parishioners accorded to their rector proper respect as a gentleman. But of him as a priest, upon whose mediation hung the issues of eternity, they knew nothing. This was just the problem. For the rural French things were different, their curés, in addition to their sacerdotal anointing, had an influence arising from oneness with the ordinary people, with whom they shared a common life. Allies by contrast was perceived as remote and condescending.

For Wordsworth the apparent immorality and instability of French society only confirmed his belief in the superiority of the English establishment. He was impatient with those of its members who were attracted to Rome, dividing them into three classes: the profligate seeking easy absolution, those brought up in ignorance of the visible Church, and 'spinsters and widows of a certain age':

> The very same principle which leads some of this class to squander their sympathies on parrots and lapdogs, seems to lead others ... to fall victim to the arts of proselyting Romanists.[123]

The sentiment would have exasperated Allies; Wordsworth represented what he most disliked about the Church hierarchy: a complacency that did not feel the wound of separation, or accept that there might be spiritual riches upon which Anglicanism had turned her back. Allies had none of these failings; rather his temptations lay in the opposite direction. When, in 1849, he published a book detailing his own reaction to the continental Church, his friend, William Palmer of Magdalen, said that it was particularly valuable as 'an an antidote to Christopher Wordsworth's Establishmentarian Journals ... however, he disfigures the French Church, you throw yourself *too completely* into its spirit.'[124]

In the summer of 1845 Allies arranged with Robert Aris Willmott to be his curate while he travelled. Three years before he had examined him for ordination at Fulham Palace. Having arrived at Launton the day before Wilmott rose early on 4 June to bid farewell to the rector, who was travelling to Eton to join his wife.[125] Three weeks later, after taking Eliza and the children to stay with her father at Bideford, he went with Marriott to spend a few days at Hursley with John Keble. They crossed the Channel on the Southampton–Le Havre packet.[126]

It had been arranged that they should visit the township of Yvetot, not far from the port, just north of Rouen, where there was a Catholic school and junior seminary. Clerical education was Marriott's particular interest. In 1838 he had been involved in the founding at Chichester of the first seminary established to prepare graduates for Anglican holy orders, becoming its first principal. But he was there only briefly before ill-health compelled his resignation and return to his Oriel fellowship. At Oxford he had been visited by two French teacher-priests, Pierre Labbé and Charles Robert, who, among other reasons for visiting England, wished to meet the celebrated Newman. Being introduced to other Tractarians and learning of Marriott's interest in theological education they were insistent that he should visit France and inspect their school, which had been established to serve the needs of the community and the Church. Now, three years later, he took up the invitation.

For Allies visiting Yvetot was a seminal event on his spiritual path and he later had much to say about the Petit Séminaire and its staff. Having no obvious sense of the ridiculous, he never mentions the township's principal claim to fame, that before the Revolution it had its own crowned monarch and was described by Voltaire as a 'kingdom infinitely small'. Its extraordinary history might have been forgotten had there not been published in 1813 an anti-Bonapartist squib, *The King of Yvetot*, which when set to music was sung all over France and immensely popular.[127] Thereafter, the small community became a by-word for presumption; witness an 1838 edition of the *New Monthly Magazine*:

> As for the capital itself, at present existing, it possesses a post office, an under-prefecture, a small free school, one street a mile and a half long, ten thousand inhabitants and an immense number of cisterns, which, as they are generally empty, does not prevent this metropolis from being almost entirely without water for nine months of the year.[128]

Ignoring all this the visitors found the religious character of the Petit Séminaire very impressive. Its principals, the Labbé brothers—Xavier and Pierre—worked to ensure that a good proportion of their scholars would proceed to the Grand Séminaire and become priests. Their efforts were successful: in the period 1830 to 1876, of the 446 pupils who graduated, 332 were ordained to the priesthood.[129] For Allies also, Yvetot was a place of spiritual education, contributing significantly to his eventual conclusion that he had never been a true priest. In Pierre Labbé, he found a friend and confidant, who whispered encouragement on his journey and who would be with him when he took the final step. He and the other Yvetot teachers introduced the travellers to the leading clerics of Rouen, where they visited the churches that had so impressed Allies in 1843, especially the soaring St Ouen.[130] With Marriott he joined in the Catholic life of the city and attended High Mass in the cathedral. Allies welcomed the absence of a sermon: 'The really edifying thing is the devotion of the people, who look upon it as a sacrifice, and do not require that perpetual stimulating of the *understanding* as among us.'[131] However, both visitors were unhappy that they could not '*hear* and follow' the priest as he uttered 'words so very grand and touching.'[132]

After a week in Normandy they travelled to Paris. Arriving there on 2 July their first call was on Miss Young, who was residing at the Abbaye aux Bois. It is not clear whether this was Isabella or her sister Jane, both recent converts who were travelling on the Continent. The Abbaye was both a convent and a fashionable address: the sisters let rooms to upper-class ladies. For example, living there at the time was the celebrated Juliet Récamier, once at the centre of Parisian intellectual and social life, who was still visited by notable figures such as Chateaubriand. Miss Young introduced her visitors to her Catholic friends, one of whom, a nun, escorted them on a tour of her convent of St Vincent de Paul on the Rue de Bac. In its chapel Allies was impressed to hear of how the miraculous medal that had become so popular among Catholics had its origin in the Marian visions of an anonymous sister still resident.[133] Among other notable Parisian churchmen, they met l'Abbé Carron, a former secretary to the archbishop, who explained the work of the celebrated seminary of S. Sulpice, a subject that had interested Wordsworth the year before. They also waited on the publisher, M. Bonnetty, who took them to see the Abbé Guéranger and Emmanuel d'Alzon, the vicar-general of Nîmes; both men were visiting Paris. The former was the founder of the restored Benedictine community at Solesmes and had unsuccessfully urged d'Alzon to join him. D'Alzon had, as a young man, once fallen under the influence of Lamennais but unlike his mentor had become a committed and consistent advocate of Ultramontanism. He was a charismatic figure and a remarkable preacher: Allies was astonished at his histrionics, remarking on the contrast with Newman's pulpit style.[134] D'Alzon believed his great vocation was to combat secularism and Protestantism, and was most interested to learn of the latest developments in the Church of England. He had founded a secondary school in Nîmes, believing that education was key to re-christianising France. To this end also he worked for the revitalisation of the religious orders and had become the spiritual director of Marie-Eugénie Milleret du Brou, the founder and first superior of the Sisters of the Assumption, who owed her religious awakening to the ministry of Lacordaire.[135] He was in the process of forming an order for men and with five others was about to begin his novitiate. D'Alzon took the two travellers to visit the Assumptionist sisters where Marie-Eugénie spoke warmly on the centrality of the religious orders to the educational mission of the Church. Allies was greatly impressed by what he learnt of this practical work, observing to his hosts 'I am sure there are thousands of young persons in England who would enter into religious orders if we had them.'[136]

On 15 July the two met Lacordaire himself and had 'very animated talk'. They were distinctly impressed; Allies said that he was 'St. Bernard as it were, returned again in the vigour of manhood', and 'it was worth coming to Paris to see him'. But the experience was disquieting: their vigorous defence of the Catholicity of the English Church elicited little sympathy. Allies asked him whether he would consign a person who was 'firmly convinced that the English Church is a branch of the Catholic Church', 'out of the pale of salvation'. The reply was not reassuring: other than invincible ignorance, which in the case of the Tractarian leaders was 'out of the question'; only 'corruption of the will' could prevent perception of the truth, and any one guilty of this stood condemned. The French divine was unmoved even by Marriott's testimony as to the holiness of one unnamed Anglican friend. The visitors put his dogmatism down to ignorance: 'He did not seem acquainted with the peculiarities of our position. He spoke with great energy and ability. I can fancy what his force in the pulpit must be.'[137] In his view of Anglicanism Lacordaire was not alone; Allies noted resignedly that despite their Gallican heritage all the French clerics he spoke to asserted that 'the first thing' was to 'be in communion with Rome. Without unity they can conceive no holiness, nor self-devotion, nor even sincerity'.[138] Allies, in meeting so many, was not able to perceive the different nuances in the reaction of the French clerics to Anglicanism, but the published account he later gave of their opinions has been of value to students of the clash of parties in the French Church.[139]

The two returned to England on 28 July. Both were deeply affected by what they had seen of the revival of religious life in France. Marriott wrote in his journal:

> I am, I may say, fully convinced that neither the worship of saints, nor the use of images, nor the withholding of the cup, at all affect the life of the Roman Church. What I have seen has led me to reflect bitterly on Mr Bowdler's *Quid Romae Faciam?*[140] The answer is, all that you try in vain to do in England ... [H]ow to get ecclesiastics to live in primitive brotherhood and primitive poverty? How to bring people to confession? How to induce candidates for holy orders to submit to education? How to get the opportunity of restoring the daily sacrifice? How to warm our churches with devotion ... It requires every allowance for the reserved and retiring character of the English to hope that we are not, even in comparison with the French, a fallen people?

Nevertheless Marriott's belief in the Catholicity of the Church of England was unaffected and in the remaining few years of his life he never contemplated leaving the Church of his baptism. Returning to Oxford one thing alone unsettled him:

> Still, were it not for *one* person who thinks otherwise, I should take our failings calmly, as a mere hindrance to be

surmounted, and even take easily the painful separation between us.¹⁴¹

Allies, by contrast, was badly shaken by his experiences. He wrote in his diary on Sunday 10 August:

> Since my return home I have been more troubled in mind than for near eight years past I can remember to have been. I think this has arisen from a general and very vivid sense of the deficiencies of the English Church, and of her very dubious position, which has been impressed on me by what I have heard and seen in France.¹⁴²

More comfortable and composed in mind

The next day he went to Littlemore, wishing to consult Newman 'as a confessor and director'. But the latter no longer considered himself a priest and there could no longer be a sacramental aspect to their relationship. Nor could Newman say anything to reassure his troubled friend, telling him that for almost four years he had lived under the conviction 'that there was no choice between the Church of Rome and infidelity' and for this reason his conversion would not long be delayed. He said he wished now to complete the book he was writing, would resign his fellowship in October, and 'after publishing cannot say how soon the final step may follow'.¹⁴³

This was a direct challenge, but for Allies not a difficult one, for he felt no divine call to abandon his Anglican ministry, and, despite his unsettlement, he was increasingly conscious of an inner call to stay with his Launton flock: an assurance that he was not required to follow Newman. It led to a sense of liberation, and the following Sunday he noted in his journal:

> Blessed be God, since my visit to Oxford I have been more comfortable and composed in mind. I seem to feel that it is the will of God that I should remain quiet where I am in

> the discharge of everyday duties, and this is all I can desire. I have felt my interest in things around me restored. I have been quietly arranging for studies to come—I have finished my [travel] diary, and hope soon to recommence sermons, or a steady course of reading.[144]

Yet later, when reflecting on this time, he spoke also of a divided conscience, quiescent for much of the time but with intellectual doubts never fully answered and returning to trouble him each time he thought of the Catholic practices that had so impressed him:

> I well remember also the disconsolate feeling with which I began to compare the ritual of the Catholic with that of the Anglican Church, and as the thought came full before me that perhaps it would be my duty to become a Catholic, I said to myself, the divine command ought to be as clear as that given to Abraham, for the sacrifice would be as great.[145]

Preference for a ritual was not the compelling call of God: the worship of the Church of England could be changed and its bishops revived. However, whilst not sharing Newman's conviction that the English Church was a dead branch severed from the living tree of Christendom, Allies still valued his counsel above all others. Now, however, they talked at cross-purposes: as at their last meeting as Anglicans on 11 August, when Allies, quite insensitive to the true situation, sought his mentor's reassurance that in its essential beliefs Anglicanism had emerged unscathed from the Elizabethan settlement. For Newman the question was beside the point, simply a technicality; all that mattered was the judgment of the *orbis terrarum*.[146] Nevertheless he was still able to offer his friend some spiritual counsel, and Allies left Littlemore that Monday morning in good spirits. He called on Marriott, who told him it was his duty to remain with his flock and spoke of the many grounds for optimism: that Tractarianism was making great strides in the parishes. One shining example was the Oriel graduate, Edward Monro, the incumbent of Harrow Weald. He had achieved the religious transformation of this newly created rural parish. According to Marriott, from a regular congregation of 700 he had 100 communicants, of whom 'all speak to him before communicating; thirty-five regularly confess'. Allies, who could not point to similar success, noted in his diary, 'this is no work of man'.[147]

On Friday 10 October, Allies again met Marriott in Oxford, who told him over breakfast that Newman had 'gone over'. It made less impact on him than might have been expected: 'I had been so long expecting the blow that it was almost a relief when it came.'[148] He was one of the select few to receive a personal note dated the day before. It was waiting for him when he returned to Launton:

> I am to be received into what I believe to be the one Church and the one Communion of Saints this evening, if it is so ordained. Father Dominic the Passionist is here, and I have begun my confession to him. I suppose two friends will be received with me.[149]

✣ 3 ✣

The Church of England is not in Schism

Transplanted to another part of the vineyard

For most of the Tractarians who remained the impact of the Littlemore conversions was muted. They felt that they had moved on and that in their monastic isolation Newman's little company had failed to discern the movement of the Spirit. Pusey drew comfort from the thought that now his friend could again take up arms for the Cross in the sister Church, infusing new life into it:

> Our Church has not known how to employ him. And since this was so, it seemed as if a sharp sword were lying in its scabbard... because there was no one to wield it... He seems then to me not so much gone from us, as transplanted into another part of the Vineyard, where the full energies of his powerful mind can be employed, which here they were not.[1]

Writing in the *Christian Remembrancer*, the journal that he edited, J. B. Mozley acknowledged the power that Newman had wielded. With his departure 'a general sense of inward safety, security, and peace is disturbed. The mind likes a patron.' Yet because most of those who had journeyed with him and whose thinking he had so influenced—men like Allies—remained behind, Mozley questioned whether Newman himself had ever been 'truly Anglican'. It was as if the converts were a detached group who had viewed the Church from the outside, seeing it as 'a book religion, not an acting one'. Thus the relevance of what had happened was discounted, although in developing his thesis Mozley advanced an unfortunate hostage to fortune:

> A movement thus external in its origin is no sign against that Church in which it arises, in the sense in which the departure of her genuine children, who had had genuine natural feeling and faith toward her, would be. Where this decided note is shown, and a large mass of genuine sincere faith is seen deserting a cherished ground against its will, where a movement shows this spirit, not in some of its followers only, who simply yield to the influence a superior has over them, but in its leaders too, and, as one whole movement, exhibits this type; that is a peculiar sign, certainly.[2]

By this token the exodus in 1850 and the years after was surely a 'peculiar sign'. Yet perhaps Mozley was right, of the three acknowledged leaders of the movement only Newman doubted that the Church of England was a true branch, and the immovability of Keble and Pusey was for many assurance enough that she did not lack the note of holiness. Allies, among those comforted, turned now to Pusey to become his confessor and spiritual director, and both were among those who—not many days after Newman's conversion—travelled to Leeds for the consecration of the new parish church of St Saviour's. It was Pusey's creation, built to infuse the blessings of Tractarianism into a community blighted by rapid industrialisation. No one knew who had funded the work. Hook, the vicar of Leeds, was told that the money came from 'a penitent', and over the west door ran the inscription 'Ye, who enter this holy place, pray for the sinner who built it', words calculated to inspire misgivings among the defenders of the Reformed faith. Longley, the bishop of Ripon, who counted himself among their number, had to be assured that the donor was still alive.

Allies travelled to Leeds on 27 October. At Bicester he joined Pusey, who had been up all night writing the sermons he was to deliver. They journeyed together to Blisworth station, Northampton, and there, while waiting for the train to Derby, talked at length about the English Church in the light of Newman's secession. Pusey conceded that her position was 'weak'. Allies commented that the Roman case was 'much more easily stated logically', and Pusey agreed, observing that once Rome's Catholicity was accepted, 'our position becomes strictly defensive, and lies in points not easily stated'. Nevertheless, he was 'full of hope' because of 'the contrast between the Church of England, as he remembered it, and as it is now'.[3] And indeed the grounds for his optimism were evident the following day, the Feast of St Simon and St Jude, when two hundred and sixty clergy assembled for the consecration. Longley, concerned to dampen any excessive Catholic zealotry, preached on 'the blessings which we enjoy as members of the English Church, and the dangers that would be incurred by ungrateful abuse of them'. Allies was very harsh on him, judging it an address of 'deplorable feebleness' and a 'most calumnious misrepresentation of the Church of Rome. He made out our peculiar blessing to consist in the possession of the Bible, "the instrument whereby the soul is new-born to God" ... I have rarely been so disgusted as by this sermon'. Thomas did not keep his opinions to himself: 'Dr P ... corrected me more than once for a rather free exercise of my opinion on the Bishop's proceedings.'[4] He accepted the rebukes, but later, when Pusey tried to convince him that the bishop's view of scripture was 'susceptible of a right meaning', he remained profoundly unimpressed,[5] a difference which foreshadowed an eventual estrangement.

The following week Allies went to Littlemore, having resolved to give three years to considering 'this dreadful Roman controversy'. He sought advice on 'a course of reading and moral and intellectual discipline for that time'. But Newman, unwilling now to take responsibility for any delay, told his former penitent to 'wait and read his book and then consult him on any particular point. It was such a *sea*.'[6] It was not a long wait; on Thursday 27 November, Allies wrote in his diary:

> Went into Oxford to get J. H. N.'s book, so anxiously waited for, and with a combination of opposite feelings—love, fear, curiosity; ... returned in evening with my treasure.

He read *An Essay on the Development of Christian Doctrine* 'with avidity'. There was much to please him and with Longley in mind would have warmed to its image of a mythical vast deluge which had swept away all trace that the 'divine efficacy of the Scriptures' had ever been a historical doctrine of the Church.⁷ In truth, Allies had been so stirred by the continental Church that he was largely untroubled by the developments that the book strove to justify, and as he read, it was with the recurring thought that one day he would become a Roman Catholic. For the present he reflected anxiously on the validity of his priestly ministrations, concluding that any call to conversion would have to be an inescapable crushing conviction; there was so much at stake: 'if one left one's present communion, one would be so utterly torn up by the roots, and dashed on the sea shore to perish like sea-weed'.⁸

The Church of England cleared of the charge of schism

Despite the power of Newman's example and the cogency of his arguments and despite his own disturbing presentiment, Allies would remain in the Anglican ministry for another five years. His intellect was not to be easily subdued, even by such a magisterial authority as Newman: close historical investigation was to convince him of the Catholicity of the Church of England. Whether he found the answer that he was unconsciously seeking cannot be answered, but it is certainly true that he would not accept his mentor's scholarship on trust. He must prove for himself that submission to the see of Rome was an inescapable duty. Here papal supremacy was the key. Tractarians believed that the Church of England taught all that the primitive Church deemed necessary for salvation; if it could be shown that a monarchical papacy was a usurpation, then their duty was to stay and work, so that its essential Catholicity could be revealed.

In the introduction to his book Newman had turned his fire on Anglo-Catholicism's founding charter, the Rule of St Vincent: *quod ubique, quod semper, quod ab omnibus creditum est.*⁹ He said that by applying this test the doctrine of papal supremacy had greater authority than another doctrine the Tractarians considered fundamental for salvation:

> In truth, scanty as the Ante-Nicene notices may be of the Papal Supremacy, they are both more numerous and more

definite than the adducible testimonies in favour of the Real Presence.¹⁰

For Catholics, Roman and Anglican, and for the Orthodox, the Real Presence was a precious truth beyond debate, but Canterbury and the East were as one in refusing to obey the pope in all things. Newman's challenge was that the supremacy was *jure divino* and that those who rejected it were schismatics and outside the Body of Christ. No one who sought to obey the will of God could remain separate: 'the question of schism is a question of salvation.'¹¹ In his conversion Newman asserted that papal sovereignty was implicit in the truths vouchsafed to the apostles by their risen Lord: that there was an absolute need of a monarchical power.¹² Peter's successor spoke with the voice of Christ and, despite infallibility not having yet been promulgated as a binding doctrine, the papacy was the ultimate guarantor of the indefectibility of the visible Church:

> As creation argues continual governance, so are Apostles harbingers of Popes ... [A]ll Catholics agree ... first that the Pope with General Council cannot err either in framing decrees of faith or general precepts of morality; secondly, that the Pope when determining any thing in a doubtful matter, whether by himself or with his own particular Council *whether it is possible for him to err or not, is to be obeyed* by all the faithful.¹³

Allies wanted the evidence that this full-blooded sovereignty was written—albeit in embryo—in the ancient texts. Armed with his own extensive collection of the Fathers, he resolved to document what the primitive Church had to say on the subject. 'I thought that by appealing to those who lived so many ages before the Reformation I had found judges beyond the reach of corruption, and of conclusive authority.'¹⁴ He began his quest by writing to his mentor, seeking guidance on the authors who had studied what the Fathers had written on the papacy. In reply Newman could only direct him to a forthcoming new edition of Kirk and Berrington's *Faith of Catholics*, with its extensive patristic quotations, and to Feuardent's notes to the third book of St Irenaeus's *Adversus Haereses*.[15] But the comprehensive analysis Allies sought did not exist; a somewhat disconcerting reply. Yet, such was his confidence in Newman that he feared that his investigation would have but one outcome: the authority of Rome would be confirmed and the call to convert would become irresistible

In the spring of 1846 in the hours that he could spare from pastoral duties, Allies grappled with the Fathers. What he concluded would decide not only the validity of his priesthood, but his family's future standing and prosperity. And at first he found what he expected to see: 'Roman Primacy confirmed on all sides'. But as he accumulated references he began to see that the apparently closing trap could be side-stepped; slowly he reached the conviction that whilst the primitive Church did acknowledge the primacy of Rome as a practical matter, its authority was not regarded as *jure divino*, not absolute:

> the unanimous testimony of Christian antiquity represented the Church as governed by a Patriarchal system (as I call it) at the head of which was the Bishop of Rome, whose power was limited by the canons and by usage.[16]

This scholarly riposte to Newman's challenge allowed him to remain a conscientious priest of the Church of England for another four and a half years. Other Anglicans, also disturbed by Roman claims, found his answer to the charge of schism conclusive, and most of these, unlike the author himself, never lost faith in the Catholicity of the Church of England.

After just three weeks of intensive work, by the beginning of April 1846, Allies had written an article proving patriarchal government in the primitive Church and thus establishing by the Vicentian rule the rights of the English provinces. He intended to publish it in the July number of the *Christian Remembrancer*. However, some who read the draft, in particular Edward Coleridge, thought this reply to the theory of development so powerful that he was persuaded that its impact should not be lost in the pages of an avowedly Tractarian journal. Expansion into a book would enable more evidence to be included, and William

Palmer of Magdalen pointed him to a rich vein of material, which he apparently had not consulted: the works of the Gallican theologians and Church historians, Bossuet in particular.[17] On the face of it it is surprising that given his sympathy with the French Church he was unaware of the significance of these writers, particularly considering the extent to which the Tractarians had already identified themselves with the Gallicans in opposing the universal primacy of the bishop of Rome. For example, in his standard work on the Church 'designed chiefly for the use of students in theology', William Palmer of Worcester College, one of the founders of the Oxford Movement, had defended Anglican liberties by quoting extensively from Bossuet's *Defensio Declarationis Conventus Cleri Gallicani*. It was the other Palmer—Allies's friend 'Deacon Palmer'—who lent him a copy of the *Defensio*:

> To my astonishment, I found that he seemed to take the same view as I had done myself. Often he quoted the same passages, and he carried his argument into the third and fourth Councils. I kept on as I was preparing my article for the press, adding matter to it, chiefly out of him, so that, in a very short time, on June 3, it increased to about double its first size. I thought my original view was thus confirmed by independent witnesses, and I published my little book in June with the greatest possible confidence in its truth.[18]

The full title he gave to the book explains Allies's purpose in writing: *The Church of England Cleared from the Charge of Schism upon Testimonies of Councils and Fathers of the First Six Centuries*. He was convinced that the historical evidence he had uncovered contradicted Newman's superficial reading of Church history:

> What Mr Newman asserts is, moreover, entirely in accordance with the Patriarchal system, as we have attempted to describe it, 'that the writers of the fourth and fifth centuries fearlessly assert, or frankly allow, that the prerogatives of Rome were derived from apostolic times, and that because it was the See of St. Peter.' I confess that these words set me upon the

> search, and that I have found such testimonies in abundance; but then they are invariably to the Bishop of Rome as holding the first see, not as *Episcopus Episcoporum*: they bear witness to the Patriarchal system not to the Papal. For instance all lovers of truth would be obliged to Mr Newman to point out, in all the works of St Augustine, a single passage which is sufficiently distinct and specific to justify the Papal claims, nay, which does not consider the Pope the first Bishop, and no more. It is little to say I have searched for such in vain.[19]

In Allies's opinion the attitude of the North African bishops to Roman claims paralleled the later assertions of the Eastern Patriarchs. He quoted the words of St Augustine to Pope Boniface:

> To sit on our watch-towers and guard the flock belongs in common to all of us who have episcopal functions, although the hill on which you stand is more conspicuous than the rest.[20]

Allies saw a primitive Church in which an ideal balance was maintained between the authority of each bishop and the primacy of Rome. He cited St Cyprian as a leading advocate of episcopal autonomy and dated the relentless progress towards universal jurisdiction as beginning in the reign of Leo the Great, whose papacy began in 440, ten years after the death of Augustine.

> The combination of the Patriarch's, and still more, of the Universal Primate's power with that of the Bishop is a nice point. If this be pushed too far, it issues in a monarchy; if the other alone be allowed, it converts the one Kingdom of Jesus Christ into an unlimited number of petty republics. On the one hand there is a danger pregnant to the high priesthood of the Church; on the other to the sacrament of unity. The one-sided development of St Leo's teaching has produced the Papacy, in which the Bishops who represent the Apostles, are no longer the brethren, co-ordinate in authority,

but the delegates of St Peter's successor: but the one-sided development of St Cyprian's teaching has rent into pieces the seamless robe of Christ. Yet this need not be so. Surely the first six centuries of her existence are not a dream.[21]

The Church of England Cleared was read avidly by those unsettled by the 1845 conversions and by the theory of development. It became an important weapon in the Anglican armoury as her theologians sought to answer Newman, and was extensively quoted in the *Christian Remembrancer's* review of the *Theory of Development*.[22] In a powerful but ultimately unsatisfying critique, the reviewer tackled the key points of Newman's analysis, arguing that the tests purporting to identify illegitimate developments were inadequate. For example, they could not cope with subtle changes arising simply through exaggeration; as with moral qualities so with doctrines, they may become corrupted without losing their original essence, as courage may shade imperceptibly into recklessness or prudence into meanness. Similarly, a sensitive reserve about matters of faith has become Jesuitism, and in the same way has a right belief in the eternal felicity of the holy departed become the questionable doctrine of saintly intercession.

Newman had argued that denying the validity of developments would lead to the unsatisfactory conclusion that the creeds of the ecumenical councils must be unsound, because these represented an advance on the inchoate faith of the ante-Nicene Fathers. For the reviewer conceding this could lead to a juggernaut of doctrinal change:

> Starting from the small and seminal beginning ... it gradually grows and enlarges ... Truth gains fresh augmentation at Nice, at Ephesus, at Chalcedon, at the Lateran Councils, at Florence, at Trent: its first one is at Nice, where our Lord's divinity is declared; that step gained, in course of some centuries it proceeds under the infallible sanction, to establish the cultus of St. Mary.[23]

If the process thus develops through its own inner logic then it would seem the Christian must chose between the creed of Rome and no creed at all. The reviewer was, however, unconvinced, arguing that the 'Nicene Creed only asserted and guarded a doctrine that had been held from the first'.[24] Indeed, Newman's argument pushed to *reductio ad absurdum* 'appears to us to run, distinctly and quite inevitably, into a denial of the doctrine of our Lord's divinity as an original doctrine of revelation'.[25] Moreover, and here the reviewer turned to Allies, whether the doctrines of the modern Rome were legitimate developments, or as traditionally taught, somehow known from the beginning, was unimportant beside the fact that they were binding on the faithful under the 'infallible sanction'. At the heart of the Catholic case was the universal authority of the see of Rome:

> The doctrine of papal infallibility comes out as the keystone of Mr Newman's whole argument and according as he proves, or fails to prove, that doctrine, that argument stands or falls.[26]

In the light of this the reviewer was struck, as Allies had been, by the meagre attention given in the essay to this key issue; 'the actual proof of it hardly catches his eye as he turns over the pages'. Newman's case for an inerrant authority rests on the 'necessity of a continuance of a Revelation once given'. If the original revelation was guaranteed then its true development must also be guaranteed. The reviewer was unconvinced:

> With the formula—some uncertain truths are results of certain truth: if they are, they are certain themselves—he gets something out of nothing, converts uncertainty into certainty without a medium; and transmutes the known into the unknown by a stroke of legerdemain.[27]

A more realistic perspective was provided by Bishop Butler, who maintained that there can be no presumption against a partial revelation and no reason to assume that 'from the fact of its incompleteness that it will go to fill that incompleteness up'.[28] The argument from analogy 'leaves the Revelation ... exposed to the same chances of abuse, perversion or neglect in carrying out, which attends the course of nature'.[29] After

The Church of England is not in Schism

discounting the inevitability of an infallible tribunal, the review turns to practical and historical considerations: must the Church of Christ have a centre of unity? Allies's work had proved the contrary. And Orthodoxy's long history of sanctity and missionary zeal answered Rome's contention that severance from her is slow death. In examining the vexed issue of the evolution of governance in the early Church the article cites Allies to prove that the primitive model was patriarchal, not papal.

Newman received his copy of *The Church of England Cleared* on 25 June and could not have been surprised when unsettled Anglicans with whom he was in correspondence found comfort in its arguments. One such was Mrs Elizabeth Bowden, the widow of his dear undergraduate friend, John Bowden.[30] He challenged her as to whether the practice of the primitive Church could be used to establish a rule of faith. Indeed he would not have dissented from the *Remembrancer*'s judgment: 'Mr Newman himself admits that his presumption is the strongest part of his argument; and alludes to the historical evidence for the Papacy, as a subordinate and secondary part of it.'[31]

He told Mrs Bowden that antiquarianism could not substitute for the authentic voice of the living Church.

> How are you qualified to decide on the historical questions which are in debate? How can you tell whether Collyer is right or wrong?[32] Or whether Allies or my reply to him would be right? If I said that, *as* Allies shows that the fourth century was patriarchal not papal, *so* I could show that the first three centuries were Arian not Athanasian, what means would you have of judging between us?[33]

Henry Wilberforce had turned eagerly to the book to counter his old friend's relentless undermining of his Anglicanism. Newman, after chiding him for being so quick to read *The Church of England Cleared* whilst disregarding the *Essay on Development*, summarised his response:

> There are men, as I suppose T. W. Allies who have been converted to the Catholic Church by their belief in the divine

> mission of S Peter and his successors; I on the contrary ... mainly received it [papal supremacy] on the word of the Universal Church, that is, on faith. I believed that our Lord had instituted a Teaching, Sacramental, organised body called the Church and that the Roman Communion was as an historical fact its present representative and continuation.[34]

Some Catholics pressed him to reply to Allies, and he told Lord Adare[35] that 'in time I shall take it in hand' and repeated his argument:

> I have made the papacy, *a doctrine*, which may be fairly taken on faith without a bit of evidence in its favour, on the Church's warrant, supposing there be no great antecedent objection to it, and no facts clearly irreconcilable with it ... whereas Allies, I believe, takes it as a primary and elementary point, to be proved simply by historical evidence in order to the determination *which* is the Church. This is just the reverse of the mode of reasoning in my book.

He suspected that Allies may not have understood the primary reason for his conversion. Certainly there was no common ground between them, so that even by the end of his letter to Adare, Newman had changed his mind: 'On these grounds it is that I suspect I shall have nothing to do with Allies.'[36]

With the passing years he became increasingly irritated when potential converts continued to cite Allies's book as grounds for their security as Anglicans. In November 1849 Henry Bittleston, on the brink of converting, was still quoting it. Newman responded that it would be futile to answer it; 'It is not argument that keeps them, as the Last Day will show': *decipi vult populus ergo decipiatur* ('the people wish to be deceived, so let them be deceived').

> Now to say that a theory of religion is true, which is at present held by half a dozen people only on the face of the earth (for not many more hold the Pope to be as great as Allies does and no greater,) is to my feelings and judgment a simple

absurdity—and I do not know how with patience to argue against it.[37]

Newman esteemed Allies highly as a classicist, not as a logician or historian, and his sweeping dismissal of historical investigation as a guide to the perplexed was somewhat unfair. After all, the object of his *Essay on the Development of Christian Doctrine* had been to examine the evolution of the Church's doctrines to confirm that these could be traced back to the original deposit of faith, the 'idea of Christianity'. Thus Anglican critics believed they could legitimately call Allies's investigations in aid when responding to this new theory. W. G. Ward, now himself a convert, challenged them in the *Dublin Review*, denying that historical investigation could ever provide the solid ground they claimed to have found:

> *All* history is, on the surface, difficult and perplexing; why should we expect church history to be an exception? Were church history, indeed, the Catholic's *rule of faith*, as it seems to be Mr Allies's, the question would be very different; but there is no one statement on which all the great Catholic doctors are more unanimous than on this, that not individual study of ancient records, but the living voice of the Church, is the appointed interpreter of Apostolic Tradition.[38]

Allies has read the records closely, but had come to the wrong conclusion because he lacked an integrating principle of interpretation:

> it is interesting to mention that more than one of the recent converts, who had been especially given to the study of the Holy Fathers, and had been drawn towards the Church mainly by that study, have declared that, since their accession to the light of the Catholic faith and the grace of the Catholic Communion, their former reading has been invested with so much of new significance and of deeper meaning, that it appears as though they had never before really understood it.[39]

Catholic critics emphasised the contradictions and lack of clarity that they found in Allies's book, and it was not hard for them to make a case, for he sought to defend a communion of which he despaired against a Church that he much admired. Ward mercilessly exposed what he considered the weaknesses of his old friend's thesis, saying he was anxious to express 'sympathy with the *moral* aspect of Mr Allies's work, because (to say the truth) we have the meanest possible opinion of its *intellectual*.'[40]

> In fact the intense dislike which we fairly profess to entertain towards the reasoning of Mr. Allies's work, arises in no small degree from vexation that so paltry a theory can have the power to detain one moment in a mind, apparently well fitted for a far worthier and higher position.[41]

Ward identifies Allies's central idea not as the patriarchal system which was 'not of divine right' but as being 'the high priesthood of the bishops ... the recognized doctrine of Anglicans of his school.'[42] Granting the apostolic authority of each in his diocese it follows that no bishop could possibly be schismatical:

> We have only further to carry our minds gradually onwards from the fourth century, and recall to our memory the innumerable new questions on faith and practice which the church has had to encounter in her course, to form some idea of the Babel-like confusion, the indescribable hubbub, in which the whole church would be involved, by the time she came down to the nineteenth century.[43]

Ward's review drew heavily on the work of another recent convert, Edward Healy Thompson, whose rebuttal of *The Church of England Cleared*, entitled *The Unity of the Episcopate*, appeared early in 1847.[44] The book did not attempt to reinterpret each of Allies's historical examples but rather to challenge him on the issue that eventually proved decisive: the source of jurisdiction in the visible Church. Thompson argued on theological grounds that from the beginning the episcopate was an organic unity bound together in its head, the bishop of Rome, Peter's successor, contrasting this with the confusion inherent in episcopal 'equality and parity' posited by his opponent. Just what sort of primacy did Allies concede to Peter and his successors?[45] And whence was the authority of the Anglican bishops derived? Thompson agreed that universal jurisdiction had been bestowed on the whole apostolic college, but the jurisdiction of individual bishops was local and specific; they could not act outside their own dioceses. When the apostles died their ability to grant jurisdiction died with them. How then could the need of the Church for a continuing episcopate be provided for? The answer was that the universal jurisdiction of Peter, the accepted head of the apostolate, continued in an unbroken chain of acknowledged successors. 'The pope is therefore, *jure divino*, the ultimate source of all ordinary jurisdiction.'[46] Moreover, 'papal infallibility is the necessary logical corollary of holding the unity of the Episcopate in conjunction with Peter and the indefectibility of the Church.'[47] Thompson set aside the question of the validity of Anglican orders but asserted that separate from Rome the Anglican episcopate has no legitimate jurisdiction, having exchanged 'the cramping fetters of the state from that service of perfect freedom.'[48]

Allies took the opportunity of answering this criticism in the second, greatly expanded, edition of his book: 'from June 1846 to October 1847 I was constantly engaged in reading, extracting, arranging, and adding. Then the book was passing through the press till February 9, 1848, when it came out six times the bulk of the original article, and thrice that of the first edition.'[49] The revised title indicates the search for even greater authority: *The Church of England Cleared from the Charge of Schism upon the Decrees of the Seven Ecumenical Councils and the Traditions of the Father*. The book was dedicated to Edward Coleridge:

> Fervent in love, in labours unwearied,
> For the sacred cause
> Of our Mother the Church
> This Defence
> Of the rights of the Catholic Episcopate
> Is dedicated by the author,
> As the fittest offering he can make

> To the guide of his youth
> And the firm friend of his maturer age.

In a preface of sixteen pages he responds to *The Unity of the Episcopate* as 'vigorously *asserting and reasserting* ... the very primary Idea in dispute, *without any proof of its truth*.' His answer to the challenge of jurisdiction was to allege that it was a theory worked up by 'the school of St Ignatius Loyola' when it was shown that the Decretals upon which the popes had previously based their claims were a fraud.[50] He brands the division of episcopal authority into orders and jurisdiction as 'very clever, but wholly arbitrary, and moreover *ex-post-facto* defence of the plenitude of Papal power' and says that he will quote Bossuet and Van Espen as rejecting the theory in the 'strongest terms.'[51]

Thompson must have found it frustrating that his argument was so summarily brushed aside. In due course he was able to take up the debate with his opponent directly. The occasion was a review of Allies's later work, *Journal in France*, that he was preparing for the new Catholic periodical, *The Rambler*, which in an early issue had noticed the second edition of the *Church of England Cleared*:

> Few controversialists write with the same good temper and sincerity as the author of this volume. He will not therefore be either surprised or irritated, if we say he appears to be still far from comprehending his own theory or that of Mr. Thompson's *Unity of the Episcopate* which was written in reply to his first edition.[52]

Allies was unmoved by the Catholic response, and when he debated with French ecclesiastics his patriarchal theory formed a wall of defence against their strong advocacy of papal claims. Some of these conversations are recorded in his *Journal*, and one of these gave Thompson a reason for approaching him directly. He explained that he would have waited until after review appeared before telling him he was its author, 'but there is one observation you have made in the work which seems to call for immediate notice.' After some flattering references to Allies's 'candour and fairness', he referred to the author's account of an exchange with Lacordaire:

> I said that I by no means impugned the primacy, but entirely recognised it; my defence was in the difference between a primacy and an absolute monarchy... He quoted Bellarmine as saying it was a monarchy tempered by aristocracy and democracy. The Pope could not destroy the episcopate. I said our new converts maintained that he could: that if all the bishops of the world were on one side, and the Pope on the other, he could make a new episcopate.[53]

As a new convert, and on behalf of his fellow converts, Thompson described this as a 'monstrous proposition ... as extraordinary a misapprehension as any the most ultra Protestant ever conceived of the doctrines of the Church or of the opinions of her members.'[54] He said that he was 'thinking of writing' to Lacordaire to assure him that in none of the converts' works is to be 'found even a seed or a germ of so strange an opinion as that which you say they all distinctly maintain.' He asked Allies to look again at his own book (*The Unity of the Episcopate*); for example, at page 106: 'Bishops are not mere *delegates* or *vicars* ... [they] do not act merely *for* the Pope, as his *representatives*; they act *with* him—*in essential union* with him—as organs of that divine system of which he is the head'. The supposed opposition is 'an impossible one, it is simply absurd'. This Thompson asserts is the doctrine of the Church:

> You are perhaps not aware that not a single publication has appeared from the pen of a convert which was not carefully looked over by some Catholic divine, commonly a bishop or professor of divinity.[55]

Allies's reply, which came almost immediately, has not been preserved, but he clearly expressed some puzzlement, to which Thompson responded—'I do earnestly long to put you at the right point of view from which all that looks at present so perplexing to you would be harmonious and plain'. But all he could do was to propose different metaphors, such as foundation and superstructure, before displaying a little of the intolerance that Allies thought he had detected among the converts:

The Catholic no more holds that the Church can ever become Peter again than he holds that the body of a man can become again that germ or atom that it was when life was first breathed into it in the womb. The Church is not *Peter* only and can never be *Peter* only. What is your *principle* of unity ... what is it that makes many Episcopal units one episcopal body? I never could get an answer.[56]

The defeat of Gallicanism

Thompson's question was the reason why in the end all of Allies's extensive readings in the Gallican divines, which provided most of the additional material for the second edition of his book, proved fruitless. Papal authority was integral to the Catholic Church; the French theologians could not reject it, but neither could they define clearly its extent and limitations. Manning had pointed this out when thanking Allies for the first edition of his book (August 1846). After describing the work as 'the most candid, and therefore the most satisfactory, we have had on either side of late', he alluded to Gallicanism's failure to speak to the Anglican position:

> The point in it I should like to know your further thoughts upon is, how you distinguish between Bossuet's view of the Roman Primacy and your own.
> 1. Does he hold that jurisdiction inheres in the Primacy, or,
> 2. Does he hold that the Canonical Supremacy or jurisdiction by Canons is so engrafted into the Primacy and united by affinity of nature as to be inseparable?
>
> In either view we should have subtracted obedience, according to his judgment.[57]

Others shared Manning's foreboding, and Allies too, though delighting in Gallican scholarship, always acknowledged that it had no answer in logic to the growth of Ultramontanism, no account to match the clarity and power of Cardinal Bellarmine's stark assertion: 'The ordinary jurisdiction of bishops descends immediately from the pope.'[58] However,

The Church of England is not in Schism

in both editions of *The Church of England Cleared* Bossuet's response to this is quoted:

> One objection of theirs remains to be explained, that Bishops borrow their power and jurisdiction from the Roman Pontiff, and therefore, although united with him in an Ecumenical Council, can do nothing against the root and source of their own authority, but are only present as his Counsellors; and that the force of the decree, as well in matters of faith as in other matters, lies in the power of the Roman Pontiff. Which fiction falls of itself to the ground, even from this, that it was unheard of in the early ages, and began to be introduced into theology in the thirteenth century; that is, after men preferred generally to act upon philosophical reasonings, and those very bad, before consulting the Fathers.[59]

'Philosphical reasonings' they might be, but Allies accepted them as 'the true logical development of the Papal Theory ... Grant but its postulate, that the Pope is the sole vicar of Christ, and all which it requires must follow'.[60] Against such a potent idea the Gallican case lacked coherence:

> On the other hand, that school which ranks Bossuet at its head, and which sought to limit, in some degree, by the Canons the power of the Roman Pontiff, and maintained that Bishops were, jure divino, successors of the Apostles, in a real, not in a fictitious sense, however well-founded in what it maintained on the one side, was certainly inconsistent. It gave either too much or too little to the Roman See;—too much, if its own declarations about the succession of Bishops and the authority of General Councils be true, and founded in antiquity, as we believe; too little, if the Pope be indeed the only Vicar of Christ on earth, and the supreme Ruler of His Church; for then these maxims put their partisans very nearly into the position of rebels, and, in truth, brought the Gallican Church to the brink of a schism in 1682. However

this may be, that school is extinct; the ultramontane theory alone has now life and vigour in the Roman Church. It seems to absorb into itself all earnest and self-denying minds, while the other is left to that treacherous conservatism which would use the Church of Christ as a system of police, for the security of worldly interests.[61]

Indeed, having at great length and with many examples proved to his own satisfaction that the ancient Church was patriarchal in its government, as he surveyed subsequent centuries Allies was almost swept away by the grandeur of the emerging vision of papal supremacy. In a sentence of prodigious length he cites one champion of papalism after another: 'saintly Hildebrand... our own St. Anselm... St. Bernard, the last of the Fathers'. It was the cause for which 'our own St Thomas shed that noble blood... for which St. Francis, the spouse of holy poverty ... and St Dominic ... and one greater yet, the warrior saint, Ignatius, raised their myriads of every age and of both sexes ... That power is, indeed, the most wondrous creation which history can record.' And then, remembering his purpose in writing, he adds:

> and one to which I am not ashamed to confess I should bow with unmingled reverence, had not truth a yet stronger claim upon me, and did not the voice of the early Church, its Fathers, Councils, Martyrs, sound distinctly in my ears another language.[62]

Yet the French Church had succumbed; Gallicanism was dead. Perhaps the Anglican scholars had misread antiquity? Allies was sure that they and he had not, because there existed a compelling witness

> who take[s] away from our opponents their proudest claim ... of being by themselves the Catholic Church. Let it never, then, be forgotten, that any argument which would prove the Church of England to be in schism would condemn likewise the Eastern and Russian Church ... It is not the Catholic Church against a revolted province, as our adversaries would

have us believe; it is the one Patriarch of the West, with his Bishops, against the four Patriarchs of the East, with theirs.[63]

Indeed, the East's unbroken traditions of orthodoxy and sanctity put Allies's own communion to shame:

> Here, at least, are no sympathies with the heresiarchs of the sixteenth century: the Synod of Bethlehem has anathematised Luther and Calvin as decidedly as the Council of Trent. Here was no Henry the Eighth fixing his supremacy on a reluctant Church by the axe, the gibbet, the stake, and laws of premunire and forfeiture: no State using that Church as a cat's-paw for three hundred years, and ready now to offer it up a holocaust to the demon of liberalism. Here is the ancient Patriarchal system, the thrones of Constantinople, Alexandria, Antioch, and Jerusalem, subsisting still. Here is the same body of doctrine, the same seven sacraments, the same Real Presence, the same mighty sacramental and sacerdotal system, which Latitudinarian and Evangelical, statesman and heretic, dread while they hate, as being indeed the visible presence of Christ in a fallen world, the residence of a spiritual power which controls and torments the worldling,—while it disproves and falsifies the heretic.[64]

The challenge posed by Orthodoxy to those who would equate Catholicism to communion with the see of Rome was answered from his retreat in Jura by the youthful Peter Le Page Renouf. As a student of Pembroke College he had converted in 1842 at the age of eighteen. In a most cogent pamphlet (*The Greek and Anglican Communions*) he emphasised the deep divisions that Allies strained to minimise, pointing out that the Book of Homilies unequivocally condemned the Western Church as the communion of the antichrist, whereas both the Synod of Bethlehem and the Council of Trent were as one in anathematising the Thirty-Nine Articles.

The Anglo-Catholic scholars bewailed the broken unity of the Church. Renouf denied the premise: it was accepted by neither the

Roman nor the Greek Church; if Allies admitted the Catholicity of either communion then that of Anglicanism must be denied. He pointed out that over the millennia numerous churches had fallen away from Catholic unity, citing in particular the Donatists and the Monophysites. Both cases paralleled Orthodoxy in terms of the large numbers involved and the long duration of the schism.

> The existence of the Russian Church for eight or nine centuries is no proof of its truth. It is not nearly so wonderful that it should still exist after eight or nine centuries of almost undisturbed tranquillity, as that *the Monophysite Communion should still exist after fourteen or fifteen centuries*, during which it has undergone the most fiery persecutions.[65]

This argument would not have resonated with Allies, in whose eyes the Eastern Church was a model of sound doctrine and sanctity compared with the degenerate state of his own communion. 'Truly all that was deficient on our side seems made up by the Greek Church. And this living and continuous witness of a thousand years is to be added to that most decisive and unambiguous voice of the whole undivided ancient Church.'[66] This ancient patriarchal model remained the ideal and the existence of division, in particular

> all so-called national churches, unless they be subordinate to the law of this kingdom, are so many infringements of the great primary law of unity, in that they set up a member instead of the Body ... Certainly it is a difficulty, that we must admit this essential law to be at present broken. But I do not think it is fair to argue against a provisional and temporary state, such as that of the Church of England is confessed to be—which, too, has been forced upon her—as if it were a normal state, one that we have chosen, a theory of unity that we put forth over against the ancient theory or the present Roman one. Nay, thousands and ten thousands feel, the whole rising mind of the Church feels, that we are torn 'from Faith's ancient home,' that we groan within ourselves,

waiting until God in his good time restore a visible unity to His Church.[67]

Allies's longing for unity was tempered with pessimism about his communion. Perhaps he had answered the charge of schism, but that of heresy lay open: that a project like the Jerusalem bishopric[68] could be countenanced demonstrated how far Anglicanism had become detached from its apostolic moorings.

> Fare-well, indeed, to any true defence of the Church of England, any hope of her being built up once more to an Apostolical beauty and glory, of recovering her lost discipline and intercommunion with Christendom if she is by any act of her rulers, or any decree of her own, to be mixed up with the followers of Luther, Calvin, or Zuingle ... A persuasion that nothing short of the very existence of the Church of England is at stake, that one step into the wrong will fix her character and her prospects for ever, compels one to say that certain acts and tendencies of late have struck dismay into those who desire above all things to love and respect their spiritual mother.[69]

Whilst the Church of England remained Allies's spiritual mother, a note of desperation marks the close of the book. Only because her isolation was 'provisional and temporary' might he continue as her minister. Indeed his denunciations were so ferocious that he must have been very sanguine as to the likelihood of change:

> If she is to become a mere lurking-place for omnigenous latitudinarianism; if first principles of the faith, such as baptismal regeneration, and priestly absolution, may be indifferently held or denied within her pale,—though, if not God's very truths, they are most fearful blasphemies—the sooner she is swept away the better. There is no mean between her being 'a wall daubed with untempered mortar', or the city of the living God. I speak as one who has every

thing commonly valuable to man depending on this decision; moreover, as a Priest in that communion, whose constitution, violently suspended by an enemy for one hundred and thirty years,[70] yet requires that every one of her acts, which bind her as a whole, should be assented to by her Priesthood in representation, as well as by her Episcopacy. If the grace of the sacraments may be publicly denied by ministers of the Church, nay, by a Bishop ex-cathedra, with impunity,[71] in direct violation of the most solemn forms to which they have sworn obedience, while the assertion of Christ's Real Presence in the Eucharist draws down censure on the most devoted head, the communion which endures such iniquity requires the constant uninterrupted intercession of her worthier children, that she be not finally forsaken of God, and perish at the first attack of antichrist.[72]

Thus the question of heresy remained open, Allies believed that the Catholicity of the Church of England hung upon the continued allegiance of those who thought like him. Renouf's pamphlet had questioned whether the Established Church had ever been other than the congerie of views so eloquently condemned by Allies and whether the Anglo-Catholics would ever be anything other than a small party mainly of the wealthy and having no resonance with ordinary English people:

> The Gospel was meant to be the religion of the poor, yet whoever heard of a poor 'Anglo-Catholic' ... an Anglican of the lower classes, who believes in the 'Apostolic Succession', 'Baptismal Regeneration' (etc.) ... is a phenomenon which *may* exist but is utterly unknown in the world, and is certainly a great rarity.[73]

Despite Allies's exasperation with her, his scholarly assurance that nevertheless the Church of England was not in schism was warmly received by those shaken by Newman's defection. As was the author's custom, many complimentary copies were distributed. The general response was gratitude for the 'patriarchal theory', but irritation at the sweeping criticisms.[74] Gladstone was particularly critical of the book's tone, and Baron Alderson was concerned that attacks on 'heterodox Bishops' would damage his friend's prospects. On the other hand, H. E. Manning shared Allies's concerns 'as to our dangers'.[75] *The Christian Remembrancer*'s reviewer was greatly impressed:

> This is a book of great value ... It is proved ... that the Church of the first six centuries never recognised, nor knew of, and therefore, of course, never submitted to that wonderful claim, which, rising out of small beginnings, and gradually developed into a perfect theory, has at last risen to such height that, according to the theory most current in the Romish communion, it is said that 'Christianity rests entirely upon the Sovereign Pontiff'.

After summarising and endorsing Allies's historiography, the reader is, nevertheless, cautioned: the author is far too impressed with the Catholic viewpoint, teetering on the brink of Ultramontanism:

> Indeed, it is in respect of some of his casual admissions respecting the primacy of Rome, that we feel the only considerable drawback to our otherwise unreserved admiration of his volume ... He abundantly, in many passages, recognises in Rome the sort of primacy which we should ourselves be disposed to grant; yet occasionally he drops expressions which carry a different sound ... not without some danger, lest a primacy of Rome, such as they seem to indicate, might be, by no very distant process of logic, converted into the very supremacy against which he argues, and ... issue in a sovereign, and even an infallible Pope ... [W]hen he is making concessions he is apt to be a little profuse, a little over-bountiful; his heart seems to be open in concessions; and so he hardly stints his words so much as prudence and truth seem to us to require.
>
> When, then, Mr Allies says that the see 'of Rome had the undoubted primacy, not derived from the gift of Councils,

or the rank of imperial city, but from immemorial tradition as the see of S. Peter', we own to a slight uneasiness.

... in reading his volume with no ordinary care, and with very great general satisfaction, we have felt uneasiness from time to time; lest, whilst he was disproving the supremacy claimed for Rome, he might be conceding a sort of primacy which might, argumentatively, lead to exactly the same end.

But his book is destined to live. It is the completest argument against the supremacy of Rome, as derived from the examination of the first six centuries, which we possess. If we have misunderstood his expressions in particular passages, it is at least a proof that they are capable of being misunderstood and without unfriendliness of intention. We shall have gained our point if he should be induced to modify a few probably casual expressions in his second edition.[76]

The Ecclesiastic went even further in endorsing Allies's conclusions as to the desired future for Anglicanism:

We gladly adopt, therefore, Mr Allies' conjecture that the present position of the English Church is merely *provisional*, and that a time is coming when, Rome requiring no other allegiance than that which was gladly yielded to her in the earliest ages of the Church, we may return to communion with her. So may it be. For then the claims of Trent would yield to those of Nice ... That those of our erring who have gone from us, may in some providential way be designed to effect this reunion, is our only ground of consolation at their departure. It only remains to thank Mr. A. for his valuable and seasonable work, and to recommend it heartily to the perusal of those of our readers especially, whose minds may have been unsettled by recent controversies.[77]

The English Review noticed Allies's work soon after it was published and it too was quite complimentary.

> A more important subject that that which Mr. Allies has here taken in hand cannot be well conceived; and we are bound to say that he has executed his task in a manner which reflects the highest credit on his abilities, research, and honesty of purpose.[78]

A year later it returned to the subject, and by now was far more circumspect. It found his attitude to his own communion to be reprehensible:

> But do not let us, while we are proving that the Church of England is not in schism, declare at the same moment, that it is in the most fearful state of corruption, and that it presents few of the attributes of a Christian Church. This is, we say, a defence so weak, and so undecided, that the effect on the mind must be to leave the whole question as it found it. For this reason, we cannot think Mr. Allies's work suitable for general reading. Its effect on the whole is uncertain.[79]

For a great many Anglicans, confused by Newman's invective against the ambiguous status of their communion, Allies's book settled the issue—the bishop of Rome had no claim on their allegiance. For the author himself, as he accumulated evidence for an expanded second edition, the intellectual case was self-evident. Though his heart might call him to Rome, in conscience he must resist; his scholarship had erected 'an insurmountable barrier'.[80] Yet he took no care at all to disguise his disgust with his communion. It was an unstable equilibrium that put severe pressure on his family.

> As I went on, a sense of the hollowness and sham of the present Anglican Communion—of its timid, indefinite, truckling statements of doctrine; of its base subserviency to the civil power; of the dangerous conclusions as to the very being of the Church Catholic to which one's historical enquiries seemed to lead—a sense, in short, of living in an atmosphere thoroughly alien to one's feelings and convictions—became almost overpowering.[81]

He recalled discussing his book with Wall of Balliol, who asked him whether he really thought that the Anglican hierarchy shared his belief that Anglicanism could be justified only on the patriarchal theory. 'I walked away feeling that the ground was cut from under me, yet certain that there was none other to take.'[82]

Across the Channel

Allies thought often about his two visits to France: the Church he discovered there had become the ideal for which he yearned. In the summer of 1846, after the appearance of the *Church of England Cleared*, and smarting from Bishop Wilberforce's command that he must marry a Wesleyan couple, he left his temporary curate to read the banns and crossed the Channel once more. This continental tour was to be disappointing. The problem was his travelling companions, all dyed-in-the-wool Anglicans determined to resist the allure of Rome. They were Edward Coleridge and another Eton master, C. J. Abraham, who was soon to join the New Zealand mission and become the inaugural bishop of Wellington. A Mr Butterfield completed the group. This was the architect, William Butterfield, to whose design a new training college for High Church missionaries, St Augustine's at Canterbury was being constructed. Edward Coleridge was secretary of the organising committee. Butterfield was also involved with the refurbishment of the parish church at Ottery St Mary in Devon at the instigation of Sir John Coleridge, Edward's brother. The travellers spent most of their time examining church architecture in Belgium and down the Rhine valley. Allies wanted to revisit some of the French ecclesiastics he had met with Marriott the previous year, but none of his companions would accompany him to Paris. He summarised the excursion: 'We saw but the outside ... it had no deeper interest, like the visit of 1845.'[83]

The following year he was able to take the tour that he yearned for. In June he appointed the newly ordained F. G. White as curate and so freed himself to spend two months on the Continent. It was to prove a memorable experience. He went with two men who were themselves to become Roman Catholics, John Hungerford Pollen, a fellow of Merton, seven years younger than him, and John Henry Griffith Wynne, fellow of All Souls, six years younger. Both were recently ordained. Their elder brothers had been Allies's contemporaries at Eton: Richard Hungerford Pollen and Charles Griffith Wynne. Their two families were linked by marriage and a shared adherence to the High Church cause. Charles Wynne, who was married to Laura Pollen, John's sister, was one of the founding members of 'Project Canterbury', the Anglican scheme to settle New Zealand, the prime mover of which—along with Edward Gibbon Wakefield—was John Robert Godley, who was married to Wynne's sister, Charlotte.

Unsurprisingly, John Pollen and John Wynne, who arrived in Oxford in the late 1830s, became close friends. These years were the high-water mark of Tractarianism, and both fell under Newman's spell. His defection shook them badly. Pollen, who had been ordained in May 1844, was guided through this crisis by William Beadon Heathcote, a fellow of New College, and briefly minister of St Peter-le-Bailey, whom he served as an informal curate. He and Heathcote studied the *Development of Christian Doctrine* together, which Pollen said that he read only after praying to be kept safe. They emerged with their Anglicanism intact. Wynne, however, was more shaken, writing in his journal:

> Upon the news of Newman's conversion, fain would I have followed him. I had a sudden intuition that in doing so, I should be carrying Tractarian principles to their legitimate consequences... But I was very young and properly diffident of my own capacity; and the example and advice of those older and more learned than myself, kept me back.[84]

It was especially the counsel of Edward Bouverie Pusey that helped to keep Wynne on the 'right side of the Tiber'.[85] Allies too, who visited him in the wake of Newman's departure, could well have met the younger man along with other troubled Tractarians in Pusey's Christ Church rooms.

Struggling with a disastrous parochial ministry, Allies had concluded that Anglicanism was ill-fitted to reach the poor. Pollen also was disappointed with the results of his parish work. He wrote in his diary on 26 July 1844 of unresponsiveness and the difficulty in getting candidates for confirmation, 'All day in the parish. Terrible state it seems to be in! we must sow in hope, for there will be little result for us, I should fear'.[86] In contrast to this, Allies when talking with his Oxford friends would surely have expatiated on what he had experienced of the great influence of French Catholicism on the lives of ordinary people. Pollen was intrigued and he and Wynne agreed to accompany him on a journey to France and Italy to investigate the continental Church's parochial ministry. They were excellent like-minded companions, and Pollen in particular had some useful connections. The day of their departure (29 June 1847) was the feast of St Peter, and the three went together to Eucharist at Margaret Street Church and afterwards made their final calls, one of which, to Sir John Pollen, the traveller's uncle, was particularly important. He had no children of his own and liked to indulge his nephew and had agreed to be their banker for the journey.[87] His brother-in-law was the eminent classical architect Charles Robert Cockerell, who was an experienced traveller, a founder of the Travellers' Club;[88] and being on good terms with many eminent Europeans he had provided the young men with valuable letters of introduction.

During the next two months the travellers journeyed through France and into Italy, visiting seminaries, charitable works, monastic institutions and missionary establishments. Their first stop was Paris. Allies's *Journal*, which he published in 1849, documents his travels, though it gives less information about his conversations with French ecclesiastics on this tour than that of 1845, but the powerful impressions made upon him before were reinforced. His companions shared his enthusiasm; Pollen later extolled the Catholic Church's educational work and concluded that in France a powerful assault was being made on infidelity and not just among the poor. He noted that, compared with the situation in the previous generation, religion was now encouraged and 'in the salons of the rich an interest is shewn in religious questions and practices'.[89]

Among Cockerell's French friends was Marcellin de Fresne, an ardent monarchist and former counsellor of state. Allies had met him briefly in 1845, and the three friends called on him shortly after arriving in Paris. He was deeply involved with European intellectual life and commended these earnest young men to his friends, prominent among whom was Alessandro Manzoni, the celebrated author of *I promessi sposi*. De Fresne admired the philosophy of Rosmini and he would later write about it in the form of a dialogue with Manzoni, also an enthusiast. As a philosopher Rosmini's star has waned, but he was, and indeed still is, revered as the founder of the Institute of Charity, a religious order indelibly linked with the mission to England of Father Aloysius Gentili and the revival of Catholic life centred on the Leicestershire estate of Ambrose Phillipps de Lisle. By the middle of July the travellers had arrived at Genoa and on the 23rd were at Milan, where they met with Manzoni. They were fortunate to be invited to his villa some five miles from the city; Mary Wollstonecraft Shelley, who sought but failed to meet him in 1843, described him as an 'ardent and devout Catholic' but 'by disposition, excessively shy'.[90] Manzoni may have been intrigued by the fact that Wynne's aunt had married the Sardinian envoy to London and that her son, John's cousin, Carlo Ludovico d'Aglie, was active in the Piedmontese cause. He was also interested in the English Catholic movement in the wake of Newman's departure. As regards the prospects for Anglicanism, the travellers would have found Manzoni resolute on the need for submission to papal authority as the only basis for Church unity.[91]

Allies had a particular interest that he wished to explore: the continuation of miracles in the Catholic Church. In 1842, England's premier Catholic peer, Lord Shrewsbury, had startled the religious world by publishing an account of a journey he had made to two young women in the far north of Italy, both of whom bore the stigmata and lived in the odour of sanctity, withdrawn from society. In Caldaro, Maria Morl, called the 'Estatica', remained motionless in silent prayer, 'a sort of supernatural existence—dead indeed to this world, but most feelingly alive to the other.'[92] Shrewsbury reported that he had found the ecstatic just as the German writer Johann Joseph von Görres had first described her in his 1834 study, *Christliche Mystik*. For the peer she was an object of 'surpassing interest'. The pilgrims who journeyed to Caldaro would often travel on to the 'lonely village of Capriana among the mountains of the Tyrol' to behold another woman of 'surpassing wonder', Domenica Lazzari, called the 'Addolorata'. She displayed the wounds of Christ; 'perhaps more distinctly marked than they have ever yet been known in any human being.' Shrewsbury said she endured great suffering, that it had been almost eight years since she hade eaten, slept or drunk, 'receiving nothing but the blessed sacrament ... and this alone has ever proved any sensible relief to her.'[93]

Shrewsbury, as a leading Catholic layman, was convinced that his eye-witness testimony—published as a pamphlet soon after his return to England in May—provided powerful confirmation of the truth of his faith.

> Will, then, the hardiest declaimer against the veneration of the cross, and the sacrifice of the Mass, dare to look upon the ecstatic of Caldaro, and the prodigy of Capriana, and repeat those atrocious calumnies, and those revolting blasphemies, with which Catholic doctrine has been so often and so long assailed.[94]

The Protestant press had responded to this as might be expected. The *Churchman's Monthly Review* speculated on the vast income to the diocese of Trent from the sale of prints, and the *Christian Remembrancer* spoke of 'some nervous affection giving rise to a double consciousness or personality.' Manzoni, however, assured Allies that his stepson had seen the Addolorata and was convinced of her genuineness. The travellers were bound for Venice, but considered a diversion of one hundred miles a small price to see such a 'marvellous thing'. The hardships of their passage from Milan to Trent—'the place whose very name recalls the first great victory of the Anti-reformation'[95]—may have caused them to reconsider, as they journeyed with six others in a 'rickety *legno*' designed for two passengers.[96]

On 1 August Allies penned a long letter to his wife, describing what they had witnessed in the Tyrol. First, the open wounds of Domenica Lazzari, 'very terrible to look at ... the blood flows as it would flow if she were suspended, and not recumbent.' He was sure beyond doubt of a 'phenomenon which sets at utter defiance all physical science, and which seems to me a direct exertion of Almighty power, and of that alone.'[97] At Caldaro, he was entranced by the ecstasy of Maria Morl, who had now moved into a monastery: 'the most unearthly vision I ever beheld ... like a statue ... extremely beautiful and full of devotion.'

The Church of England is not in Schism

Unfortunately he and his companions were allowed only a brief audience and thus 'did not leave her with that full satisfaction we had felt in the case of the Addolorata'; nevertheless 'what we saw was very strange and very striking.' Allies was quite sure that

> it appears to be a design of God, by means of these two young persons, to impress on an age of especial scepticism and unbelief in spiritual agency such tokens of our Lord's passion, as no candid observer can fail to recognise.[98]

His two companions were similarly impressed. Of the Addolorata, Wynne wrote:

> if He who does all things to bring back our erring race to Himself destines her merely to be a living representation of the sufferings of the Son of God ... men of faith will not fail to derive benefit to their souls, amidst their thanks for a token of divine goodness, in contemplating this memento of our Lord's Passion, while it may serve in some cases we may hope, to warn the scornful that a day will come when they will in like manner have to 'look on Him whom they pierced.'[99]

After his return to England Allies was anxious to share his enthusiasm, and sent a copy of his account of the ecstatics to the *Guardian*, the newspaper founded following Newman's departure as the voice of the Oxford Movement. Its publication was declined.[100]

At the beginning of August the three were in Venice, reached by the railway from Vicenza. Even the unaccustomed rain could not spoil the travellers' delight in a city 'floating on the sea.' Here they recognised several Oxford faces, including one 'college head', who later remarked with disapproval on their regular attendance at Roman services. Allies was defiant. Visiting St Mark's he noted 'that vision of the Blessed Virgin and Child ... inexpressibly consoling' and rejoiced that he and his companions 'were generally very unanimous, liking the same buildings, the same pictures, and the same principles.'[101] After some days in *La Serenissima* they travelled to Padua, where Allies, needing to return to his family, bade farewell to Wynne and Pollen. Resting at Milan, he could not resist returning to 'the deep religious gloom of the duomo'. It was 15 August, the Feast of the Assumption;[102] of this experience he wrote: 'It certainly looks to me very like reality.'[103]

Does Anglicanism have a future?

The return to Launton and ministry under the episcopate of Samuel Wilberforce was like a cold douche. Allies, hard at work on a greatly expanded second edition of his work in defence of the Church of England, spent as much time as he could with his Tractarian friends. With Manning on the Continent, Dodsworth's wife and family had stayed at Lavington rectory over the summer and Allies made at least one visit there. By the autumn, however, he was back in his parish, and occasionally visiting Oxford. On 19 October he was with Pollen and stayed overnight at Merton; that night they saw the aurora borealis.[104] Perhaps it was a harbinger of better things? Having weathered the crisis of Newman's secession there seemed to be an air of optimism among the Tractarians who remained. The focus of activity had switched from Oxford to London and the clergy there were full of plans for mission and work among the poor.

Pollen remembered that when Allies visited him that October he had just finished writing the second edition of *The Church of England Cleared*. The next few months were spent in seeing it through the press, but after it was published in February 1848 Allies felt 'heartily sorry to lose a subject round which my studies could group themselves'.[105] He consulted Pusey as to whether he should now begin a work aimed at settling his doubts by exculpating the English Church from the suspicion of heresy. His spiritual mentor sensed danger and sought to discourage him. Pusey was sure that there was no heresy in the Articles or elsewhere, but 'that our present weakness and want of unity were the result of indecisive and ambiguous language' adopted at the Reformation, yet this was not sufficient to *unchurch* the English Communion. As regards the proposed investigation he questioned whether any clear conclusion could be reached because it was not possible to say 'how far the allowance of heresy destroys a Church'. Allies accepted this advice, agreeing to study 'theology in itself' rather than 'the special circumstances of Anglicanism'. But on return to Launton he remained troubled about his Church's doctrinal purity, remarking that 'as soon as one was out of his [Pusey's] presence all the doubts came back'.[106]

His agreement not to probe the sore of Anglican doctrinal insufficiencies certainly helped Pusey's campaign to consolidate the Tractarian position, as did the encouraging signs that the Church of England was reasserting her Catholicity. On their return from the Continent Pollen and Wynne had seriously engaged with Heathcote on plans to establish Anglican monastic institutions. But these came to nothing as Pollen became embroiled in the increasingly divisive circumstances at St Saviour's, Leeds.[107] More encouraging was the success of the project to establish an Anglo-Catholic missionary training establishment, which came to fruition on 29 June 1848, St Peter's day, when St Augustine's College, at Canterbury, was consecrated. It was a momentous occasion and Allies was there along with his closest friends, including Edward Coleridge, William Dodsworth and Baron Alderson, and over a thousand other guests, including the most senior Anglican dignitaries with some 600 other clergy. It was a splendid morale-raising occasion when the whole communion seemed to embrace its Catholic wing. Pusey took especial pleasure in noting the apparent healing of the strained relationship between the rector of Launton and his bishop, an outcome he had worked hard to achieve.[108] Butler of Wantage wrote to his wife describing the day, saying how he had seen the 'Bishop of Oxford, with Trench on one and Allies on the other arm.'[109]

This *rapprochement* with Wilberforce was to be short-lived, but there was none at all with Blomfield, who finally crushed any hope that Allies might have had of returning to London. He longed to quit Launton in favour of a city living and was quick to raise the subject with anyone whom he thought might be able to help him, especially clerical colleagues with metropolitan congregations, such as Dodsworth. In March 1848 his persistence was rewarded when he received a proposal from the rector of St Ethelburga's in Bishopsgate that they should exchange livings.[110] This was a tiny city church that had survived the Great Fire: it served a population of 600 and had just 23 pews but its value was roughly equivalent to that of Launton.[111] The obliging clergyman was the

Reverend John Medows Rodwell, whose High Churchmanship was later to bring him unto conflict with anti-ritualism agitators. He explained that he and his wife wished to move to the country for the sake of their health. Allies cited the same reason as to why it would be good for Mrs Allies to move back to the capital. He believed that another benefit would be that because the living entailed 'little pastoral labour' he would have 'a large time for study, in behalf if God so please, of the Church, according to my degree.'[112] All that was required for the exchange to proceed was the approval of the bishop of London, the patron of both livings, but when Allies saw him on 17 March he met with a point blank refusal. Shocked and in despair he wrote to his eminent legal friends Judge Coleridge and Baron Alderson, seeking their intervention. He also wrote rather more diffidently to W. E. Gladstone, the opposition member for Oxford University:

> The remembrance of Eton and Oxford and the kind attention you gave both to my sermons and my book in defence of the church two years ago, moreover, may I say the sense that we are fighting though in very different spheres, on the same side, encourage me on the one hand: on the other I am aware that the slight intercourse we have had for many years hardly justifies me in obtruding any personal concerns of mine on you. However, I trust to your excusing it.

His described his disastrous meeting with Blomfield:

> Nothing can be conceived more harsh, unkind, and unsympathising than both his word and his manner. He said it was out of the question bringing me to London at all; that he felt it a public duty not to do so. I enquired what had I done. He answered that I had dedicated a volume of sermons to Mr N, 'when his Romanizing views were well known.'

Despite Allies vehemently denying that he was guilty of 'Romanizing' and claiming indeed that the first edition of his work on schism 'was of help to keep some minds in the Church of England,' Blomfield was not to be moved. 'He treated me throughout as a malefactor.' Gladstone was entreated 'either alone or in conjunction with others' to assist by 'any mediation or intervention'. Allies concluded his letter by claiming that this was not 'altogether quite a personal matter': his rebuttal could have wider consequences:

> Those, alas, who are now enemies, are continually saying, 'It is all very well for you to take up a certain line in a book, but we know very well this is not the view of the C of E; which of her Bishops would sanction it? Which would not reject it.' Now the fact that a Bishop thinks fit to proscribe its author, would give some weight to these remarks; and how much more would this be the case, if it be indeed the fact that professing the belief of the Ancient Church, of St Augustine, St Cyril and St Chrysostome, disqualifies for service in the diocese of London.[113]

Although his friends were sympathetic they were reluctant to become involved in so sensitive a matter.[114] Rodwell remained as rector of St Ethelburga's until his death in 1900. He did not, however, waste the opportunity for study that his situation provided and in 1861 published a highly regarded English translation of the Koran.

Revolutionary France

Allies was worried by the strong case for Anglicanism made by his book on schism, fearful that his convincing arguments would encourage isolationism and complacency, erecting another barrier against the teaching required to transform his Church. He had been changed by what he had seen in France and Italy and wished that others of his fellow countrymen might undergo the same transformation. Owing such a debt to the continental Church he judged it his duty to make some payment in return. As the idea germinated, in the early months of 1848 he asked Wynne and Pollen for their opinions on whether it would be right to use his travel journals and their letters home as the basis of a book of reflections on the continental Church. It was a sensitive matter: his material was most un-Anglican, almost a paean of praise for Roman Catholicism. Nonetheless, encouraged by his friends to proceed, he decided that before writing he should revisit France in order to confirm and where necessary update his original impressions.

It was an exciting time to go to Paris. 1848 was the 'Year of Revolutions'. In February Louis Philippe had been overthrown, and throughout the spring and summer there was a bitter struggle for control of the new French Republic. In June a rising by socialist radicals had been suppressed by the National Guard, loyal to the conservatives. There was much bloodshed and one very distinguished victim: on 25 June, Mgr Affre, archbishop of Paris, seeking to mediate, was killed on the barricades. Given his ecclesiastical contacts in Paris Allies would have followed these events closely and was anxious to see for himself their impact on the Church. Unfortunately, neither Wynne nor Pollen were able to travel, but James Laird Patterson, a 26-year-old graduate of Trinity College, agreed to accompany him for part of the time. He was working as a curate at St Thomas's Church in Oxford, and as treasurer of the Oxford Architectural Society was already beginning to establish a reputation in ecclesiological circles as a student of the gothic. As an undergraduate he had been profoundly affected by Tractarian views; but attending the lectures of Robert Hussey, Regius Professor of Ecclesiastical History, he had been troubled by the contrast between the beliefs of mediaeval religion and those of High Church Anglicanism. He questioned with Bishop Wilberforce whether, with his fears about his communion's orthodoxy, he should proceed to ordination. His doubts were over-ruled but they did not diminish and by 1848 Pusey was counselling him to lay aside his studies and immerse himself in parish work. It was not a sufficient remedy and by his own admission this journey with Allies was to be an important step towards his conversion: the 'absolute faith and discipline' of the Catholic Church convincing him of the inadequacy of Anglicanism.[115] Hussey, never a Tractarian, would have been disappointed with the effect of his teaching, and in 1851 published three lectures strongly antagonistic to the development of papal power.[116] Allies, on the contrary, drawing from the same pool of historical data was to arrive at very different conclusions. But in 1848 as he returned to France he still believed in the Catholicity of the

English Church, despite its rejection of the papal authority. It was to be the widespread Anglican condemnation of his *Journal in France*, when it was published the following year, that persuaded him that he might be wrong and that he should look again at the question of supremacy.

Arriving at Le Havre on 8 July a visit to Yvetot was obligatory. Here and at Rouen Allies remained entranced with all he saw. On Sunday he and Patterson attended Mass but also 'had the privilege of saying our English office in their chapel, where the single lamp marks the presence of the Holy Sacrament. How great a blessing is this, that the Lord of the Temple dwells bodily in it—how great a realising of the Incarnation'. This was to be one of the statements that the bishop of Oxford was to seize upon for censure when the *Journal* was published, quoting Article 28 against the reservation of the Sacrament. The following Sunday they spent six hours in Rouen Cathedral and once again Allies's ruminations, when they were published, drew the wrath of his diocesan. Reflecting on how the worship was pervaded with a sense of the reality of the Incarnation he was led to write on the rôle of Christ's Mother. 'She, most of all, whose most pure substance He took to make His own for ever: so that what came of her is joined in hypostatic union with God and is God'. When this appeared in the *Journal* Wilberforce was outraged, citing 'most pure substance' as contradicting Article 9 on the universality of original sin.

Moving to Paris the travellers considered the worship less impressive: 'The churches in Paris have a certain official air. I like them better in the provinces.'[117] Patterson was able to stay for another week and they filled the hours with activity, visiting members of the clergy, both grand and humble and looking at the work these men were undertaking. Allies was particularly interested in the organisation of foreign missions and the training of missionary priests. At the Seminary of the Foreign Missions Society on the Rue de Bac they inspected a room given over to the relics of priests recently martyred in China. Again, Allies's journal record was to display a rather cavalier disregard of Anglican theology. 'The young missionaries make a visit here every evening, and pray before these relics of their brethren, soliciting their intercession,—a fitting preparation, I thought, for so difficult a task.'[118] Wilberforce was to assail him with Article 22: 'The Romish Doctrine concerning

Purgatory, Pardons, Worshipping and Adoration, as well of Images as of Reliques, and also invocation of Saints, is a fond thing vainly invented, and grounded upon no warranty of Scripture, but rather repugnant to the Word of God'.

The political ferment in the city could not be ignored, and the travellers, after encountering large numbers of the National Guard camped at the railway station and in many other places, 'passed the spot at the entrance of the Rue du Faubourg S. Antoine where the late Archbishop received his death wound'. Overall, Allies concluded that 'the insurrection has left much fewer traces than one could have expected.'[119] He later mused on the assassination of Archbishop Affre: 'If ever any sacrifice was voluntary, it was his: and this notion of making expiation by his blood for his flock seems to have given him supernatural force.'[120] Wilberforce added this conjecture to the long list of offensive statements that he found in Allies's published *Journal*.

Patterson left him on 24 July: 'I dread exceedingly the being alone in Paris, but for the object I have in view I must try to get on a few days'. In fact, Allies remained another three weeks pursuing the miraculous. Following his experiences in the Tyrol he had become an enthusiastic believer in the supernatural as compelling evidence to the authenticity of Catholicism. He spent some time accumulating evidence of the healing of a Sister of Charity, seemingly mortally ill[121] and an example of restoration of sight. The *Journal in France* included lengthy medical testimonials to the cures and the lack of scientific explanation. Both miracles were attributed to the intercession of St Vincent de Paul.[122] Earlier he had been fulsome in praising the work of the Foundling Hospital in Rue d'Enfer[123] founded by St Vincent in 1632. Much to Wilberforce's disgust he was later to write that what he had seen awakened 'all one's feelings of admiration and love' for St Vincent:

> If ever charity flowed in any human breast, it was his. When people scruple at admitting some material miracle ... they forget that the whole life of this saint was a spiritual miracle ... It is simply an exercise in God's *creative* power that a malady is removed by the intercession of a saint whose relics are approached in faith.[124]

Sometimes despairing of his communion, Allies had not yet given up hope that a restoration of her Catholicism would produce the fruit of ecclesiastical miracles. It was thus an encouragement when in 1849, writing up his Journal for publication he was informed by Bishop Forbes of Brechin of 'two results, approaching at least, to the same miraculous character, following immediately from the reception of our Lord in the Holy Eucharist.'[125] For Allies believed still that Anglicanism was a true branch and it would be schism to abandon her, no matter how attractive Roman Catholicism might seem. Yet no French ecclesiastic seemed at all convinced by his denial of a papal monarchy and asked him from whence the Anglican bishops derived their authority if it did not come from Rome? As he prolonged his stay in Paris, he gnawed away at this issue of jurisdiction and on Wednesday 26 July discussed it with Père de Ravignan, the respected Jesuit Superior in Paris, who promised to read his book on schism. The following Monday, he returned to the subject with M. des Billiers, a priest whom the bishop of Langres had appointed to escort Patterson and himself around Paris.[126] Allies records that being 'attacked', he countered by asserting that 'the ultramontane theory ... demanded the infallibility of the pope singly but that this was denied by large schools among them.' His parting sally was the familiar refrain: 'I said that, if they would prove the Greek Church to be in schism, I should give up our cause.'[127]

The following day he had an hour's talk with Lacordaire when again the primacy was discussed. Allies recalled the strong line his opponent had taken three years before, and told him that after much more study his conclusion was unaltered: he believed that Rome possessed primacy of order but not of jurisdiction. After finding he had met his match in arguing from history Lacordaire remarked that 'without living in a system it is nearly impossible to understand it', that the oral tradition circulates in the veins of the Church. Allies admitted the difficulty and applied it in reverse—he could not explain the Anglican position, but he remained convinced of it:

> The question was, whether I was *forced* to become a Roman Catholic; to deny all my past life; supposing we had the succession, and formularies which conveyed the episcopate

and priesthood,—whether I should be forced to affirm that the grace of the Sacraments was intercepted by the sin of schism or heresy.[128]

It was during this encounter that Allies observed that the English converts believed that the 'Pope could destroy the episcopate', the remark which led Healy Thompson to write to him in protest.[129]

Reflecting on the encounter Allies concluded that his opponent was 'weak in facts, but strong in principles; and this seems to apply to the whole Roman controversy on this point.'[130] It was only the conviction that history proved that Rome's power was not absolute that kept him in a communion he considered so feeble compared with the French Church, for there were few, if any aspects of its beliefs and practices with which he disagreed. For example, a titled Anglican lady living in Paris confessed to him that she was puzzled by the apparent efficacy of prayers addressed to the Virgin. He replied that the communion of Saints involved such intercession and this 'being granted, the pre-eminent position of the Blessed Virgin accounted for the effects wrought by her intercession.' He went even further, speculating that 'the greater tenderness and devotion of spirit discernible among Roman Catholics must be on account of their so vividly realising the Communion of Saints, and this specially in the case of the Blessed Virgin.'[131]

Before quitting France Allies travelled by train to visit the cathedrals at Orleans and Bourges. He went to examine architecture, but took every opportunity to probe the issue of primacy. Discussing matters with one priest he was given a glimmer of hope: 'I thought he intimated that the Gallican feeling was not extinct ... I said my great difficulty was that all history was for Gallicanism, while the Ultramontane theory was the only entire and consistent one, which would bear out all the acts of Rome.'[132] On 14 August he returned to Paris, and the following day had arrived at Folkestone, and then, probably via London, travelled to Lavington, where Manning had just returned from Rome. Allies, who had written to him from Paris the week before, wanted to talk with him, to discuss his French conversations and his deep dissatisfaction with Anglicanism.

✣ 4 ✣

THE PROCESS OF DISILLUSIONMENT

Allies and the bishop of Oxford

Allies felt a strong compulsion to publish his reflections on the continental Church. But would it be wise? Edward Coleridge, who was also visiting Lavington, encouraged him to write up his Journal but to refer the manuscript to Manning before considering publication. By September this task was complete and Manning delivered his judgment at the end of the month: 'It interests me most deeply and contains most valuable and useful matter, but I have seen enough to make me doubt whether its publication would not be a signal for making your life a burden.'[1] He wrote again on the matter a few weeks later; his friend's observations had touched a nerve, had filled him 'with all manner of thoughts such as Rome used to awaken day by day'; indeed the 'whole effect' of the proposed book would be 'persuasive of going over to Rome ... dissuasive of rest in the Church of England'. He repeated that if it was published his friend would take on 'a burden. I mean that the self-sacrifice of a Curtius would be nothing to it.'[2] (Marcus Curtius gave himself for the life of Rome by leaping a chasm in the Forum, which closed after him.) Allies responded the following day, Wednesday 11 October:

> I do not see how I can publish in the face of such an opinion because as much as I should desire to be an instrument in any way to making the truth known as to the Roman Communion I do not want to unsettle, but to build up our own. I would devote myself in the way you describe if there were a probable chance of the gulph being filled up, but if the only result should be the precipitating of myself and perhaps some others into it, I feel inclined to await

more light ... I feel no doubt that further reflection will only corroborate my present purpose of showing it only to friends.³

Allies asked that his manuscript should be sent on to Oxford for Pollen to see.

Then Manning had second thoughts. Just a few days after his discouraging letter he wrote again to Launton, saying that he now thought publication might be possible: 'I think your Journal has matter to be recast if you have the patience.'⁴ This about-face followed a conversation with Henry Wilberforce, who had wished to read the manuscript himself. Allies required little persuasion, and thereafter progress towards publication was inexorable. Manning wrote to him on 27 October outlining the main areas that Henry Wilberforce felt should be revised; these included the unqualified acceptance of Marian devotion and the criticisms of Anglicanism, which were 'too wide and too sharp'. He then added a caveat, 'I should like to know how Dr. Pusey would agree in my view of this'. He was anxious that Pusey should act as censor, because

> the Church of England is so overwhelmed by your comparison which is formed of the best parts in Rome, and the worst in us that I am afraid it would lift people over the question of Primacy and Supremacy. If you could revise it marking for omission such parts as Dr. Pusey would judge to have this tendency I think the publication of it would be very useful.⁵

The suddenness of Manning's *volte-face* is hard to explain. Reflecting on it years later Allies was somewhat cynical: 'Dr. Pusey, in the autumn of 1848, hearing erroneously that I was bent at all hazards on publishing it, wrote to Manning to suggest the revision, in order to lessen, at any rate, the evil.'⁶ The Catholic Allies was was never slow to accuse Pusey of deviousness, but when the latter wrote to Manning it was on 19 December and by then the ship had already sailed: 'I hear you have taken the responsibility of sanctioning Allies's *Journal*, I do most earnestly hope that you will undertake the additional responsibility of revising for the press.' He was disturbed at the prospect of publication, the author's mind being so 'sharp, hard, angular, controversial, acrid' that his work was bound to be distressing for members of the Church of England, 'raising questions but affording no clue through them.'[7] In explaining why the *Journal* came to be published it was probably the impulsive Henry Wilberforce—without considering carefully what Allies had written—who believed that such an account of the zeal of so many Roman Catholic churchmen might challenge their Anglican counterparts to emulate.

Manning's guidance, aimed at softening Allies's abrasive tone, did not result in any significant changes. There were a few, but as the Journal was prepared for publication there is no record of Pusey being consulted in any detail nor that Manning took on any editorial responsibility. Allies attempted to reassure anxious friends by showing the draft to Pollen's friend Beadon Heathcote, who was at the heart of Tractarianism and well respected, having close links to John Keble, whose Hursley living had been occupied by his father. Allies probably thought he would be more pliant than Pusey. In this he was correct; and encouraged by Pollen and Wynne, he sanctioned publication with only limited changes, although, anticipating controversy, suggested that on publication the only name to appear should be his own, as editor.[8] Allies declined, preferring to 'stand on his own javelin.'[9] On 1 December, a month after he had written to Manning saying that it would be difficult for any editing to be conducted by post, Allies wrote again, explaining how far matters had advanced:

> After writing to you I put my *Journal* into Heathcote's hands, of New College, as one having a most dispassionate judgment and deeply involved with Mr Keble's mind. He suggests certain omissions e.g. direct comparisons, depreciating expressions of the English Church, but otherwise was in favour of publication and has even offered to publish it himself as editor.[10]

He said that Marriott also supported publication and had sanctioned the inclusion of material from his own 1845 travel diary and that they had discussed whether Murray would be a suitable publisher. For Marriott, a staunch Anglican, his involvement with the *Journal* was to become a source of embarrassment. In February 1851, by which date Allies and Wynne had converted, *The Times* printed the following report under the heading 'University Intelligence':

> We understand on good authority that the Bishop of Oxford has inhibited the Rev. J. H. Pollen from officiating in his Lordship's diocese. Mr. Pollen was one of the gentlemen who travelled to France with Mr. Allies, now a member of the Romish Church. The Rev. C. Marriott another of the party has stated that Mr. Allies, in his journal of his travels, made an unwarrantable use of his [Mr. Marriott's] name.[11]

Allies's letter to the editor appeared a few days later. It casts an interesting light on the use he made of Marriott's journal:

> The facts are these:- the journal was put into my hands when he [Marriott] knew that I was preparing my own for publication, with liberty to use such parts of it as I might wish. Having done so I called on Mr. Marriott with the manuscript, to show him what I had taken. He did not wish to go over it in detail, observing that I was welcome to insert any part of his journal. There was only one page, indeed, he said, he should not wish to be inscribed, but that was one he intended not even to be read in manuscript, and so [had] doubled it down. I replied that there was no sheet doubled down when I received it from another friend, and that I might have therefore selected the very page, and I asked him which one it was, that there might be no mistake. On reference it turned out to be the very passage which he meant not to be read. Upon this he said, at first, that he could not agree to its being inserted, but after reading it over once or twice, on my remarking that I attached a particular value to the statements in it, he left out a line or two which I thought very immaterial, and allowed the rest to be printed.

> From that moment to this Mr. Marriott has never, that I can recollect, objected to me for any use of his journal by me as unfair or unwarrantable; and I leave it to you to judge how it was possible for him to do so.[12]

With Oxford friends having reviewed and revised the draft, its publication seemed inevitable. On 14 December 1848 Allies took it to Manning and Henry Wilberforce in London. They did not examine the manuscript in any detail, Allies recalled that Manning 'contented himself with approving what I described as having been done'.[13] In fact, although it is unlikely that the author emphasised the point, the changes to the original text were minor: some matter had been omitted, there were slight revisions to the references to the Blessed Virgin, and most of the general observations about Roman Catholicism were moved to the conclusion.[14] Why did Wilberforce and Manning not read at least these last few pages? Or, if they did, why were observations such as these allowed to remain in the book?

> I do not wonder at the Roman Catholic, who regards the English Church as a sheer apostacy [sic], a recoil from all that is controlling, ennobling, and transcendental in faith to a blank gulf of unbelief...[15]
>
> Thus the perpetual recurrence to the doctrine of the Real Presence, the prominence given to the Intercession of the Saints, especially of the Blessed Virgin, and the real putting forth of Apostolic power in the tribunal of penitence, are striking features in the Roman Communion. By these she proves she has living power as a portion of Christ's Church ... 'Believe that I am the Church, for behold me exercising the supernatural powers of the Church.' This is the inward proof that convinces, which is nothing technical, merely intellectual, or matter of argument, but like St. Augustine's *Securè judicat orbis terrarum*,—'A city that is set on a hill cannot be hid.' And the Anglican portion must prove in act as well as in theory, her identity with this of Rome, from whom she has her succession.[16]

Manning wisely declined to be the book's dedicatee, saying it would put him 'in the position of being asked by everybody, "Do you believe these things which have been written by an intimate friend of yours, and dedicated to you?"' A question that he preferred not to answer. He suggested an alternative dedication 'to our Spiritual Mother, the Church in England', which Allies used unaltered.[17] The manuscript was left with Murray the day after the London meeting. As Longman became the publisher, it must be assumed that their rivals declined the honour. Even at this stage, Manning, hoping to draw others in, recommended that Heathcote should read the proofs and advised that any doubts should be referred to Dr. Pusey, adding 'Both these points seem to me of real importance.' On the draft of this letter Manning subsequently wrote, 'Neither of these directions was complied with.'[18] Allies was indeed anxious to avoid Pusey's involvement, fearing that his text would be emasculated. Despite their encouragement his Oxford friends were not without some anxieties; as early as November Pollen had noted in his journal 'Mrs. Allies is in a great fright about the *Journal in France*', but her husband 'did not in the least share her misgivings.'[19] On balance, Pollen believed publication would do more good than harm: 'It will, I fear, give great offence. On the other hand, there is so much truth in the book, that one does not like to check its publication.'[20]

Manning, in an invidious position, tried to maintain a certain detachment. He agreed almost entirely with what his friend had written, but as a senior dignitary in the Church of England—he was archdeacon of Chichester—he was understandably reluctant to confront the logic of his evolving sympathies. Allies later implied that Manning shared responsibility for the furore surrounding the book by encouraging publication but declining to become involved in the substance of the text. He said that he wrote and 'offered Manning himself the revision' but 'To this for some time *no answer came*, until, tired out I offered the task to Heathcote.'[21] This is unfair. After receiving Manning's letter dated 27 October encouraging publication, Allies replied immediately, ruling out editing by post. He did, however, highlight the contentious areas, asking whether, for example, concessions should be made to Anglican sensitivities as regards the patronage of the Blessed Virgin:

> I freely confess that I should not venture from my own knowledge of scripture and antiquity to ascribe to her the mediatorial power which she certainly holds both in the Eastern and Western Church—but when I see that fact existing, countenanced, nay warmly supported by men who led the most holy self-denying life, I know not how to resist it without resigning my belief in the Church of God.

He was also aware that comments regarding the weaknesses of his own communion would be upsetting: 'That the Church of England is overwhelmed by my comparison, I admit it. But how in any comparison of the two communions as practical instruments was this result to be avoided?' Manning had likened his friend to Marcus Curtius and Allies was prepared for martyrdom:

> I should be grieved to be unjust to my own communion. These thoughts are to me a daily sorrow, but I can see no answer to them. Now if they are false, one sided and unfair, the sooner they are corrected the better ... But if they are true they ought to be brought before English Churchmen, as they will never listen to a Roman Catholic on such a point, it would seem it must be done by one of us. Doubtless if the thing excites any notice, he will get impaled for his pains. The truth is crucified and then believed.[22]

A terrible storm was inevitable but for his own reasons Manning decided to stand back.

The great storm

When Allies received his copies of the new book on Monday, 19 February 1849, he was elated:

> I went into the garden and read the whole conclusion. The publishing of this book gives me extreme gratification. It so exactly sets forth my mind; it pays a debt which I seemed to

owe to the Roman Church ... My feeling is that these things ought to be known. I would bring things to an issue if I could, i.e., make it fairly seen whether the Church of England really and practically holds the whole truth or denies it.[23]

He expected outrage in the popular press, and was not disappointed. It was a few weeks before the *Record*, the organ of Evangelical Anglicanism, noticed the book, but the tone of its attack was reflected in most of the provincial press:

> It is the most flagrant instance of absolute Popery within our Church—published and avowed by an incumbent of our Church—that we have yet seen. We apprehend that the right course to be taken is for six or twelve incumbents of the diocese to make a selection of the erroneous and mischievous passages in the book and lay them before the Bishop of Oxford with a view to ulterior proceedings.[24]

It was not just the Protestant press; even the High Church periodicals were negative. The *Guardian's* immediate response was withering:

> we say with sincere regret that we think the general tone of it uncandid, the whole impression which it desires to produce very far from just, and we question the discretion of publishing it at all. It is a very common, though a dangerous *sophism*, so to narrate facts as to insinuate a conclusion from them, which they may warrant, undoubtedly, but which it is far from certain that they *do* ... A very heavy responsibility lies on those who, without a plain and overwhelming call, utter, when they might be silent, words which are sure to be misunderstood, upon fiercely controverted and irritating subjects.
>
> But we must object altogether to this fairness being extended to one side, to Roman Catholic Bishops and institutions being looked at in a generous and cordial spirit, and our own in one of grudging and dislike, and it being

assumed rather than asserted that wherever the Churches differ we are in the wrong.²⁵

In the *Journal* Allies lamented the spiritual impoverishment of Anglican parishes, compared with those in France. He thought the explanation lay in the Anglican neglect of confession: 'Not one Anglican priest in a hundred has ever been called to receive a confession, or unfold the terms of reconciliation to a guilty soul. Indeed so much is this the case, that the notion of the priest in most parishes is extinct.'²⁶ The *Guardian's* response to this was succinct: 'We doubt whether an English flock would refuse to confess to a pastor who was worthy to receive confessions.'²⁷

The *Christian Remembrancer*, an organ established to promote High Church views, was more sympathetic and reviewed the book twice. It was first noticed in April 1849:

> We must begin with stating, that we regret the publication of this book, and are far from agreeing with all that the writer advances, either on the side of the French Church, or to the disadvantage of our own. Having said this, however, we gladly acknowledge that the book contains much interesting information with respect to various religious institutions in France.²⁸

The article that followed was more critical of the French Church than it was of Allies, although he must have been surprised that his book demonstrated that institution's 'deficiency in coping with existing facts'. The next issue of the *Remembrancer* accorded the book a lengthy review:

> The book has been made the subject of much unfavourable remark... not without reason. For professing to be a peacemaking book—a book to correct prejudices, to soften asperities of feeling, to explain misunderstandings, to awaken sympathy—it fails in the first requisites for such a character and undertaking—calmness of temper...
>
> A peace-maker cannot afford to be indignant, impatient or even unguarded; it will not do for him to have enthusiasm for one side, sarcasm for the other.

Nevertheless,

> We make these remarks with regret, both from our recollection of Mr. Allies' former services to the Church, and because attacks have been made on him so unwarrantable and so bitter ... that we are loth to appear on the same side with such assailants. There is very much in this book which ought not to be there—much that is grating and harsh in tone ... All the information which he has given us might have been given, we do not say without offence to the ignorant and prejudiced, but without affording them such a plausible ground for clamour. But we should be very sorry if in the controversial feelings which the book has excited, this information is neglected.[29]

The reviewer went on to quote at length Allies's descriptions of the educational activities of the French Church: and allowed them to be 'a rare and touching picture of self-devotion', before countering with Rosmini's criticisms of their deficiencies, 'in some of the very points which are the first to strike an Englishman—that it is too much of a drill and not enough of an education.' After noticing Allies's information about missions the article concludes, somewhat equivocally: 'The general impression left is one highly favourable to the zeal, energy and self-devotion of the French Clergy where Mr. Allies came into contact with them'. However, 'he would have produced, we think, a better and more convincing book, if he had allowed himself more freedom of judgment, and not thwarted altogether the natural suspiciousness of a foreigner in his strong efforts to be perfectly fair, and to keep down insular and English prejudices'.[30]

Most of Allies's readers found it difficult to suppress their 'English prejudices' and strong feelings were not confined to the Protestant press, even among Allies's close friends there were was sorrow at perceived disloyalty. Judge Coleridge felt the journal form was ill-suited to the aim of making Anglicans 'know more and feel better about the Roman Church'. Instead the truth was conveyed 'in the most careless and offensive way—every bit of cake is accompanied by a slap in the face. This seems to me *now* so obvious that I almost wonder it did not occur

The Process of Disillusionment

to me when you mentioned your intention to me in London; but I really wonder it did not occur to Manning when he read the journal'. He characterised the book as 'one-sided' with broad conclusions based on narrow premises.[31] Charles Marriott was deeply offended and wrote to Allies about 'a want of sensibility' and a 'flout upon the English Church' and pointed out that those who would really suffer were loyal Tractarians 'fighting for our lives for every little bit of *practical* good that can be accomplished'.[32] Once his old friend had converted, Marriott strove to distance himself from the book. William Palmer of Magdalen underlined the danger that Manning had pointed to: that the book's portrayal of the superiority of the French Church would be for some overpowering and completely overwhelm the last redoubt of Anglicanism: the distinction between papal primacy and monarchy.[33]

From those Tractarians who were not personal friends, to whom Allies sent copies of his book, there was a harsher response. Gladstone wrote that he believed 'the evils and corruptions' of the Church of Rome were 'intense, and that any picture to exhibit the whole truth must develop largely elements at the existence of which you have scarcely glanced'.[34] In sending the book to Keble Allies had written: 'To speak candidly, the existence of you, Dr. Pusey, Archdeacon Manning, and some others in the Anglican Communion is the strongest proof I can see at present of its being part of the Catholic Church. To such a degree does it appear to me to have sacrificed, and to sacrifice at present, all objective proof'.[35] Keble waited two months before acknowledging the gift. In a letter dated 19 April, he confessed that he 'hardly knew what to say' being so 'deeply pained' that Allies's continuation in the Church of England was apparently contingent on certain individuals remaining in it. 'I think you must have written in a hurry, and could hardly mean what you say', but this remark had led him 'to put a more unfavourable construction upon parts of the *Journal* and especially on the conclusion', than he might have done. The letter stops abruptly, being resumed the following day. In the interval Keble had welcomed W. B. Heathcote to his vicarage, who had 'much comforted me as to what I had so greatly dreaded'—presumably Allies's immediate defection. But his strictures remained severe; in the *Journal*'s treatment of Anglicanism, Keble detected 'a certain tone of something almost like scornfulness'. Nor could he share the writer's view of Roman Catholicism: a religion that had dared to propound 'definite statements on points which Scripture and antiquity had left indefinite.'[36]

As was predictable, across the Channel there was more enthusiasm, with a number of complimentary reviews published in France and Belgium. At home Catholic opinion was somewhat mixed. The *Tablet* predicted that Allies would receive no mercy from the 'High-Church' party: 'for no offence other than giving his testimony on plain matters of fact which fell under his observation, and which happen to tell in favour of a body which they profess to regard as a sister-church. Very "sisterly" in truth is the Anglican Establishment's demeanour to the Church!'[37] However, the reviewer had no hesitation in asserting that 'Mr. Allies has assuredly done no small service to the object he has so near at heart—the promotion of Catholic unity', and quoted extensively and enthusiastically from the book. The *Dublin Review* was also impressed, describing it as a 'very interesting and delightful volume.'[38] Nevertheless both organs—both closely associated with the new converts—were disgruntled by Allies's blunt dismissal of his ex-colleagues: 'The moment they had left us, it seemed their object to depreciate to the utmost the Church of England ... they delighted to condemn us *en masse* in the most harsh and insulting manner.'[39]

The *Tablet*, in protesting at this, rather confirmed his statement, by condemning the 'Anglican system as a whole simply external to Christianity.'[40] The *Dublin Review* was more measured but Allies had touched a raw nerve. In stressing the danger of 'trifling with Catholic emotions' it hit back, 'Mr. Allies is now just in the state of mind from which some before him have emerged into the Catholic Church, and others fallen into the depths of scepticism.'[41] Like other journals the *Dublin* remarked on the coincidence that Allies's work had been published at the same time as *Nemesis of Faith* and claimed that its author—J. A. Froude also a one-time disciple of Newman—had been 'bitten by German Rationalism', a 'hungry demon' devouring 'so many who started back from Catholicism, when Catholicism started to show itself the way of the Cross'. Nor was it alone in this opinion; the Protestant *Examiner* reviewed both books in the same article, and from an opposite perspective drew a similar conclusion:

What the Heads of the English church and failing them the Government from which its worldly authority proceeds, have now plainly to consider, is whether the doctrines of such believers as Mr Allies are not the source of the doctrines of such non-believers as Mr Froude ... [T]here is a large class ... who cannot remain protestant and papist both; in whom the beliefs, thus admitted side by side, are so apt to contend for mastery that the whole spiritual life is endangered by the strife; and who end as Mr Froude has ended.[42]

The *Dublin* regretted that Allies had not noticed the work of the 'Roman Church in England':

Does he hold it to be a schismatical intruder, or a member of the great Catholic community ... If the *latter* why ignore our very existence? If the former is he prepared to maintain among his foreign friends, that the only communion which *they* recognise in England, is in his judgment, divided from the Body of Christ ...?[43]

The one Catholic whose opinion mattered to Allies was J. H. Newman, and he found the book a 'hopeful' foreshadowing of eventual conversion because of the impossibility of the author's current position: it was alarming that he and his Oxford friends could 'put themselves forward as teachers of a system, which they cannot trace to any set of men, or any doctor before themselves; who give up history, documents, theological authors, and maintain that it is *blasphemy* against the Holy Ghost to deny the signs of Catholicism and divine acceptance, as a *fact*, in the existing bearing and actions of their Communion'. Hence, he explained, the vehemence of the English converts so deplored by Allies: 'It is impossible then but that a convert, if justifiable in the grounds of his conversion, must be an enemy of the communion he has left, and more intensely so than *a foreigner* who knows nothing about the Communion at all.'[44]

Allies may have been grieved by Newman's lack of sympathy, but was unconcerned by the furore in the popular press or of having wounded the feelings of the converts. The judgment of friends and reviewers he respected was a different matter and above all, as soon as the book was published, he was anxious to know Manning's opinion, possibly indicating a rather uneasy conscience. He wrote on 13 March, 'Pray let me know whether you think the omissions are sufficient'[45] and a week later wrote again: 'I am very anxious to know whether you think the Journal was sufficiently pruned or not. Do pray tell your mind without fear of offence. I need not enlarge on the particular state of things which led me to choose so strong and direct a challenge to the adversary.'[46] Manning's censure when it came was severe; he called Allies a 'black crow';[47] the manuscript had 'been chastised' but 'not up to the conditions' that he had outlined. In particular,

> The miracles ... will ... perplex and sway people towards a communion which claims this as a witness against us.
> The Invocations are accepted to the extent of approval, or seem so.
> The conclusion ... Although it is much chastened, and the censures upon the English Church reduced, yet ... the effect will be in the direction of Rome.

Manning mentioned a number of points which favoured the English Church that Allies had disregarded, adding that 'with so full and moving a synopsis of the Roman Catholic and French Church, either we ought to have been passed over in silence or treated *in extenso*.'[48] This was not the reassurance that Allies had hoped for. He wrote back, 'I assure you that had you expressed so definitely what your feeling was about the conclusion before, I should have suppressed it ... I fear it is the truth of what I say, which is so angering people, instead of *thinking no evil* they cannot bear to *think any good* of the Roman communion.'[49]

Bishop Wilberforce acts

For a month after publication of his book and despite all the criticism, measured and unmeasured, Allies, was untroubled, believing he had discharged a sacred duty, and sought to put the most favourable interpretation on the comments of friends and sympathisers. On 3 March

The Process of Disillusionment 157

he had written to Manning: 'I have had very encouraging letters on the whole. Of course I expect kicking and cuffing: the beast would be quite dead if he did not resort to that. One man writes to me that he found a neighbour in a violent state of irritation against me for "assisting at a Mass" which he supposed to mean taking part in the administration.'[50] He knew, of course, that the bishop of Oxford was under extreme pressure to take condign action. Such a flagrant provocation could not be ignored and after reading the book Wilberforce had to agree with almost all his clergy who regarded the rector of Launton as the 'enemy within'. The question was whether he would respond to the clamour by immediately referring the matter to the Court of Arches: an unsettling prospect for all Anglo-Catholics. When at last he did act, handing Allies a letter after a confirmation service on 19 March, at which Wynne and Pollen were present, there was no threat of legal action. But he was severe enough, emphasising his distress at the *Journal*'s tone regarding 'the Church of which you are a minister, seeming as it does to me depreciating and even insulting' and showing 'complete alienation from her and addiction to the Roman Communion ... I must call to your most serious attention the variance, which in my judgment, exists between its language and the dogmatic teaching of the Church of England'. Although the bishop confessed to a difficulty in transcribing discrete passages that 'fully exhibit this contradiction' he attached an appendix of statements culled from the book exhibiting Roman Catholic doctrines that had the author's unreserved endorsement, and setting alongside them the Prayer Book Articles that he believed they contradicted:[51]

> The freedom of the Virgin Mary from original sin:
> Article IX: 'Original sin ... is the fault and corruption of the nature of every man, that naturally is engendered in the offspring of Adam.'
> Article XV: 'Christ came to be the Lamb without spot ... all we the rest ... offend in many things; if we say we have no sin we deceive ourselves and the truth is not in us.'
>
> Expiation achieved through suffering other than that of Christ:

Article XI: 'We are accounted righteous before God, only for the merit of our Lord and Saviour Jesus Christ.'

Catholicism's possession of 'a vast body of doctrine ... uniform, coherent, and systematic':
Article XIX: 'As the Churches of Jerusalem, Alexandria and Antioch have erred, so also the Church of Rome hath erred, not only in their living and manner of ceremonies, but also in matters of Faith.'

Miracles associated with the intercession of the saints:
Article XXII: 'The Romish Doctrine concerning ... the invocation of saints is a fond thing vainly invented.'

The adoration of the Sacrament:
Article XXV: 'The Sacraments were not ordained of Christ to be gazed upon or to be carried about, but that we should duly use them.'

The reservation of the Eucharist:
Article XXVIII: 'The Sacrament of the Lord's Supper was not by Christ's ordinance reserved, carried about, lifted up or worshipped.'

The Mass a 'tremendous Sacrifice':
Article XXXI: 'the sacrifices of Masses, in which it was commonly said that the Priest did offer Christ for the quick and the dead to have remission of pain or guilt, were blasphemous fables and dangerous deceits.'

Transubstantiation:
Article XXVIII: 'Transubstantiation is repugnant to the plain words of Scripture, overthroweth the nature of a Sacrament and hath given occasion to many superstitions.'

In each instance the bishop required Allies to provide

such explanations as shall show that I have mistaken your meaning ... or failing that, their unqualified retraction. Failing one or the other of these, nothing will remain for me but to call upon you solemnly, in the name of God, to discontinue that ministry and renounce those emoluments which you exercise and enjoy on the condition of holding articles of religion which you publicly contradict.[52]

Thus did the contest begin which was to prove an epic trial of strength between two parties, both convinced that they were fighting for the soul of Anglicanism. And despite irritation with Allies's perceived obstinacy and insensitivity there was a detectable closing of ranks among the Anglo-Catholics. Thus after several weeks had passed and the impasse seemed unbreakable, the *Guardian* editorialised strongly against legal action (9 May),

> the consequence of which might be more lamentable than we like to contemplate. Time enough has passed since the volume issued from the press ... We had thought the book was already half forgotten: a year hence it will probably be completely so ... [if] a rigid scrutiny seconded by the ingenuity of a professional advocate should lead to Mr. Allies' conviction we cannot but suggest that proceedings which will very generally be regarded in the light of persecution should procure for him more sympathy than he has yet obtained, and are certain, at any rate, to exaggerate the importance of his publication and to cause other questions to be mooted, which it is far better for the present, to leave alone ...
>
> Let it not be said, that, while the press teems with infidel and heretical publications, the Church of England has a voice only to condemn a book which accuses her clergy of indolence, and her system of want of life; that she is indignant only when the virtues of her neighbours are extolled by one of her children, even though he has unduly deprecated his own. It is not by punishing him that you can disprove his statements; they must be answered by the lives of fourteen

thousand clergymen, recalling to the bosom of the Church the millions of England.

At each stage of the struggle Allies's Tractarian friends offered support and advice. Thus before replying to Wilberforce's first letter, he consulted Heathcote and Pusey as well as Pollen, Wynne and Patterson. He wrote to the bishop denying that the *Journal* contained any insult towards the *Church* he served, 'meaning the system of the Prayer Book'. Rather he was indignant towards the 'Puritan virus' active within her that denied 'certain essential parts of the Catholic faith and practice'. As regards an alleged 'addiction to the Roman Communion', he disclaimed having any *view* but rather had examined it *simply as a fact*, which exhibited her operations 'in that one point of view in which they are regarded by those who hold them'. His own convictions he had already made clear in another work defending his communion, 'until I withdraw that defence, no one, I humbly submit, has a right to impute to me that I am disloyal to the Church of England'. Citing 'the threatening tone of your Lordship's letter' Allies declined to reply to his detailed accusations and confined himself to general comments about the extent of Catholic teaching in the Anglican formularies.[53]

He was anxious to enlist supporters outside Oxford, and sent copies of the bishop's letter and his reply to William Dodsworth in London: 'Would you be kind enough by *tomorrow's post* to send both to Manning and request him, after reading them, to forward them to H. Wilberforce ... and ask him to return them as soon as possible'.[54] He wanted to know what they thought, especially as to whether 'Fust can touch the book'.[55] Sir Herbert Jenner-Fust was dean of the Court of Arches, the archbishop's court. After seeing the correspondence, Manning urged him to be 'patient, calm and charitable' and to seek counsel before writing to the bishop again. Replying to him on Saturday 25 March, Allies confirmed that he would do nothing without 'full deliberation with others', adding 'it is lucky that you are at two posts distant so I cannot drag you into the mêlée'.[56] He stressed that the points at issue had implications well beyond his own situation: 'I have not the least apprehension as to myself. If Sir H. J. Fust can touch me, he will touch the Catholicity of the Church of England through me.'[57]

Like the editors of the *Guardian*, Allies's friends were anxious to avoid any legal ruling on the compatibility of his views with the Church's official teaching. The comprehensiveness of the communion could only be damaged by too much clarity. But the new wine of Catholic teaching was sorely testing the old wineskin. George Cornelius Gorham, the vicar of St Just-in-Penwith in Cornwall, had in 1846 come to the attention of his bishop by advertising for a curate 'free from Tractarian error'. And when, the following year, Gorham was presented to another living, also in the diocese of Exeter, Henry Phillpotts, the bishop, questioned him closely as to his theological opinions before declining to institute him. He had decided that the Calvinist clergyman's refusal to accept the regeneration of every infant in baptism was contrary to the received teaching of the Church of England. Gorham appealed to the Court of Arches. At the same time that Allies's *Journal* was published, Fust was listening to arguments as to the sense in which a clergyman of the Church of England must accept 'one baptism for the forgiveness of sins'.

It was an issue on which most Tractarians felt they were on safe ground. The extreme sacramentalism endorsed by the *Journal* was another matter. Yet numbered among those who sympathised with it were men of standing in the Church of England who were regarded in a much different light from Allies, who most said was an extremist. Bishop Wilberforce was by nature a conciliator, quite unlike the pugnacious Phillpotts, but his previous experience with the rector of Launton did not persuade him that there could be a happy outcome. Manning had detected a note of personal animus in his letter condemning the *Journal*. Its recipient had no doubt: 'I have certainly the feeling that the Bishop has been acting ever since he came into the diocese and is now acting in the spirit of a private and personal enemy to me.'[58] Having sent his remonstrance, on Thursday 22 March Wilberforce went to London to consult with Blomfield, whose responsibility it was that the Oxford diocese contained such an irritating clergyman. Returning to Oxford on Saturday, Allies's response awaited him. He wasted little time in dismissing it; immediately taking up his pen again he focused on the areas where he felt his opponent was most vulnerable:

> To my quotations of passages in which you justify (1) 'the adoration of the Holy Sacrament', though it is distinctly condemned in the Articles...; (2) the Invocation of Saints; (3) the use of Relics &c. you say nothing. You cannot, I conceive, acknowledge the authority of my office, without allowing that you are bound, on my requiring it, as again I do, to explain, justify, or retract distinct passages in your published work against which I except as directly contradicting the letter and spirit of our Articles and Formularies.[59]

Allies knew that he had no convincing answer to this direct challenge. Yet, he believed himself a loyal servant fighting for the future of the Church of England as a living branch of the universal Church, standing on ground mapped out by the Caroline divines. He was sincerely convinced that the Reformers intended the Articles to be instruments of peace and inclusion, so that for the bishop to brandish them as 'dogmatic formularies' was contrary to the genius of Anglicanism. In writing to Manning (28 March) he quoted Bramhall, 'neither do we oblige any man to believe them but only not to contradict them'. But how far could this be taken? Tract 90 was an unfortunate precedent and Allies knew his ground was not firm. Much was at stake: as he wrote to Manning, 'unless the 22nd Article (condemning the 'Romish Doctrine concerning Purgatory, Pardons, Worshipping and Adoration, as well of Images as of Reliques, and also the Invocation of Saints') be moderately and wisely construed it will bring us into direct conflict with the Fathers, the Eastern and Western Churches and make all further union impossible'. Thus it would be a serious mistake to reply in detail 'setting forth my defence', because the bishop might well, 'after hearing and pooh-poohing it hand me over to the tender mercies of the Fustian tribunal. So that (unless I had the assurance he meant to limit his proceedings to the appeal to my conscience) he would be acting like a judge who took the accused apart, begged him to state all his case in confidence, and then turned his own defence against him in Court.'[60]

Advised that he owed no legal obligation to answer Wilberforce's questions, but desiring 'peace in truth' and after consulting Heathcote, he drafted a reply. His long letter, dated 27 March, was approved by various

Oxford friends, including Pusey. It was armed with a battery of quotations from 'divines of the Anglican Church', all intended to demonstrate that 'persons of high name and office, names as distinguished and offices as high as your own' shared his sacramentalism: 'I know not why any son of the Church of England should abdicate a liberty which they have exercised; I know not any power in a bishop of the Church of England to censure a priest for doing what they have done'. He went on to contrast the bishop's present stance to his tolerant attitude towards the vicar of Bicester, whose puritan views on the Sacraments Allies described as 'the most formal heresy'. 'I ask you very respectfully, why should you deal in a different spirit towards me?'[61] Keble, when shown this letter was sanguine; 'I trust that your very striking quotations will have their effect'.[62] He reckoned without the popular press: in the face of strident demands for decisive action Wilberforce had little room for manoeuvre. By the end of the month it was being widely reported that 'the Rector of Launton, the Papistical tendency of whose work on France and Italy has excited great astonishment and disgust, has been induced by the Bishop of Oxford to retire from his living, with a view to render legal proceedings unnecessary'.[63]

At Blomfield's suggestion, Wilberforce had written to the bishop of Lincoln, John Kaye, who had been Regius Professor of Divinity at Cambridge, seeking his guidance as to 'what further steps I ought to take in the (probable) event of the uselessness of my private remonstrance'.[64] Whilst sharing his exasperation that Allies was 'only looking for authorities to justify him in adopting Romish opinions and practices, while he still continues as a beneficed minister of our Church', Kaye advised against legal action. However, after studying Allies's second letter Wilberforce concluded that this course could not be excluded and approached Stephen Lushington (since 1828 judge of the consistory court of the diocese of London, and destined to succeed Fust as dean of the Arches Court) asking whether the author's '*words* make his *meaning* plain enough' for legal action to succeed. The response in a letter dated 8 April was unequivocal: Lushington urged action in the courts to prevent the propagation of 'Romish doctrine'. Moreover, 'the publication of this book is a matter of notoriety. It has not only come to your knowledge, but you have taken notice of it; if evil consequences should arise there are some certainly who would attach blame to your Lordship, and as this undoubtedly would be a mischief, so ought care to be taken to avoid such a result.'[65]

By now the newspapers were in full cry. On 11 April the *Bury and Norwich Post* delivered its judgment:

> We are inclined to fear that the announcement we lately copied from some other paper, that Mr. Allies at the recommendation of the Bishop of Oxford has resigned the rectory of Launton—was 'premature' or ill-founded. We now hear that Mr Allies disregards the Bishop's hint, and persists in retaining the benefice until forcibly ejected. If this is the case, the duty of the diocesan will be quite clear.

The fear of 'popery' was very deep and very diffuse, but among a growing number of the clergy, especially those newly ordained, the Oxford Movement was acting as a leaven and Wilberforce was worryingly conscious that on doctrinal matters two of his clergyman brothers[66] sympathised strongly with Allies. Of these, Henry was closest to Newman and should Allies be condemned his own continuance as a priest of the Church of England was doubtful. The bishop knew also that Archdeacon Manning was most anxious to protect the Tractarians against insinuations of 'Romanism'. Manning was his brother-in-law and they shared a deep emotional bond; both were widowers, united in grief. So, after consulting with Charles Sumner, the bishop of Winchester, on Easter Sunday 1849, Wilberforce decided to make one more attempt to reach a settlement. The following day, 9 April, he wrote to Allies for a third time in response to his catena of extracts from Anglican divines:

> It would not, I think, be difficult to show that the passages you have quoted in justification of your statements either do not apply to the matter before us, or taken in their full context do not fairly bear the meaning you put on them, or are from writers who are of no authority on this subject.

The quotations which were so reassuring for Allies did not move the bishop at all; they were no answer to the charge that 'your words directly contravene the plain letter of the Thirty-nine Articles.' But, anxious to avoid 'the scandal and the pain of calling you into a court of law', the letter contained a proposal. The *Journal* and their correspondence about it should be referred for judgment to the archbishop of Canterbury, or alternatively, to the three Regius Professors (Divinity, Pastoral Theology and Ecclesiastical History) in the University of Oxford.[67] This was quite unacceptable, but before responding, Allies decided to consult Manning in person. On Wednesday 11 April, he left Eliza at Launton, although she was now, probably because of the strain of the controversy, feeling quite unwell with symptoms identified by Thomas as influenza. Returning on Friday 'much comforted' by the visit he found that she was no better, so they agreed to try the curative powers of sea air and on Monday travelled to Brighton via its now well-established train line to London. There they stayed at a hotel for several weeks, whilst the crisis played itself out.[68]

An impasse had been reached. Allies had agreed the outlines of a response with Manning but both felt that it would be better to wait before once more defying the bishop. Wilberforce, increasingly impatient, wrote again to Allies demanding a response. He eventually replied on 25 April declining the proposed mediation on the grounds that no Catholic could accept that any individual, however eminent, should now rule on 'what the sense of the Articles is on certain disputed points ... a matter which for three centuries has been left open by the Church of England'. Of course, he added, the 'Church of England herself, either assembled in Synod or represented in her courts of law' could so decide.[69] It was almost a challenge for Wilberforce to do his worst. But it was bravado: neither Allies nor any of his sympathisers really wanted the issues tested in this way. Indeed, any hope that Anglican doctrine could be safely left to the mercies of an English court was soon to be shattered. Fust had not yet delivered his verdict in the Gorham case and few Tractarians had considered the implication that should his decision be appealed the final interpretation of Anglican doctrine would rest with the civil authority, the judicial committee of the Privy Council.

Continuing his letter, Allies turned again to his familiar argument, that historically the Church of England had ever sought to embrace its Catholic wing. His Anglo-Catholic forbears had subscribed to the

Articles in their 'literal and grammatical sense', 'not as articles of *faith* but of *peace*'.

> This therefore reduces the question to a single point, whether I have in any statement contradicted the literal and grammatical meaning of any Article. Your Lordship considers that I have. I feel convinced that I have not; but the Church of England alone, and no individual, can decide the point; for such decision will fix a certain sense on particular Articles which at present is not fixed on them.[70]

Prosecution avoided

It was of course impossible for Wilberforce now to retreat and upon receiving Allies's reply he instructed counsel to proceed in the Arches Court. It was at this stage that Baron Alderson intervened. He was on good terms with both parties and felt that a prosecution would do great damage. On Friday 27 April he wrote to the bishop 'out of the very great affection which I have long felt and still feel for Allies'. His opinion was that the legal position was far more 'problematic' than Lushington allowed. Moreover, if the Court found against Allies the risk was incalculable: 'I do really believe, and that from good authority, that this proceeding against Allies will produce probably a schism and will drive out some whom we all and you especially wish most ardently to retain within our Church'. Alderson, echoing the counsel of Gamaliel (Acts 5:38–9), argued that those 'whose tendencies go towards Rome ... will die out if judiciously left to themselves'. Thus it would be better to leave Allies alone:

> I admit his errors, which I agree are errors, but I would set against them a self-denying life, a liberal spirit to which money is really as dross, an unimpeachable morality, a great mass of learning, and having written one of the best books against the vital principle of Rome—her supremacy ... Is it desirable to drive out of the Church such a man ... or ... by showing him

kindly his errors, letting them expend themselves noiselessly and without mischief, to retain within our own Church one of its most learned and holy—even if erring—members?[71]

Wilberforce must have been relieved to receive this letter from such a distinguished intermediary and after meeting Alderson agreed to delay proceedings to see whether an agreement could be reached. Allies travelled to London on the first train the following day, which was Sunday 29 April. After Holy Communion at Margaret Street, at which Manning preached, he went to Alderson's home, 9 Park Crescent, where along with the baron he met Edward Coleridge and his brother Judge Coleridge, Pusey, Manning and W. U. Richards (the incumbent of Margaret Street). Allies stayed in London, resisting the considerable pressure put on him to compromise; he was to describe this period as a 'fight' lasting ten days.[72] Convinced that the bishop had acted unfairly in pursuing him but not clergy who denied baptismal regeneration, he was reluctant to retract in any way. Resting in his confidence that the Church of England was part of the universal Church Allies could not believe that what he had read in the Fathers and seen practised on the Continent could be condemned by her formularies, properly interpreted. Meeting his friends again on Monday he was immovable. But the constant pressure told on him, and by Tuesday (when some of his advisers had to leave) he had reluctantly agreed not to republish, but would not admit to any error. Alderson was so relieved by even this small concession that in writing to the bishop he was guilty of a slight exaggeration, intimating that Allies was 'Quite willing to say that you having expressed an opinion that scandal had been justly given by the publication, a consequence he did not contemplate and one which he deeply regrets, he is anxious to prevent it in future by making no further publication of the book'.[73]

The baron was too sanguine. Allies prepared a draft letter declaring he would not republish but not accepting any fault. Dated 3 May (Thursday) he sent it to Wilberforce, although Manning and Pusey had agreed that the bishop would be justified in rejecting it as insufficient—which he did. In it Allies had dismissed criticisms of his book:

> If I had believed any matter contained in it to be either at variance with the doctrine of the Church of England and not to promote the cause of faith and charity, nothing would have induced me to publish it. My intentions and desires were to produce effects the very reverse, and to promote, as I hoped, both truth and charity and I regret that in your Lordship's judgment a contrary effect has ensued. While I still believe that nothing contained in that book was contrary to the doctrine of the Church of England I am nevertheless ready, as an act of obedience, to cease from publishing any further editions of it.[74]

On Saturday Allies met again with Manning to discuss his options and an amended response was drafted. William Palmer joined them and 'suggested a distinction between matters of faith and of opinion, which was inserted'.[75] Manning met with Wilberforce the following evening, spending two hours with him. On Monday he met with Allies along with with Henry Wilberforce and Baron Alderson and outlined the sort of statement the bishop required. Although 'much disgusted', Allies was persuaded to draft a new letter. Now quite weary but confident that his words were more than sufficient to satisfy the bishop, on Tuesday 8 May he returned to Brighton and to a very anxious Eliza. Unfortunately, Wilberforce—presumably after taking advice—was not satisfied and told Manning, who remained in London, that he wanted 'an entirely new letter'.[76] On Friday Allies travelled back to London with Eliza, spending the night with the Aldersons. The following day he called on Manning, who told him that the matter was far from resolved. After this, he and Eliza returned to Launton 'dispirited and uncomfortable'.[77]

Allies was by now quite prepared to submit to the decision of the court; but none of his High Church friends would countenance this. They wanted another letter from him. By Sunday he was back in London, and by 4pm, after a great deal of pressure, a fresh draft was agreed, which Alderson agreed to take to Wilberforce that evening. Allies was deeply unhappy and penned a note for the baron:

> The letter, as now amended, is really the very utmost point

to which my conscience will allow me to go and in going so far I am yielding against my own desire and judgment to the authority of others. If the Church of England will censure me for anything in my book *de fide* I am quite content to be censured and to be cast out: for in my opinion she would cease by such a judgment acquiesced in by Episcopate and Priesthood to be part of the Catholic Church. The *certainty* therefore of losing the case would not deter me from going into court (at the same time I think the issue far from certain).[78]

At their meeting Alderson persuaded the bishop to accept Allies's revised letter along with an unadorned statement of his subscription to the Thirty-Nine Articles. This Allies was prepared to give, and he sent it to Manning from Launton on Tuesday 15 May:

I send you the subscription—in doing which I act, as I have acted throughout this business more in accordance with the judgment of others than my own. If anything in the world is repugnant to me it is to have to *shuffle* with the truth: which seems to me to have been the proper function of the Anglican Episcopate since the Thirty-nine Articles were imposed.[79]

Manning sent it on the following day along with with his own explanatory letter, which Allies considered sufficiently supportive of his case to reproduce in his *Life's Decision*. Manning aligned himself almost entirely with his friend, in a statement regarding the book, that must have left his brother-in-law quite shaken:

In language, sentiment and opinion there may be parts which, in the present disorder of our ecclesiastical courts, and the present confusion of our theological interpretations, might give occasion to an adverse judgment.

But I believe that such a judgment would put not so much Allies' book in opposition to the Thirty-nine Articles, as the Thirty-nine Articles, and the living Church of England, in opposition to the faith of the whole Church, both East and

West, according to Bishop Ken's rule, from the beginning.

It is not, therefore, Allies' book, nor Allies himself, that is alone at stake.[80]

The final letter sent by Allies and accepted by Samuel Wilberforce is dated 15 May 1849. Reproduced in the bishop's *Life*, it is hardly a fulsome submission:

> My Lord,—I regret that anything in the book that I have published should appear to my Diocesan to be contrary to the Articles of the Church of England, or calculated to depreciate that Church in comparison with the Church of Rome; and I undertake not to publish a second edition of that work. I declare my adherence to the Articles in their plain, literal and grammatical sense, and will not preach or teach anything contrary to such Articles in their plain, literal and grammatical sense.[81]

In his letter to Wilberforce Manning had pleaded 'that what is written may be used as a private record on which such a verbal reconcilement of this issue may rest' and that 'nothing more will be published than that you are satisfied'. However, things had now gone too far for the press meekly to reproduce Wilberforce's reassuring phrases: the submission had to be made public. He therefore decided to send Allies's statement along with his own gloss on it (in a letter dated 18 May) to Archdeacon Clerke,[82] asking him to make it known to his diocesan clergy. Wilberforce wrote that by his submission the errant clergyman was 'expressing his regret that there is anything in his recently published work, which has brought upon him the censure of his bishop, withdrawing it from future circulation (the first edition being now sold), and pledging himself to teach and preach in future in the plain, literal and grammatical sense of the Articles.'[83] Yet, despite the impression given by Wilberforce's biographer, the matter did not end with his letter to Clerke. If it was ever sent the archdeacon was stopped from doing anything with it, because the apparent concordat broke down almost immediately. It was discovered that the printers had a stock of the books, could these

The Process of Disillusionment

be sold? And Allies himself, almost immediately regretting what he had written, used the opportunity of a meeting with the bishop—convened ostensibly for them to discuss their future relationship—to present his superior with a note, the terms of which he outlined to Manning in a letter dated Wednesday 23 May:

> I wish to state simply what as a matter of conscience I can do (though it is grievously against my feelings, and as far as I am personally concerned I would rather the thing went into court). There remain I believe several hundred copies of the first edition to be sold: when these have all been sold in ordinary course I will undertake to publish no second edition *provided that at the same time I state that in doing so I withdraw no proposition in the book*. I decline being bound by any engagement whatsoever as to my future teaching other than what I am already bound by as a beneficed priest. I feel that it is impossible for me as a matter of conscience and with regard to my own peace of mind to go beyond this.[84]

Wilberforce was concerned that the book was still being sold. As for Allies, having seen the bishop's covering letter to Clerke, he was dismayed at its tone and the implication that he regretted what he had written; this was quite unacceptable. He told Manning that the failure of the agreement was a relief to his conscience:

> My interview with the bishop has completely revealed to me the view on which he and his colleagues have been acting and I confess that in spite of the opinion of my six advisers I think my letter of May 15, *combined with the act of engaging not to publish a second edition* would have been interpreted by the world as the Bishop intended it to be interpreted and not as we did. I have been saved from this by the Bishop's own letter which you advised him *not* to write.[85]

That an agreement was eventually reached that stopped the matter being referred to the lawyers is a tribute to the perseverance of Manning, Pusey and Alderson. Allies was very reluctant to compromise. He felt that the very legitimacy of the Church of England as a branch of the universal Church was at stake. His advisers were desperate to avoid the issues being tested in the courts because the almost inevitable outcome would be defections to Rome. Manning's concerns were more immediate and more personal, should Samuel Wilberforce—to whom he was so closely bound in human terms—bring the matter to a head, he hardly dared to contemplate the consequences: Lavington with all its associations was so dear to him. When Manning told him of the breakdown in negotiations Alderson was exasperated. Allies's fear that his statement would be regarded as a capitulation was 'utterly unworthy of a sane man':

> I account for it by supposing that he is very unhappy at being condemned to labour in his vacation at a mere country place like Launton where he sits in poring over old books until his understanding gets addled and things appear in a perverted light to him—I should prescribe, instead of a straight waistcoat a dose of rational and agreeable conversation with a few persons of common-sense and understanding.[86]

The baron expressed his admiration for the bishop's 'kindness and forbearance towards this odd little learned man.'[87]

Wilberforce was adamant that the offending book should no longer be available for sale. This impediment was removed when—much to its author's discomfit—all remaining copies of the first edition were purchased in one transaction. Allies knew the name of the buyer's agent, not that of the buyer, but surmised that it was Pusey.[88] He suggested to Manning—apparently in earnest—that as Wilberforce only required the publisher's stock to be cleared the agent might himself offer copies for sale. The one remaining stumbling-block was Allies's insistence on asserting publicly that he retracted nothing of what he had written. Such a declaration was of course quite unacceptable to Wilberforce, still under enormous pressure in the popular press. Manning sought to resolve the *impasse* by drafting a statement as to the circumstances of the agreement and the intentions of both parties. Allies took his draft copy of this into Oxford (Wednesday 6 June) to consult with friends as to its adequacy.

The Process of Disillusionment 173

William Palmer in endorsing it wholeheartedly agreed with him that the 15 May letter standing alone would have been misinterpreted, saying 'I would rather have cut off my finger than have signed it'.[89]

Unfortunately Manning's initiative proved insufficient to satisfy either party. Far from accepting any statement of non-retraction Wilberforce now decided he wanted a pledge from Allies as to his future teaching on the points he had originally raised. The latter's response was almost contemptuous:

> Although in the whole course of my pastoral teaching hitherto I have never touched upon such subjects, which I should have hoped would be the best pledge of my conduct in the future yet as an act of further obedience to my Diocesan I will engage not to preach in favour of the Reservation of the Holy Sacrament, the worshipping of Relics, and the Invocation of Saints without giving your Lordship full notice of my intention so to do.[90]

For Manning this was most unhelpful as he strove earnestly to conciliate his brother-in-law. He wrote again to him on 23 June, 'I fear the arrangement with Allies is still unsettled' and appended another note from him:

> In as much as I have never touched in my pastoral teaching on the points specifically referred to by your Lordship... nor am likely in time to come to do so I should have no hesitation in saying that no occasion could hereafter arise, as in the present case, for your Lordship's animadversion. But in as much as the Church of England has, in my conviction, ever allowed a liberty of belief in the matters involved in this question I am unable to assent to conditions on myself which could in truth impose a limitation on the liberty which is the common possession of her members.[91]

Manning knew this would be deemed unsatisfactory; perhaps the bishop could accept a much briefer statement from his adversary? Another note was submitted: 'These were or are my honest convictions, I believe them to be not inconsistent with the Thirty-nine Articles, nevertheless in deference to you I will publish no second edition'. Along with Alderson, Manning sought to convince the bishop of Oxford that his clergyman's beliefs were unshakeable and that all that he could render was act of external obedience: 'Allies's interior belief being left to his conscience and subscription'.

> The issue is left untouched: your office being satisfied by expressing itself and receiving an act of obedience. To go beyond this seems to me to attempt to obtain without sentence what nothing but a sentence can obtain: or something which in the nature of the case is impracticable, the appearance of a retraction where none is made.[92]

Yet, so far from backing down, at the very height of these sensitive negotiations Allies found a most provocative way of re-affirming what he had written in the *Journal*. In its issue of 19 May, the Catholic periodical the *Tablet* had supported his diocesan's condemnation of him:

> Mr. Allies has at least half-a-dozen times in his life most solemnly declared that the Prayer-book 'containeth in it nothing contrary to the word of God:' that book says that the adoration of the Most Holy Sacrament is 'idolatry to be abhorred by all faithful Christians.'[93] Yet, notwithstanding these principles which he maintains at home, abroad he denies them, and performs more than once, without any misgivings, those actions which he had already pronounced to be idolatry.

Allies responded without hesitation in a letter published a fortnight later (2 June). He denied that the formulae of the Church of England prohibited him from adoring the presence of Christ in the Eucharist as distinct from the 'corporal presence of Christ's natural flesh and blood'.

> Accordingly, what I have done in the churches abroad, I am in the habit of doing, and trust to have the grace always to

do, as often as I am present at the celebration of the Holy Eucharist in the English Church,—I adore that is with the adoration due only to God, the Lord Jesus Christ, truly, really and substantially present, under the species of bread and wine.

The editor of the *Tablet* dismissed his attempt to argue that the 'conversion of substance' cited by the Articles in condemning the doctrine of transubstantiation differed from the 'formal conversion' taught by St Thomas and which Allies accepted. When the English press reported on this correspondence they had no time for such casuistry. On 9 June the *Exeter and Plymouth Gazette* featured an article entitled 'The Rev. T. Allies' Declaration of Belief in Transubstantiation'. The article, which had originally appeared in the *Morning Herald*, would have made difficult reading for Bishop Wilberforce had he seen it:

The Rev. T. W. Allies... is determined to let people understand that 'there is no mistake, and shall be no mistake,' so far as he is concerned. He has taken up the duty of avowing Romish principles upon all occasions, and he prosecutes it manfully. How long his superiors in the Church will allow this to go on is a question we must leave to *them*.

He admits in his book that among the French Priests with whom he conversed, there was not one who did not plainly tell him, that, *holding such views*, he ought to leave the Church of England. To which his answer was 'Ah! but there are *peculiar circumstances*, with which you are not acquainted.' Foremost among these circumstances, obviously, was the snug rectory of Launton with its £600 or £700 a year.

However, leaving Mr. Allies we feel more inclined to ask, whether we have any governors or overseers in our Church? Or whether it will be possible *ever* to exclude a man, in future, on the ground of false doctrine, if such cases as this of Mr. Allies are to be passed over in silence?

The day before this article appeared Allies wrote to Manning:

> Do not put it down to pugnacity but to *conscience*, if you light upon a letter from me in last Saturday's *Tablet* (which will be in the *Oxford Herald* tonight) it purports to be an answer to an attack of theirs, its intent is to gather up the doctrine of my *Journal* on the Holy Eucharist in a few plain words and reassert it, as a proof that I have withdrawn nothing on the fundamental point. If all that I say there may *not* be fully expressed and taught in the English Church I do not see how anyone can henceforth defend her from heresy.[94]

Tractarians desperate to keep the matter out of the courts were infuriated at this development, but to their relief the bishop did not respond. Allies rather hoped he would and on 15 June wrote 'I suppose the Bishop swallows it, which is no slight disappointment to me.'[95] In fact it was not until 27 August that Wilberforce raised the matter with him saying that because he did not read the *Tablet* he had only just seen a reference to it in the Oxford paper. He asked Allies whether his words were 'reconcilable with the doctrine of the Prayer Book and Articles of the Church of England taken in their strict literal and grammatical sense', being the criterion to which he said he would adhere.

That an agreement was finally reached tolerable to both parties is testimony to the doggedness of Allies's friends, because as time passed he seemed to become increasingly recalcitrant and quite reconciled to the Court of Arches. Frequently close to despair, they persevered in seeking to persuade him to allow his letter of 15 May to be shown to the diocesan clergy. The last stumbling-block was what the bishop would say about the nature of his submission. In July Allies travelled to London at least twice to discuss the terms on which his letter—that had now been with the bishop for two months—could be made public. In Oxford too, pressure continued to be applied; Pusey pleading with him that the Catholic future of the Church of England was in his hands. Allies recalled the negotiations culminating in a day of extreme tension: 'In the last interview, when I was very near refusing to come to any terms, Dr. Pusey cried with vexation.'[96] This may have been the occasion described by Anne Pollen: 'As a last hope, Mr Lenox Prendergast brought

Mr Allies down to John Pollen at Oxford. It was late at night; Allies yielded, not before dawn.'[97]

It was due largely to Alderson's persuasion that the bishop held back from legal action and that he penned an accompanying letter that Allies was cajoled to swallow. On 25 July he wrote wearily to Manning, 'Penelope's web has been finished at last.'[98] The bishop's letter to Archdeacon Clerke was dated 3 July:

> I think it right that my Clergy should know what has taken place between the Rev. Mr. Allies and myself; and as you are the most proper person by whom I can in this occasion act, I will thank you to communicate this my letter to them.
>
> I felt it was my painful duty to censure Mr Allies's volume as in my judgment contradicting the 39 Articles. My censure has drawn from Mr Allies the following letter, which (there being no copies of the first edition remaining in his publisher's hands) is held by the Archbishop of Canterbury, the Bishop of London and myself to be sufficient to allow me not to originate legal proceedings against him. Mr Allies's letter is as follows ...
>
> This letter of Mr Allies, my dear Archdeacon, you will observe, applies to two distinct subjects.
>
> 1st As to the publication which I have censured, Mr Allies regrets my censure, and now proposes not to publish any second edition. Under the circumstances which I have before stated as to the first edition, I treat this if he had originally showed me his book, and on my expressing my disapprobation of it had, in deference to the opinion of his Diocesan, abstained from publishing it. I accept this act of deference to my office on his part.
>
> But 2dly, I deem it my duty as Bishop, in consequence of this publication having already taken place, to require an assurance that Mr Allies will not, in his parish, teach contrary to the doctrines of the Church of England. As to this, I apply the same test which I have applied to other cases before. I ask Mr A. whether he, as the rule of his teaching, accepts, in

conjunction with the Prayer Book, the Articles of the Church in their plain, literal and grammatical sense. By this letter he assures me that he does so, and I accept his assurance.[99]

Allies was immediately overcome by regret at this ambiguous denouement, a feeling which intensified when some newspapers described his letter as a recantation.[100] He was later to blame his counsellors, especially Pusey, for keeping the matter out of the courts, reflecting that the inevitable condemnation of his Catholic beliefs would have unsealed 'many eyes'.[101] But his 'burning anger' was reserved for Wilberforce, who had acted against him whilst tolerating heterodox puritan clergy. It was damning evidence, he concluded, that the bishop was merely 'acting in harmony with the spirit' of a communion founded on 'hatred and opposition' to the Church of Rome and in consequence the praise for her in his *Journal* constituted 'the one inexpiable heresy'.[102]

Wilberforce could claim to have acted decisively in removing the *Journal* from the book sellers,[103] but it was a pyrrhic victory: the furore generated had encouraged a number on their journey to Rome. And Allies was comforted that even without a legal ruling eyes had been opened, revealing an infuriated Church of England as essentially Protestant. He said that it was this illumination that 'made both myself and my wife Catholics, and helped on many others.'[104] But not in the summer of 1849: he remained an Anglican, disillusioned and distressed. Why did he stay? Perhaps it was another manifestation of the same profound failure of imagination that prevented him understanding, let alone sympathising with, the pressures Wilberforce faced. Assailed on every side,[105] what must the bishop have felt when, a few weeks after the 'retraction' was announced he came across Allies's letter to the *Tablet*? This took 'Romanizing' to a new level, as he explained to Sir Stephen Lushington:

> It appears to me that 'substantially under the species of bread and wine' is a direct assertion of Roman doctrine: and not capable of admitting the excuses & solutions applied to his book of his being a mere detailer of what was held by others etc.[106]

Writing also to the bishop of Ely he encapsulated his dilemma—was it in the interests of the Church of England 'considering the difficulty and nicety of the point at issue that I should endure the scandal of leaving Mr. A. uncensored or ... proceed against him in the Courts'.[107] He wisely chose the former path. But it was not comforting for him to know that the offender was so close to his brothers and brother-in-law and when, a year later, Allies quit the Church of England, this only brought new pain as Henry Wilberforce followed him almost immediately. A few weeks later came the frenzy generated by the restoration of the Catholic hierarchy. Wilberforce reeled under personal tragedy and the onslaught of Protestant petitions demanding that he condemn 'Papal aggression' and answer charges that his own High Church sympathies were subversive. All this may explain his somewhat panicked reaction to an advertised 'general meeting of lay members of the Church of England ... for the purpose of protesting against the late insolent and insidious attempt of the Bishop of Rome and also of invoking her Majesty's aid to suppress the various Romish innovations recently introduced in some quarters into the services of the Church of England'.[108] Alarmed that yet again his travails at Launton would be publicised he wrote to Lord Ashley, who was to chair the meeting, protesting that he had been unfairly blamed for encouraging 'Roman opinions':

> The alleged proof has been mainly my alleged toleration of Mr. Allies. Such an impression is quite natural, but it is quite untrue ... *now* I believe the interests of the Church require and circumstances allow of my justification ... I have written down therefore, a short statement of the case; and I trouble you with it, with the request that if the charge is again made you would contradict it ... my clergy well know how firmly I have set my face against such views as those of Mr. Allies. It is, however, natural, perhaps unavoidable that with such a press as we have at this time, with my poor brother's notorious course and with my own distinctly High Church opinions, that I should labour under the unfounded reproach of holding secretly that I have always opposed.

Lord Ashley replied that he would do all in his power to 'avoid personalities' and that the meeting was to oppose Tractarianism, which 'drove whole congregations to Dissenting chapels'.[109]

The turmoil and anxiety of those weeks in 1849 spent fighting the bishop of Oxford shattered Eliza's health, and as July ended she went with Basil and Cyril to Lowestoft, to stay near the Aldersons. Her disillusionment with the manoeuvrings of the Church of England was greater even than Thomas's:

> I attribute, so far as human means go, and in the order of second causes, the conversion of my wife to the effects produced by the publication of my *Journal*—not merely to the persecution, but to the inward view of the want of principle ... It left her not a stick for the affections to rest upon in the Anglican Communion.[110]

Within eight months Mrs Allies would become a convert, anticipating her husband by several months.

Among those who obtained a copy of the *Journal* was Mrs Charlotte Wood, the widow of the vicar of Fulham, who became a disciple of Newman and converted to Catholicism at the same time as him. She lived on the Isle of Wight, and when her son, a Royal Navy officer, was home on leave, he picked up the book simply to pass the time and was immediately struck by its account of the *Ecstatica* and the *Addolorata*. On looking further into the matter he became convinced of the veracity of the travellers' reports and was converted. Later he was called to the priesthood, entering the newly founded St Bueno's College in north Wales; in 1854 Father Francis Wood was ordained and entered the Jesuit Order. He died in Malta two years later.[111]

Kneeling before Pio Nono

As the confrontation with Wilberforce took its toll Allies became increasingly restive, anxious again to visit the continental Church and immerse himself in its certainties. He wanted especially to go to Italy and if possible to be received by the pope and present his *Journal* to him,

The Process of Disillusionment

and it was in this hope that he had translated its concluding chapter into Italian. John Wynne—who loved Italy and had travelled in the country with Edward Lear—agreed to accompany him. With Eliza and the children safe at Lowestoft and a curate at Launton, by the beginning of August 1849 he and Wynne had arrived in Rome. He had a letter of introduction to Dr Grant,[112] the head of the English College, and under his guidance the travellers explored the eternal city, its churches and catacombs. It was fatiguing tourism under a broiling summer sun: 'eight days under the dog-star' was how Allies described it.[113]

Rome at this time was a hot-bed of republicanism and anti-clericalism. After a popular uprising the previous November, the pope had been forced to flee to the castle of Gaeta in the Kingdom of the Two Sicilies and there he remained in exile. Leaving Rome, and after a brief stop at Albano,[114] the travellers set out for Naples, having it in mind to visit Gaeta—some seventy five miles to the south—on the way. Grant provided them with a letter of introduction to Monsignor Stella, the pope's private secretary and confessor, who had accompanied him on his flight. On 18 August they arrived at the village of Mola di Gaeta and stayed overnight near the tomb of Cicero. The next day was Sunday and they tried to find a boat to take them across the bay to the papal residence. Allies afterwards recalled a providential train of events that led them into the presence of the pope. Detained on the shore after refusing to pay what they considered an exorbitant fare, a distinguished gentleman approached them and offered to take them in his boat and also to give their letter to Father Stella. Upon landing their companion took charge, ushering them past policemen and soldiers. Allies whispered to Wynne: 'It seems we are under St Michael's guidance',[115] and indeed they had been taken up by Prince Odescalchi, the doyen of one of Italy's most distinguished families. He took their letter to Stella and after a short wait they were summoned to meet Pius IX.

Perhaps the prince had briefed them as to protocol? Allies recalled that as they approached the successor of St Peter they genuflected three times. Pio Nono had also been briefed and knew about the *Journal* and its author's battle with the bishop of Oxford. Allies gave him the translated final chapter and said that it expressed the aspirations of 'the ecclesiastics among us' who 'feel how great a calamity it has been to

England ... that she has been separated from the Holy See. They ardently desire her reunion with it.'[116] After some conversation in Italian the pope gave the travellers his blessing and valuable gifts: a cameo of the crown of thorns for Allies and an intaglio of Saints Peter and Paul for Wynne.[117] It was an exhilarating experience and when Allies next wrote to Manning he exclaimed: 'I reckon St Peter's benediction to have effaced the Episcopal censure.'[118] Allies later recalled the impression made upon him by the exiled pope: 'His manner and look were very pleasing; much more so than his portraits. He is a little above the middle height, very corpulent his white soutane seeming to bulge out very much; looks about fifty-five, and in good health; light eyes. The most simple dignity characterised his bearing.'[119] In retrospect Allies identified the visit as a turning-point in his life:

> The comfort which this interview gave is indescribable, and I feel sure that from the time S. Peter's successor gave me his blessing and promised me his prayers, the heavy cloud of confusion and misapprehension which had rested so long upon me, in spite of prayers and the most resolute efforts after the truth, began to dissolve, and the day-star to rise.[120]

Moving on the travellers spent 'a delightful fortnight at Naples, Sorrento, and Capri'[121] before returning to the north. Allies left Wynne at Genoa and sailed to Marseilles, arriving in England on Thursday 13 September. Despite the papal prayers once he was back at the rectory autumnal feelings of gloom and uncertainty returned. Standing before the altar of Launton church he was plagued by the fear that Anglican sacramentalism was 'a thorough nonentity, a gross sham.'[122]

For almost a year the *Journal* had dominated concerns and conversation in the rectory. Its publication had brought the satisfaction of a debt repaid but also the pain of rejection and calumny: the saddening realisation that the English Church would never accept any transfusion of Roman Catholicism. Allies tried to continue with his theological studies, and, bearing with Pusey as mentor and confessor, he sought to distil what an Anglican could legitimately believe about the Eucharist. A year before in September 1848 after reading Augustine and Ambrose he

The Process of Disillusionment 183

had made 'a great discovery... that they spoke of it as the practice of their day to worship Christ in the Eucharist'. He believed that the adoption of this practice of the ancient Church was incumbent upon Anglicans, and it is in this light that his provocative letter to the *Tablet* should be viewed. On returning from Italy he at once set to work to write an essay encapsulating the patristic understanding of the Eucharistic sacrifice and the Real Presence. He resolved that if this—a carefully considered and theologically accurate treatise—were to be formally rejected by the bishops then his way would become clear.

An Anglican still

But this was for the longer term, now back at Launton Allies was so beset by worries about the legitimacy of Anglicanism that he felt incapacitated even for routine pastoral duties. On 1 October he went into Oxford to open his heart to Pollen, who had just returned from a troubling few months at St Saviour's, Leeds. Nothing that his friend told him about the policy of the diocesan bishop (Longley of Ripon) and the difficulties encountered by the clergy of what was intended to be model Tractarian Church would have reassured him as to the legitimacy of the Church of England.[123] Quite restless now, he set aside his research on the Eucharist and took up again a document he had drafted the previous year, a summary of weaknesses in the Anglican position. He now added a list of points for and against Rome. Entitled *Thoughts of an English Churchman on the Roman Controversy*, it was finished by 6 October. He sent it to Tractarian friends, hoping that their reactions and explanations would illuminate the path he was being called to take. His preference was clear: the document pointed to Rome's unbroken apostolical descent, its unity and extent, and defined dogma, resolutely maintained. It was a Church 'living and in action, and exercising the most awful functions: sacraments, counsels of perfection', including, crucially, the celibate life. But there remained a fundamental and still unresolved problem: Allies could not accept the papal claim to monarchical supremacy and by implication the dogma of personal infallibility. For this reason alone he remained an Anglican. The 'objectionable features' in the popular Roman system, in particular 'saint-worship', would not have held him back, though like Manning he remained puzzled, even disturbed, that the general state of society and standards of morality did seem to be lower in Catholic than in Protestant countries.

Against these few matters telling against Rome, his documented criticisms of Anglicanism were a multitude. If the branch theory was true then 'the Church has ceased not only to be one, but likewise to be the pillar and ground of the truth.' He was disquieted by the fact that his communion's separation from Rome seemed to be widening, believing this was an inevitable consequence of 'private judgment'. Even more damningly the Anglican Reformation had been motivated by politics, 'the subjection of the spiritual to the civil power' and 'the overthrow of the principle of authority'. The national Church that resulted had 'no inward coherence and unity, but intestine opposition of formularies: the Prayer Book in the main reflecting, though faintly, the old Catholic system; the Articles and Homilies representing the intruding Protestant virus'. The result was not coherent theology but a mixture of opinions on key issues such as the Eucharist, baptism and holy orders, which involved the allowance of 'heresy on the Protestant side, as respects the whole Church system and justification'. More than this, the general denial of the Eucharistic sacrifice and the Real Presence, as well as the doctrine of the priesthood and the power of the keys, tainted the whole communion. He echoed Newman's solemn judgment: the Church of England spoke with 'the stammering lips of ambiguous formularies, and inconsistent precedents and principles but partially developed'. He then cited a long list of specific infringements of Catholic discipline at the pastoral level—for example, the marriage and burial of dissenters—to which he could bear personal witness. To his mind the great witness against his co-religionists was that they were 'as sensitive about any approach to Rome, as Catholics in all ages have been about heresy'.[124] So why did Allies remain a minister of the Church of England, if he could find almost nothing to say in her favour? When he later asked this question of himself he explained it as arising from the fact that he was speaking from within the system, serving as a parish priest and her theological apologist, who took for granted Anglicanism's rights and fundamental coherence.

He longed to discuss his difficulties with Manning, whose counsel he valued more highly than that of any Oxford friend, not excluding Pusey. But it was a long journey to Lavington and Manning, plagued by his own doubts, would have had mixed feelings about a visit which could only unsettle him further. Allies, however, needed to go down into Sussex, having decided to send his eight-year-old son Edward, whom he described as being 'of an active turn', to Park House School, Shoreham, established the year before by Nathaniel Woodard, the curate there, and now under the headmastership of the newly ordained Charles Moberly. The school owed its establishment to Woodard's anxiety about the low standard of education for the growing middle class and his desire to establish an institution with a Tractarian ethos at its heart. This school—soon to be renamed Lancing College—was to be the first of many Woodard schools, the beginning of an educational movement that still thrives.

Thus it was on Thursday 11 October, a few days after completing his treatise on Anglican difficulties, and after leaving Edward at Shoreham, that Allies took the train to Arundel and then walked nine miles across the Downs to Lavington. The following morning he gave the document to Manning, who, having read it, at first 'replied nothing'. When, a few hours later, Allies pressed him to respond he was most reluctant, saying little beyond 'a single remark on a subordinate point'. He asked Manning whether he should publish on the Eucharist, who agreed that he should, and pledged that he would not now counsel withdrawal in the face of opposition. Clearly, both men had been scarred by the fate of the *Journal*.[125] Somewhat fortified, Allies returned to Launton and to his studies on the Eucharist. He felt that by getting to the bottom of how far Anglicanism had preserved the essence of patristic theology he would find the light he sought. The next few months passed uneventfully, but developments in the Church of England were not encouraging. The Gorham case continued its slow progress through the ecclesiastical courts. On 2 August 1849 Sir Herbert Jenner-Fust had delivered his judgment in the Court of Arches. After speaking for four hours he concluded that in denying that infants were always regenerated in baptism Gorham had contradicted a key doctrine of the Church of England and the bishop of Exeter was justified in refusing to institute him. For the High Church party it was a victory, but one tempered with foreboding. At the end of his determination Fust had stated that the issue was too important to rest on his opinion alone and that there should be an appeal. This, however, would deliver the matter from the Church to the state, in the form of the Judicial Committee of the Privy Council, whose judges were laymen owing no allegiance to ecclesiastical authority and without any pretension to theological expertise.

Allies was not following the case in meticulous detail, his attention remaining focused on clarifying the Catholic inheritance of the Church of England and whether she could ever be led to accept the full implications of this tradition. The insidious issue of the state's power to legislate her doctrines did not seem to be his immediate concern. In November he wrote to Manning, wondering whether anything could be done for Alfred Dayman, whose High Church views had led the bishop of Worcester to demand his resignation. Allies felt it 'a monstrous iniquity that a man should be summarily dismissed for the expression of doctrines which we consider vital and essential'.[126] The bishop complained that the curate was indistinguishable from a Roman Catholic priest, such was his predilection for that communion's usages: 'incense, images, candlesticks, and such errors in doctrine as the *Sacrifice* of the Eucharist.'[127] At about this time another curate, the Rev J. A. Hanmer of Tidcombe, with whom Allies had been in correspondence, announced his conversion to Catholicism, to be followed by Dayman a few weeks later.

In December 1849 the fourth and last volume of Manning's Anglican sermons was published. Allies gave them close attention; he was much more interested in what they revealed about the author's state of mind than in their intrinsic spiritual value. Thus he was intrigued by Sermon IX, 'The Analogy of Nature', commenting that pages 164–75 were 'so many hammer blows dealt at Anglicanism':

> You certainly ought to be cited into the Court of Arches. I consider it very unfair you are not. You have been not so much attacking a single point here and there in the Articles of our Faith, as overthrowing the whole ground on which the Anglican Church originally went and now stands. When you

speak of 'inhering in the infallibility of the Church catholic', it is a language and a thought unknown to all her writers and utterly alien to her action and *esse* for three hundred years. How has she lived save on criticism of the text of Scripture, criticism of antiquity, entrenching herself in her insular position ignoring any such doctrines as that 'original inspiration has descended in a perpetual illumination'?[128]

Still working on the doctrine of the Eucharist, Allies was particularly sensitive to Manning's treatment of the subject. And here he perceived a deficiency, a hint of 'receptionism': teaching that might be acceptable to the 'pious Lutheran' or a follower of the 'subtlety of Calvin'. Perhaps, however, he speculated, the author's design was by conciliation to lead his readers on to the truth. 'This would be most like that lovingness of nature which is apparent throughout the whole work'. He recognised that Manning could influence his communion in ways that he never could: 'you are a bee revelling in the sweets of Roman theology and coming home to the Protestant hive with wings laden with the sweet things your poor unsuspecting fellow insects will use up in the winter hours and turn Papist bees themselves'.[129] Allies, however, held up a mirror to matters that Manning was reluctant to acknowledge: 'I cannot help saying that comparing your sermons with those of J. H. N's I do not think that when he left us he had bestowed on us a volume so advanced in Catholic feeling, so clear and so loving as yours'.[130]

Where does authority lie?

In January 1850 the Privy Council heard Gorham's appeal. Among Allies's friends there was mounting anxiety that this demonstration of the civil state's power to determine the acceptability of a clergyman's beliefs negated the Church of England's claim to apostolic descent. On Sunday 27 January Dodsworth preached on 'The things of Caesar and the things of God ... with especial reference to the claim of the State to exercise power over the Church in decisions of doctrine'. He confessed that hitherto he had not realised that a civil court had such power: the only hope for the Church of England was the repeal of 'those laws which have thus, we may hope inadvertently, enslaved the Church to the State.'[131] This hope was unreal. Anglicanism was an intricate fabric; the Reformation settlement had been finely woven and could not be unpicked. Another Churchman who had publicised his deep concerns was William Maskell, the bishop of Exeter's chaplain. The *Western Times* saw him as the *eminence grise* in the Gorham affair: 'They say down here that this Maskell it was, who supplied the stale and fusty authorities on which the good Bishop thought to back the cart of the Church of England to a state of things anterior to the time of the Reformation.'[132]

In February 1850 he published a *First Letter on the Present Position of the High Church Party*, which unpacked the Acts of Parliament that had established the absolute jurisdiction of the Crown in the Church of England:

> Whatever it may have been, good or bad, right or wrong, the supremacy is part and parcel of that pure and apostolical branch, the reformed church of England; and as she has made her bed, so must she lie on it.
>
> The actual exercise of the royal supremacy, now (as some have said) brought into operation before us all in a manner which touches upon doctrine, is a very startling fact ... We have managed to forget it; but it has all along been a living, real, power; waiting its time, if we may say so; ready to interfere, or rather, ready to exercise the authority which the English Church declares to be inherent in the sovereign.[133]

As was his custom, on his thirty-seventh birthday (12 February) Allies put his Eucharistic studies to one side in order to reflect on the progress of his spiritual journey:

> As to my own mind I find it in a curious state, which must surely be transitional. I am profoundly dissatisfied with the Anglican Church; its first principles, so far as it has any, seem to me founded on misconceptions of doctrine, and confusion as to the proper relation between the civil and spiritual power; and more than all, its moral atmosphere

chokes me. Again, as to the Roman Church, I am at one with it on principles. I admire its spirit of asceticism, and its maintenance of independence. I think the Papal Primacy of divine institution, and that in the doctrinal controversies between the two communions Rome is right, especially as to the whole sacramental and sacerdotal system, and justification. And yet I feel unable simply to accept Rome as the Church; unable to throw myself upon her with the calm conviction that I am doing right, and quitting a heresy and a schism. Intellect points that way; but heart and will are divided, not through any fear of consequences as to temporal interests, but through incomplete conviction; and for such a step I feel that the whole Trinity within one, body, soul, and spirit, should be of accord. What can I do but wait, and pray 'send out Thy light and Thy truth.'[134]

The light he sought would not be long in coming. His eyes were opened by an issue of which hitherto he was but dimly aware: the key importance of valid jurisdiction in the ministry of the Catholic Church. On 15 February he wrote to the *Guardian*, the Tractarian newspaper, in response to a leading article advocating that Parliament establish a supreme appellate tribunal on doctrine comprising only ecclesiastics. For Allies this did not go to the heart of the problem: 'I assert then as a proposition self evident to every churchman, but likewise born witness to by the principles, the acts, the position of the Church for 1800 years that the whole question whether any particular court be a Church court or a state court depends upon this one point, *whence does it receive its jurisdiction?*' The same objection could be raised to another option advocated by some: a return to the ancient system of appeals being heard by the Court of Delegates. Yet, although comprised solely of clerics, this too was a state court, originally established under Henry VIII. Allies said that the fundamental question now facing Churchmen was '*where is the source of spiritual jurisdiction?* ... To whom then has our Lord, the Head of His Church given spiritual jurisdiction within that Church?' It, surely and only, was the gift of Christ 'to the apostolic body and in them to the bishops ... [G]overnment resides in the bishops and not in the civil power'. Therefore any court, however constituted, established by the state 'would not relieve the consciences of churchmen'. The *Guardian*, sensing the implication of this letter and another on much the same lines from Henry Wilberforce appearing in the same issue, countered that these were extreme views and that the 'Church may legitimately authorise' a court appointed by the Crown.[135] Thus was the battlefield demarcated, as Anglicans sought to understand the implications of the pending judgment of the Privy Council.

Yet, despite his strong statements, Allies remained where he was. That the question of jurisdiction would remove the final barrier to his conversion remained hidden from him. Illumination came as 'a sudden unblinding of the eyes'[136] on Wednesday 27 February, the very day that his letter appeared in the *Guardian*. In his work on the Eucharist, seeking to understand the metaphysical underpinnings of transubstantiation, he had found the work of Francisco Suarez particularly illuminating. This Jesuit theologian was also a distinguished jurist, noted for the *Defensio Catholicae Fidei contra Anglicanae Sectae Errores* (1613), a powerful assault on the Anglican theory of the divine right of kings, the identification of Church and state in the person of James I. That Wednesday, whilst reading Suarez—presumably seeking light on the implications of Gorham—Allies made a startling discovery. He suddenly saw that in the national Church established by Henry VIII a monarchical pope had been replaced by the king of England. State control was not 'an abuse by those in power' and hence in theory remediable; it was 'the real basis of Anglicanism'.[137] This was a dawn that in a moment flooded the whole ecclesial landscape with daylight. To confirm that he had not misunderstood the Reformation settlement Allies turned to authorities accepted in the Establishment: to his near-contemporary at Oxford, Edward Cardwell (now the Camden Professor of Ancient History), and to Edmund Gibson, the eighteenth-century bishop of London. The former had spent years collating the documentary basis of the Church of England[138] and Gibson had published on the rights and duties of the Anglican clergy.[139] After reading them Allies found 'overwhelming proof of the Sovereign being made by English law accepted and acted upon by the Church the source of spiritual jurisdiction and the supreme judge of doctrine'.[140]

Royal supremacy—the root of Anglicanism—was the 'very simplest point, one which it would be thought a student of such a controversy ought to have secured at the very beginning of his work.'[141] Why—he again asked himself—had he hitherto been blind to it?

> For two reasons, I believe. First, because men, my superiors by far in character, reputation, learning, age, wrote and spoke, and replied when consulted, that it was far otherwise, and I had naturally assumed their hypothesis. And secondly, nothing being taught in Anglicanism systematically, an individual mind, with the very honestest intentions to arrive at the truth, did not proceed to the subject in any logical order.[142]

He blamed 'Puseyism' for simply asserting 'the spiritual order's independence of the civil', when in fact Anglicanism sprang from 'its exact contradiction.'[143] On the day after the scales fell from his eyes, he wrote to Henry Wilberforce: 'I see full warrant now for Pope Pius V.'s Bull, *Regnans in Exelcis*.[144] The *real* Church of England was in fact a perpetual denial that there was any Church at all upon earth ... I hope as soon as Pope Joan's decree comes out we shall meet in London and see what is to be done.'[145] His faith in Anglicanism having received this shattering blow Allies immediately felt it his duty to shine the strongest possible light on this crucial issue. In this he was stimulated by reading Maskell's *First Letter*, and, having put it down, at once wrote to congratulate him (1 March):

> As long as I can remember the Royal supremacy has been a sensitive subject with me, yet it was only two days ago that I saw it in its full and true light. I then came to the conclusion:
> 1st That the law of England sanctioned by the Church, regards the Sovereign as the source of spiritual jurisdiction;
> 2nd as the supreme judge of doctrine;
> 3rd that the whole history of 300 years is but a consistent carrying out of this Idea.
>   I had just made up my mind to set this forth in a pamphlet

when this morning I received yours and am happy that you have done it already as to 1 and 2.

As regards his third point Allies said that he would now publish a letter to illustrate 'how completely past history has been the carrying out of Henry VIII.'s Idea.'[146] The result was a pamphlet on the royal supremacy, completed in a matter of days.

The Gorham judgment delivered

On 8 March 1850, the Judicial Committee of the Privy Council delivered its verdict, upholding Gorham's appeal against the bishop of Exeter's refusal to institute him to the vicarage of Brampford Speke. It was the humiliation that the Tractarian clergy had feared and was met by vocal protests aimed at reaffirming Anglicanism's Catholicity, and proposals for the introduction of measures to establish her autonomy in matters doctrinal. But for some, like Allies, it was now clear that the situation was irremediable: the royal supremacy could not be abrogated because it was the very essence of the national Church. And with this insight he now appreciated, as never before, the force of the Catholic polemic: that valid jurisdiction—with its ultimate source in the successors of St Peter—was as essential to the life of the Church as valid orders. On 3 April he wrote to Manning that a correct understanding of this had now 'vitiated altogether my book [*The Church of England Cleared from the Charge of Schism*] as a defence of the Church of England, for I presupposed a state of things to which the actual state bears no resemblance.'[147]

Manning, unwilling to look the issue in the face, sought to be positive:

> Do take up your work again, and show that these 'royal vicars' were subjects of another sovereignty, and that only the external coercion, not the internal judgment, was in their hands. These men do not believe the Catholic Church to be infallible, and therefore see no infidelity in giving doctrinal jurisdiction to princes. You will see that the clergy here have moved well. There is great goodness and firmness of heart in

The Process of Disillusionment

many, but all falls within the four seas. The Royal Supremacy seems to me exhausted by 1688, 1828, 1829, and the whole subsequent development of religious and civil dissolution. The Gorham case is the *Dirige*.[148]

In meeting the Chichester clergy on 19 March Archdeacon Manning stated that it had not been the Reformers' intention 'to transfer the determination of any matter involving doctrine, or discipline purely spiritual, from the Courts of the Church to any tribunal of the temporal power'. But the position was difficult because the Church had no formal procedures by which it could overrule an erroneous decision. A new concordat was required to avoid a 'trial of strength' with each appeal from a Church court.[149] Allies disagreed with him; the transfer of jurisdiction from pope to monarch was essential to the Reformation: 'the power given seems directly to be intended to be given, contrary to what you seem to say at the meeting of the Archdeaconry'.[150]

The fruits of his rapid theological research appeared later that month in a pamphlet entitled *The Royal Supremacy Viewed in Reference to the Two Spiritual Powers of Order and Jurisdiction*. It went beyond Maskell's letter in a careful analysis of the principles of jurisdiction in the universal Church and on this basis, by historical examples, proceeded to lay bare the illegitimacy of Anglicanism. On the title page Allies quoted from Athanasius:

> When was such a thing heard of before from the beginning of the world? When did a judgment of the Church receive its validity from the Emperor? Or rather when was his decree ever recognised by the Church? There have been many Councils held heretofore, and many judgments passed by the Church, but the Fathers never sought the consent of the Emperor thereto: nor did the Emperor busy himself with the affairs of the Church.[151]

The author accepted that the Reformation monarchs had made no attempt to intrude into the divine commission of the clergy deriving from their apostolic holy orders. However, beside the apostolic succession, the visible Church requires a system of interior and exterior jurisdiction, the latter being the power that exists in the Church for its governance:

> This power is spiritual and supernatural, requiring indeed, and presupposing orders, but not given in them indelibly as their character, for it is capable of increase or diminution in individuals, and exists in different degrees in those who have the same rank of orders. It can also be taken away, and given again, which is not the case with any power given by consecration.[152]

This right 'belonging to the rulers of the Church, by positive grant of Christ' had been seized by the Reformation monarchs and

> annexed to the imperial crown of their realm. That which in end, in origin, and in subjects, was entirely distinct from the civil, that which sprung from the gift of Christ to St. Peter, and the apostolic body, they appropriated as an engine of temporal government ... And what was the result? – that within ninety years after this *new thing* had been finally settled by Elizabeth, and the power of Christ attributed to an earthly sovereign, another *new thing* was beheld, an awful prelude to the last times of lawlessness. In that monarchy which had thus laid hold on things divine subjects were seen to rise against their sovereign, dethrone, imprison, judge and execute him, and bathe in the blood of its wearer the crown which had stolen Christ's prerogative.[153]

Although Henry VIII took to himself 'the full powers of the Papal supremacy' his bishops still possessed valid jurisdiction in the universal Church but with the Elizabethan settlement the existing episcopate was abolished. The bishops who consecrated Matthew Parker had no jurisdiction; he was in effect installed as archbishop of Canterbury by royal *fiat*. In his analysis of these events Allies drew heavily on the work of the Oxford convert, David Lewis, whose 1847 pamphlet on the royal supremacy[154] he had only recently come across:

> Supposing that the consecrators of Parker were themselves Bishops validly ordained, Parker's consecration was good, *so far as episcopal character is concerned*. It appears, however, that his consecrators had no authority to consecrate him from any Bishop in the actual use of his jurisdiction: which makes the act *defective in the point of authority*.[155]
>
> Supposing them to be true Bishops ... and under no canonical disabilities, they could not confer orders which should be valid in respect of execution: as they had no jurisdiction themselves, they could confer none upon Parker, and that defect must still inhere in Parker's successors; time cannot cure it.[156]

Whilst Allies was prepared to accept that Anglican priests had received valid orders, he argued that the dependence of the Anglican episcopacy upon the sovereign meant that there was great uncertainty as to the efficacy of their sacramental ministrations within the Church of England. This was Lewis's argument:

> All, therefore, admitted to orders in the Anglican Church—supposing the orders to be valid—are disabled from exercising their ministry, whatever it be: they are not called to their several places by persons having authority to do it; their ordinary ministrations are irregular; their extraordinary ones, such as hearing confessions and absolving penitents are absolutely null and of no effect, because the Bishops do not authorise any person to this work. And by reason of the general defects—the want of jurisdiction in the hierarchy—no authority can be given; whosoever, therefore, hears confession under these circumstances, involves himself in the sin of sacrilege, and deprives his penitent of the grace of the Sacrament of penance.[157]

It was this aspect of 'jurisdiction *in foro interno*', the power of remitting sins upon individual confession of them, that Allies concentrated upon. All validly ordained priests receive this authority but as regards its exercise, 'a person is made the proper matter of the power of Order by means of Jurisdiction, and so no one can use the keys upon one over whom he has no jurisdiction.'[158]

> though this power is in itself a part of Order, and of the sacerdotal character, which is indelible ... yet the *lawful exercise* of this power belongs to Jurisdiction ... which descends from superiors to inferiors, and must be used according to the limitation imposed by the superior. And there is another most important distinction between acts flowing from Order and acts flowing from Jurisdiction. Acts flowing from Order, though done wrongly and illicitly, are yet, when done, *valid*; but acts flowing from Jurisdiction, if done upon those over whom the doer has no jurisdiction, are absolutely *invalid* and *null*.[159]

The result of the Crown's arrogation of papal authority was 'inextricable confusion ... rendering dubious all spiritual powers most necessary for the soul's good.'[160] Even if—a most unlikely prospect—an English bishop sanctioned the hearing of confessions his priests could not grant absolution, which are 'acts flowing from jurisdiction ... which comes from the grant of Christ and not from the temporal power.' Allies proceeded to turn the knife in the wound: 'if such acts are absolutely *null* and *invalid*, I leave it for others to trace in this respect the result of the Royal Supremacy on the Church of England.'[161] The pamphlet concludes by dismissing the Gorham case as marking any sort of turning-point. Such appeals were only to be expected: 'supremacy of spiritual jurisdiction carries with it necessarily the right and the burden of supreme judgment as to doctrine.'

> It was the very idea of Henry VIII. and Elizabeth to put supremacy in his [*sic*] single person ... [it] has descended by act of parliament, or a prerogative inherent in their crown and quite unique in the history of the world, together with their ample temporal dominion, on the shoulders of the kings and queens of England.

But what is the effect of this on the status of the Church of England? It is the actual bond of her existence—her characteristic as a religious communion—that which makes her whole—it is the right of the civil power, now lately exercised, to be the supreme judge of her doctrine.[162]

What then should I do?

Yet Allies did not resign his parish; did he still hope that there was more to be said, some rock to which he could anchor in the storm that engulfed him? He sent his pamphlet to a number of Anglican friends, desperately concerned to hear what they had to say. Yet in the terms of the pamphlet's logic there could be no answer. The only responses he elicited were impatience and resentment. He pressed Manning for a reaction: 'But I want you, seriously, to tell me what you think of the points raised in my pamphlet, and especially to answer the four questions which I send along with this. I shall send them also to Keble, Pusey and others.'[163] Yet he despaired of these two founding fathers of Tractarianism, about whom he had written in exasperation to William Maskell, 'it is impossible to make them see the first principles, or is their filial love so tender, that no proof however damning will ever convince them that their mother has committed suicide?'[164]

Allies's four questions were intended to bring matters to a head:

> Has not the Papal supremacy, as it existed in England up to 1532 been transferred to the Sovereign by an Act of Parliament recognised in the 37th Article[165] and sworn to by all Bishops and other Church officers?
>
> Was not Dr. Parker confirmed in possession of the See of Canterbury by an exercise of the Royal Supremacy, and did he not consequently thence derive his jurisdiction...?
>
> Is not therefore the jurisdiction of the Anglican episcopate as derived from Dr. Parker, and through him from the Crown, invalid, and all acts flowing from jurisdiction, external or inherent, void *ab initio*?

> If so, is there any remedy within the bosom of the English Church?[166]

Allies saw no incongruity in sending the *Supremacy* pamphlet to the most senior Catholic bishop, Nicholas Wiseman (Vicar Apostolic of the London District), asking him whether he considered its theological statement of jurisdiction was 'correct'. 'I am aware', he wrote 'that considering my position, and that of your Lordship this is a somewhat singular request—but the whole position of things is more than singular, and I feel convinced that you will pardon any defect of form and listen without hesitation to one sincerely desirous of seeing and following truth.'[167] Unsurprisingly, the bishop's response was very positive, although even he, in common with many others, wondered if the argument might be 'found complex and abstruse by persons who have never read or thought on the subject.'[168] Allies then met Wiseman in London on Monday 22 April.

Judge Coleridge agreed with Wiseman's note of caution. His acute legal brain certainly did not find the concept of jurisdiction incomprehensible; but, in this context, he judged it abstract and unreal:

> I look at my country parish, where my little property is, and see a poor clergy, schools ill supplied, many ignorant people willing to be taught, and I feel I can do them and myself, by God's grace, some good now; and I ought not to risk a change which could put an end to all this, unless upon a conviction based upon an inquiry, and resulting from a knowledge of all the circumstances, *quite out of my power to attain to*, or follow out.

He confessed himself: 'startled to see with what undoubting ease and positiveness conclusions are drawn in limitation, as it seems to me, of God's ways with the Church, from what I may call parchment premises.'[169] This was not an uncommon response. When Manning expressed his own fears about the dangers of over-intellectualising, Allies felt obliged to defend himself:

> I assure you I have ever before me the dread of following any false light of the intellect I have had but one continual prayer for many years 'Oh, send Thy light and Thy truth etc.' ... But then it surely cannot be a false light of the intellect to apply to our own case those rules and principles which we have been inculcating ... for ten or fifteen years past.[170]

He dismissed Anglican responses that tried to divert attention by pointing to weaknesses in the Catholic position. Bishop Forbes of Brechin, for example, who sought to avoid responsibility by asking his brother to review the pamphlet, warned Allies that an over-sophisticated historical analysis was dangerous 'as it would invalidate the Pope's own orders'.[171] Archdeacon Wilberforce, perhaps the most eminent of Tractarian theologians, observed, 'I should be sorry to have to defend Parker's consecration against you ... I suppose the thing which most weighs with men is the subsequent history of the English Church, which seems incompatible with a belief that it was a mere creature of Royalty'.[172] Allies commented, 'This is all he could say'.

But it was from Anglicanism's doughtiest defender that he was most anxious to hear. Although seemingly unshaken, Pusey found the part he was expected to play in the wake of Gorham hard to bear: 'Pamphlets come like hailstones, by every post, and from the hands of friends ... Mr. Allies has sent me his pamphlet: I have no heart to read it, unless I must.'[173] His answer was enshrined in a work on the royal supremacy, which appeared in May 1850.[174] With detailed scholarship, the pamphlet attempted to demonstrate that the powers claimed by the English monarchy in relation to the Church did not exceed those exercised by Constantine or Justinian. He had met with Allies at the end of April and had reiterated his own conviction that the Church of England had 'made itself good' by continuance.[175] For Allies this was not good enough. His response was dismissive and the passing years only hardened his judgment on one who became an adversary, one who had deliberately blinded himself to the truth and sought to inflict this wound on others:

> Dr. Pusey never could be brought to face the question. He wrote, indeed, this year a first part upon 'the Royal Supremacy not an arbitrary authority, but limited by the laws of the Church, of which Kings are members.'[176] But this first part only quoted ancient precedents totally removed in principle from the relation set up between Church and State by the Henrician and Elizabethan settlement; and he never went on in a second part to treat of this settlement and the actual condition of things. During the thirty years which have since elapsed he has preserved silence on that subject a silence which I venture to think more significant than any defence could have been. Clearly the subject would not bear touching; but perhaps it might be *ignored*.[177]

It was left to Archdeacon Manning, who was profoundly and personally involved, to attempt to meet his friend's challenge. He defended Anglican holy orders, citing the 1723 work of the French Jesuit, Pierre François le Courayer.[178] Allies was sceptical about this priest's scholarship and said that it was notorious that he was tainted by unorthodoxy as regards the divinity of Christ. The validity of Anglican orders was, however, a complex issue, Allies believed that his continuance in the Church of England hinged rather on the more immediate question of whether the English episcopate exercised valid jurisdiction. Turning to this front Manning built his defensive line: citing the *Tentativa Theologica* of the Roman Catholic author Fr Antonio Pereira, originally published in Portuguese in 1766, and recently translated into English.[179] Pereira sought to establish that under the pressure of necessity bishops could be consecrated without papal confirmation. Its translator, E. H. Landon, described the work as dealing 'a death blow' to Ultramontanism, by proving that 'an absolute control over his diocese is vested, by Divine Right, in every bishop'. He ranked Pereira's book alongside Allies's work on schism as a key defence of the Church of England, and an effective answer to Roman claims that a bishop's authority derives only from the pope. Pereira argued that 'Bishops being necessary, both by Divine and Natural Law ... may be consecrated (taking into consideration the present condition of things,) without the Papal Confirmation.'[180]

The Process of Disillusionment

But did Pereira's argument cover the circumstances of the Reformation? Manning was now having to deal with Anglican consciences disturbed by Allies's new certainties. To a female relative who told him that the issue of jurisdiction now rendered doubtful the absolutions she had received from Anglican priests and that her only course was submission to Rome, he replied:

> As to absolution, the view of the pamphlet [Allies's] is one of two, both tenable, and therefore neither absolute.
> The Spanish and Gallican Churches both hold the validity of jurisdiction as to sacraments to go with valid Orders.
> But apart from this, the whole Church holds that contrition with a desire for absolution reconciles the soul with God.[181]

Allies believed that history had invalidated Gallicanism. Whilst agreeing that there was an intrinsic jurisdiction attached to the episcopal office, he was certain it could only be exercised by an individual validly appointed. In extinguishing the ancient hierarchy Elizabeth had cut the link connecting the English episcopate with the jurisdiction of the universal Church. As he explained to Manning:

> The designation of the Bishop comes from the Pope as an *extrinsic* condition, but the jurisdiction is given immediately by Christ ... Now this will cover Henry's Episcopate and perhaps Edward's but I want you to point out to me how it reaches that of Elizabeth. If Parker was ever *designated* to the see of Canterbury by any power which up to that time had *ever* been acknowledged or even supposed to be able to designate a Bishop to a See, I grant the point. But the Pope did not designate him, the existing Episcopate did not designate him, or accept him ... He and all descended from him, appear intruded by the exercise of a power in its principle utterly anti-Christian i.e. the claim of the civil power to grant ecclesiastical jurisdiction.
> Now is this not a most remarkable provision of Providence that when one examines the historical facts that there should

be at the moment when the actual schism (and heresy) took effect, a complete break of the jurisdictional succession. How different was the case in Henry's time had his intention been Christian (instead of the devil's) much might have been said on the old Cyprianic ground. But did not his bastard daughter procreate a bastard church?[182]

✣ 5 ✣

CROSSING THE TIBER

Journey into the unknown

Allies lived in two worlds. In the study he grappled with the issues he regarded as of the profoundest importance, but he did not share this intellectual turmoil with parishioners or even, in any depth, with Eliza. Insofar as his developing theology might have practical consequences those who looked to him as husband, father or pastor, were expected to submit with gratitude. He thought the issues beyond their comprehension: 'It is not, I suppose, by the way of study that either the female sex in general, or the poor, or the great mass of mankind, are intended to arrive at truth'.[1] For her part Mrs Allies had had little patience with her husband's intellectual agonising and at first found his 'incipient tendency to Rome'[2] a great irritation. But with the furore surrounding the publication of the *Journal*, she knew instinctively that there could be no going back to the old certainties, that Thomas had burnt his boats with the ecclesiastical authorities. Moreover, she could not blame him, feeling that he had honestly reported what he had found, and was reassured by knowing that her trusted friends, Pollen and Wynne, shared his opinions. The opprobrium heaped upon them worried and perplexed her. In her heart Eliza knew that there was no future for her or her family in the Church of England, and that it would be better to accept this, and to begin again by taking their place among the Roman Catholic laity. This at least would resolve the domestic tensions created by Thomas's agonisings over what was expected of him as a priest.

It does not seem that she fully opened her heart to Thomas although he was aware that her attitude towards Catholicism was perceptibly softening. She was a woman of clear and decided opinion and he must have known that she had no patience with his prevarication. In her biography of her father, Mary Allies quotes approvingly 'the striking portrait' that Bishop Gillis drew from her mother's handwriting:

> Good-natured and kind. Caring much more for the reality of things than for their outward appearance or expression ... Would more willingly deal with generalised views of a subject than care to analyse its details. Impulsive and apt to rap out what she thinks or feels without much consideration of those in whose presence she speaks.[3]

Yet, with Thomas, she kept her counsel. These important and sensitive matters were not openly discussed between them. Hence, in the early weeks of 1850, he resorted to what might be regarded as improper means to obtain information about her state of mind:

> so entirely was I in doubt as to her feelings, so entirely also had I abstained from any attempt directly to influence her mind, that the first intimation I received of what her real judgment was I got from a letter to a cousin who was like a sister to us, which I opened on the supposition of its containing something on the subject, and which said, 'If Tom does not make haste I shall go over before him.'[4]

In the loneliness and isolation of her life at Launton, with her husband often away and little companionship in the parish, Eliza began to find comfort in Catholic books of devotion. Her views and her reading were probably being influenced by a developing friendship with Mrs Wootten the widow of a well-known Oxford physician, who was receiving instruction from a Catholic priest. At last, in February 1850, emboldened by her husband's increasingly bitter words about the Church of England, she told him that she was convinced of its falsity. Some weeks passed until, soon after the Gorham decision, she announced that she no longer felt 'any reality in our ordinances' and told Thomas that she wished to become a Roman Catholic. This was on Saturday 16 March. Allies was just back from London, where he had had anxious discussions with Manning and Henry Wilberforce about the judgment's implications. If she thought that Thomas would move with her she was to be disappointed: notwithstanding his complete disillusion focused on the issue of jurisdiction, something still held him back. On Sunday 17 March he read to his congregation the protest that Dennison, the vicar of East Brent, had delivered in his church the previous Sunday and which had been published in *The Times* on Friday. Although solemnly worded it did not go to the heart of his concerns:

> Whereas the Church of England is a branch of the One Catholic and Apostolic Church, and in virtue thereof holds absolutely and exclusively, all the doctrines of the Catholic faith; and whereas George Cornelius Gorham, clerk, B. D. priest of the Church of England has formally denied the Catholic faith in respect of the Holy Sacrament of baptism ... I ... do hereby enter my solemn protest against the said sentence ... I do also pledge myself to use all lawful means within my reach to assist in obtaining without delay, some further formal declaration, by lawful synod of the Church of England, as to what is, and what is not, the doctrine of the Church of England in respect of the Holy Sacrament of baptism.

As it was Lent Allies persuaded a reluctant Eliza to defer any action until after Easter, when perhaps the response of the Church of England to Gorham might have become clearer. But nothing happened. Easter Sunday was 31 March, and in the weeks that followed it became apparent that there would be no cataclysm. The Established Church would muddle through, as it was wont to do. Allies was unsurprised:

> ferocious grumbles of the party, but no action: a vast number of tracts and pamphlets: laments over the injured faith of the Church: distress of individuals: but all this grief and indignation far within the mark of doing anything. The political and the religious adversary alike could well afford to pass them over in silence, and gather the fruits of what

was a real victory to the Royal Supremacy on the one hand, and to the Evangelical party on the other.[5]

And he had an explanation. Although 'the defenders of the Creed', might complain, their fight with the state would 'stop far short of endangering the safe reception of their tithes and rents'.

Eliza could no longer visualise herself as the dutiful clergy wife: at the rectory things were moving to a crisis. On Saturday 11 May she was staying with friends whilst Thomas joined with forty old Etonians for Edward Coleridge's fiftieth-birthday celebrations. Afterwards he remained in London for a few days. When he returned to Launton Eliza told him that she would wait no longer. Accepting the inevitable, he wrote at once to Newman, who replied immediately (23 May) expressing his delight but saying that he personally would not be able to receive her until 30 May, the Feast of Corpus Christi. Eliza would not be delayed and took up Newman's alternative suggestion.[6] Father Wilds, a priest ordained in the previous century and living quietly in retirement in London, received her into the Catholic Church on Friday 24th. The elderly priest—who a few years before had received Mrs Bowden, the mother of one of Newman's closest friends—felt the responsibility very heavily and as he administered conditional baptism asked the convert, 'Have you felt the water, my child?' to which she mischievously replied, 'not a drop'. On leaving his rather dingy rooms she was exultant and turned to Thomas with the words: 'Now you are heretic, and I am not.'[7] A little while later Eliza was able to meet Newman, assuring him that her husband's conversion would not be long delayed. Her concern was for the children. They had been baptised by their father and she was sure everything had been done correctly; would they too require conditional baptism, before the whole family could be considered Catholics? Newman considered the point and later wrote to her: the decision would lie with the bishop of the diocese within which Allies himself was received, should the children be with him.[8]

Who holds the keys?

Thomas knew that soon he must join her.[9] But to the exasperation of his Anglican colleagues he lingered. Claiming to be waiting for inner assurance, a 'final call', he felt no need to retire into obscurity; just the opposite. Whilst still enjoying the rewards of his living he put himself forward as one of Anglicanism's loudest and sternest critics. Loyal Protestants were sure that he was already a Roman Catholic and acting in bad faith. In truth his motives were complex. The pamphlets that he wrote during his last few months as the rector of Launton were undoubtedly aimed at undermining the national Church. Believing that he now knew where the true Church was to be found he wanted to open eyes, to show those unshaken by Gorham's vindication that they were 'without excuse'. Yet this was not all. Even as he dismissed the English episcopate he genuinely wanted to hear the arguments of those who did not agree with him. Perhaps there was still something to be said, some steps that might, even yet, establish the theological *bona fides* of the national Church. Not until everything had been done could he conclude that he had not mistaken the call of God.

There were other clergymen on the brink of converting, lumped together by the Protestant press as 'the transitionists', who, in the opinion of their opponents, were intent on making mischief. One was William Maskell, whose *Second Letter to the High Church Party* appeared on 8 April. Subtitled *The Want of Dogmatic Teaching in the Church of England*, it argued that if Anglicanism had any coherent theology at all, it was that of Gorham, not Pusey. The founding fathers of the English Church had embraced doctrinal Calvinism; any lingering Catholicism was mere sentiment. Indeed he charged the Church of England—through its union with the Church of Ireland—with being implicated in formal heresy:

> Another established Church in full communion with our own, using our ritual, unaltered, unmutilated, had obliged its clergy to subscribe and to accept articles of faith, 'for the avoiding of diversities of opinion, and the establishing of consent touching true religion', not merely making doubtful the catholic doctrine of regeneration in baptism, but positively and undeniably contradicting it.[10]

Allies thought the case unanswerable and challenged Manning to read the *Second Letter*, 'What a *find* Maskell has made in those Irish Articles: how can you answer his *demand* in page 32?'[11] This was that those Anglicans who had joined Manning in denouncing Gorham and asserting baptismal regeneration was unequivocally the belief of the Church of England should also demand that their communion free itself from guilt by association. There was no response. The pamphlet was Maskell's swan song. Soon after its publication he resigned his living, lamenting that the Anglicanism 'I have worked for, dreamt of, prayed for, will not and may not be'.[12] Poor Manning, who was beleaguered by Allies's doubts, was also being assailed by William Dodsworth, an even closer friend. He too was convinced that royal supremacy had cut off the English Church from the only valid source of episcopal jurisdiction[13] and was regularly shocking his well-to-do and influential London congregation with apocalyptic warnings about the perilous state of their communion. In the face of this onslaught, Manning could not remain silent, and in July 1850 published his own pamphlet: *The Appellate Jurisdiction of the Crown in Matters Spiritual*. If the disease was yet to be healed, radical surgery was required. Parliament must now act to 'relieve the Princes of these realms of a burden too weighty for any royal head, by repealing so much of the Acts of Henry VIII as invests the Sovereign with this perilous and unnatural judicature'.[14]

Dodsworth assured him that this was an impossible dream, for no one could doubt that the only strong feeling of the English people 'is against priestcraft and the exercise of spiritual power. NO, IT CAN NEVER BE; and with this conviction have I any *right* to be where I am?'[15] Maskell, Dodsworth and Allies were all to convert, as indeed was Manning, though many Tractarians remained, convinced of the Catholic status of the Church of England. Their leader was Edward Pusey. If Allies had respected him once, he did so no longer, and had dismissed his spiritual direction as very thin gruel, writing in 1849: 'Pusey's guidance was a poor substitute for Newman's. I found he did not touch the wound which festered. He does not seem to see the Church of England as she is, but through such an atmosphere of filial love as disguises or sublimates her features.'[16]

Allies was sure that Pusey had worked actively to suppress *The*

Journal in France, and also to deflect him from attempting a defence of Anglicanism from the charge of heresy. This was surely sufficient evidence that his confessor's overriding objective was to prevent further conversions. It was, he reflected, 'the sort of conduct, which seems to wear an aspect of inward dishonesty, and refusal to meet the light.'[17] He was accordingly unsurprised when Pusey sought to come to terms with the Gorham decision by giving his opinion, that the integrity of the Church of England could be safeguarded if the bishops met and re-affirmed the doctrine that original sin was remitted in baptism. Dodsworth told his congregation that this was just wishful thinking because any statement acceptable to all the bishops would inevitably fall far short of a full Catholic understanding of the Sacrament. Both men went into print. It was a final parting of the ways. Pusey added a long postscript to his pamphlet on the royal supremacy defending his position on the Gorham judgment.[18] Dodsworth wrote a short essay containing the dire warning that attempts by Pusey and other 'moderates' to maintain unity by conciliating the Evangelicals would lead to disaster:

> We may not 'do evil that good may come;' and surely it is evil that we should advocate the admission of those to the cure of souls who deny the doctrine of baptismal regeneration. You hope that in time they will be brought to a more orthodox faith on this point. But in the mean while, what is to become of the souls which they are leading astray by the denial of this fundamental doctrine? For this denial is not, as you say, a mere 'breach in the wall,' but an undermining of its very foundations.[19]

In a postscript to his short tract Dodsworth commended Allies's work on orders and jurisdiction, observing that, despite its length, Pusey's treatise on the royal supremacy had not answered his opponent's challenge: 'if your object be, as it seems to be, to shew, that the Church may safely, or without forfeiture of her birthright, allow to the State *jurisdiction* in matters purely spiritual ... *all* your precedents ... tend to show that the Church has never allowed such an interference as this.'[20]

The forgiveness of sins

Allies's arguments regarding episcopal jurisdiction were perhaps somewhat arcane. But there were serious practical implications; in particular, did Anglican clergy have authority to forgive sins in virtue of their orders alone? Pusey and his followers believed that confession and sacramental absolution were at the heart of spiritual growth. Yet, in accepting penitents priests were almost invariably acting in defiance of their bishops. Allies told Manning that the bishop of Oxford had denied Pollen a faculty to hear confessions, and even Phillpotts of Exeter had refused a curate's request to absolve penitents.[21] Both bishops reputedly held High Church views. Pusey having no parish received penitents who came to him, regardless of the opinions of their incumbents and their diocesan bishops. But what jurisdiction did he have? What authority to forgive sins? For troubled souls this was a question of personal salvation. Allies was sure that in consequence of its separation from Rome the Church of England had forfeited the authority to grant absolution. Maskell and Dodsworth were troubled about the lack of jurisdiction of clergy who privately heard confessions despite episcopal opposition. They shared these concerns with Allies, who agreed to draft a joint letter to Pusey to see what he had to say. Sent to him on Ascension Day 1850 (9 May) it drew heavily from Allies's pamphlet on the royal supremacy:

> What authority is there for supposing that the acts of a Priest are valid who hears confessions and gives absolution, by mere virtue of his Orders, without ordinary or delegated jurisdiction from his Bishop?
> We believe it to be the undisputed law of the Church that as it flows from Order, acts done wrongly and illicitly are yet, though when done, valid — the reason of which is that the power of Order being given by consecration and indelible, cannot be taken away; but that acts flowing from Jurisdiction, if done upon those over whom the doer has no jurisdiction are absolutely invalid and null; the reason of which is, that jurisdiction being a relation of command

between a superior and a subject, one who has no subject can bear no jurisdiction, and accordingly cannot exercise a power which he has not received.

After citing various (largely Roman Catholic) authorities the letter concluded:

> the authority which for some time past has been exercised by some among us, and especially by yourself, not only in our own dioceses, but in other dioceses,—often without the knowledge, and probably (were it known) against the consent of both the Parish Priest and Bishop,—has not been based upon true and sufficient foundation; nay more, has been (however ignorantly) in opposition to the Catholic rules from the first ages to the present time. And further, a point to which we allude with reluctance and sorrow—it would follow likewise that the vast majority of those persons to whom you and others have given absolution in this manner, are still, so far as the effect of any such absolution is concerned, under the chain of their sins, because they have not made confession to Priests who had duly received power to absolve them.[22]

Pusey was terribly wounded by the personal nature of the challenge and wrote a stinging response to Allies:

> I write to you, because the letter, which has been countersigned by others, is written in your hand, and I am not called upon to write circulars.
> I cannot express the pain which both the tone and object of your letter gave to me; and I do most earnestly protest against the practice which has recently been pursued by one who signed your letter to me, of putting questions on sacred subjects, and then publishing the answers in any secular newspaper to be read at alehouses and made the subject of profane jest and merriment.
> I am the more pained at the letter coming from you, calling

me to account for my acts, and for the very acts for which you yourself sought me. You sought me, not I you. And now, having used confession and received absolution through me, you ask me as an abstract statement, and a point to which you 'allude with reluctance and sorrow' whether 'so far as the effect of such absolutions are concerned' they (and yourself among them) 'are not yet in their sins'. People do not write so, who are thinking about their own souls.

I cannot look upon the letter which you have sent me, as one of reality: I cannot think that you want to be satisfied. Had this been so it would not have been written as a circular. It looks like the manifesto of one, who has made up his mind to quit the English Church, and wishes before he does it, to make out a case against her. You seem to me to be intending to employ your position as a priest of the Church, to unsettle peoples' minds, before you leave her, and while preparing to do so.

Your statements as to my self (especially with the insertion, apparently in Mr. M's hand[23]) are calculated to give an erroneous impression of what I have done. But if you *think* I have acted against the discipline of the Church of England you can institute a suit, and you yourself can be a witness that I have received confessions. The irregularity according to you (since I have no cure of souls) is my receiving anyone whatsoever, who come to me with a burdened conscience. It applies to one as much as to all.

I do then most solemnly protest against your publishing any letter to me, you are not any ecclesiastical superior that I should give account to you. Nor were you led to confession by me, or first used confession with me. I am not then responsible to you in that way. And for your own satisfaction you would have asked me in a very different tone. I am satisfied about the answer, although it would not satisfy you, who found your objections partly on the practice of the Ancient Church, as to reconciling public penitents, and *removing excommunications*, partly on the discipline of the later Western Church, which our own held a right to discontinue.

You and I shall have to give an account of our actions before the judgement seat of Christ. Whether it will then appear that I did right in ministering to wounded consciences who came to me, or you and your colleagues in trying to unsettle consciences, which have received healing and peace, as seen in their lives afterwards, He is the Judge.

I stand at His Judgement Seat, or at that of His Bishops in this Church, not at that of the public press, or an ex-parte and exaggerated statement.[24]

Allies cannot have been surprised by this reaction, as he told Manning: 'He writes to me most grievously angry, as if we had made a personal attack on him, whereas we want to clear up a most important point, which makes every absolution that one has received invalid and debars one from ever obtaining another in the Church of England.'[25] He sought to pacify Pusey, whose reply to him also attempted to recast the issue in a less confrontational form:

If you please to send me your question, apart from all personality, as a case whether the power of the Keys can be validly exercised by a priest of the Church of England towards those over whom he has no jurisdiction, either by cure of souls or sanction from the Bishop of the Diocese.

But then I should be glad that you should distinguish whether you doubt (a.) whether such use of the power of the keys is allowed by the discipline of the English Church or (b.) whether it is allowable for the Church of England to permit it, if she so does. In a word whether your question relates to the lawfulness of the acts of individuals or the lawfulness of the acts (if so be) of the Church in not allowing the *use* of the power of the keys, without giving authority distinct from the act whereby she gives the power itself...

If ... you persist in this personal attack upon me for irregularity, I can have nothing to do with it. I know not why you make all your attack upon [me] rather than upon Archdeacon Manning and others, except that the influence which many years of labour have given him will be exerted in the same direction as your own, mine in a different.[26]

By this time Maskell, close to converting, was living at St Edmund's College at Ware in Hertfordshire, a Catholic seminary. Allies met him there on Wednesday 15 May. Dodsworth was in Paris, but assuming his concurrence they wrote to Pusey declining to withdraw what they had written: 'We cannot press you to give us an answer, but propose as soon as possible to print that (the original) letter and the present one, with some remarks. We shall not do so, however, for a few days, until we have learnt your final decision as to sending any answer.'[27] Pusey was very angry: 'You might as well stab a man and say "I meant nothing personal"'. He objected to 'vague generalities' and demanded that those paragraphs in the first letter asserting the inutility of his absolutions be removed from any published correspondence.[28] He asked that their reply should wait until Dodsworth could be consulted in person because

> he has done the same as my self though not in degree: you (if it had been an irregularity) would have been in part an occasion of it, by coming to me, and Mr. M. by sending one to me. And then you turn around and write as if I had been an intruder in your dioceses. Yours in sorrow, EBP.[29]

Whether Dodsworth was consulted or not it was Allies's opinion that they could not compromise, he wrote to Maskell on 19 May, saying of the paragraphs referred to by Pusey, 'they contain the very gist of the matter.'[30] Three days later the two sent a third, uncompromising letter:

> We are surprised and deeply regret that you continue to suppose that our letter referred to, or tended to implicate yourself, personally, in any degree more than many others, who, during the last few years, have been in the habit of receiving confessions and giving absolution. We can most sincerely say that we selected you as the person to be publicly

addressed on this very solemn matter, on account of your position in the Church, your acknowledged learning and long practice of administering in various dioceses the Sacrament of Penance. We must therefore leave our first letter as it was originally written, and unless we receive your answer, we propose to publish these three letters without further delay.[31]

It was in the course of this—as yet private—correspondence that Dodsworth had published his own *Letter to Pusey* condemning his response to the Gorham judgment. It was a cry of distress at what he saw as his friend's fall from the Catholic teaching that they had both embraced, which included 'your constant and common practice of administering the sacrament of penance—by encouraging, if not enjoining, auricular confession, and giving special priestly absolution.'[32] It must have seemed to Pusey as if his critics had deliberately opened a second front. Not content with undermining his ministry among Tractarians by denying the efficacy of his absolutions, they were now exhibiting him to Protestant England as an insidious agent of Romanism. And indeed there was furious reaction in the popular press:

> Does it not become the duty of every sincere and honest member of the Church to do what in him lies, in order to her being set free from the obloquy of including such persons as Dr. Pusey or Mr. Dodsworth amongst her authorized teachers. Is it not, if possible, even more incumbent on every true son of the Church, to require that Dr. Pusey be deposed from the Professorial Chair at Oxford which he occupies as much to the Church's peril, as to his own disgrace and that of the University in which he holds so important a position? … We live in times of imminent peril. There are interests at stake which must no longer be trifled with.[33]

Pusey knew that Maskell was in earnest in threatening to publish the joint letter and had complained to Allies that it was scandalous that the former's correspondence with the archbishop of Canterbury had been published in the press.[34] Maskell had written to the prelate after his parishioners had petitioned him not to resign, seeking guidance on 'what doctrines I ought to teach my people to believe'. He wanted from Sumner an explicit statement that Catholic doctrines formed the official teaching of the Church of England: baptismal regeneration, the transmission of orders, and the power of absolving penitents. The archbishop's reply cannot have come as a surprise: 'there are many subjects connected with our holy religion, upon which we have no reason to expect the dogmatic teaching of the church', and 'The church can only speak as scripture speaks, and does not intrude into "the secret things which belong to the Lord our God"'. This exchange of letters, which occurred during the last week of April 1850, was forwarded by Maskell to *The Times*, which published them on Wednesday 1 May.

Pusey was deeply concerned to defend and promote the practice of sacramental confession. He felt the attack keenly. Keble commiserated with his old friend, observing that the sole aim of Maskell and his allies was 'to stab the Church of England through your sides'.[35] Many years later Pusey's official biographer agreed with this judgment, detecting a wanton insensitivity: 'It must be hoped that the writers of this letter afterwards felt regret at the consequences to Pusey of such an appeal. To themselves it can have made little difference, for their own convictions had reached a point at which it must have been almost a matter of indifference whether confessions were received at all in the English Church.'[36]

Pusey wrote to Allies: 'I can only ask for the sake of others, whose peace I prize to give me time to prepare my answer. Amid these distractions and University duties, I can only get little fragments of time.'[37] Of his three assailants he felt closest to Dodsworth—believing him at least still to have the interests of the Church of England at heart—and at the end of May assured him that he was working on his answer. It was not published until the end of July as a *Letter to The Rev W. U. Richards, Minister of All Saints, Marylebone*, with the self-explanatory additional title: *The Church of England Leaves her Children Free to whom to Open their Griefs*.[38] He knew that Allies's work on jurisdiction and the letter questioning the efficacy of his absolutions (which although not yet published had been widely circulated) had unsettled many, indeed had led to at least one conversion.[39] He was accordingly very anxious to establish the legitimacy of his practice and to answer the charge that no bishop would approve of it:

> I cannot believe it possible that any English Bishop would bid us send away those who came to us with burthened consciences ... Still less can I imagine that any Bishop, to whom any of us could tell, in general terms, the blessed fruits of this ministry, could hesitate for a moment to bless God for His work.[40]

Pusey argued that when the Church of England released her people from the obligation to go at least annually to their parish priest in auricular confession the position regarding jurisdiction changed. She had 'returned to the same state as in the time of St. Chrysostom or St. Augustine, "when many were corrected as Peter; many were endured as Judas; many not known until the Lord comes"'.[41] However, auricular confession was undoubtedly permitted because the Book of Common Prayer through a number of revisions continued to put the following exhortation into the mouths of her priests: 'if there be any of you who ... cannot quiet his conscience ... let him come to me, or to some other discreet and learned minister of God's Word, and open his grief; that by the ministry of God's holy Word he may receive the benefit of absolution'. The implication was that at the Reformation the Church legitimately 'gave her children leave to go to whom they willed, having placed them under no "jurisdiction"':

> The words in her exhortation are living words; they are an actual reality; they are renewed whenever they are pronounced; they speak whenever they are read; they have spoken to thousands and tens of thousands of broken, anxious, burthened hearts; they are the voice of the Church of England and of God through her speaking to people's consciences, and they were heard and understood.[42]

As regards Allies's 'abstract' arguments regarding orders and jurisdiction Pusey commented that it was not known what was the practice in the primitive Church, but that the Anglican Church had the power to relax the restrictions established by the Lateran Council. Not until October, by which time both he and Allies had converted, did Maskell publish the correspondence on absolution along with his critique of Pusey's pamphlet. By this time, however, loyal Anglicans could safely ignore his *Letter to Rev E. B. Pusey*, as simply another piece of Roman Catholic propaganda. Newman wrote to Allies:

> I have just received Maskell's able and settling pamphlet, but I am very sorry the three letters did not appear, as you intended, immediately on their being written. Then they would have produced an effect, the question would have been before the world, and the *doubt* would have thrown the *onus probandi* on Pusey. Now, it is to be feared, the *onus probandi* will be upon the 'Why should I read Maskell?' The more I think of it, the more I regret it.[43]

Maskell sought to expose the weakness of his adversary's position: who, he says, asserts but does not prove that at the Reformation the Church of England intended to change the disciplines of the Catholic Church as regards jurisdiction. Nevertheless, this admission—necessary for Pusey's case—was embarrassing to one anxious to assert Catholic continuity despite the rejection of papal authority. Pusey had argued that for practical reasons the Roman Catholics themselves had made many exceptions to the general discipline not least in seeking to resolve the thorny problem of determining who could absolve the pope. On these grounds the Church of England was entitled to allow those with wounded consciences to choose their own confessor. But, asked Maskell, did Pusey really speak for his communion? He asserted her Catholicity because she had the apostolic succession, the rule of the episcopate, yet he could find only one Anglican bishop willing to countenance the practice of sacramental confession, and then only in exceptional circumstances.[44] Pusey's biographer returns to the familiar criticism that Allies's attack was based on abstruse reasoning, 'abstract theory derived largely from Suarez' and that Pusey's practical approach mirrored that of the primitive Church.[45]

After both had converted Allies expressed his exasperation to Maskell. It was to become his usual response to Pusey's steadfast loyalty to the Church of England. 'It seems he *will* not look in the face the real matter which one has at heart; he strives to shift the question to the rightness of confession, from the point we urge, whether the Anglican Church provides for it, sanctions it, or even endures it.'[46] Stung by Maskell's criticisms, Pusey wrote a *Postscript* to his *Letter to Richards*, dated Advent Eve 1850; it was almost as long as the original pamphlet. Their positions, however, were irreconcilable and by now there was little interest in their argument. The *Christian Remembrancer* spoke for most Anglicans in opining that the Schoolmen and the great Catholic canonists were all agreed that practical necessity should ever outweigh the 'technical difficulty of a pettifogging objector':

> Mr Maskell and Mr Allies, in quitting the Church of England, thought to strike a parting blow which would sever from her many Catholic minds, by casting a doubt upon the validity of her absolutions given under her free system of choosing a confessor. It is curious enough to see their argument completely overthrown by Roman authorities, who are compelled by the necessity of the case, and by the practice of their own Church, to acknowledge the kind of jurisdiction *in foro conscientiae* which is claimed for priests in the Church of England.[47]

Allies was unconvinced, and passed harsh judgment on his one-time spiritual director:

> He contented himself with settling the question of jurisdiction, as far as it touched himself in *foro interiori*, by hearing confessions wherever he pleased, as if every priest had, in virtue of his priesthood, unlimited licence to hear all confessions and grant absolution, and by disregarding the fact that, even were his priesthood real, all his absolutions would be null and void. In other words, he assumed to himself, within his own communion, a power which in the Catholic Church is possessed by the Pope alone. Many, also, since have

followed his example; but none have ventured to enter into the whole subject of spiritual jurisdiction, and justify either the Anglican position in general, or their own practice in particular; they have preferred to ignore both points, and assume each in their own case papal faculties.[48]

Where Maskell's pamphlet was known about it only served to inflame Protestant suspicions of Pusey's pernicious influence. The popular press pounced on its 'revelation of certain *hidden practices*, of which before we had only an indistinct impression'. Moreover, 'after all this secrecy and contrivance ... the poor dupes who make Dr. Pusey their pope are *absolutely taken in by him*—for that he assumes a power to which he can show no title whatever'.[49] The bishop of London was equally discouraging when he delivered his charge at St Paul's Cathedral on 2 November, having Pusey very much in mind when he asked:

> what can be better calculated to lead the less learned or less thoughtful members of our Protestant Church to look with complacency upon the errors which that church has renounced, and at length to embrace them than to have books of devotions put into their hands by their own clergymen, in which all divine honour is ascribed to the Virgin Mary, a propitiatory virtue is attributed to the Eucharist, the mediation of saints is spoken of as a probable doctrine, prayer for the dead is urged as a positive duty, and a superstitious use of the sign of the cross is urged as profitable. Add to this the secret practice of auricular confession, the use of crucifixes and rosaries, the administration of what is termed the sacrament of penance; and it is manifest that they who are taught to believe such things are compatible with the principles of the English Church must also believe it to be separate from that of Rome by a faint and almost imperceptible line, and be prepared to pass that line without much fear of incurring the guilt of schism.[50]

Allies—from many conversations with Blomfield—could not have been surprised at all this. However, Pusey's biographer, concluding that the bishop had drawn his list of objectionable teachings from Maskell, who 'had already gone to Rome', and Dodsworth, who was then 'meditating secession', commented that 'it was indeed strange that a prelate who had known Pusey so long should have thought it right to judge his real work and motives on the evidence of those who were in such a position'.[51] By this time Protestant England was in uproar regarding the re-establishment of the Catholic episcopate and Blomfield was not immune to the frenzy. It all added to Pusey's embarrassment. A little while after his conversion and whilst winding up his affairs in Launton, Allies came across Pusey when they were travelling on the same train. It must have been a difficult encounter, but they were able to talk, and the practice of confession in the Church of England was alluded to. A few days later when staying with his wife's family at Nelmes, Allies read Blomfield's *Charge* and could not resist writing to Pusey, to turn a knife in his wound:

> I have often reflected on your conversation with me lately on the railway, and especially on what you said that all you did in the diocese of London as to hearing confessions etc. was with the cognisance and approval of Dr Blomfield—so much the more was I struck on looking out his charge yesterday to see a most pronounced and explicit censure of 'the secret practice of auricular confession, the use of crucifixes and rosaries, the administration of what is termed the sacrament of penance' and then of people being 'taught to believe that such things are compatible with the principles of the English Church.'
>
> Indeed, I cannot reconcile these words, which seemed especially aimed at you with the cognisance and approval of which you spoke. Or can you doubt that your view of your right to exercise ecumenical jurisdiction in the matter of penance is not at least in accordance with that of Dr Blomfield.
>
> You cannot wonder that such a letter as Maskell's is addressed to you, under such circumstances.[52]

Unsurprisingly, he received no reply, although two months later Pusey published another long pamphlet protesting his complete devotion to the Church of England: *A Letter to ... the Lord Bishop of London in Explanation of Some Statements contained in a Letter by the Rev. W. Dodsworth.*[53] But by this time Allies had pronounced judgment on his one-time confessor, a verdict that he never found reason to modify.

The shining of a great light

In the spring of 1850 Allies still hesitated and prayed daily for more illumination. Why did he remain an Anglican? A great light had shone from the Gorham judgment, which, he said, revealed the 'distinctive character' of Anglicanism in the royal supremacy, a 'power which alone makes it a whole', its 'Cathedri Petri'. And in view of the importance of national cohesion it was inevitable that the queen's judges should seek to be as accommodating as possible in the interpretation of her Church's doctrine. For those Anglican clergy who considered themselves the guardians of an objective Catholic faith, this was profoundly humiliating, but for Allies only to be expected: '*any* error and *any* heresy are innocent and innocuous compared to the tenet that error and heresy are indifferent. The Royal Supremacy and the Church of God are two ideas absolutely incompatible and contradictory.'[54] Yet even after his Damascene experience, still he delayed. Throughout the summer of 1850, despite the embarrassment of having a Catholic wife, and despite the pleadings of friends who had already 'gone over'[55] Allies continued to officiate as rector of Launton. The press of course had no difficulty in accounting for his inertia:

> The Oxford Herald asserts that Mrs. Allies has also gone, but our contemporary does not add that her husband has not followed her. Mr. Allies remains rector of Launton; and in spite of his suppressed book, and his notorious sayings and doings, he is looked upon by the Tractarians as a man in the right path. That they should think so is natural for they know whither he is going. People are apt to ask, when Mr Maskell wends, why does Mr Allies tarry? We do not know why. We only know that Mr Maskell's income (derived from the church

preferment he held) was a very small one indeed, and that the rectory of Launton is a valuable living—a golden incumbency. This does not explain the new respective positions of the two gentlemen, but it will flash across the mind when the latter is occupied with the subject.[56]

In August the *Cheltenham Chronicle* was sure of his intentions:

The report of Mrs. Allies's secession is fully confirmed, and we are informed that the reverend gentleman is on the point of establishing himself at a fashionable watering place and taking pupils! Thanks to his indulgent diocesan, the Protestant endowment of Launton, amounting to £800 p.a., is for the present retained, as a matter, we presume, of convenience.[57]

Where this information came from is a mystery, but it was incorrect, although by now he had resolved to take the final step. It was quite a recent decision. Pusey had been unfair in accusing him of bad faith; even after Eliza had been received he was still desperately probing whether anything more could be said in favour of Anglicanism. Indeed on the very morning of her baptism (24 May), he slipped into a London church and took communion, later saying that not for another two months did he lose 'the sense of reality in Anglican ordinances'.[58] A fortnight later he and Eliza returned to the rectory and the following day (Tuesday 9 June) he wrote tortured letters to various Anglican friends: 'I am most anxious not to take a final step without giving myself every chance'. Their responses led him across his Rubicon. To Manning especially he appealed as 'a doctor called in on a desperate case',[59] citing five issues on which he was 'unable to acquit the Church of England ... I consider that to be wrong on any one of these points cuts off a province of the Church from all the privileges of the one mystical Body'. These comprised: 'unity, infallibility, heresy, schism and jurisdiction'.[60] Quite what response he expected is unclear. Manning could only refer him back to 'your book upon the question of Schism' as 'ample ground for doubting any contrary conclusion'. But, in his heart Manning knew that the patriarchal theory—even if true—could not justify a Church which owed its *raison d'être* to the supreme authority of the monarch. He could offer Allies no comfort at all:

> If I could offer to you anything you have not weighed, I would gladly; but you have, I know, far outgone me in real study ... All that I can say is that my time has been given to serving my neighbour, how poorly I well know. This is a worthless letter to send to you. But I have no better. I trust to be led to the truth in these points, on which I feel to need rather than to be able to give such help as you require.[61]

The bishop of Brechin could offer no help except to refer to the distaste of Roman devotions expressed by the Caroline divines:

> I confess that even if these are weak in first principles, they are strong in uncomfortable facts, which would be sure to haunt one when over. The nearer I approach Rome the less I feel drawn to it. I cannot understand Newman's line; it must be a cardinal defect to seek to impose the devotions fitted for an Italian mind on our Saxon real selves and may not our insularity, after all, be more of a subjective argument than we admit of? I feel quite the grand intellectual position of the Roman Church, and yet how far is intellect to be the measure of faith?[62]

This echoed Judge Coleridge's response to the *Royal Supremacy* pamphlet. Neither man was to convert. Once he was a Catholic Allies found it almost impossible to comprehend how a Church of England minister could describe himself as a priest of the universal Church. Believing the Roman case to be overwhelming he ascribed the failure to grasp it as coming from either intellectual or moral weakness. Thus he explained Edward Pusey: despite his great learning, he still possessed a Protestant mind, 'destitute of all organism and coherence ... "ever learning and never coming to a knowledge of the truth"'.[63] Perhaps if he had reflected on the spring of 1850 when he continued to minister the Anglican rites whilst believing her to be in schism, Allies might have been better able to sympathise with those who continued to be nourished by her teachings and sacraments, who never lost 'the sense of reality in Anglican ordinances.'[64]

The Tractarian clergy who did not convert were held fast by a sense of continuity: that the pre-Reformation buildings in which they ministered the sacraments were validation enough that they were the inheritors of St Augustine's little band. They could not envisage abandoning the souls of those in their care, when the ecclesiastical issues over which Allies agonised seemed so abstract. Gladstone, who thought deeply on these matters and who had written on the identity of Church and nation, found Rome's case unproved and later argued against papal infallibility and the threat of 'Vaticanism'. In 1880 he read Allies's *A Life's Decision* and at the end of the book drew up two lists: one, the names of eminent personalities who had gone over to Rome, the other, a longer list, of the equally illustrious individuals who had remained at their Anglican posts.[65]

The primacy of Peter

A few days after Thomas and Eliza returned to Launton in June, she now as a Catholic, they were visited by John Pollen, who was anxious to learn about Thomas's intentions. They discussed the recent news that Wynne and Patterson had converted, which had come as no surprise to Allies, who had received letters from Wynne[66] and knew that like himself both men so admired continental Catholicism that their faith in the Church of England had been eviscerated. Patterson in particular had agonised so much about the validity of his ministry that his health was affected and he had been advised 'to go abroad for a year to rest.'[67] Thinking that a deeper knowledge of Orthodox Christianity might restore his belief in the branch theory he asked John Wynne, whom he described as 'like-minded and very earnest', to travel with him to the Middle East. Observing the Copts at close quarters, however, did nothing to reassure them and both men became convinced that unity was to be found only in Rome. In Holy Week, 1850, they were in Jerusalem, and there, in Patterson's words 'we received and obeyed the Divine call, and submitted to the One, Catholic, Holy, and Apostolic Church.'[68]

Allies said that before long he would follow them. Pollen asked when, concerned about the falseness of his position, particularly as he was the author of a celebrated book defending the Church of England from the charge of schism. Surely it was his duty to give the 'reasons for so great a change of opinion on the subject of the Primacy?'[69] Allies felt the force of this. Maybe the process of systematically ordering his thoughts on this key issue might help him to take the final step? For it was not only the popular press who referred contemptuously to the 'transitionist clergy', many of the Anglicans who had borne sympathetically with his soul-searchings were losing patience with him. Bishop Forbes hearing that he was writing in support of papal supremacy, rebuked him for disloyalty verging on hypocrisy:

> I think you ought to take great care of tampering with your convictions. You should fix a time for the solution of your doubts, and then act at once consistently. I doubt the morality of writing a pamphlet such as I hear you are at present, while Rector of Launton. Indeed, I think you should abstain from writing anything at present, till you are settled, as the 'transition style' is less satisfactory in literary fame than in orders of architecture.[70]

It was a valid criticism, but Allies believed that he was preparing for a great sacrifice and in the interim had little choice, because from 'the moment I gave up my living I should be tossed about for some time from place to place, without books, and unable to collect my thoughts. If anything was to be written, it must be done at once.'[71]

These were desperate weeks. Was there now nothing to be said for the Anglican episcopate? Despite the damage inflicted by the Reformation, his Tractarian friends insisted that existing facts must be reckoned with: the Church of England had inherited an episcopal order. This was her link with the universal Church. Might the royal sovereignty not have become—in the divine will—the guarantee, not the enemy, of episcopal autonomy? The state's role was not to define doctrine but to identify and diffuse the episcopal consensus and it was notorious that almost every bishop had condemned Tract 90 and approved of the decision in Gorham. Was it really the case that Anglicanism possessed no more authority than any Protestant denomination? Five years before Allies had refused to follow Newman, claiming that the monarchical papacy was unjustifiable, an infringement of episcopal liberty and an arrogation of power unknown in the primitive Church. So was he now fully convinced that every Christian owed final allegiance to the bishop of Rome as the source of all ecclesial jurisdiction?

How could he answer his own formidable scholarship that underpinned the second edition of the *Church of England Cleared of the Charge of Schism?* Allies's second conversion was based on a new and overwhelming sense of the importance of a divinely established jurisdiction in the ordering of the universal Church. There had to be an ultimate source of authority for the promulgation of doctrine and for the allocation of pastoral responsibilities. What or who could fulfil this role if not the pope? Healy Thompson had argued this in his work on the *Unity of the Episcopate* written in direct rebuttal of the *Church of England Cleared*, which Allies had read but not understood. Now, in the light of Gorham, he read it again and wondered why he had ever thought the patriarchal theory could withstand the crushing logic of the Roman position? He blamed the Anglican ecclesiology in which he had been trained, which lacked, he said, any integrating principle. 'I was lost in an endless search for facts, without having any grasp of the principles required for interpreting those facts and giving them their due value'.[72] Thus he had missed 'the single elementary distinction between the powers of order and jurisdiction'.[73]

In re-reading *The Unity of the Episcopate* Allies was aware how heavily dependent it was on a more substantial tome, Giovanni Bolgeni's *L'Episcopato*.[74] It was to this classic study that he now turned and after reading it could only bow before its central thesis: that all sincere Churchman must embrace an infallible papacy as the seat of ultimate jurisdiction, the guarantee of unity. According to Bolgeni:

> The Pope's universal jurisdiction comes immediately from God. The Pope being deceased, there is no one in the Church of God who has universal jurisdiction over all the bishops and Christian people. Not even the body of all the bishops has

> it; since without the Pope it does not represent the universal Church, and is not that body on which in the person of the apostles united together with Peter, Jesus Christ immediately from Himself conferred the episcopate for the general governance of His Church.[75]

Allies recalled the early summer of 1850, when he was grappling with these issues as the most intense period of his life:

> I gave up my mind entirely to the question of the Primacy; from June 16 to July 30, I devoted every moment of time I could spare to form my view, collect and classify my documents, and draw out the programme of my treatise. This done on July 30, I began to write, and in three weeks completed the seven sections of the work, then sent it to press.[76]

His pamphlet was published early in September, timed to coincide with his reception into the Catholic Church. It was entitled *The See of St. Peter, the Rock of the Church, the Source of Jurisdiction, and the Centre of Unity* and was dedicated to W. E. Gladstone, whose own recent pamphlet defending the royal supremacy had dismissed Allies's work on *Order and Jurisdiction*:

> I have read with some surprise and much grief in the work of a clergyman of great ability and undoubted theological learning the assertion that in the time of Henry VIII. the See of Rome was both 'the source and centre of ecclesiastical jurisdiction' and therefore the supreme judge of doctrine; and that this power of the Pope was transferred in its entireness to the Crown ... That the Pope was the source of ecclesiastical jurisdiction in the English Church before the Reformation is an assertion of the gravest import, which ought not to have been thus taken for granted. It is one which I firmly believe to be false in history, false in law—which in my view as an Englishman, is degrading to the nation, and, as a Christian, to the Church.[77]

In dedicating to him this, his last book as an Anglican, Allies accepted this challenge: 'The assertion was not made by me lightly and offhand. I knew what an immense body of proof existed for it; and I had too much respect for you not to wish to bring such a portion of that proof as the time allowed before your notice.'[78] *The See of St. Peter* seeks to demonstrate how existing facts point to a papal monarchy as ordained for the government of the universal Church, a position derived from logic and supported by a mass of Scriptural evidence: 'Now, in all this I have hitherto gone on the mere words of Scripture, which are so plain, so coherent, so decisive, that I cannot imagine a candid mind drawing any other conclusion from them.'[79]

Such a *volte-face* entitled the critics to respond that only two years before he had drawn a very different conclusion from the same evidence. In the second and subsequent editions of the *See of St. Peter* (1855) the author sought to explain himself: in writing as an Anglican, he noted, his mind had been in thrall to a national prejudice,

> a modern contradictory tradition inculcating as a first principle of belief that the primacy of S. Peter, as continued in the Pope, is a corruption of Christianity, had then possession of his mind ... and prevented his even studying what is said in Holy Writ with regard to this particular subject. Such a tradition makes a mind incapable of exercising candour, however much it may desire to do so.[80]

Yet light had dawned on him and he believed that truly candid minds must also see that the unity of the visible society established by Christ necessitated an episcopate united in the successor of St Peter. Where he speaks 'you have one faith, one homogeneous and harmonious system of teaching'; but 'Go to those who left Peter denouncing him as a corrupter of God's truth ... and you find this divine system broken into fragments.'[81] Now, 'the *end* for which the Primacy was instituted (unity) guides us then to the nature of its *power* which is jurisdiction, universal, immediate and supreme.'[82] After adducing a mass of historical testimony to the Roman primacy and the necessity of communion with the pope Allies reviews the impact of the Reformation. The author is now sure that his bishop—a successor of the Elizabethan hierarchy not the apostles—possesses no divine legitimacy.

> For myself, now that after long years of pain and distress, of thought, of enquiry, and of prayer, since by the mercy of God the light has broken upon me, let me say as much as this ... let those who can put their trust in such a Church, and such an Episcopate, those who can feel their souls safe in such a system, work in it, think for it, write for it, pray for it, and *trust their souls to it*. But the duty which I owe to Almighty God, and the regard which I have for my salvation, compel me to declare my belief, by word and act that it is an *imposture*, all the more dangerous to the souls of men ... because it pretends to be a member of the Catholic Body, with which it has broken the essential relation, and to possess spiritual powers which it has indeed forfeited.[83]

The pamphlet concludes with a challenge to those Anglicans who claimed their communion as more authentic than Rome because more faithful to the Bible and to the primitive Church:

> And now, I have given the *Scriptural* authority for S. Peter's Primacy, carried on in his successors;
> Where is the *Scriptural* authority for the Primacy of Queen Victoria?
> I have given the *Patristic* authority, and that of the Councils, for S. Peter's Primacy;
> What Fathers and what Councils acknowledge a temporal supremacy of the State over the faith and discipline of the Church? ...
> But for the Royal Supremacy you have *nothing* to bring from Scripture; not one word; unless you like, 'Render unto Caesar the things that are Caesar's, and unto God the things that are God's.'
> And as for tradition, King Henry and Queen Elizabeth set themselves against the current of fifteen hundred years;

they tore up what had been the root of their own Church for well nigh a thousand. They severed themselves from S. Peter's See, and they sowed throughout their realm divisions never ending.[84]

In 1850 there were many conversions leading to a plethora of pamphlets urging the claims of Rome; few were noticed in the daily press. But Allies was notorious, and he was reported. The *Morning Post* judged his conversion more than ordinarily reprehensible:

> Genius is proverbially eccentric: so we account for Dr. Newman. Feebleness easily imposed upon, so we account for a score of others. But what are we to say or think of the middle class of persons—faint imitators of genius—hair-breadth convicts of mediocrity—the garment of whose erudition (scantily as it hangs on them) distressingly displays all the seams and joins, not of a thrifty antiquity, but a novel patchwork of pieces new and old? What can be our feeling at the painful sight of an arduous and awful position usurped or travestied by incompetency? Whatever such feeling must necessarily be, even in its most mitigated form, our readers may impute it to us as undeniably ours on a recent perusal of a thick pamphlet of Mr Allies, the late Rector of Launton in Oxfordshire, directed against the Church of England, which, he informs us, he has just deserted.
> We can imagine a man of highly-wrought and sensitive mind, varied acquirements and scholarly habits ... We can picture him to ourselves resigning his college, vacating his parish, retiring into privacy for months or years, with the frightful idea growing upon a diseased mental vision, that, after all his toil he was not a members of the true Church ... It may be no imaginary portrait. Possibly (so, at least, some have believed) this was such a conversion as Dr. Newman's. We say not; but is it necessary to contrast with this the tarrying among us of busy writers, doing in our midst a deed which can only be likened to that of one who should have

admission to our household, and use his position there to win and abuse our confidence at our domestic hearth, and without changing countenance, aim to destroy us in the very home that harboured him?

The newspaper's critique of Allies's actual argument was less powerful. It criticised his translation of ancient documents, 'he softens down every strong word or phrase unmanageable to his theory of supremacy'. However, only one example is cited: 'Our readers will hardly expect more of us, after this specimen'. Its sharpest barb was saved to the end:

> Ambitious beyond his knowledge ... he has put forward a pamphlet which only displays his own *animus*—bitterness against the communion in which he has been so long cherished, with the vain eagerness to fix the charge of heresy on a Church whom he so late affected to 'clear of the charge of schism'—an eagerness so ill instructed that, while proceeding to rebuke probable heresy on baptism, he falls into positive heresy as to the Holy Spirit (p. 43), attributes the unity of the Divine Father and the Eternal Son, not to their consubstantiality, but to the uniting power of the Holy Spirit![85]

Compared with the *Church of England Cleared*, *The See of Peter* is a slight book, the work of weeks, not years. Criticism more considered than that of the daily papers still asked the same obvious question: how could so rigorous a historian after so short a time take up the same documents and draw quite opposite conclusions from them? The *Christian Remembrancer* was excoriating:

> To the great masters of disputation of old, it used to be a light thing to prove indisputably conclusions on one side only. Their pride was to maintain what none could answer but themselves; to prove incontrovertibly all but themselves wrong; and then as incontrovertibly, themselves also. Nothing but victory on both sides would content them. Mr Allies seems

disposed to emulate them, and to aim at the uncommon yet somewhat delicate experiment of refuting himself.[86]

Prefacing the second edition of *The Church of England Cleared* Allies had answered his Catholic critics by dismissing papal sovereignty and infallibility as unhistorical: this 'great primary Idea' was a modern theory 'unsupported, nay, denied by the whole history of the Church, down to the separation of East and West.'[87] In *The See of St. Peter* he sought to explain his reassessment of the evidence:

> I went over again the testimonies of antiquity which I had before put together, and many others besides; and I found that one or two confusions and incoherencies of mind—especially the not understanding accurately the distinction between the power of Order and the power of Jurisdiction, and their consequences—had alone prevented my seeing, not merely a Primacy of divine institution, but how full, complete and overwhelming was the testimony of the Church before the division of East and West to the Supremacy of S. Peter's See, *as at present claimed*, the very same, and no other.[88]

Not having shared Allies's sudden enlightenment his Anglican critics felt this would not do. The *Christian Remembrancer* thought that an apologist

> who as positively pronounces the same facts to run all one way in 1850, as he did that they went directly in the opposite way in 1848... rather mild to himself... How far in any parallel case, a writer, a lawyer, or a politician, by such an explanation could save his reputation from the charge of random and reckless hastiness, we have no difficulty in determining.[89]

The *Remembrancer* was unfair; conversion is of the essence of faith, and Christian history studded with sudden enlightenment. Allies was quite unembarrassed by his change of opinion. Why should one who had been blind apologise for receiving miraculous sight, for the fact that now he saw what hitherto was shrouded in darkness, that the bishop of Rome alone was the foundation and keystone of the Church?

The Catholic reviewers were understandably exultant. The *Tablet* indeed confessed itself perplexed how one whose 'right-minded researches' and whose 'generosity' and 'singleness of mind' it lauded had hitherto failed to 'recognise the truth when it was before his eyes'. Their reviewer, however, offered a solution: 'the Gorham case has wonderfully cleared up the atmosphere of controversy', although 'all or most of the facts were known to him before, but he had not got into the right perspective to see them'. As a measure of his thanksgiving and esteem Pius IX ordered an Italian translation of Allies's work and before the year was out this had been published in Naples.[90]

Allies knew that Protestants would dismiss his pamphlet as merely theoretical, a logical mind seeking to prove that in accepting royal authority, the Church of England had taken the path of schism. The Reformation based its claims on the Bible. Against this, what weight could be given to 'mere theology', the decrees of Church councils or the arguments of canonists? Only an overwhelming weight of scriptural proof might convince his opponents that Christ had unequivocally designated Peter as his vicar, the ruler on earth of all Christian believers. For this reason he was delighted to come across a work published in Latin in 1850 by the Jesuit scholar, Carlo Passaglia: *Commentary on the Prerogatives of St. Peter, Prince of Apostles, as proved by the authority of Holy Writ*.[91] Allies was immediately struck by its strong biblical basis, ideally suited to those 'brought up in the prejudices of Protestantism'. 'Is it possible' he asked 'that they who specially profess to draw their faith from the written Word of God, would refuse to acknowledge a doctrine set forth in Holy Scripture with at least as strong evidence as the Godhead of our Lord itself ...?' He considered Passaglia's 'chain of evidence ... so strong, that, when I first saw it completely drawn out it struck my own mind ... with the force of a new revelation'.

Thus the Catholic Allies set out to condense and popularise Passaglia's work for English-speaking readers. It was published in 1852 under the title: *St. Peter, his Name and his Office, as set forth in Holy Scripture*.

I have considered his whole work as a treasure-house of

learning, whence I might draw at my pleasure 'things old and new,' adapting them, as I thought good, to the needs of the Protestant mind, as familiar to me in England. Thus I have not scrupled to translate, to omit, or to insert matter of my own, according to my judgment.⁹²

The book is a detailed and painstaking analysis of the Scriptural references to Peter based upon the key importance of his being given—as was Abraham—a new name. Thereafter it traces the steps by which Peter was prepared for the office of supreme ruler, leading to the great events of Passion Week and the Forty Days, during which he was designated with authority as the one who would 'confirm' his brethren. Following Passaglia, Allies draws out the fulfilment of his unique ministry in the Acts of the Apostles and—despite some apparent tensions—in the writings of St Paul. The analysis does not seek to prove that Peter's authority was transmitted to his successor bishops of Rome; here the author refers readers to his *See of St. Peter*, 'especially in the fifth section which ought to be preceded by this Treatise.'⁹³ In opinion of *The Month*—a Jesuit periodical—Allies's narrative was compelling in its flow of argument:

> There is no single book in English on the Catholic side which contains the Scriptural argument about St. Peter and the Papacy so clearly or so conclusively put. It embodies all the learned and elaborate argument of Passaglia, from whose work it is derived, but the matter is condensed and arranged by the hand of a master, and thus the book is anything but a mere translation.⁹⁴

Given the nature of the argument what one side found compelling would fail to convince the other. In his history of the papacy, Dom John Chapman commented:

> I think, few people could read Mr. Allies' admirable digest of Passaglia, *St. Peter, His Name and Office*, without acknowledging the proofs to be overwhelming. But then, Protestants do

not study the place of St Peter in the Bible, they pass it over. They do not read Mr. Allies' excellent book: they either have never heard of it, or they avoid it.[95]

Yet, not every Anglican disregarded it, some within the High Church fold valued its analysis but without drawing the conclusions that Allies would have wished. A young woman whose sympathy for things Roman was disturbing her mother, later threw some light on their response to its analysis. Recounting her conversion, Caroline Young recalled:

> We had a High Church acquaintance at Clifton, Mr Linlithgow Scott ... To [whom] we were indebted for a perusal of Mr Allies' book *St Peter his Name and his Office*. If one of our convert friends had offered to lend my mother this work, probably the offer would not have been accepted. But Mr Scott was a thoroughly good Churchman. He said that he had been surprised to find how very much there was about St Peter in the Bible. Mr Allies had collected all the texts and facts which bore upon that great Apostle. It really was a very fair work, and very instructive. We should be interested in it, and as members of the English Church we might at all events recognize the *Primacy* of St Peter. When the book came I found that Mr Scott had left off reading it just at the place where the demonstration of the untenableness of the Anglican position began ... Some instinct must have warned good Mr Scott that it was better for his peace of mind that those pages should remain uncut.[96]

Elsewhere the Anglican response was predictable. *The Church of England Quarterly Review* said that the book had earned for its author 'whatever credit or discredit he may attach to a leadership of the ultramontane sect'. It did not attempt any direct rebuttal but rather confined itself to a reinterpretation of key proof texts:

> Of the general character of the book, it will suffice to observe that his style is involved—that there is a constant repetition of

the same things—and that he seems to aim at overpowering and harassing the mind into a compliance with his views, rather than to win the conviction of an unbiased intellect.[97]

The unfairness of his polemical style was a frequent complaint of his Protestant opponents, who found it hard to answer him on his own terms. Indeed, later in the same journal the difficulty was fairly acknowledged:

> We never shall, and indeed we never can, shake the belief of a conscientious Roman Catholic in his peculiar tenets by merely proving them adverse to the natural interpretation of Scripture, or even to the deductions of sound philosophy. He will always entrench himself within the assertion that his Church possesses the same kind of authority as that by which the apostles wrote or sanctioned the New Testament; and whatever objections lie against the one, do against the other.[98]

The final step

The last weeks that Allies spent as rector of Launton were clouded by a sense of unreality as he continued to officiate in a Church that he believed to be in schism; his conscience a little eased by the fact that Bishop Wiseman—soon to be elevated as cardinal—had agreed that he should stay whilst completing his pamphlet on the papacy. Those closer to him were less forbearing: 'My wife was waiting anxiously for me to take the decisive step, for no situation could be more embarrassing than that of the Catholic wife of an Anglican parson at his living.'[99] Newman, sympathising with her difficulties, invited her to Birmingham, where she arrived on Friday 9 August, lodging in a house in Warwick Street occupied by a changing population of women, converts and others who were helping with the nearby Oratory's pastoral work. Eliza stayed until Monday week, a time of spiritual and emotional refreshment.[100] It was much needed because she returned to a disturbing situation: an outbreak of typhus fever in the parish.

No epidemic had happened in my parish during my residence there, nor had so many people ever died, and I could not help feeling that if I was taken ill myself and had to be received on a death-bed, the force of my witness would be diminished, and I should be accused of having delayed through love of my worldly position.[101]

The disease—called the 'Irish Fever' because of its association with immigrants fleeing the famine—was associated with insanitary conditions but was no respecter of persons,[102] and on the Sunday morning following her return Eliza herself developed alarming symptoms. That she survived Thomas attributed to the special protection of the Blessed Virgin. In honour of her conversion Newman had sent her a Marian medal, recommending that she regularly prayed the *Memorare*,[103] whilst kissing it. During that anxious Sunday Allies said that he uttered the prayer 'hundreds of times … and the symptoms disappeared'.[104] Despite his assiduously attending the sick he and the children remained unaffected.

By the end of August the manuscript of *The See of St. Peter* was ready; he had told Newman that his conversion would coincide with its publication.[105] In early September, and apparently coincidentally, Labbé, his old friend from Yvetot, was visiting England—now becoming a fascinating place for French Catholics praying for Anglican conversions—and Allies invited him to visit the rectory, anxious for his support over the days to come. At evensong on 8 September, the Feast of the Nativity of the Blessed Virgin, the Launton congregation heard their rector declaim on the scandal of doctrinal confusion within Anglicanism. He then announced his resignation from the Anglican priesthood. He recalled this as coming 'to the great astonishment of everyone'.[106] Perhaps this was because having hesitated so long it was generally believed he would continue in the parish, having in some way satisfied his conscience that this was reconcilable with obedience to the pope? After the service concluded, but before he could retreat to the safety of the rectory, an infant—whose parents presumably had no doubt as to the efficacy of his sacramental ministrations—was brought to him for baptism. This he could not refuse and later reflected that it was somehow fitting that his priesthood should end with a new birth, for it had begun, he remembered, with a death: the first service at which he had officiated, very much against his will, was a burial.

The rest of that Sunday evening was spent in visiting the sick and wishing farewell to those few parishioners with whom he remained on good terms. The following day, just as *The See of St. Peter* arrived in the book shops, he and his family accompanied by Labbé went by carriage to Buckingham, from where the children (who were not to be baptised) were sent on to Nelmes, whilst the adults took the train to Birmingham. On arrival they found that Fr Newman had gone to Cotton Hall in Staffordshire.[107] Until recently, it had been occupied by a group of converts under the leadership of Frederick Faber, who had constituted themselves as Oratorians. They had now left for London, but their legacy there was a fine Pugin church, St Wilfrid's, and Newman visited the property regularly to enjoy a temporary release from the bustle of Birmingham.

Eliza stayed at Birmingham while the men travelled on to Cotton. The day after arriving, on Wednesday 11 September, Allies made his general confession, received absolution and was conditionally baptised by Newman.[108] They then went to St Wilfrid's church, where Allies made his public profession. The *Te Deum* was sung. Some newspapers reporting the event noticed the coincidence that it was on this same day that Gorham had delivered his first address in the parish church of Bramford Speke, taking as his themes baptism and confirmation.[109] Allies received his first Roman Catholic communion on Friday. The weekend was spent at Birmingham and on Monday he was confirmed by Ullathorne, bishop of the Midland District, in the chapel attached to his episcopal residence on Bath Street. That afternoon he and Eliza went with the bishop for the consecration of a new Catholic cemetery. On Wednesday they visited Oscott College.[110] It would have pleased him to know how, in all the rites of his reception, the matter of jurisdiction was carefully considered. A few weeks later Maskell was to write to Newman, seeking his opinion on the validity of Anglican absolutions, those of Dr Pusey in particular. He was told that proper authority was essential: 'M. Labbé, who came here with Allies, could not even publicly reconcile him to the Church—I was obliged to do it.—He *could* give him Communion for this requires no faculties.'[111]

The reaction of the Protestant press was to exhale a collective sigh of relief that the notorious crypto-papist had at last had the courage of his convictions. Let Charles Dickens—a notorious anti-Catholic—in summarising the events of September 1850 speak for all:

> Of other home incidents there are not many that call for remark, unless exception be made for another batch of Popish converts, including a weak-minded Lord, the relative and the sister-in-law of a protestant bishop, two well endowed vicars, a richly beneficed rector, and a few sentimental lovers of Roman Catholic fopperies. These Puseyite secessions to Rome are to be regarded with no feeling but of satisfaction by good Protestants. The danger is not from those who go but from those who stay. The difference is between a fair and a treacherous enemy; and as good Arnold says, we would honour the one and hang the other. To take a notorious instance Mr. Allies, the vicar of Launton, has only held his post in the English church (to the disgrace of those who for the last four years have suffered his continuance there), in the hope and with the purpose of betraying it; and there is nothing in the fact of his now openly joining Rome, but a gratifying confession of the failure of his treachery. The heart of the great body of the English people was never sounder in regard to all such matters as it is at present. There would be more danger in the secession of one member of the sturdy, thinking, middle-class population, than in fifty such apostacies [sic] as those of the latest batch recorded.[112]

✛ 6 ✛

A New Life

Allies enters a new world

At the age of thirty-seven Allies had reached the end of his pilgrimage; all his thought, all his prayer had led to this: he had submitted to the see of Rome. What else remained? He and Eliza had not prepared for this moment, had given almost no thought to their future outside the Establishment. Where were they to go, what were they to do? Faced with the immediate prospect of having no home and no income Allies had no practical plans at all. He was indeed as Judge Alderson had said completely unworldly. Wrapped up in pursuing the right path, obeying the will of God, he had made no arrangements at all for the future security of his wife and family, and was even to overlook collecting the accrued rent income due to him before resigning his living.[1] Money was indeed as dross to him.

Hitherto Thomas had relied on Anglican friends—those in Oxford, the London judges, Coleridge at Eton, among many others—for wise counsel and practical assistance. Now he and Eliza were cast adrift in an alien environment, and the autumn of 1850 was an especially difficult time to be a Roman Catholic. English identity was built on anti-Catholicism. When he was sure of Allies's impending conversion, Palmer, the rector of neighbouring Mixbury, had sent his daughter to urge the Launton servants to flee the rectory lest they too be infected with the virus.[2] Within a few weeks, throughout the land the usual suspicion and distrust of Catholics was to give way to an almost visceral hatred. The trigger was the restoration, after three hundred years, of the Catholic hierarchy in England and Wales, promulgated by the Bull, *Universalis Ecclesiae*, issued in Rome on 29 September, dividing the country into thirteen Catholic dioceses ruled by bishops having territorial titles.³ The offence taken at what was seen as a 'land grab' by an alien—even an enemy—power exploded, when Wiseman—now elevated as cardinal archbishop of Westminster—issued a triumphalistic pastoral letter entitled *Given out of the Flaminian Gate of Rome this seventh day of October MDCCCL*, celebrating 'the English Church's restoration to its orbit in the ecclesiastical firmament, from which its light had long vanished'. He and the pope were burned in effigy on 5 November, and there were acts of vandalism against Catholic churches.

As the new converts lingered in Birmingham this storm was impending. Eliza was lodging with Mrs Wootten, her old Oxford friend, who had recently moved there, having converted a few months before.⁴ Thomas stayed at the Oratory, daily seeking 'strength from that "bread of the strong," for that period of bitter trial that was coming.'⁵ Food that was sorely needed; hitherto Thomas had shaped an identity as priest, preacher, theologian: now this was taken away. They were reluctant to leave, but confronting the new reality could not be delayed indefinitely.

> We had to go back to Launton, pack up, and remove our things, and we knew not even where to go. In vain we asked advice from Father Newman, and turned our minds in every direction. No occupation or maintenance for the future presented itself; as to temporal matters, a more arid waste of years could not stretch itself before the fainting traveller than then encompassed us. The convert in the first three centuries often met at once the Roman axe, or the torturing hook or scourge, and was released after a glorious conflict; but here the trial, if not so sharp, was far more prolonged. An indeterminate space of time, dark and unredeemed by hope, opened its illimitable lowering desert before us.⁶

They returned to Launton on Thursday 19 September, knowing that within a few weeks they would have to vacate the rectory. Where should they go? Allies wrote to Newman with the vague idea of moving to Clifton, a place he knew well, and where he could perhaps take pupils. His friend replied immediately, urging caution, 'Clifton is a *most eligible* place and I shall be glad if you go there. But I cannot advise you to move all your goods there or to take a lease of a house.' He hoped rather that Allies would find a new home near the Oratory; 'We shall be most sorry to lose you from Birmingham. We want a boy's school there, and at this moment have seven boys from 11 to 16 to offer.'[7] Becoming a school master in Birmingham was not an attractive prospect. Newman also addressed a more immediate problem: the storage of the furniture and the many books that filled the rectory. He told Allies that he had found among his papers a fourteen-year-old bill for the storage of the effects from his mother's house in Iffley in 'a room above the Billiard Room in High Street Oxford' for which he had paid £3 a year.[8] Allies took the advice and rented a large room from a local farmer to deposit his possessions, 'till some prospect opened.'[9]

The passing days brought no illumination. Thomas wondered whether they might move to Paris,[10] but instead he and Eliza decided to go Ventnor on the Isle of Wight to visit his mother and sisters, 'to see if any light would spring up there.'[11] From his sternly Evangelical family there would have been little sympathy, but—reluctant to return—he and Eliza stayed until almost the end of the month, long enough to smooth offended feelings and perhaps to receive some practical help from his mother, who was comfortably off. After returning to Launton it took a fortnight of strenuous effort to clear the rectory. Eliza stayed just a week. The circumstances of her leaving for the last time burnt deeply into her husband's memory. On Saturday afternoon 12 October she and Thomas went together to Bicester railway station[12] to catch the Oxford train; during the long wait his old enemy, Mr Watts, the town's vicar, arrived, and there 'undesignedly witnessed his triumph.'[13] Over the weekend they stayed with their Oxford friends, Pollen and Dean—who evidently did not regard him as an apostate—before Eliza travelled on to Nelmes to be reunited with her children. Thomas returned forlornly to the rectory to finish the packing:

> I had estimated that this would take a day or two. It took the whole week, of unremitted toil, and I could only just get away on Saturday evening by the last train. I felt in that week pushed to the utmost. My wife's presence hitherto had wonderfully cheered me. We worked till all was removed, and

> I sat on a basket in the kitchen to get a bit of food. At last it was done. Everything was stowed at Hawkins's, or in one room, the haunted room, at the Rectory. Emma, the maid, had continued with me to the last; and now, all being concluded, I looked once more into our bedroom, and thought how often little Basil had slept beside us there, and then hurried down to Bicester, caught the train, and arrived for supper at Pollen's room, Oxford, like a bird escaped out of prison, casting aside, at least for the time, the heavy burden of care which had lain upon me.[14]

What next? Where should he go? On Monday 21 October he travelled from Oxford to London, where he posted the formal resignation of his living. He then joined Eliza and the children at Nelmes. The embarrassment of his position at the home of his brother-in-law may be imagined. He and Eliza talked about the future but had no sense of direction at all. There was the immediate problem of arranging schooling for their eldest child, Edward, who on the day the children were taken away from Launton had celebrated his ninth birthday. He had been a pupil at Woodard's school at Shoreham, where he clearly could not remain, so it was decided that he should be enrolled at Oscott College school and that his father should take him there as soon as possible and at the same time go himself to the Oratory to seek counsel about his future.

Before being left at the school, Edward went with his father to Newman and, perhaps surprisingly, received from him conditional baptism.[15] Allies then spent a week at the Oratory seeking some sense of direction. Still a young man, with a young wife and family, his circumstances reflected the wider problem of what the Church should do with a growing number of married clerical converts, who had lost the income and security of their Anglican livings. Seven months after his conversion he wrote to Newman, 'I always used to think a turtle laid on its back an unfortunate animal but this is nothing to an ex-Anglican minister with wife and children.'[16] Newman wrote that these men had 'together an amount of talent, which the unmarried clergy converted have not.'[17] The dilemma was never resolved; many of these men had

A New Life

life experiences and connexions which might have been of great value to their new Church. But her organisation and resources were quite inadequate to provide them with commensurate employment and income. Accepting this, Allies nevertheless felt that more could and should have been done:

> I am sometimes grieved that there is not a religious sect of importance in England, as, for instance, the Puseyites, the Evangelicals, the Scotch Free Church, or the Wesleyans, who as a *body* would have treated the converts as the Catholic body have done. Whether it is powerlessness or apathy, or want of perception, or disunion, or that many who have the will have not the means, while the few who have the means have not the will, but so it is that I see us (for I speak as one of a class) simply let fall to the ground. I speak here, of course, of the married ex-parsons, for their 'occupation's gone'—and it is a sheer impossibility to find another.[18]

Pauline Adams in her analysis of the circumstances that befell the Oxford Movement converts, comments:

> The special hardship of the converted clergyman was not— what he must have taken for granted in becoming a Catholic— the sacrifice of his former way of life, the loss of home and livelihood and friends; but, as Allies soon came to see, the blankness of his future as a Catholic. They had talents, a position in society, they understood the Establishment. They now had time on their hands, and were eager to use it in the service of their new faith. It was the Church's misfortune as well as theirs that she did not know what to do with them.[19]

In considering the proposal that he should open a school in Birmingham, Allies doubted whether instructing young children was his calling. Mary Allies wrote: 'My father was no more qualified for teaching rudiments *rudibus* [i.e. to the immature] than a Mozart would be for teaching scales. He forgot that explanations were necessary, and if a pupil showed denseness would pinch his ear and pass on.'[20] Newman sympathised, writing to him on 30 September, 'I feel what you say about boys, and it had grown on me before your letter came. You are not specially fitted for a small boy school, and I fear that, unless you had as many as would deserve that name, small boys would not answer. On the other hand, you would not *quickly* get youths at a proper sum. I think you would ultimately ... It would be a great thing, could you manage to be independent of receipts for a year or two, for you must reckon, I should think, on doing little at first.'[21]

The week he spent at the Oratory was a short time of 'rest in a beautiful land-locked harbour ... after being tossed by a tempest'[22] but Allies left there confused and uncertain, returning to London via Clifton, where on All Saints' Day (Friday) he stayed in Maskell's house, Maskell himself being away. He could not escape a renewed tempest: the furore created by the restoration of the hierarchy was far from abated, and in London on 5 November he was 'curious to see what form hatred of Catholics would take'. His curiosity presumably satisfied, the following day he was back with his family at Nelmes. It was a time of deep anxiety, not least as he had not yet finished with his old Church. Having been harried by Bishop Wilberforce to leave the rectory, he was now being pressurised financially: 'Then anxious thoughts afresh where we should go; longing to get to Rome, but troubles about dilapidations stopped that.'[23]

The gathering pace of Anglican conversions following the Gorham affair presented the leaders of the English Catholic Church with a tremendous challenge at a time when the flood of Irish immigration was putting parish life in London and the great cities of the north under severe strain. Cardinal Wiseman wanted to help the converts, particularly one of the eminence and obvious ability of Allies, but he had many other concerns. If his intemperate proclamation of the revived episcopacy had served to inflame Protestant feeling he was now contributing significantly to dampening the fire, not least through his masterly pamphlet entitled *Appeal to the English People*, published on 18 November. Shortly before this date Allies had joined him along with several other converts at Danesfield, the home of Charles Robert Scott-Murray, near Marlow.[24] There, no doubt, the plight of the men in

Allies's position was discussed. Soon afterwards, perhaps as a result of these conversations, Thomas, Eliza and their two younger sons moved to London, taking lodgings in Golden Square, two doors from the archbishop's official residence. It was a rather run-down neighbourhood, far removed from the splendours of Regent Street, so close by. Their new life highlighted the sacrifice they had made: a country house exchanged for 'one dingy-sitting room' and no garden for the boys to play in. They were required to provide accommodation for meetings of the newly created chapter of Westminster, which given all the circumstances might be considered a rather unthoughtful arrangement; Newman certainly believed that the clergy should have found alternative premises.[25]

Nevertheless, being in London and mixing with 'polite' Catholic society could bring useful introductions. They were befriended by the Welds, a celebrated recusant family who had done much to relieve the distress of French exiles in the Revolutionary period. Mrs Weld introduced Eliza to another friend and distant relation, Mrs Carrington Smythe, whose home, Wootton House at Wootton Wawen, had long been a centre of recusancy and had sheltered mission priests during the days of persecution.[26] It was now the location of a Benedictine mission which served Stratford-upon-Avon. Next to the hall was an Italianite church, erected by the Dowager Lady Smythe in 1819. Mrs Carrington Smythe, on learning of the Allies's straitened circumstances, invited Eliza, Basil and Cyril to live in her house. They moved there in June 1851, whereupon the tenancy at Golden Square was given up. Thomas remained in London, staying with Catholic friends. He found sanctuary at the London Oratory in King William Street, which Frederick Faber and his 'Wilfridians' had established in 1849, and joined himself to the laymen who constituted the Brothers of the Little Oratory, which included converts such as Dodsworth and W. G. Ward and other old friends, as well as members of the Catholic nobility. They met regularly for prayer and undertook charitable works. Allies sought counsel from Faber, who perhaps at times found his importunity a little trying. He wrote to Newman in July 1851: 'Dodsworth is constantly here, and works for us; Allies *lives* here nearly, and wanted to lodge here, but I would not let him'.[27]

As the months went by, although never doubting the rightness of his decision, Allies agonised about its impact on his family and what the future held for his children, concerns that were not alleviated when Eliza told him she was pregnant. Perhaps indicating his lowness of spirit, in January 1852, a few weeks before the birth of his first daughter he wrote to Newman to ask if he would consent to be appointed guardian to his boys. His friend declined: it was against 'the spirit, if not, which it almost is, against the letter of our Rule'.[28] It was deemed prudent that Eliza and the children should remain at Wootton beyond her confinement. Cyril was five years old and Basil almost eight when their sister was born on 2 February 1852. Named Mary Helen, she proved to be closest of all the children to her father. Educated at home, 'feeding on the marrow of his mind',[29] she shared his temperament, was scholarly and thoughtful, and an ardent Catholic. In adulthood she became invaluable to him as amanuensis and colleague. She was the author of a number of books, and a historian in her own right, and she memorialised her father's life in a biography published in 1907, four years after his death. Eighteen months after her birth came a second daughter, also named Mary—Mary Frances. Of all five children only she and Cyril were to marry and provide Thomas and Eliza with beloved grandchildren. On 4 February 1855 Eliza gave birth to another son, Bernard Joseph, who lived for only a month. The last of their children, he was buried in a borrowed tomb—the Gallini Vault—in Our Lady's Church, Grove Road, St John's Wood. Thomas was profoundly affected: 'I bought lilies of the valley and snowdrops for him, and Eliza wove a crown of lilies which she put round his head. Yet still the thought of his pretty little face continually comes over me, wakening regret for his loss.'[30] Eliza became pregnant again but in March 1858 suffered a late miscarriage. At the time Thomas was working hard, heavily involved in an office move. The experience left her very ill and both of them in low spirits.[31]

Wootton was an unhappy place for Eliza; she saw little of her hosts and felt isolated, with Thomas visiting only occasionally, as he remained in London seeking light and direction in the society of other Catholics. The lack of a family home was a great concern to them both. On Easter Day 1852 he wrote to Newman, saying that the solitude of Wootton House 'has so pressed on Mrs. Allies' that they planned to return to London by the end of the month; they were seeking lodgings, but in

A New Life

the meantime had accepted an invitation to stay with the Bethells in Putney.[32] On 21 June they moved into The Priory, an attractive new villa on North Bank, St John's Wood,[33] which in outward appearance may have reminded them of Launton rectory. They were to stay there until the end of 1856. However, the move did not inaugurate a time of tranquillity, placing an even greater pressure on their limited finances. With the arrival of Mary Helen there were four children under eleven years and the education of the boys was a major concern. Edward, the eldest, had exhibited little disposition for academic subjects and found it hard to settle, a restlessness perhaps exacerbated by the tensions that his father had brought into the rectory and then the turmoil of departure, leaving him with a life-long sense of insecurity. At the age of seven or eight he had been sent to board with Allies's friend Edward Dean, who was rector of Lewknor, about twenty-five miles away from Launton.[34] When Woodard opened his first 'school for the middle classes' at Shoreham he was enrolled there and first attended in October 1849.[35] His name was removed from the school register in December 1850 but he had left in October, going to Oscott College, but did not thrive there. So when it was judged that Basil was old enough to start school, just before his eighth birthday, in the spring of 1852, Thomas took him and Edward to Labbé's school (*petit séminaire*) at Yvetot.[36] Around the time of his seventh birthday (7 July 1853) Cyril joined them.

The boys were a continual anxiety. On 17 December 1853, Thomas was at the school, reporting to Eliza that Edward in particular was quite unhappy.[37] 'I have to settle this evening and tomorrow whether Edward stays here or not; it is a great perplexity.'[38] He stayed, but his unhappiness was distressing. Around this time Allies wrote in his diary,

> I have had a novena of the children for my intention, that I might have confidence in God, for this has been the great trial of these four years. I have suffered intensely from anxiety, and suffering has brought with it no sensible consolation … It is especially the sight of my children and the thought of their futurity, which has in the last month so come upon me.[39]

At least by the summer of 1853 some clouds were lifted when Thomas secured well-rewarded employment. Hitherto he had been compelled to take pupils, work which he found most uncongenial. Their numbers fluctuated. For a while in 1851 he had taught the fifteen-year-old son of Newman's close Anglican friend, John William Bowden, whose mother was concerned that he was insufficiently studious, a sentiment with which Allies undoubtedly sympathised. Charles Bowden left him when the Golden Square accommodation was given up and he moved to Ushaw College.[40] Ordained eight years later, Bowden was to live out a useful life as a priest of the London Oratory. On moving into The Priory Allies searched for more pupils, but there were never enough, and by October 1852 just two, which did not provide a sufficient income.[41]

Thomas received support both emotional and practical from London Catholic society, and there was spiritual help too, especially from Fr Faber of the London Oratory, whose encouragement he came increasingly to value. On Ascension Day 1853 he went to Mass there. Moved by Faber's homily on Our Blessed Lady he reflected 'More grace given to her than to all other creatures put together'. Yet still he was not entirely satisfied: 'he has too great facility in preaching, and I think, a certain tone of exaggeration, which is quite Faberistic diminishes his force. He conveys to me a greater notion of power in intimate conversation.'[42] The following year, in answer to the prayers of Faber and many others, Pius IX declared the doctrine of the Immaculate Conception to be *de fide*. Wiseman had fears that some potential and actual converts might find this a stumbling-block, but he was to be reassured. In Allies's case his experiences in France had made him an enthusiastic advocate of the cause.

Not all Catholic society treated the converts sympathetically; some indeed were inclined to criticise. For example, not many months after his conversion Allies met A. W. N. Pugin at a dinner-party. Pugin was appalled to discover that he, like several of the 'new men', did not worship at the shrine of gothicism. Perhaps Thomas had been too enthusiastic in extolling the beauties of the Italianate church at Wootton? Pugin described the encounter in a letter to Ambrose Phillipps de Lisle:

> I met Allies at dinner on Tuesday last and he was open mouthed against the whole thing. In fact the principles he laid

down were those of a *new religion* which they do not blench to acknowledge—but saith that people *antiently* served God in *fear & reverence* but that the whole was changed to love and openness & that people might flock up to the altar steps & almost on it on occasion—& he is only a fair specimen of the school. I can assure you that I spoke very strongly & represented the dangers of this new system so repugnant to Catholic traditions. We shall live to curse the hour these people ever came amongst us—for they are a curse in themselves & to me ten times more hateful than sincere Protestants. Allies classes you and me together as two ultramen ... I repeat again the recent converts with some few exceptions are a pest & I look on them with great suspicion.[43]

Pugin's mental health was becoming somewhat fragile and Allies, who as an Anglican had been vaccinated against all criticism, would not have been discountenanced had he known of this harsh judgment.

The search for employment

Wiseman was sure that the Church had much to gain from using the talents of the converts. He also believed that in the time of the 'second spring' a new Catholic newspaper was needed to present the faith with greater clarity, vigour and urgency, and that Allies was well qualified to be its founding editor. However, despite some generalised conversation between them about this in the early months after his conversion, very little was done to formulate detailed proposals and in particular the vital question of how the venture could be funded remained unanswered. There the matter rested. In all the busyness of the cardinal's life—in particular dealing with the ramifications of the restoration of the hierarchy—the newspaper scheme remained long months in the pending tray and Allies was left in limbo, knowing little of the true position. Newman, who had little confidence in Wiseman's efficiency, on learning early in 1851 that his friend had given up a plan to visit Paris in case there should be any rapid developments regarding the editorship, urged caution:

> I hoped indeed you were stopping for some good,—certainly the Cardinal's wishes were not sufficient. He is a kind hearted sanguine man, who never sees difficulties in any thing and in consequence often promises what in the event he cannot make good.[44]

So that when Allies met the cardinal in March he was disabused of any immediate hope of a journalistic career. But the matter was not dropped and at last, in the closing weeks of 1852, Wiseman entered into negotiation with Thomas Richardson, the proprietor of the *Catholic Standard*, to purchase his interest and relaunch the newspaper as a new force in the propagation of Catholic opinion. For Allies, who still had no settled employment, the prospect of establishing a prestigious newspaper offered him what he so much desired: a regular income and a position of some importance in the expression and perhaps shaping of Catholic opinion. But the prize was cruelly snatched away. After five weeks of discussions no agreement could be reached. When he became aware of the outcome, Allies wrote, 'the prospect was suspended before me in the most provoking manner and at last disappeared like a ghost.'[45]

Newman was not disappointed. He had never approved of a new convert being appointed to edit a popular newspaper, believing that it would be some years before any one of them would be sufficiently steeped in the traditions and assumptions of English Catholicism. In Allies's case in particular he doubted whether his studious character really equipped him to be an effective communicator to a wide audience:

> As to your qualifications, your only danger, as I think, is, that they are too great for your work. You write with a gravity, a power, and a dignity, as well as eloquence, which is more fitted for a work, than a newspaper...
> The *Guardian* is flippant but I should have some apprehension you would fall into the opposite extreme. You might take things too seriously.[46]

Money was the principal stumbling-block in the negotiations. About the time of the restoration of the hierarchy an attempt had been made to

A New Life

interest the Catholic public in a new paper. The leaflet that was circulated seeking financial support rather confirms Newman's reservations about the gap between what it was thought was wanted and what a scholarly editor could supply. The paper, to be called *The Investigator*, was to be:

> a Weekly Journal of Catholic interest, which will promote the great cause of Free Trade, Parliamentary Reform, and Social Progress, as embodied in the views of the Irish Brigade, the Manchester School and the Peel party,—the only liberal sections now remaining in the House of Commons ...
>
> The great want of a Catholic Journal, written in a high tone and vigorous spirit, has long been acknowledged ... Great care shall be taken that no language appear in its articles unworthy of the meek Christianity they defend.[47]

A Catholic university

Despite his scepticism Newman did make practical suggestions as to the sort of employment contract that any new editor should negotiate. But his heart was not in it, being sure that Allies would be far better occupied in serving the new university that the Irish bishops wished to establish. When Dr Paul Cullen was appointed archbishop of Armagh in December 1849 he arrived with a vision for the establishment of an important Catholic seat of learning to which the English-speaking faithful could send their sons, as an alternative to the recently established 'godless' Queen's Colleges. Cullen 'was in the confidence of Rome, he was zealous against Mixed Education, and he had come from Rome with extraordinary powers for the furtherance of the Holy Father's wishes.'[48]

In August 1850 Cullen summoned his brother bishops to a synod at Thurles, where higher education featured significantly among the matters considered. They resolved to establish a university modelled on Louvain in Belgium[49] and to this end to appeal to the faithful for funds. A standing committee was established, and on 15 April 1851 Cullen wrote to Newman seeking his advice on the appointment of academic staff. In July he visited him at the Oratory and invited him to become its first Rector. For Newman the establishment of a new university was exciting and providential. Perhaps contrary to the wishes—and best interests—of the Irish bishops,[50] he envisaged not a school to serve the professional needs of the Irish middle class but a centre for higher studies open to Catholics from across the English-speaking world and staffed by the 'best minds' including 'married converts, who have been clergy-men in the Protestant Church, such as Mr. Allies.'[51] Anxious to share some good news, on Easter Sunday (20 April) he wrote to Allies:

> What would you think, if an offer was made to you, of undertaking a Professorship in the new Catholic University in Ireland?
>
> A greater field of usefulness cannot be. It will be the Catholic University of the English tongue for the whole world. And I shall think I have [done] much, if I can accomplish the settlement of you and other Saxons in it, to do the great work.
>
> I am supposing such Professorships as Classics, History, Polite Literature, etc. Is there any one you would like more than another?
>
> P. S. As to the pay. I know no more than you, but it *must* be enough to keep a married man, or they will get no one to come.[52]

As Newman had not yet been formally appointed Rector all this might be considered somewhat presumptuous. A few days later he wrote again and at length to the archbishop, recommending a number of married Oxford Movement converts: either Allies or Henry Wilberforce would make 'a first rate Professor of History.' He expatiated on Allies's attributes: well qualified as a scholar and a writer he 'would be invaluable as Greek Professor, or Latin, or Professor of Ancient History or Modern, or of Metaphysics. He is a person I value very much, and take great interest in, from the painful difficulties in which he is at present.'[53]

Allies never moved to Ireland and delivered only one lecture in the university, but his involvement with its establishment was to exercise a profound and continuing influence on his life as a Catholic. In the summer of 1851, rather than an academic appointment, he was offered the secretaryship of a committee, comprising Newman, Dr Leahy and

Myles O'Reilly, charged with reporting on 'the best mode of commencing the University, on the course of studies, etc.'.[54] Accepting the position, he visited Newman (on 30 July) and later met with Leahy. His first task was to correspond with those who could supply relevant information, for example with J. R. Hope (later Hope-Scott), on the courses of study pursued at Catholic universities on the Continent.[55] At the end of September he and Newman (accompanied by Fr Philip Bathurst of the Oratory) travelled to Thurles, the designated meeting place. Following the discussions there Allies drafted the 'Report of the Sub-Committee on the Organization of the University', which, after some amendments by O'Reilly, was presented to the standing committee on 12 November 1851. On the same day the Irish bishops confirmed Newman as Rector. He had already told Cullen that in taking on the role he would be acceding to the wishes of the Oratory brothers.[56]

The bishops were optimistic that an immediate beginning could be made with establishing the institution, acquiring premises, appointing staff and selecting students. But it was not to be. Ireland had been devastated by the famine, and the relief of suffering was a prior call on any funds that could be spared. Many of the Irish—lay and clerical—instinctively dismissed—fairly or unfairly—the proposed college as irrelevant, simply a way of providing employment for English ex-Anglicans. Months passed; for Allies it was a frustrating time with the prospect of a professorship the only light in his gloomy circumstances. In March 1852 he wrote in some exasperation to Newman, asking him about the state of things in Ireland. 'I have heard today that the farmer in whose house my goods are is moving and ill treating our furniture, and it is certainly at his mercy ... it distracts our equanimity.'[57] He noted that if his professorship was to begin in October, it would have been eighteen months since the appointment was first mooted. In response to this *cri de cœur* Newman asked Archbishop Cullen whether he might safely advise Allies to move his furniture and books to Dublin, 'which is in fact a guarantee in private, that he will be Professor'.[58] The reply was discouraging,

> I think we shall have no difficulty in getting him appointed professor—yet I would not counsel him to take any steps, as if

the matter were finally arranged. We have a set of Newspaper editors and others who are trying to excite prejudices against everything English. We must avoid giving them any motive to attack us for a little while longer.[59]

Allies could be forgiven for wondering quite when anti-English sentiment would abate sufficiently for him and his family to be welcomed to Dublin. In passing on the discouraging news Newman's tone was far from reassuring: 'I confess I do not see an end to your suspense speedily … I am most sincerely sorry for your trial, but trial is the way we all get to heaven'. He then added a revealing post-script: 'Don't suppose that Irishmen are going to be put about me. I should object to them distinctly, not of course as Irishmen, but as persons whom I do not know, who were not of the same school as myself, on whom I could not rely.'[60] He dreamt of recreating Oxford in Dublin, but it was not to be. Not until 1854 did Allies receive an—honorific—academic appointment: Reader in the Philosophy of History. On 21 December he delivered his only lecture, which might be thought surprising as his discourse was judged a great success. The occasion was reported in the *University Gazette*:

> at eight o'clock, an inaugural lecture was delivered by the Lecturer in the Philosophy of History. As might be expected from the fame and talents of the distinguished lecturer, a more satisfactory conclusion to the business of the first term … could scarcely have been desired than was afforded by Mr Allies on this occasion.[61]

Among Catholics there was widespread approbation. The lecture was reported (and later reprinted) in the *Tablet*:

> An inaugural lecture was delivered on Thursday se'nnight, in one of the academical halls of this institution, by the Rev. T. M. [sic] Allies, A. M. Oxon. The subject of the lecture was the very interesting one of the 'Philosophy of History'. The audience was crowded, and of high respectability, including a large section of the Catholic Hierarchy, Clergy, and laity of

A New Life

Dublin. Not alone the important and interesting character of the subject, but also the name and fame of the lecturer, one of those gifted men whose adhesion to the principles of the Catholic Church has been fresh testimony to the truth of her doctrines, tended to render the occasion of this inaugural lecture specially interesting.

Amongst the visitors present, might be noted several distinguished members of Trinity College. Mr. Allies opened his lecture by putting clearly and succinctly before his audience the subject of his lecture defining in terms at once concise and intelligible the meaning of what was called the philosophy of history. He evinced powers of mind of a high order, regulated by judicious study and habitual training, and showed himself to be thoroughly the master of his subject in all its bearings.[62]

In March the following year he was appointed to the Chair of Modern History (to which the philosophy of history was joined). It was another honorific appointment; there was no student interest in the subject, Allies gave no more lectures and his connection with the university lapsed.[63]

Thus after years of waiting did the prospect of an academic career prove to be a *chimera*, as did any lingering dream of becoming a newspaper editor.[64] Two and a half years after Allies became a Catholic he was still without regular employment, and finding enough money to support his family was a constant anxiety. A few pupils, and the articles and book reviews he wrote could not suffice. Newman returned to the idea that he should open a school for small boys, and in 1852 had urged his fellow Oratorian Ambrose St John, who owned premises in Edgbaston, to let them to Allies for this purpose. St John was deeply sceptical: 'I hear nothing but the most dismal forebodings on all hands about my prospects with A. as tenant.'[65] Never good with money Allies was paying for the storage of items from the Launton rectory and may not have been regular with his rental payments. Newman intimated as much in April 1852 when he wrote to Archbishop Cullen that Allies's books and furniture were 'ill treated or exposed to ill-treatment where they are—a continual threat of their being put out of doors—and he not knowing where to put them.'[66] All this, however, was beside the point, for Allies had no intention of opening a school.

Allies's apologetics

The opening months of 1853 passed with nothing to lift Allies's mood. He wrote in his journal on 4 May:

> I think again and again over the sufferings of our Lord, of our B. Lady, of St Paul, and all the saints. I have known the law of suffering long ago. I have preached it to others: I have dwelt upon it for years in my own thoughts, and yet no sooner does it come to be exemplified in oneself than one's faith is tried to the utmost.[67]

A month later no relief had come:

> During the past month I have suffered at times extreme depression of spirits; the root of this is always the same— the utter destitution of my temporal fortunes, and the hopelessness of the prospect, as if the rest of my life was to be heaping up sand hillocks by the sea-shore. The grievance is that I long to study, to produce some work for the glory of God, and I am condemned to the most anxious thoughts as to what I shall eat and what I shall drink, wherewithal I shall be clothed, I and mine, and to the drudgery of teaching dunces. It is a terrible trial certainly, and has been upon me with the weight of a mountain for three years now, and in anticipation long before.[68]

The cloud lifted when in July 1853 he applied for, and was elected to, the post of secretary to the Poor-School Committee[69] at a salary of £300 pa. But it was not the occupation he would have chosen for himself, and after beginning work on 1 August wrote grudgingly: 'The state of constant anxiety and fret has subsided. I discourage myself from looking at the future ... my trial has a little sifted. Its real force consists in living the life of a clerk ... when my natural desire is to study and write.'[70] Allies was just one of many gifted writers who had converted and who were left to feel alone and forsaken. In the autumn of 1850 Newman had contemplated acquiring the *Dublin Review* to provide an outlet for their talents and an income for those with family responsibilities, and wrote to Maskell floating the idea. But the significant capital required proved to be insuperable problem.

However, for Allies during the barren years, writing articles for the *Dublin* did provide a sense of usefulness as well as a small income.[71] He also contributed to *The Rambler*, a review established in 1848 by a convert, John Moore Capes. It was 'essentially the organ of the lay converts'[72] and its September 1851 issue contained Allies's review of Robert Wilberforce's rather agonised attempt to come to terms with the Gorham judgment. He was archdeacon of the East Riding, and his pamphlet (*A Sketch of Erastianism*) whilst accepting the Church of England was at present subservient to the state sought to argue that this was not a necessary consequence of the Reformation. Allies was dismissive:

> The sovereign in England ... was bent on taking the Pope's place over the spirituality, and he took it in spite of all absurdities and anomalies; he mounted the chariot of the sun: what wonder that the hearts of Anglican Churchmen are fainting for fear, looking for vital warmth and kindness they find death instead![73]

The December 1850 issue of the *Dublin Review* contained the first of a series of articles by Allies; a stinging attack on the Church of England, occasioned by his reading Dr Russell's edition of Leibniz's *System of Philosophy* published a few months before.[74] Allies noted that the sympathetic attitude of this great thinker towards Catholicism was shared by the eminent Dutch jurist Hugo Grotius, although both were, and remained, Protestants. He contrasted their eirenicism with the anti-papal frenzy that the restoration of the Catholic hierarchy had inspired, a Protestant zeal from which the Anglo-Catholics had not dissociated themselves. In the piece Thomas rebuked his old adversary, the bishop of Oxford, who having received as a 'Lord-Lieutenant *in spiritualibus*' his jurisdiction from the monarch, had fanned the flames of outrage at the re-establishment of a regular Catholic episcopate. Noteworthy among the protest meetings held all over the country there was

> a deeper and darker disgrace—an assembly of the diocese of Oxford, on the very spot where the Anglo-Catholic movement went forth—an assembly embracing, it would seem, almost every clergyman in the diocese, and a vast number of laymen, presided over by a Bishop so kind and amiable in the ordinary intercourse of life as Dr. Wilberforce, at which only fourteen voices were raised against the word idolatrous applied to Catholic rites—of which fourteen the Bishop's was *not* one.[75]

The theology of the two Protestant scholars is examined in some depth. Allies concluded that Leibniz spoke for them both when he 'sweeps away every particle of justification which the Reformers claimed for their acts'. His impartial analysis of Catholicism is contrasted with the prejudice of Her Majesty's bishops:

> Let us try to discover, among the Anglican clergy, among the declaimers at public meetings, among the Episcopate itself, who are the equals of Grotius and Leibniz in learning and knowledge of antiquity. Leibniz saw 'the only sacrifice not unworthy of God's infinity' where they see 'idolatry'. Grotius saw 'the points which had everywhere, always and perseveringly been handed down, remaining in that Church which is bound to the Roman'; to them these same points are 'corruptions'. Both Grotius and Leibniz saw in the Roman Pontiff, the successor of St. Peter, the necessary bond of unity; the Anglican episcopate, clergy and laity, see in him the rival of Queen Victoria, and one who has committed an act of aggression on her crown by appointing a diocesan episcopate.[76]

A New Life

Russell had noted the part played by Leibniz—who was librarian to the Elector of Hanover—in the 'numberless plans of Church Union set on foot by the Sovereigns of Germany during the course of the seventeenth century.' All ended in failure; their history furnishing

> no lesson so significant of the hopelessness of all such general movements, and of the folly of an individual member of any Church, when once convinced of the necessity of communion with the great Catholic body, perilling his private and personal happiness on the more than problematical expectation of an approximation of the Churches themselves and bartering his own yearning desire of peace and rest within the bosom of the common mother, for the brilliant but elusive prospect of enjoying that happiness in the restoration of his Church to the privileges of Catholic unity.[77]

In the next volume (no. 30) of the *Dublin*, which appeared in March 1851, Allies had two articles. One was a review of a new book by Ernest Silvanus Appleyard (*The Greek Church—A Sketch*) and the other an analysis of the education of the Anglican clergy.[78] The former was a slight work, enabling Allies to deplore the subjection of any Church to civil control. Appleyard was determinedly optimistic, believing that with just a little more good-will amongst all shades of opinion a reunification of Christendom was not an impossible goal, even venturing the opinion that something positive could be said for the insights of Arius! Allies in contrast prided himself on an unflinching regard for the truth:

> Really, we can only rank this gentleness towards heretics with the mawkish compassion felt by some of the public towards murderers. The latter springs from an inadequate sense of sin in moral crime; the former from an inadequate sense of the exclusive obedience due to dogmatic truth. If Protestantism were to triumph it would efface both the notion of sin and the notion of truth.[79]

It was in writing about clerical education that Allies gave full vent to disillusionment with his Anglican inheritance. He took the opportunity created by the recent establishment of a royal commission to subject the roles of Oxford and Cambridge as Anglican seminaries to an excoriating analysis. His starting point was the High Middle Ages, when scholarly life—permeated throughout by Catholicism—underwent an intellectual and spiritual renaissance and although, as he acknowledged, there was a falling away after 1350, the universities remained 'nurseries of the Church'. In 1559 came the cataclysm: the extinguishing of the ancient hierarchy, and a complete change in the spiritual government and worship of the English Church. This compelled the universities radically to re-assess their syllabuses, leaving no place for canon law, and most philosophy condemned 'under the sentence passed on the scholastics'. Above all, the Reformation resulted in 'a radical and fundamental subversion of the highest faculty—theology: 'Not only *ought* there to be no science of theology known in the Anglican establishment and in the Universities which are its high schools, from the year 1559 unto the present day, *but there has been none.*'[80]

In training the clergy, the instruction offered by the universities—the Greek and Latin languages supplemented, at Oxford, by some Aristotelian philosophy and at Cambridge by mathematics—had proved woefully defective. The question of vocation was not even considered: 'lectures are given, not consciences directed'; indeed 'one thing is plain': their graduates will be 'moulded according to this world, and not according to that which is to come'. In Allies's opinion—the fruit his own experience—the competitive intellectual atmosphere of the universities provided a signally inappropriate preparation for the work of the ministry. Their most able scholars pass their student days with the thrill of academic success which becomes 'the pleasing poison of praise' and infects the whole being. But,

> how will it brook hereafter the obscurity of a country village, the reforming of clownish minds, the stirring up of consciences sunk in the pettifogging of daily trade, the converse of those 'whose talk is of oxen'?... Should we expect such to be ready to inhale fevers over sick beds, or teach the first articles of the Creed to the children of ignorance?[81]

Allies's Catholicism

Allies was acute in his condemnation of Protestantism, but what sort of Catholic would he become, as he sought to make sense of a new theological landscape and began to interact with a variety of new influences and ways of thinking? In the articles he wrote in the months after his conversion some intellectual inconsistency may be detected. Both Hugo Grotius and Gottfried Liebnitz, whom he admired and praised, are best known for their contribution to the 'Radical Enlightenment', and in this were the heirs of Bacon. Yet, in a December 1851 article—a review of the address of the Irish bishops on the Catholic University[82]—Bacon is excoriated as an unwitting tool of the antichrist. When this piece, centring on the inefficacy of Protestant education to the true needs of mankind, was reprinted in *Per Crucem ad Lucem* (a two-volume compilation of Allies's polemical writings published in 1879) it was under the suggestive heading of 'Christian and Antichristian Education'. For Allies the Scholastic exemplified the former, and he used the writings of St Bonaventure to summarise and extol their thinking. At the Reformation a wrong direction was taken as Luther succeeded in freeing 'the individual mind from submission to the general mind of Christendom'. The consequences were incalculable: 'We are far, indeed, from asserting that Luther knew what he was about. There was a great and subtle combining spirit using him as an instrument, who had formed his plan, a vast and skilful one, though the agent had none.'[83]

In this changed intellectual climate Bacon formulated his philosophy by disregarding a vital first principle: 'that each individual possesses a *something* incomparably more precious than the discoveries of all the physical sciences'. 'We are not underrating the *quantity* of light thus diffused; but we are remarking on its *quality*, that it is mainly the *inferior* and *outward* light, with so much of the *interior*, as embraces the physical and mathematical, but not the higher speculative and metaphysical sciences.'[84] Looking on Victorian Britain with profound distaste, Allies concluded 'we are witnessing, in political anarchy and moral socialism, the *denouement* of individualism' and in demonstration pointed to the quasi religious language used by *The Times* in describing the culmination of a national triumph: 'thus the spirit of this age describes the closing of the Great Exhibition, in language which a Medieval Christian would have thought more appropriate to the last judgment.'[85]

> Withdraw from the world the Christian idea, that is, a society divinely constituted, to which the possession of spiritual and moral truth is guaranteed, by incorporation with which man is taken into the circle of higher existence, brought under divine influences, and taught to labour through the course of this passing life for a superior inheritance; withdraw this, and the hopes, the desires, the passions of men become fixed on material wealth, as the standard of this world without reference to the next.[86]

It was Newman's request that he should lecture on the philosophy of history at the Catholic University[87] that stimulated Allies to engage more formally with the relationship between Catholicism and the legacy of the Enlightenment. He accepted the challenge, although admitting to being puzzled as to what exactly such a subject could involve. Newman sought to help: 'My notion of the Philosophy of History is the science of which historical facts are the basis, or the laws on which it pleases Almighty Providence to conduct the political and social world'. It was from this perspective that the work of the celebrated scholars both he and Allies had read could be assessed: 'The fault of Schlegel's work so far as I recollect it, is that it has no *view*—only a number of detached remarks. Gibbon's is a philosophical history i.e. a history written not as Fleury writes, *viz.* a collection of facts, but with reference and subservience to a certain philosophy, and a bad one!'[88] Accepting the Catholic Church as the pillar and bulwark of the truth, Newman's ambition was that in his university historical investigation should be conducted on the basis of academically respectable philosophical principles. Whilst eschewing overt Providentialism he was confident that rigorous scholarship would uncover laws of cause and effect pointing to divine superintendence. The secularist historians could be challenged on their own ground, and he encouraged his friend in words that Allies would use in his lecture:

> Bacon seems to me to state correctly that the doctrine of final causes (when actively introduced) spoils physics ... Depend upon it when once the laws of human affairs are drawn out, and the philosophy into which they combine, it will be a movement worthy of the Lawgiver, but if we begin by speaking of Him first of all, we shall never get at His laws, I can quite understand a professor drawing religious conclusions from historical laws or ordinances as from physical but he must first find His laws.

Allies was daunted, unsure how he might meet this challenge: 'Have you not set me a science almost new, about the meaning of which even people are not agreed? On the Continent the Philosophy of History seems to be mixed up with Psychology.'[89] He feared Newman envisaged a more subtle scholarship than his lecturer could deliver. Hence on the evening of 21 December 1854, addressing his distinguished Dublin audience, Allies began with a disclaimer:

> I have not sought a post, but obeyed a call. It is a call the nature of which I had never thought of till it was made; in following it I obeyed another's judgment, not my own. I put my feebleness under the shield of his authority. I recognised him, indeed as one of the chiefs among the sons of thought, and felt that it was glory enough for me to serve under him.[90]

What he went on to say provides the context for his subsequent historical writings. The tone was unashamedly apologetic: only Christianity could provide the interpretative key to history as the unfolding of human experience under divine superintendence. In understanding this process Augustine's *De Civitate Dei* was central, a work which planted a slowly germinating seed that bore its precious fruit in the revival of learning in the Middle Ages:

> Then, at length, the province of the historian is recognised to consist, not merely in the just, accurate, lively narrative of facts, but in the exhibition of cause and effect ... What then

had happened in the interval? Christianity had happened; Christendom had been formed ... From the time of the Great Sacrifice it was impossible to sever the history of man's temporal destiny from that of his eternal; and when the virtue of that Sacrifice had thoroughly leavened the nations, history is found to assume a larger basis, to have lost its partial and national cast, to have grown with the growth of man, and to demand for its completeness a perfect alliance with philosophy.[91]

Believing profoundly in the reality of 'Christendom' Allies maintained that divine revelation must underpin the philosophical understanding of history.

No one can be a great and true historian if his history be not written with a full conviction that 'three great powers move through the whole course of human events. There is a Divine Providence, which shapes all things to its own ends ... and never leaves the mastery of results to the blind or iron force of chance or fate. There is a free will of man, left sacred in every human breast by that Divine Providence, not the slave of outward circumstances nor of inward pleasure, but the very basis of our moral being, and its inviolable citadel. And there is, by the permission of that same Providence, an ever active power of evil, universal in his operation, and tempting every human free will to a false pleasure and an unreal good. If the human mind could not discern and recognise these three powers for itself from the mere contemplation of the outward facts of history, yet, at least, when they are disclosed by revelation, it sees infallible proof of their presence in those facts; nor has either of these ever been denied or ignored by the historian without manifest injury to the truth and the completeness of the view he takes of human affairs.

Nay, I am prepared to maintain that it was the very discerning and reasoning on these three powers and their joint operations in human affairs, which gave birth to that

A New Life

philosophy of history, of which we are now treating.[92]

But what of his master's warning about final causes? Believing as he did that God had intervened in human history—above all in the Word made flesh—how could Allies avoid teleology? Divine purpose had overcome self-will in his own life and history too was ultimately the resolution of a spiritual battle (Ephesians 6:12). In his historical writing Allies would never be able to distance himself sufficiently from these beliefs to satisfy the rigorous tenets of the 'scientific' historians. In examining his conscience, he was sure that his calling had a higher purpose than mere academic distinction: 'If the Philosophy of History be not exactly the subject I should have chosen, it lends itself at least to the illustration of the Church, and its ἔργον in the world, the one subject of predilection to my mind.'[93]

He was confident that this underlying objective did not conflict with the academic respectability he earnestly sought, and in taking the supernatural as foundational he was in exalted company, for had not his academic superior once condemned Dean Milman's philosophy of history?

> A living dignitary of the Established Church wrote a History of the Jews;[94] in which, with what I consider at least bad judgment, he took an external view of it, and hence was led to assimilate it as nearly as possible to secular history. A great sensation was the consequence among the members of his own communion, from which he still suffers. Arguing from the dislike and contempt of polemical demonstrations which that accomplished writer has ever shown, I must conclude that he was simply betrayed into a false step by the treacherous fascination of what is called the Philosophy of History, which is good in its place, but can scarcely be applied in cases where the Almighty has superseded the natural laws of society and history. From this he would have been saved, had he been a Catholic; but in the Establishment he knew of no teaching, to which he was bound to defer, which might rule that to be false which attracted him by its speciousness.[95]

What were the 'laws of history' and how could it be determined when and how the Almighty had suspended them? Newman was confident that historical data could be assembled and analysed to demonstrate a purpose behind apparent randomness. Allies concurred; his purpose would be to identify 'the natural laws of society and history'. Thus in securing academic respectability

> history and philosophy have an equal share. It [the philosophy of history] rests on a basis of facts; it results in a science, the scope of which is to set forth the laws by which the political and social world is governed. How can we attain to the knowledge of these laws? ... by a cautious and conscientious induction of facts, an induction which needs to be as patient, as rigorous, as scrupulous, as extensive, as little warped by preconceived fancies or extraneous theories, as the induction on which physical sciences are built, and which has been the main instrument in their wondrous advance.[96]

All this is encapsulated in his declaration 'I would apply to events of the moral order what a famous philosopher says of physics, that the doctrine of final causes, when actively introduced spoils them.'[97] Yet recently, in writing for the *Dublin*, Allies had identified this same philosopher as the enemy of Christian scholarship: 'The principle of authority, of tradition, of deduction and development, having been overthrown in things divine, what more natural than that Bacon should propose the principle of induction, that is, proceeding from the particular to the universal, as the foundation of all human science.'[98] So that without overt dishonesty the Dublin lecture strains unsuccessfully to accommodate divine authority and supernatural purpose with the principles of objective enquiry. Guizot[99] is both commended as having elevated the philosophy of history into a science by 'a careful study of original authorities, a patient induction of facts, a cautious generalisation', but also rebuked for a failure to give due weight to the 'great spirit and his personal operation. Strong as he is, he has been apparently too weak to bear the scoff of modern infidelity, "he believes in the Devil"'. Allies finished his address with a ringing denunciation of those who seek to 'construct histories,—and philosophical histories too,—which either ignore the existence, or disfigure and misrepresent the operation of the city of God. The grand exploit of these writers is to blot the sun out of the world.'[100] It would take a decade before he resolved the intellectual contradictions apparent in the Dublin lecture.

Allies believed that he would soon be called upon to teach students, and this gave a shape and structure to the reading that filled the hours not taken up by paid employment. What sort of historian would he become? His friendship with J. H. Newman was foundational but as they had taken different paths on their journeys to the 'one fold' so as Catholics, differences in understanding and emphasis would draw them apart. Allies had found his security in St Peter's successor, the unchanging source of jurisdiction and infallible shepherd of the flock, speaking truth to a society in the grip of the antichrist. Newman looked less towards the Magisterium and more to the witness of the Church as a living body: clergy and laity indwelt by the Spirit. In the 1850s this difference in perspective had no impact on their friendship; if there was any 'party-spirit' in the Church it came from the unease of some 'old-Catholics' with those converts who enthusiastically embraced Wiseman's Italianate devotions. But for most Catholics the 'Second Spring' was a time of optimism; with the restoration of the hierarchy fuelling a renewed sense of being at one with the universal Church and of gratitude and loyalty to the new pope. Allies wrote in 'Christian and Antichristian Education' of a Church that had been 'collecting itself up more and more in its supreme head and feeling that its strength lies in the chair of Peter. Its children more than ever trust their mother. Faith leads them to knowledge, and love preserves harmony between the intellect and the will.'[101]

Allies was in regular contact with the priests of the London Oratory, and Faber was his confessor and confidant. Honoured today as a devotional writer whose hymns are still popular, he was in increasingly poor health, and seems to have found the converts who flocked to him rather trying. He criticised their practice of going to confession 'only for the purpose of direction', and their sensitivity about forms, 'making their devotion only a new capability of censoriousness.'[102] He was steadfastly loyal to Pius IX and fostered devotional practices favoured by Rome, for example instituting at the Oratory a confraternity devoted to the Precious Blood (a feast made universal in 1849).[103] He was, however, mindful of the sensitivities of Catholics unable to share his joy at the proclamation of the Immaculate Conception by papal decree in 1854.[104] Faber did not make Allies an Ultramontane but nor could Newman lead him in another direction. Whilst still an Anglican Allies had sworn loyalty to Pius IX in his heart. He valued both men and was troubled by their estrangement, with Faber drawing closer to Wiseman and thus to Manning, and Newman isolated in Birmingham increasingly suspicious that the influence of the London Oratory was directed towards turning the converts against him.[105]

The Rambler and the *Dublin Review*

A Catholic who attracted the interest of Newman and Allies was Sir John Acton, who in 1854, while still a minor, had proposed the American convert scholar Orestes Brownson for the chair of philosophy of history at Dublin.[106] He had written to the Oratory from Munich, when studying under the celebrated German historian Ignaz von Döllinger,[107] whose rigorous approach to Church history he had adopted as his own. By applying critical and analytical tools to original documents the German was becoming a disrupter, questioning, for example, the historical evidence for the pope's temporal authority. For some this was an uncomfortable challenge to the 'new Ultramontanism': an increasingly accepted mindset among Catholics that looked to the unchanging authority of Peter for security in an uncertain world. Döllinger, who was both a scholar and a nationalist pledged to a union of the German peoples, believed that one great obstacle to this would be removed if Catholic and Protestant scholars could agree on principles of interpretation as a first step towards healing the wounds of the Reformation. Ultramontanism challenged this agenda, and as early as 1850 Dollinger had characterised it as an attempt to 'impose ... what another nation [Italy presumably] according to its own traits in religious matters had formed and developed and then, like an ill-fitting coat, sought cumbersomely to make the German people wear.'[108]

In 1857 at the age of 23 Acton returned from his studies to his seat at Aldenham, which was within 30 miles of Birmingham. He had lately been in Rome, where he and Döllinger had been received by Pius IX. Unlike so many, not least Allies, neither man was captivated by him. Late in life Döllinger recollected, 'Pio Nono addressed us in somewhat commonplace fashion, to the effect that the pope was the supreme authority over all, and only when the world had learned to bow before the apostolic chair would the welfare of the world be assured.'[109] According to Bishop Mathew, Acton, too, was 'cold at heart toward the Roman Pontiff'.[110] However, though a loyal son of the Church and committed to the temporal power, he rejected the allure of Ultramontanism, believing that only sound scholarship could demonstrate that papal claims were historically well founded, firm enough to withstand critical attack. Acton's *bête noire* was propagandist history: the use of 'arbitrary facts and authorities'. He pointed, for example, to the Ultramontanist writings of Dom Guéranger lauded by some as 'the learned Abbot of Solesmes', whom he stigmatised as the 'most outspoken of these systematic adversaries of modern knowledge'—an approach he contrasted with that of the Abbot's scholarly adversary, the Prince de Broglie, who at least 'recognized in history, besides the action of Providence, the operation of natural and secondary causes'.[111]

Acton soon became a presence in London Catholic society and Allies the academic was drawn to him as representing the world of modern German historical studies. They had a shared interest in Catholic education, and although Allies had no wish to teach children, he was concerned for schooling, not least that of his own children. He wrote in January 1858: 'there is not I suppose a convert of Oxford or Cambridge who is not forced into a feeling made up of despair and disgust at the condition of scientific teaching among us, compared with that existing in the best Protestant schools'.[112]

Acton too believed in the need to raise educational standards among Catholics and joined with Allies and a number of influential laymen, mainly converts, university men, to urge on a sympathetic Newman the establishment of an Oratory school. This, it was hoped, might become a 'Catholic Eton' to strengthen young men both in faith and intellect. Their work led to the opening of the school in May 1859, with Cyril Allies one of its early scholars. Other similar schools followed, but a lack of suitable higher education for their sixth-formers remained a problem for many years. In 1872 in a report for the bishops Allies advocated university education:

> Catholic youth on their entrance into manhood betray a certain apathy and listlessness in comparison with non-Catholic youths of corresponding position ... Of course it follows that no adequate remedy can be applied save by giving education its proper crown and completion. Catholics were in prison for nearly three hundred years. We were let out in 1829 but after more that forty years we still wear the prison dress. Have we discarded the prison spirit?[113]

Despite Newman's hopes his Dublin foundation did not draw English students and eventually some Catholic parents would begin to send their sons to study at Oxford and Cambridge. But as the 1850s opened the religious tests remained an obstacle to this, and there was within the traditional Catholic community some resentment at the criticisms of ex-Protestants who flaunted their own degrees. Acton insisted that the Church could not ignore the intellectual challenges to dogmatic Christianity, symbolised by the publication in 1859 of two unsettling works: Charles Darwin's *On the Origin of Species* and John Stuart Mill's *On Liberty*. The so called 'Liberal Catholics', of whom he soon became a recognised leader, believed that rigorous dispassionate scholarship was not a threat to faith; indeed that it would ultimately vindicate the Church's claims. In his mission to educate the laity Acton's chosen vehicle was *The Rambler*, which under the guidance of its assistant editor, Richard Simpson, was by the end of 1857 no longer the house paper of the converts but an aggressively campaigning review, of which Acton became part-owner.[114] Despite their degrees Acton did not see the converts as his natural allies; in 1862 he wrote that they had been spoiled by 'sickly' Puseyism, making them 'advocates, workers out of a view, aprioristic, also devoted to authority, anxious for mental repose, and no question asked'.[115] They were not all dismissed; after all Simpson was a convert, and Allies, although he was never detached

A New Life

from Brompton orthodoxy, was to prove a useful intermediary, perhaps even a temporary fellow-traveller. In sowing the seeds of 'Döllingerism', the role of *The Rambler* was vital. Its publisher was James Burns, whose firm had issued the *Church of England Cleared* in 1846. However, he was apparently unpersuaded and converted the following year; continuing his work as a Catholic, he took Allies's *The See of St. Peter* through the press. The two men were now on good terms, with Burns confiding in him his fear that Simpson's forthright style might alienate subscribers to *The Rambler*. Early in 1858 he suggested a solution: that Allies and some other converts should form an editorial advisory council. Acton was dismissive, 'For my part I should like to hear occasionally what they would have to say, not so much for the sake of their advice to be followed as of their errors to be made a note of and incidentally combated.'[116]

The Rambler's principal rival for the attention of the Catholic intelligentsia was *The Dublin Review*, established by Wiseman and still his vehicle. By 1858 it had fallen on hard times and when its editor (Henry Bagshawe) resigned it seemed possible it would fold. Burns, however, saw an opportunity and asked Allies to enquire whether Acton might be prepared to take it on. The latter's enthusiastic response was tempered when the expectation that Allies should be deputy editor was intimated to him. He wanted Simpson: but, knowing that Allies would be disappointed, 'begged Bellasis [a mutual friend] to gild the pill' for him,[117] confiding in Newman: 'I do not think you can have a doubt of Simpson being the most [sic] competent of the two, and am persuaded he has energy enough for both reviews.'[118] Newman did not press Allies's case, but predicted, accurately, that he would not get his way; 'As to Simpson, he is one of the cleverest writers of the day—but I shall be surprised, if you succeed in making him sub-editor against the Cardinal.'[119] And so it proved. In August Wiseman persuaded Bagshawe to return and the *Dublin* limped on. Later that year its editorship was offered to Allies. When he declined, Newman thought it a fortunate escape, 'You would have found yourself sadly entangled.'[120]

Allies was too closely bound up with Faber and the Ultramontanes for Acton to feel entirely comfortable with him and with the assurance of youth had formed a low opinion of his scholarship. So that when, early in 1858, he had learnt that Allies intended to write on Buckle's *History of Civilization* for the *Atlantis* (the journal of the Irish university) he proposed running a parallel review in *The Rambler* to demonstrate what he believed would be the former's inadequacy.[121] Allies's article did not appear. It seems, however, that Acton yet believed something could be made of him as a historian and invited him to Aldenham to meet Döllinger. Allies responded with enthusiasm and travelled there with Simpson, arriving on the evening of Monday 6 September. Also present were R. G. Macmullen, who had been a Catholic priest for ten years, and another convert, John Moore Capes, founder of *The Rambler*, who was undergoing a crisis of faith, and whose doubts it was hoped Döllinger could settle. Newman had been invited, but declined. Quite what transpired there has not been recorded. Mary Allies simply comments: 'In August 1858 [*sic*] he met Döllinger at Aldenham and was encouraged by both the German and English historian to proceed in his labours. Father Faber, whom he had consulted, somewhat discouraged him.'[122]

These labours were his historical studies. Stimulated by what he learnt from Döllinger Allies returned to London re-enthused about lecturing in Dublin. Newman, however, could give him no information on when he might be required there. He added that it was fortunate he had not accepted Acton's invitation to join the Aldenham party: 'People are, strange to say, watching me'. Among those with doubts about *The Rambler*'s orthodoxy the gathering there was being interpreted as a conspiracy with seditious intent. Newman sympathised with Acton's aspirations but Faber sensed danger. Allies wished to remain on good terms with both men, but would ultimately have to choose his side. His heart was with Pio Nono and so his head was with Ultramontanism. But he owed much to Newman and shared with him an admiration for Döllinger's scholarship, and as yet saw no reason to doubt his orthodoxy. In October's *Rambler* was an article he co-authored with Simpson, on an uncontroversial subject, but one dear to his heart as secretary of the Poor-School Committee: the parsimony of Catholics in supporting 'missionary book and education societies'.[123] The next issue featured a review of a conversion narrative and highlighted the part played by Allies's writings in an Anglican vicar's journey to Rome.[124]

Nevertheless, the more Acton knew of Allies the less reason he found to modify his verdict that his scholarship was subservient to dogma. When he learnt that he had been invited to edit the *Dublin* his comment was: 'Allies will be little more than a cat's paw of Faber.'[125] Yet, reflecting that Allies still looked to Newman as his intellectual mentor, perhaps there was hope for him? Thus, among the reasons Acton gave for supporting a proposed relaunch of the *Atlantis* with Newman as editor was that it would 'take the wind out of Fabers [*sic*] sails and would almost compel Allies and the men who have not committed themselves to join Newman.'[126] The latter had to tread a delicate path. In August's *Rambler*, Simpson had given great offence by branding St Augustine the 'father of Jansenism'. Faber protested at a layman adjudicating on theology. Acton responded that Faber, unlike the author, had not studied the sources and was thus himself unqualified to adjudicate.

When not at his office, Allies was immersed in his books, but as 1859 opened he was recruited to a convert-led scheme to relaunch the *Dublin*. Simpson wrote that its agenda would be set by 'Thompson, Ward, Lewis, Allies, Dalgairns censor, Brompton the breath of inspiration and the Cardinal the controller.'[127] As with previous schemes this too came to nothing. It would be a difficult year for *The Rambler*. In January the English bishops took exception to an article by Naysmith Stokes (a Catholic inspector of schools), criticising them for not cooperating with the Newcastle Commission established to enquire into elementary education. According to Simpson, Stokes had not 'mastered the difficulties', which could have been avoided had he consulted with Allies.[128] Simpson had been appointed editor, but he could not continue in the face of episcopal censure. In order to save the review a reluctant Newman was persuaded to take over, but in the July issue gave even greater offence to the bishops with his article 'On Consulting the Faithful on Matters of Doctrine'. He too had to stand down and Acton himself was compelled to take his place, though with Simpson in the editorial background. Burns found such sailing so close to the wind very uncomfortable and in 1861 put it to Acton that he could only continue to be his publisher if editorial policy were vested in '3 or 4 persons who could act together, and whose names would be a guarantee to the public ... such names as Macmullen, Allies, Ward, Thompson etc.' Simpson wrote to Newman that 'the names Burns mentioned did not command my confidence, nor, I felt sure, that of the Catholic public.'[129]

Acton's response was to seek another publisher, and opined that there was little to fear should Burns try to launch a rival review: 'If they begin attacks upon us, I look forward to Allies's historical articles, yea and Thompson's,[130] to scatter them to the four winds'.[131]

No new review was forthcoming. Acton found another (Protestant) publisher and decided to relaunch as a quarterly, pondering if *The Rambler* could be merged with the still moribund *Dublin*. He envisaged a new Catholic quarterly accepting communicated articles from all shades of opinion. Russell, the *Dublin*'s acting editor, favoured the scheme but was over-ruled. Divisions among English Catholics were hardening and Wiseman wished to reinvigorate the *Dublin* under a new regime. Acton retorted that he anticipated a 'stand-up fight'[132] between the Catholic reviews. It was then (April 1862) that Burns, seemingly unaware of the cardinal's thinking and after another conversation with Allies, proposed himself as the publisher of a new, merged, *Review*. Acton was approached and he drafted a letter setting out how this arrangement could benefit the Church. The agreement of the archbishop was essential, and in order to forestall the proposal being summarily dismissed he thought it prudent to use an intermediary. He decided to ask Allies:

> overwhelmed by work this week (in the wake of the annual meeting of the Catholic Poor-School Committee)... [he] will only pass on my letter, but as it is the week of his glory and persecution, he will give it an impetus as it passes through his hands ... My line would be perfectly independent, but extremely conciliatory. I would say that I loved peace much, knowledge and honesty more.[133]

Allies took the letter to Canon Morris, Wiseman's secretary. But the matter went no further. In July 1862 Acton launched *The Home and Foreign Review* and the following year the cardinal handed over his interest in the *Dublin* to Manning, who appointed W. G. Ward as the new editor. Thereafter its spirit 'was that of Ward, brilliant, logical, predominantly theological and devotional, always aggressively Ultramontane'.[134] Liberal Catholicism was swimming against the theological tide and Acton was compelled to wind up his new journal after its April 1864 edition. So strongly imbued was it with Döllingerism that it could not continue after the publication of the papal brief (5 March 1864) condemning this theologian's contribution to the Munich Conference the previous year, which had been a celebration of academic freedom. Acton wrote that by acquiescing in Rome's judgment 'the review will lose its identity, and the very breath of its nostrils'.[135]

The formation of Christendom

This was a key episode in Döllinger's long demise, confirming Allies's doubts about him, which had their origin in an article written by the professor five years before in support of Simpson's questioning of St Augustine's orthodoxy. Acton had asked his former tutor to write and after the article appeared observed: 'Of course there is war to the knife between the Bromptoratory and all theology pursued on the German method',[136] and just a few days later reported having a 'long talk with Allies, who is entirely in Faber's hands'.[137] Thereafter Allies was gradually consigned to the darkness that the liberals reserved for their theological foes. The favoured platform of the Ultramontanes was the 'Academia of the Catholic Religion', which Wiseman had established in 1861 in the—forlorn—hope of fostering greater understanding between the two parties. Allies was a charter member, as were men as opposed as Simpson and Ward, Manning and Acton. Newman was sceptical about it, understandably so when it became clear that its ethos was to be anti-liberal, wedded to the restoration of the pope's temporal power. For a time Acton and Simpson remained members and the latter was present on 26 November 1861 when Ward lectured. He wrote to Acton describing 'a common place sermon' on the misuse of the intellect and said he had upset Wiseman by offering criticism and, interestingly, named Allies as among the critics when a debate developed, saying that afterwards he and Macmullen went to Allies's home. But the incident did not betoken any abandonment of 'Westminster Orthodoxy', for when Allies himself lectured the following spring—using material that would later appear in *The Formation of Christendom*— Acton was confirmed in his low opinion of him. He wrote to Newman on 6 May:

> The demolition of a bad argument in favour of Christianity or Catholicism is I should have thought a service to religion. Allies has an argument based on a comparison of Cicero with S. Augustine, which as he puts it, is just as strong as the argument would be the other way in comparing Mark Antonine with Alexander VI. I cannot help feeling uneasy at the state of mind that rejoices in these arguments, that produces them and is encouraged by them. There is a whole party of converts in whom I cannot help discerning a sort of latent scepticism covered by a habit of flinching from difficulties, and of assuming that there is nothing which cannot be converted into a support of religion by a very superficial examination and manipulation.[138]

By this time Allies had largely written the six lectures, which along with the inaugural, were to form the first of the eight volumes that came to define his intellectual life. The subject he chose, the formation of Christendom, was the resolution of a quest that had begun in 1854: to map out the historical territory that he wished to cover. Whilst the Poor-School Committee occupied his working day, in the interstices of time that remained he accumulated source material, keeping a commonplace book of extensive transcriptions from the Church Fathers as well as modern historians: an impressive demonstration of his facility in German, French and Italian as well as his command of Latin and classical Greek. Most of the material that came to inform his own writing was from continental historians; he had little time for English scholars, for example giving short shrift to Henry Hallam's *Introduction to the Literature of Europe*:

> Conceive the twelfth century dismissed without any mention of S. Thomas and his effect on the mind of Europe. In fact this is proof of how utterly incapable of writing history at all is a mind full of the strongest prejudices against the Church and disdainful of the whole matter of religion.[139]

Under Acton's influence he valued German scholarship, in particular

Möhler and Döllinger's work on early Christianity. After reading the latter's *Kirche und Kirchen* (the first edition of 1861) he wrote 'it is full of good sense and solid views of history', and noted with approval the historian acknowledging 'how intimately the papacy is bound up with the very existence of the Church'. But later he told Newman that his confidence in its author had not survived the 1864 papal censure.[140] Allies's anti-Enlightenment instincts were deep-seated. As a young man he had written in his diary 'How I hate the substitution of the word nature for God!', and in the commonplace book quotes with approval comments by Fr Faber on the supremacy of grace. He remained unshaken in his belief that European civilisation had reached its peak in the High Middle Ages, a conclusion reinforced by studying scholars such as the Spanish thinker Donoso Cortès,[141] whose works he read in a French translation.

By 1860 Allies had prepared an outline of his planned lectures. He had concluded that he could serve the Church most effectively by an extended comparison of modern society with the high-water mark of European civilisation, the five centuries of Christendom inaugurated by the coronation of Charlemagne. In his Journal, he summarised the thesis, the unfolding of which would 'occupy me all my life'. It was 'the position, political, moral, and social, of the Church towards the State, in mediaeval and modern times'. He particularly wished to explain the position of the Church in the period since 1300, 'what Donoso Cortès calls *le morcellement et le fractionnement de la république chrétienne*.'[142] The history would be in two parts:

> the first setting forth the Church as the Mother of Nations, 800–1300; the second the gradual break up of her political power and ascendency until the upshot comes to the present balance of power i.e. force and fear keeping heathendom at bay.
>
> This work may serve as an introduction to the whole position and work of the Church in modern times, which has hovered before me for years, and now seems to assume more distinct form and substance.[143]

In taking this view he would be guided by Schlegel, 'The general idea of the

Christian empire was a universal protectorate over all Christian countries ... When this religious unity was destroyed the whole political edifice fell to pieces (and was replaced by) a mere mechanical balance of power.'[144]

In explaining why the civil supremacy of the pope was overthrown and 'a very large proportion of the faithful in all Europe ... rose in insurrection against the Church' Allies was persuaded by Höfler's[145] thesis that nationalism was at the root, beginning after 1300 and culminating in 'Luther's schism'. The Reformation was fuelled by the growth of anti-Italian sentiment in Germany, a more important causation than religion: 'it was as the *Trafen* of German feeling that Luther became a "Demigod" to his people.'[146] In fine, Allies wanted to write a history that would explain in terms of the waxing and waning of Christendom the confusion and contradictions of contemporary society. His objective was 'the glory of God' and his prayer: 'may he enable and direct me'. In November 1860, he outlined his plan to Newman: the fulcrum of his work was to be the *république chrétienne*, the 'Balance of Power', to be honoured in its medieval apogee and thereafter in its 'decomposition and dismemberment'. He asked if the subject was defined clearly enough, whether it had already been treated, and crucially, was it one desirable to be treated? His letter concluded 'I should rather have your judgment than that of any man living. And I hope that I am not led by myself alone, for I would put my design aside if your judgment is unfavourable to it.'[147]

Newman considered the matter at length. His reply was that as a historian Allies's first responsibility was to objectivity: on what basis could it be argued that one state of society was better than another? Thus he questioned the entire concept of a 'Christian society', as allowable for the historian:

> I do not see my way to hold that 'Catholic civilisation' as you describe it, is *in fact*, ... has been or shall be, or can be, a good or *per se*, desirable.
>
> St. John says, *Mundus totus in maligno positus est.* Is this the declaration of an ever-enduring fact? I think it is. If so, the world, though stamped with Christian civilisation, still *in maligno positus est.*

> Have we any reason to suppose that more souls were saved (relatively to the number of Christians) under the Christian Theocracy than under the Roman Emperors, or under the English Georges?[148]

Newman had concluded the first draft of his letter, 'I wish you would take the trouble to answer this, for I don't profess to have a clear view'. When it was sent the second clause was omitted; perhaps its inclusion would have steeled Allies's resolve, because at first he was reluctant to abandon his central thesis:

> I suppose I mean by Catholic civilisation the founding of natural society on the principle of the supernatural end of man; measuring the world by the Cross, and planting the Cross upon it.
>
> Now I entirely admit that *mundus totus in maligno positus est* is the declaration of an ever enduring fact. But is there any incompatibility between this fact and the Catholic civilisation defined above?
>
> Christianity has captivated to its sway as many minds of every degree and order of excellence as have refused to own it. In Literature, especially, its conquests have been so great that even its enemies, in spite of themselves, are half Christian. While attacking Christian dogma they have appropriated Christian morality ...
>
> I wish you would enable me to take a firmer grasp of your positive view. I am in doubt as to it at present, but it would seem to me the result of your letter would be a restriction to St. Augustine's position of a *Civitas Dei*, and a *Civitas Diaboli*, and that all beyond this may be tenable or desirable, *hic et nunc*, but not *per se*.
>
> Now is it not against this that the Church has shown the greatest reluctance to surrender her mediaeval position? Has she not stuck as it were, tooth and nail, to that consecration of the *mundus*, that taking possession of it with the cross, which I have called a Catholic civilization?

He asked his mentor to consider the temporal power surely 'the very consecration of the mediaeval system itself? And the Holy Father defends himself by anathemas against all who touch it', and of the Catholic bishops 'scarcely one in a thousand' would advocate its surrender. On the other hand it was *The Times*, a 'sagacious exponent... of the heretical mind' that advocated the loss of the papal territories 'as in itself desirable for the Pope'.[149]

Newman was unmoved and sought to clarify his position by stripping his objections to one key argument:

> My *assumption* is, that the revealed object of the institution of the Church is to save souls.
>
> My *position* is that there is no *probability in facts* (i.e., no *evidence*) that one organisation of society saves more souls than another.
>
> And further, that there *is* an *antecedent probability* the other way ... from the circumstances that the world—that is human society, *in maligno positus est* ...
>
> When has the mediaeval system acted with undeniably greater effect (in appearance) in saving souls than another system? That can hardly be said to be included in the Divine Purpose, which cannot be clearly shown to have special *fructus animarum*.
>
> How can you speak of the Gospel converting first the individual, then the State, as if the two were in the same order? The mediaeval system was a great triumph for the Gospel, and I am puzzled to say what it was in the way of benefit for the souls of men, considered as a whole.[150]

On Christmas Day 1860 Allies admitted defeat:

> I have nothing to allege, which at all satisfies my own mind, against your powerful exposition of '*mundus totus in maligno positus est*'. What I feel is the old instinctive struggle against the fact itself. This is, I suppose at the bottom what led me to dream of a Catholic civilization, not in theory only, but in

act overmastering corrupt nature, and making the empires of the world, yield a not unwilling homage to the Church. You have convinced me that it will not do. They are rebels from the beginning to the end; the single soul is the work of God, and lasts into eternity, and so brings Him glory in eternity, but all human polity and civilisation stop with this life, and have no counterpart in the eternal world.[151]

The surrender was almost total; he raised only a token objection: that in fact more souls might be saved in nations where the faith was established than in those where it was only tolerated. Newman replied: 'Is God more glorified by many saved or by great saints?'[152] Given the assurance with which in 1851 he had characterised modern society as pervaded by the spirit of the antichrist Allies's capitulation may seem extraordinary. Yet Ultramontanism did not necessarily involve an apocalyptic frame of reference. Father Faber, from whom Allies also sought advice, disapproved of the 'worship of some pet past ages of the Church' and wrote, 'to all appearances the nineteenth century is a very exceptional time. But then I have misgivings that all times seem so, as they are passing.'[153] For Allies the correspondence with Newman was a critical turning-point. Now abandoning any overt polemical intent, he decided to write about the subject foundational to his Catholicism: the establishment and evolution of the see of St Peter as the 'rock of the Church, the source of Jurisdiction, the centre of unity', and how evolving Christian societies found their coherence in St Peter's successors. This account of the formation of Christendom took eight substantial volumes and thirty five years to complete. But as a contribution to scholarship it has not endured and it is possible to lament his turning away from a project so long and carefully considered. An analysis of the wounds of contemporary society on the lines he envisaged might have served to deepen the spiritual understanding and strengthen the resolve of many Catholics bewildered by a rapidly changing world.

The first volume of Allies's history with its detailed account of the profound impact of Christianity on the ancient world—terrible corruption combatted by the preaching of the Cross—was published in 1865. Its writing coincided with the war between the American states, which added poignancy to the book's thesis that the institution of slavery underlay the moral decay of Roman society: 'The spirit of slavery is never limited to the slave: it saturates the atmosphere which the freeman breathes together with the slave, passes into his nature and corrupts it.'[154] Allies equated American with Roman slavery: only the owner was regarded as a person, the slave was 'a lower being ... a soul without a spirit ... having only the value of a thing and an instrument.'[155] He sent the draft chapter to Newman, who disagreed with its assertion of the unique immorality of slavery: 'I thought you had not guarded yourself against views different from your own, and that readers might say you had not gone to the bottom of your subject, but that you went with the age.' Why, asked Newman, had the Church not condemned it? In his eyes it was but 'one of those potent instruments of evil, which corrupt Roman civilization used', and he saw despotism and the army (a 'school of vice, crime and spiritual ruin') as equivalent, perhaps even greater evils.[156] The key was Scripture: if slavery was an evil in itself rather than in its consequences then why did Paul not tell Philemon to free his slaves, and how could he describe himself as a slave of Christ?[157] Although Allies's response is missing, this discussion must have reflected many such debates, as, for the North, the Civil War became increasingly a crusade to free the slaves, with both sides asserting that theirs was the Christian cause. It is not clear to what extent Newman influenced Allies's argument, but whilst his book did not confront the theological issues directly, its condemnation of Roman slavery remained unchanged. It was the leaven of Christianity that exalted the dignity of all mankind. For the apostles, 'the regeneration of man himself was their remedy for a world in ruins.'[158] Newman had also objected to the choice of Cicero as representative of heathen amorality—although he did not rehearse Acton's objection to this line of reasoning—suggesting Cato or Boethius; but when Allies adduced unwelcome evidence from Pliny he reluctantly accepted the force of his criticisms.[159] Despite his reservations Allies drew heavily from Döllinger's *Heidenthum und Judenthum* (an English translation had been published the year before as *The Gentile and the Jew*), which Newman had agreed was an 'awful book'—probably meaning in its description of pagan corruption—but believed there was much to commend in the work.[160]

There was to be more useful criticism of the work in progress but these early exchanges anticipated Newman's increasing unease at what was becoming evident: Allies's failure to fulfil the 'Dublin brief'—using a scholarly analysis of primary and secondary sources to confront difficult and contested issues. Nevertheless he was happy to be the dedicatee of the third volume (1875), which expressed 'profound gratitude ... for the aid which your writings gave me to discern the light of the Catholic faith'. The dedication noted that the work had arisen from the writer's appointment to the Catholic University but was less than fulsome about Newman's subsequent contribution: 'your counsels were not wanting to me in the first choice and handling of the subject'.[161] By this time the two men were walking separate paths in their understanding of the faith. Of course, Allies also consulted with London friends, Faber in particular, but the weight and direction of the different influences upon him is hard to assess. After Faber's death in September 1863, his visits to the Oratory were less frequent; the church nearest his home was Our Lady's, in St John's Wood, where Bernard was interred.

A relationship under strain

During the first half of the 1860s Thomas maintained a regular correspondence with Newman and Eliza also wrote to him: forthright letters, drafted in a large, florid, almost indecipherable hand. At the end of 1863 she was in poor health, desperately concerned for Edward and Cyril, who had in June had gone to Queensland to find their fortunes and from whom nothing had been heard. Then a letter was received and in relief she wrote to tell Newman, before venturing to give him some advice: she thought that he was too occupied, dissipating his talents, and would be more usefully engaged writing on some pressing theological subject. He replied,

> Your kind letter made me smile, I have not had one day's holiday, nor am I likely to have ... And your husband asks me if I am writing on Nature and Grace! And you ask me what bones I am cracking? The bones of old jackalls and hyenas, of foxes, rats and mice in some ancient palaeontological cave.[162]

When she wrote back endorsing her husband's plea that he write a treatise, Newman expressed himself freely to her in a letter marked 'private'. He said that tackling a theological theme was out of the question because he could do no useful work, given the constraints of 'Westminster orthodoxy'. His experience in having to relinquish *The Rambler* in 1859 still rankled and he did not wish again to 'feel a pat from the lion ... [W]hen authority interferes, one seems to feel one's breath taken away'.[163] In discussing slavery with him Allies had drawn a distinction between its Jewish and heathen forms, and said he had been influenced by Döllinger's assessment of the 'whole subject of heathen and Christian virtue, that is nature and grace'. He thought that this would be a worthy subject for his master's pen and 'no invention of mine—it had been said for a long time that you had been engaged on some great work'.[164] Newman's response was decided, echoing what he had already told Eliza:

> The more I know of Döllinger's views (I mean his German works) the more I find I agree with him ... I could not write a book and not *show* this; as well might a bird *fly* without wings, as I write a book without the chance, the certainty of saying something or other (not, God forbid! against the Faith) but against the views of a particular school in the Church, which is dominant.[165]

He suspected as well that his plan to establish a Catholic Oxford in Dublin had been thwarted by a defensive and suspicious hierarchy. Allies had clung for many years to the hope that his professorship might be a proper teaching role rather than honorific (he had been awarded a chair in 1855). However, in 1864 his offer to deliver a course of lectures—made through Newman—was, after some prevarication, declined on the grounds of cost. His friend was sceptical and wrote about the 'dreadful jealousy of the laity' having ruined things in Dublin.[166] English Catholics were unwilling for their sons to go there but were increasingly prepared to send them to Oxford or Cambridge now that the religious tests for undergraduate degrees had been abolished.[167] The hierarchy were opposed. Newman said it was the same fear of an educated laity that lay 'at the bottom of this unwillingness to let our youths go to Oxford ... Propaganda and our leading Bishops fear the natural influence of the laity: which would be their greatest, or (humanly speaking) is rather their only defence against the world.'[168]

Yet there was genuine concern for the spiritual welfare of Catholic students at the ancient universities, where religion was retreating before the advance of rationalism. One response was that of Bishop Ullathorne, who in August 1864 agreed that the Birmingham Oratory might open an Oxford mission. A well-situated plot of land had become available and, believing this to be providential, Newman launched an appeal for funds. Manning, however, who had the ear of an ailing Wiseman,[169] was opposed on principle to Catholics at Oxford and distrusted Newman's intentions, believing that his aim was to establish a Catholic college. In October he expressed his fears to Mgr Capalti, the Secretary of Propaganda:

> The leaders of this movement are precisely those who supported *The Rambler* and the *Home and Foreign Review* ... All of them ... have either kept silent when they should speak out on critical questions such as that of the Temporal Power, or about the Munich Congress, or else they have openly opposed the Catholic point of view ... I fear very much the influence, or the entry of that intellectual element in the education of our young laymen. Furthermore, the harmful effects of the intellectual tendency can already be seen among some of the younger clergy.[170]

A month later Wiseman received a letter from the Cardinal Prefect of Propaganda, asking that an extraordinary meeting of the English bishops should convene to consider the desirability of a Catholic hall at Oxford. Allies was strongly in favour; like Newman he had a deep affection for 'those glorious ancient halls' where 'still a certain humane culture has lingered on ... a certain character has been formed in them which had its greatness, and its beauty, and its classic grace.'[171] He met Newman at the Oratory on 23 November, when it was known that the bishops were due to meet and that it was likely that they would reaffirm opposition to attendance at the Protestant universities. Writing to him on 3 December Allies was dismissive, opining that not one of the thirteen prelates was in a position to judge by experience the effects of a university education on the mind. 'How many of them care sufficiently for mental culture to give an adequate consideration to the motives determining parents to send their sons to Oxford? Or understand that society in which the Catholic Church has to act?'[172] He suspected that 'this meeting of the Bishops has been called expressly to prevent your going to Oxford and the Bishop's giving you the Mission at Oxford was its immediate momentum'.[173] It was an issue that touched him deeply, so that when he was asked—along with some other converts—to respond to a list of twenty questions framed by Wiseman and endorsed by the bishops, he spoke his mind. Newman was not asked for his views, and suspected that Ward and Manning were behind questions clearly intended to elicit support for a Catholic boycott, which included, for example:

> Ought the principle to be admitted that the laity should be more highly educated than their clergy, considering the reproaches too readily cast on the latter for lagging in the progress of knowledge and solid attainments?
>
> Do you think it possible for a Professor or teacher holding the Holy Catholic Church in contempt, and perhaps execration, from day to day to lecture upon even indifferent topics without almost involuntarily allowing his feelings to escape from any amount of watchful guardedness, and insinuate themselves into the susceptible minds or imaginations of a few unnoticed Catholic pupils?[174]

Ullathorne told Newman that he thought Allies's paper which Canon Morris read to the bishops' meeting was 'very able', but that a Catholic college would not be allowed, and that an ailing Wiseman was decidedly against Catholics going to Oxford. There was, however, no immediate prohibition and the matter was remitted to Rome, giving time for a meeting of prominent laymen to be held at the home of Sir John Simeon (7 January 1865). Allies was there and supported an address urging

Propaganda to leave the question open.[175] Yet those who would question the episcopacy were struggling against an ever-harsher theological environment. Döllinger had been censured, and the publication the previous December of the encyclical *Quanta Cura* and its attached *Syllabus of Errors*[176] further constrained the limits of permitted debate. Newman was grieved by it, writing to Henry Nutcombe Oxenham:

> It would be most rash in me to pronounce, that, looking back in the year 2000 at the recent Syllabus of errors condemned in 1864, an impartial posterity will not pronounce it to be a wise, bold, and necessary manifesto. And this seems to me clear, that it condemns little which would not have been condemned by all Anglican High Church men thirty years ago. Therefore it is no trouble to me to acquiesce in its denunciations.
>
> But if you ask me what I think of its bearings in England at this moment, I certainly am deeply pained at the publication of a document, which, however necessary and wise it may be, is a great disadvantage and discouragement to us English Catholics.[177]

The publication of the *Apologia* in April had inspired a wave of sympathy for him, but this was not universally shared. In his December letter, in addition to opining that the bishops were conspiring to thwart his Oxford plans, Allies had relayed some gossip. '[E. H.] Thompson called here yesterday to tell me there was a split in the *Dublin*: he and Henry Coleridge unable to bear Ward's highhandedness leave it. But *you* are the cause of the split. They wanted to say more of you and the *Apologia*: W. would not allow it.'[178] Allies had once joined in criticisms of Ward's denigration of the intellect, but now, despite his deep debt to Newman, accepted that 'academic freedom' had its limits and that ultimately there was no middle ground between obedience to the Holy Spirit speaking through the Magisterium and Protestantism. And in this he was at one with Ward, who was soon to acquire even greater influence. Wiseman was seriously ill; on 10 February 1865 Newman wrote to Pusey, with whom he was in regular contact, 'the poor Cardinal is dying every day, and there is a great idea that Manning will succeed him, which I can't believe.'[179] Wiseman died five days later. Allies attended the Requiem Mass at St Mary Moorfields and wrote of the impression made on him by

> a most astonishing sight ... I have vivid memories of November 1850, and the scenes which then passed in London after the letter 'Out of the Flaminian Gate'. The Cardinal's body passing from Moorfields to Kensal Green, seven miles, through a line of people, sympathising and sorrowful, is one of the most remarkable contrasts with his entrance that can be conceived.[180]

In March Rome's decision on the university question arrived, followed soon after by a statement that following consultation with the Holy See: 'The Bishops are unanimous in their disapproval of the establishment of a Catholic College at any of the Protestant universities. And they are further of the opinion that Parents ought to be in every way dissuaded from sending their children to pursue their studies at such Universities.'[181] Rome then spoke on another matter and on 10 May the stunning news of Manning's elevation to the primacy appeared in *The Times*. A fortnight later Allies wrote to Newman retracting his aspersions on the conduct of the bishops and of the new archbishop in connection with the Oratory's Oxford plan:

> *Now* I *know* as a matter of fact that this meeting [that of the bishops on 13 December] was caused by a letter from Cardinal Barnabo to our late Cardinal, at a time when he could not possibly know of your having the Mission at Oxford, or having bought land there; which letter again of his was drawn forth by letters addressed to him in August last from two persons, the one Bishop Grant, the other Dr Manning. Of course they had not the remotest thought that you were likely to be mixed up personally in the question ... I wish therefore to recall the opinion I expressed that Dr Manning had anything to do with the meeting of the Bishops, so far as it bore upon your having the mission or the land at Oxford.[182]

It is not clear where Allies's information came from nor in what terms he might have discussed Manning's influence with the bishops, but he now felt it his duty to put the record straight. He wrote on Tuesday 23 May. Newman's reply came the following day, inviting him and Eliza to Birmingham for the St Philip's Day celebrations on Friday to include a performance by the Oratory schoolboys of Terence's *Phormio*. His letter concluded abruptly: 'if you write to inspire me with confidence in the archbishop, *lateram lavas*'.[183] It was a quotation from the play: if Allies sought to be a peacemaker, he was wasting his time; a stinging rebuff. Was the invitation to Birmingham seriously meant? Allies replied on Thursday: 'St. Philip has bespoken me here tomorrow, so that I cannot be with you. I wish Mrs Allies was strong enough to attempt anything like the expedition to Rednall' (for Saturday's continuation of the festivities) 'but she hardly ever is, and at present she is not well.' Then, perhaps unwisely, he too alluded to the *Phormio*: 'I have no taste for brick washing ... I wished to undo the mischief which my own tongue might have done. And I should have written this a month ago, before the late appointment but your friend Geta (a character in the play) deterred me *loquanne incendam*, I knew the Achillean temperament.' He meant that he had not wished to give Newman further reason to sulk. It was insensitive, as was his attempt to mollify him by recounting how Manning had sought to secure a bishopric for him *in partibus infidelium* after the notorious incident of the episcopal offer and its withdrawal in 1854:[184] 'It shewed a jealous regard in behalf of your honour the very reverse of what I have heard people attribute to him. Now I have done with my brick but even Geta says *purgem me lateram lavem* whereas *purgo alteram*'.[185]

Newman felt no need to respond. But Allies was not finished and wrote again a few days later using his admiration of the second part of *Gerontius* to make a further point: 'considering they nowadays claim you as a liberal ... you have given expression to the feelings of modern day liberals with regard to Catholic sanctity in those "purrings" of the demons.' He added that he had had a visit from Ward, who confided that Manning had once said that if he had been in Cardinal Wiseman's shoes, he would have written to Newman 'to say to him, we must have a Catholic University and you must be head of it.' And how could people say that it has been 'Manning's object for years to get the place he holds' when he had sought to have Ullathorne appointed Wiseman's coadjutor with right of succession?[186]

Newman brushed him aside:

> You strangely misunderstood what I said about Manning, and treated it as if it denoted *personal* feeling on my part. What I said was, that I could not trust him—'confidence' is the word I used. Confidence is an intellectual habit, not a moral... I never can trust he has not an *arrière pensée*, in any profession or offer he makes. It is not *my* feeling alone; I have long defended him; I am one of the last who have given in to it; I thought that in your last, while you expressed 'penitence', you had an *arrière pensée*, that you were indirectly trying to get me over. So I gave you open warning. *Lateram lavas*.[187]

The *Eirenicon*

It was four months before Allies wrote to him again, when on 10 October he took up his pen to congratulate Newman on the twentieth anniversary of his reception into the Church:

> I ought to have thanked you long ago for your note of June 4th, removing my misconception of what you said about Manning. I wrote as I did because I knew that the Archbishop keenly felt what he imagined to be a quite personal alienation from him, arising in your mind from the supposition that he had worked against you personally in the Oxford Education matter.

He added that he felt 'penitence' because he too had been guilty of promoting this injustice. But there was another reason for writing now: Pusey's new book, 'by which it would seem that he has learnt at least nothing in those [twenty] years of what the Church is.'[188] The book was the *Eirenicon* and it stirred many memories for Allies, who had never ceased to blame his erstwhile spiritual director for detaining him in the Church of England by concealing its subservience to the civil power. Over the years he had watched it with a jaundiced eye, noting the publication of *Essays and Reviews* (1860) as further evidence that it lacked doctrinal authority. In a repetition of Gorham the courts were asked to adjudicate on the orthodoxy of two contributors; a finding of heresy in the Arches Court was overturned on appeal to the Privy Council (1864). In despair Pusey published a pamphlet lamenting this outcome.[189] He acknowledged that some Roman Catholics would be saddened at 'what weakens her who is, in God's hands, the great bulwark against infidelity on this land', but that there were others who 'seemed to be in an ecstasy of triumph at this victory of Satan'.[190]

Manning responded to Pusey with his own pamphlet, examining 'the workings of the Holy Spirit in the Church of England'. Unsurprisingly he found none; 'I am afraid, then, that the Church of England, so far from a barrier against infidelity, must be recognised as the mother of all the intellectual and spiritual aberrations which now cover the face of England.'[191] Pusey countered with his *Eirenicon*: a vindication of Anglicanism's claim to Catholicity and a condemnation of Roman 'excesses', especially the 'vast system as to the Blessed Virgin'. To Allies's disgust Pusey drew extensively from *The Church of England Cleared from Schism*, justifying this by claiming that *The See of St. Peter* provided no adequate answer to a book 'which he wrote, not as a partisan, but as the fruit of investigations, as to whose issue he was indifferent'.[192]

This was a provocation, and Allies felt obliged to respond. As he wrote to Newman, 'not that it will do any good'; 'he has closed his eyes with all the energy of his will'; 'his work inspires in me a disgust which I cannot express'.[193] In January's *Dublin Review* Allies collaborated with W. G. Ward in reviewing Pusey's work as well as two Manning pamphlets: *The Workings of the Holy Spirit in the Church of England* and *The Temporal Mission of the Holy Ghost*. They scorned the *Eirenicon* as the work of 'Rip Van Winkle', who despite many opportunities still had learnt nothing of Catholicism: 'It is a curious proof indeed how wonderfully Dr. Pusey misunderstands Roman doctrine, that having written as aggressive a work as any Tractarian could possibly write, he calls it (and no doubt thinks it) an *Irenicon*'.[194] The same edition of the *Dublin* included Allies's own 'Letter to Pusey', dated 21 December 1865; the title it was given when reprinted in *Per Crucem ad Lucem* defines the essay's scope and intention: 'The "Royal Supremacy" and the "See of St. Peter". A Competent Answer to the "Church of England Cleared from the Charge of Schism"'. The author recounts how his eyes were opened, before going on to accuse his former confessor of bad faith: 'In the years before this [the Gorham judgment], from the end of 1845, when I went to you for advice and consolation under difficulties, your custom was to deny altogether that ugly fact of the Royal Supremacy.'[195]

Allies's tone is bitter. He recalled Pusey having written in 1850 that 'any portion of the Church which does [so] abandon the essential meaning of an article of the Creed, forfeits not only the Catholic doctrine in that article, but also the office and authority to witness and teach as a member of the Universal Church.'[196] Yet after Gorham he had remained 'a Presbyter, a Dignitary, and a Royal Professor in the Church which has so done, and you have now come forward with the exact contradictory of these propositions in behalf of the Church which has so done.'[197] A few months later Allies published a fuller rebuttal, showing how the Fathers had taught that only sees united with the Holy See could be part of the One Body. Most of this pamphlet (*Dr. Pusey and the Ancient Church*) is a reworking of familiar material, focusing on the Donatist schism. Thus he quotes Augustine to Theodorus in 401: 'we grieve over them as wandering, and desire to win them over to God through the charity of Christ, that they may possess in the peace of the Church unto salvation that holy sacrament, which, outside of the Church's peace, they possess unto destruction.'[198]

As for Dr Pusey, his 'doctrine is the most unpatristic which can be conceived, being the contradiction of that idea on which the Fathers lived.'[199] He is accused of untruthfulness as well as hypocrisy, the *Eirenicon* being

> constructed as a scarecrow to frighten troubled consciences from seeking their true home ... in it devotions sanctioned by himself for private practice are mentioned as derogatory to the honour of our Lord when used by Catholics ... [B]elieving assuredly, as St. Iranaeus did, that 'Christ will judge those who work schisms, being devoid of the charity of God, and seeking their own private advantage, but not the unity of

the Church, and who for little and self-exalting reasons cut and divide, and, so far as in them lies, destroy the great and glorious body of Christ.'[200]

Of course, it was a dialogue of the deaf. All the arguments had been heard before. The deep and enduring hostility that Allies bore towards Pusey was noted by all his reviewers, both friendly and unfriendly. The *Dublin Review* said it

> would earnestly recommend ... to Dr. Pusey and other Anglicans, Mr. Allies's most eloquent and effective exposition of their ecclesiastical attitude. For ourselves, we have a most kindly feeling towards Dr. Pusey, and do not therefore entirely sympathize with Mr. Allies's *tone*; but we cannot wonder with the *Eirenicon* before us, that many other Catholics judge him far more severely than we do.[201]

The *Union Review*, established by Anglicans to promote reunion and profoundly opposed to Ultramontanism, remained convinced that Roman Allies had not answered the arguments of Anglican Allies. Moreover:

> Of the intense personal bitterness, to use no harsher term with which Mr. Allies, both here and in his recent letter to Dr. Pusey in the *Dublin Review*, thinks it fitting to assail the venerable and venerated author of the *Eirenicon*, who was formerly his friend and counsellor, who is his senior in years, and as immeasurably his superior in learning as in Christian charity (though denounced by him as 'devoid of the charity of God') the less said the better. It was perhaps an inevitable consequence of the method of treatment he has adopted, his pamphlet, notwithstanding the occasional flashes of brilliant pungency, is one of the dullest we have ever read.[202]

When in October Allies had urged Newman to answer the *Eirenicon* his reply was that he could do it 'but not except at the expense of theories and doctrines which the Archbishop thinks of vital importance, and which I cannot receive.'[203] Eventually, however, he considered it safe to publish a partial response, a detailed defence of the Church's exaltation of Mary and of devotion to her.[204] Despite his condemning certain continental practices ('I suppose we owe it to the national good sense, that English Catholics have been protected from the extravagances which are to be found elsewhere'[205]) which was taken by some as a criticism of the archbishop, Allies joined in the widespread congratulation. He said, 'the way you have brought out the second Eve in conjunction with the *Theotokos* may be of great service to many who now stumble at the stumbling-block of our Lady', and suggested another witness to the doctrine 'older than any you have' (the epistle of Mathetes to Diognetus), a reference that Newman was to include in the third edition of the *Letter to Pusey*.[206] Allies thought his tone too gentle; 'I admire particularly your courtesy, for I have heard many remark, how intolerably offensive P.'s book is to them; and for myself his *untruthfulness* is so revolting, that I am obliged to shut the book: and can only look at it at intervals with the greatest pain: and I find it difficult not to shew one's sense of this untruthfulness.'[207]

Newman, who regularly corresponded with Pusey, was more generous:

> As to Pusey, it is hard to call any mistakes of his, untruthfulness. I think they arise from the same slovenly habit which some people would recognise in his dress, his beard, etc. ... Then again (speaking antecedently, for it is 20 years since I actually knew him) surely a habit of carelessness in stating and ruling points must be generated from the fact of his position, as being *testis, judex and magister* to so many people. He goes into print with the same heedless readiness and decisiveness with which he would say words in conversation.[208]

He always hoped that his old colleague would eventually be reconciled to the see of Peter; so that when twelve years later Pusey was desperately ill and his life despaired of, Newman wrote thus to Liddon, Pusey's close friend and protégé:

> If his state admits of it, I should so very much wish to say to my dearest Pusey, whom I have loved and admired for above fifty years, that the Roman Catholic Church solemnly lays claim to him as her child, and to ask him in God's sight whether he does not acknowledge her right to do so ... I cannot let him die, if such is God's will, with the grave responsibility lying upon me of such an appeal to him as I suggest; and since I cannot make it myself, I must throw that responsibility on some one else who is as close to him as you are; and this I do. Oh! what a world is this, and how piercing are its sorrows.[209]

Liddon replied the following day, saying that he had visited Pusey and found him 'on the whole much better than I had expected':

> I told him that you had asked for him, and he desired me to write 'a loving message'. But I did not say more about the contents of your letter. He has not a shadow of doubt as to the entire consistency of his position with the Revealed Will of God ... Only the week before last he told me how completely Mr. Allies had failed to answer his own book, 'The Church of England Cleared from the Charge of Schism'; and how inconsistent the history of the African Church, under St. Cyprian and St. Augustine, was with the modern claims of Rome.[210]

Pusey was to live for another four painful years. Allies never relented in his harsh judgment. Indeed, it took Newman's intervention to stop him describing Pusey as 'a tinker'[211] in *Life's Decision*, published in 1880, urging Allies to remember 'how ill he is. How afflicted, and how pained by Sam Wilberforce's letters now published.'[212] Unlike Newman, who never ceased to hope, Allies was sure that only a miraculous intervention could open eyes so tightly shut. But the fact that over a decade since the *Eirenicon* controversy Pusey was still reflecting on the significance to Anglicanism of what Allies had said about the North African Church might indicate that beyond the impregnable exterior he still found the need to wrestle with certainty of his opponent.

A broken friendship

As with Pusey, so with those inside the fold who sought to question the extent of papal power; Allies was harsh and Newman more understanding. After Döllinger's papal censure they disagreed about him. In a letter of 8 March 1866 Allies cautioned Newman about Henry Nutcombe Oxenham,[213] who he said was translating a work considered scurrilous (*Fables Respecting the Popes in the Middle Ages*). Newman replied briskly that his friend was translating another, quite different, Döllinger book, 'an account of how Christianity grew up out of Paganism',[214] adding it 'will be bristling with facts rather than drawing out views', before adding, 'you yourself have leant a good deal on his former work. Thank you, however, for mentioning the matter'. Their relationship was evidently under increasing strain, because in response to Allies's request that he review three articles intended for the *Atlantis*,[215] Newman had replied: 'I would gladly engage in a task so interesting as that of looking over your lectures, but I really have not the time'.[216] Allies wrote again to explain that when his informant had been unsure which book Oxenham was working on he had suggested the *Fables* to him; however, the Döllinger work being translated was one he knew well and to which he had no objection. But he now decided that he owed it to their friendship to be candid:

> you have taken so kindly to what I have said, and I am so sure of my own intentions in what I write on this, that I venture to say one word more. It is possible that you do not know to what degree Acton and Simpson and Company claim you on their side; how they say Fr. Newman never speaks more than half his mind: we speak out what he *means*. And how again, persons most opposed to Acton and Simpson are inclined to say what they say on this matter. Of course, it would help both sides to see a book of Döllinger's translated by Oxenham and dedicated to you. You probably mean it as a mark that you sympathise with what some think hard treatment received by Oxenham. But it would carry a much larger meaning to both

these classes. Few things in this world would grieve me more than not to feel that there was a deep gulph between you and Acton and Simpson, though particular circumstances lead you to sympathise in one or two points with them. Just then when it seems as if two parties were likely to grow which would be a great calamity to the whole Catholic cause in England. I mean a party taking you for their watchword, and a party taking the Archbishop, comes an act slight in itself, but associating you much in appearance with the most extreme and heterodox. And then again Döllinger is understood to be writing against the Temporal Power. Five years ago when the work O. is translating came out, to have dedicated it to you would have borne no signification. Will it bear none now?[217]

Newman did not reply immediately and his response went through several drafts, its tone marked by a restrained anger:

I am glad to hear from you that the report, that I was giving currency to some statement about 'Papal Fables' rests on no better foundation than you now assign to it. It has brought before me vividly, as never before, in what way false reports grow and take shape; and how they are proof against antecedent probability ...

Thank you for now stating your real objection to the leave I have given to Oxenham,—which lies it seems, not against the work dedicated, but against the person dedicating ...

It has to be shown that the 'understanding' that Döllinger is writing against the Temporal Power of which you speak, has better foundation than the report about 'Papal Fables' ... But antecedent probability goes for nothing against 'understandings' ...

As to certain friends of mine, whom you mention, who are reported to say that I only half speak out my mind ... All I can say is this, that I have before now spoken out my mind to you with a freedom which I have never used towards them ... This will enable you to judge of the value of this report.[218]

Allies cited Dean as the source of the misinformation about Oxenham and protested that he was innocent of giving it 'any currency'. He then explainted that it was the archbishop himself who had privately challenged him: 'Do you know what is coming upon you—Döllinger is writing against the Temporal Power'. For Manning to link him in this way with the dissentient must have been disconcerting, and he felt he should warn Newman. 'You do not read German and may not be wary enough, relying on Döllinger's great name.'[219] After this exchange of correspondence, Newman treated Allies with greater reserve. Thus when acknowledging receipt of *Dr. Pusey and the Ancient Church* (April 1866), his only comment was, 'you seem to have done your work very thoroughly ... Thank you for quoting a passage from me at p. 67. It will do me service in this season of lies.'[220] In the summer, when visiting London, he declined an invitation to stay with him and Eliza.

Their correspondence then lapsed, but was taken up again when Fr Ignatius Ryder, a priest at the Birmingham Oratory, criticised Allies's statement (in his reply to Pusey) that outside Catholic unity grace was not communicated in the sacraments, observing that 'not every schismatic was a formal heretic'. Newman referred the objection to him observing that there was a difference between active and negative schism: the Anglican's conscious rejection of the papacy was 'a definite, active opposition, a doctrinal opposition, which must be of the nature of heresy.'[221] Allies did not dispute the distinction but said that 'negative schism, if continued long would be sure to make itself a heresy.'[222] Ryder was soon to make himself the avowed enemy of the Ultramontanes when he decided to take on Ward, whose strong infallibilist views were set forth in *The Authority of Doctrinal Decisions which are not Definitions of Faith*, published in 1866, a series of essays culled from the *Dublin Review*. Some flavour of the controversy these articles had generated is contained in the author's apology: 'I really cannot admit that the confidence of my tone has been in itself a proof of arrogance. I have been confident in maintaining my main theses, because it seems so absolutely unquestionable, by any one who takes pains to examine, that the Church teaches them.'[223] Ryder believed that there was a case to be made against theological absolutism, and set it out the following year in a pamphlet, *Idealism in Theology, A Review of Dr. Ward's Scheme of Dogmatic Authority*, the tone of which may be gathered from its dedicatory quotation from *Timon of Athens*: 'The middle of humanity thou never knewest, but the extremity of both ends'. It was a frontal attack on the 'tyranny of lay journalism', and began with the declaration: 'It is notorious that in some minds the craving for ideal completeness is so strong as to overpower from time to time their sense of truth'.[224] The controversy continued in the Catholic press, with Ward making full use of the pages of the *Dublin Review* to press his case against the 'Gallicans'. Of course, the tide was running with him and he had the full support of the archbishop and, among others, Allies, who to emphasise his commitment to the cause contributed four articles to the *Dublin Review*: four chapters taken from volume II of the *Formation of Christendom*, due to be published in 1869.[225] Fr Ignatius would not have published without the approval of his Superior, underlining the distance that now separated Allies from the Oratory.

In October 1866 Allies, in his role as 'candid friend', wrote to Newman about his recent Rosary Sunday sermon, concerned that the popular press had misrepresented him as dissenting from Manning on the need for the pope to be a secular prince. Allies's friend 'Deacon' Palmer, who had heard the sermon, was sure that its publication would end suspicion.[226] Newman agreed to publish but observed that the newspaper accounts were '*in the main* accurate'. Adding, 'But of course I know nothing of what kind friends and enemies say about me privately without foundation'.[227] Allies wrote back that he was sure that the pope's temporal authority over Rome and the Latium was of unique importance: 'its end would be a victory for evil.' He branded Napoleon III's conduct towards the Holy Father as 'so atrocious that one of the things for which I most desire to live is to see him punished signally before God and man for his treachery'.[228] Newman rebuked him: surely such vehemence stemmed from a lack of faith?

> to make his temporal power necessary in *all* states, when I have no word of Scripture, tradition, the Pope or the Church to make me say so is simply unbelieving. God can support his Church by every word that goeth out of His mouth, and it is well to tell Protestants this, that we do not depend upon

man, and that, if they take away (by God's permission) the temporal power, still the Church is the Church still.

We ought to pray and to do our part for the preservation of the temporal power, but it is most undignified to shriek, most undignified to say, 'it is all along of Louis Napoleon.' It may be so, but it does not become the Church of God to imply that mortal man can do us real harm, or to be angry with those who ill treat her. All things will turn to good. The Apostles did not shriek when they were put in prison ... [A] sacred cause is lowered and disgraced by the appearance of abject fear.[229]

Allies replied, unconvinced, but thanking him for publishing his 'beautiful sermon' ('The Pope and the Revolution'), saying he had sent copies to three Protestant friends.[230]

The final act in their estrangement had to do with Newman's dream of returning to Oxford, 'home of lost causes and forsaken beliefs.'[231] Bishop Ullathorne, with the best of intentions, proposed the building of a church in Oxford splendid enough to mark so rich a harvest of converts, and that the Oratorians should take responsibility for it. Propaganda was consulted and agreed with the project but stipulated that Newman should not reside in the city: the number of Catholic undergraduates was a serious concern, and it was feared that his presence would attract many more. Unfortunately, he was not told of the inhibition and enthusiastically prepared a prospectus, which in January 1867 he sent to wealthy Catholics. However, he delayed circulating the appeal in London, telling Allies that it was unlikely that the archbishop would approve of a scheme 'connected with me'. Not until March did he ask for Allies's support in raising contributions from the capital: 'From your position, you can do a great deal in the way of distributing the Circulars; and it would be a great kindness, if you would also undertake to receive small sums ... We have promises to the amount of £5,000, but the second £5,000 will be the difficulty.'[232] Only two years had passed since Allies had written enthusiastically about the value of an Oxford education, but now that the bishops had rejected a Catholic college, the position was clear. He replied:

A New Life 303

Now ever since I came to think seriously on religion, I have detested the notion of mixed education ... I learnt this principle from you, and your life has hitherto been the strongest exhibition of it. You went to Dublin to carry out the principle that Catholics alone should educate Catholics ... I may claim then your authority and your life in testimony to the principle that Catholics putting themselves spontaneously under heretical teachers commit both a crime and a mistake: sacrifice at once both honour and safety, and in sending my token of goodwill for your mission at Oxford, I am not countenancing what I should most abhor, what would be a repudiation of your principles as well as mine in past life.[233]

He reminded Newman of what he had said sixteen years before—that it would be 'too painful' for him to return to Oxford, and stipulated that his gift of £5 should not be used to encourage Catholics to enter Protestant colleges. He apologised that a lack of contacts prevented him from distributing the appeal in London. It was the second time in two years that the merits of an Oratorian presence in Oxford had been debated, and on the previous occasion Allies had signed the following address:

> The undersigned, having heard that the Sacred College of the Propaganda is about to consider the question, whether British Catholics shall be permitted to frequent the Universities of Oxford and Cambridge, venture respectfully to hope that the Sacred Congregation will not think its active interference necessary.[234]

Despite implying that his mentor might have fallen from grace, he was conscious of no inconsistency himself. Newman denied the charge, saying that he had always believed that it was possible for even the most zealous to consent to 'schemes of Education from which Religion is altogether or almost excluded, from the stress of necessity, or the recommendations of expedience.' As regards his returning to Oxford, the pain had not diminished; it would be a 'living death', but he could not refuse a divine call. The final sentence of this letter ended his closeness to Allies: 'Certainly I should never have thought it my duty to ask you for a contribution, had I anticipated it would be so ungraciously granted.'[235] The response was immediate, Allies protested that he had long believed Newman should be at Oxford and had no intention of impugning inconsistency 'in the way you imagine.' However,

> your note drove me into a corner, because I knew people were claiming you as a patron of the scheme of sending individual Catholics to Oxford and welcomed your going thither not so much for the purpose assigned in the Bishop's letter, but for this ... You have been forced in your life to express dissent from those you most loved. Have then compassion on me.[236]

When the Vatican's full terms became known the project did not proceed, and unattributed press reports appeared in Rome, stating that Newman's orthodoxy had been called into question. At home influential Catholic laity leaped to his defence and in April a letter appeared in the *Tablet* with over 180 signatures, headed by that of the Earl Marshal, expressing 'our gratitude for all we owe you, and to assure you how heartily we appreciate the services which, under God, you have been the means of rendering to our Holy Religion'. Allies's name was not included. When, five years later, Newman returned his £5 contribution, Allies, unlike others in this position, chose to keep it.[237]

The question of Catholic access to higher education remained unresolved. In the autumn of 1867 Newman, having been told by Father Weld, the Jesuit provincial, that Manning wished to establish a 'house of higher studies', pondered what he should do if invited to serve on an advisory committee. Writing to Hope-Scott, he had little doubt that any colleagues Westminster selected would be uncongenial, citing such names as 'G. W. [sic] Ward, Allies, H. Wilberforce, Lord Petre, Lewis and Sir G. Bowyer.'[238] Thus was Thomas consigned to the inner circle of 'Intransigents'. Yet unfairly so, because he and Allies were as one on the unique value of Oxford and the harmful consequences of Catholic exclusion, a belief Allies reiterated in 1872, when, in responding to a questionnaire about Catholic higher education from a sub-committee of the bishops, he rejected any plan that did not involve a Catholic college at either or both the ancient universities. The aim of education was surely 'not so much to produce *Fachmänner*, as to strengthen, enlarge, consolidate, and exercise the mind itself ... Now from all this ... as yet, the children of the Catholic nobility, gentry, and professional classes are excluded.' This was also Newman's perspective, but not Manning's, who was suspicious of such elitism and wished to provide the Catholic middle class with relevant and practical higher education.

Allies denied that Oxford was out of touch with modern society: 'Middle education is being connected with the university. Modern history, modern languages, and law are being taken into the curriculum.' But this was not the point: was it not generally acknowledged that 'Catholic youth on their entrance into manhood betray a certain apathy and listlessness in comparison with non-Catholic youths of corresponding position'? And in remedying this, mechanistic options such as 'a central board of examiners for Catholics more or less on the model of the University of London' would not do. 'I consider the value of an university education to consist in the effect produced on the mind by a residence in it.'[239] He had little faith in Manning's favoured policy:

> As 'for the foundation of one or more separate houses of higher study, such as might form the nucleus of a future Catholic university,' I take the value of the suggestion to lie in the probability of the nucleus developing, and this to my mind is simply *nil* ... We have not a population sufficient for it. We have enough to make a good college at an existing university but not enough to make anything by itself and of ourselves worthy of that great name ... I consider the notion of an English Catholic University to be like a comet of very irregular orbit ... After watching these alternate phases and effacements for more than twenty years, I have come to the conclusion that a separate university for English Catholics is a mere phantom of cloud cuckoo land.[240]

In proposing a Catholic college at Oxford,

> I do not mean to suggest any concession to the plan of mixed

> education. What presents itself to my mind is a Catholic College, as a complete whole, teaching the entire range of university instruction within its own walls, under exclusively Catholic tutors and rulers, so that the students should never look upon any but those of their own faith as instructors.

There was no need to fear contamination from having to study a curriculum set by the Protestant authorities:

> neither in theology nor in mental and moral philosophy would any studies be required which would be dangerous to the faith. It is stated that there is a strong desire to treat us with fairness, accompanied by the wish that all should be represented at Oxford.[241]

Newman agreed that a Catholic university could not succeed. But wounded by experience he was sceptical about Allies's vision, fearing that the academic freedom of a Catholic college would be hobbled by an 'ultra clique, whose gossip is taken in Rome and by Propaganda as nothing short of gospel'. His reluctant conclusion was that 'mixed education' was the only way forward:

> I should say that the Bishops ought to have left things alone seven years ago, and that in our present straits, they will do best to undo their own work, and let Catholics go to Protestant Colleges (without their formal sanction,) and to provide a strong Mission worked by theologians, i.e. a strong Jesuit mission, to protect Catholic youths from the infidelity of the place.[242]

Manning remained wedded to the idea that a university like Louvain might eventually emerge. Following the Fourth Provincial Council of Westminster in 1873, the bishops decreed that 'the growth of the middle and upper classes of our laity, and the opening of the career of professional and public service render it necessary to lay at least the foundations of a system of Higher Education, such as are required by

A New Life 307

our youth from seventeen to twenty-one or twenty-two years of age'. The first step was the formation of a senate 'representing the experience and needs of the Catholics of the higher classes, and also to afford counsel derived from practical acquaintance with literature, science and art'. Invited to be a senator, Allies was dubious but was prepared to play his part.[243] Other senators had their own agendas; for example, some 'Old Catholics' thought that higher studies should be in the hands of the Jesuits, and free from episcopal control. Thus politics interfered. At the first Senate meeting (May 1874) an attempt was made to exclude the bishops from the deliberations. Manning's response was not to convene it again.[244] After the debacle of his Dublin professorship, Allies's second foray into Catholic higher education proved to be equally futile if far more short-lived: 'The Kensington University College solemnly opened in 1875 came to an ignominious end as a work of the English hierarchy in 1878'.[245]

A process of healing

The arguments over the expediency of defining formally the personal infallibility of the pope encapsulated the gulf that had developed between Allies and his once beloved mentor. Thus Allies was delighted to learn of the summoning of an Ecumenical Council, knowing that Pius IX wished that the belief should become a doctrine of the universal Church. Newman on the other hand made no secret of his foreboding; thus when Canon Estcourt had asked him in October 1868 to support a proposed society for the publication of Catholic educational books (principally to create employment for Anglican clerical converts), he replied somewhat sarcastically. 'It seems to me that the subject of your letter is as deserving the notice of authorities at Rome though it does not bear immediately upon the aggrandisement of the Chair of Peter, as some other matters which are watched there with keen interest'.[246] He quite accepted the infallibility of Peter's see but saw no pressing need for the first Ecumenical Council since Trent three hundred years before. A year later, after the bishops had assembled, Herbert Vaughan, the editor of the *Tablet*, asked him to join with many others in supporting the 'movement ... the cause we have at heart'; he replied 'I am not partial to what you call "movements"—In the Catholic Church I consider *rest* the better thing.'²⁴⁷ To Ullathorne on the same day in January 1870 he unburdened his heart:

> No impending danger is to be averted, but a great difficulty is to be created. Is this the proper work for an Ecumenical Council? As to myself personally, please God, I do not expect any trial at all; but I cannot help suffering with the various souls which are suffering, and I look with anxiety at the prospect of having to defend decisions, which may not be difficult to my private judgment, but may be most difficult to maintain logically in the face of historical facts. What have we done to be treated, as the faithful never were treated before?²⁴⁸

These were sentiments that Acton shared. Newman had been expending his intellectual energy in building up the walls of belief rather than those protecting Rome, and was in the process of finishing his masterpiece, *An Essay in Aid of a Grammar of Assent*. Unfortunately, coinciding with its publication in March, his private letter to Ullathorne appeared in the newspapers. A few days later on Palm Sunday (10 April) Allies wrote to the *Tablet* to voice his 'sincere desire that the present Council of the Vatican may by a clear and indubitable definition set its seal' on the doctrine that had made him a Catholic: 'that the power of universal jurisdiction, which no one can be a Catholic without admitting to reside in the Holy See requires for its exercise the gift likewise of infallible authority.' The letter marks both his intellectual distancing from, and his enduring affection for, Father Newman; he quotes a phrase from the now published private letter: 'we are all at rest and have no doubt and at least practically if not doctrinally, hold the Holy Father to be infallible.' He gently chides the author 'surely the conclusion to be drawn from all this is, that no Catholic should be allowed to deny that without admitting which it is impossible to maintain the infallibility of the Church.' But then Allies goes on to quote from the *Grammar* a panegyric on the Athanasian Creed as expressing 'all he believed.' And so, as regards infallibility:

A New Life

> I do not accept it because I cannot help it; but I exult in it as a glorious endowment bestowed on the Church ... And so I pray that ... the honour of St. Peter's See may be completed while Pius IX is its occupant in 1870. Nor can I fear the effect of this upon those within and upon those without. To the men of my own time whom I have known, the most learned, the most intellectual, the most earnest of the converts, this doctrine never was a stumbling-block.[249]

Newman wondered how much of the *Grammar* he actually understood: 'It amused me to find Allies and Dalgairns found my book difficult. I don't say it is not—but I know that, among clever men, they are the least clear headed that I know—and I have long thought so.'[250]

Once the excitement and division surrounding the definition had died away most English Catholics united around the limited and careful statement of the doctrine that had been so overwhelmingly endorsed by the bishops during a memorable thunder storm on 18 July 1870. Anglicans were less sanguine and Gladstone believed the doctrine was a threat to the integrity of the British constitution. His concerns were decisively answered in Newman's *Letter to the Duke of Norfolk*, published in January 1875, and Allies was among those who effusively welcomed this classic analysis of the relationship between conscience and the principle of religious authority.[251] Thereafter there was a gradual healing of the rift between them. The Infallibilists could afford to be magnanimous: their party had conquered the field, and Allies, seeking now to mend bridges, dedicated the third volume of the *Formation of Christendom* to his oldest friend (dated 21 February 1875, Newman's birthday), acknowledging that the origin of the work was his appointment as Reader in the Catholic University of Ireland. It was a warm tribute, not simply to the illumination that Newman the theologian had provided, but also to 'the force which your example added to follow that light into the knowledge, peace and liberty of the Catholic communion.'[252]

Contributing to their reconciliation was a shared friendship with William Palmer, the eldest son of Allies's erstwhile Anglican colleague, the rector of Mixbury. Ordained deacon in 1832, Palmer never proceeded to the priesthood; from 1838, as tutor of Magdalen College, his developing High Church sympathies led him to seek Orthodox recognition of Anglicanism's Catholicity through the principle of intercommunion. Supported by Martin Routh, the venerable college President, he went twice to St Petersburg but failed to secure endorsement of the Thirty-nine Articles. In the face of these rebuffs, in 1855 in Rome, he was received into the Catholic Church. There he settled, but was often in London, usually staying with Thomas and Eliza and regarded as an old family friend. When Thomas sent him a copy of the *Letter to the Duke of Norfolk* he praised it as an 'effective answer ... if anything can move honest Protestants or mitigate their prejudices that ought to do so ... I expect many minds will be permanently influenced by F. Newman's answer.'[253] Allies transcribed these words and sent them to Birmingham. In later years both he and Palmer were occasional visitors to the Oratory and each year Allies would send birthday greetings to Newman, sometimes in verse.

Palmer died in Rome on 5 April 1879, living just long enough to hear confirmation of Newman's elevation to the cardinalate. This honour was the culmination of a campaign of the English laity led by the Duke of Norfolk, initiated soon after the commencement of Leo XIII's papacy in 1878. On Tuesday 18 February 1879 *The Times* reported that the new pope had 'intimated his desire to raise Dr. Newman to the rank of cardinal, but that he had 'excused himself from accepting the sacred purple'. Two days later Allies attended a meeting of the Catholic Union, where resolutions were passed expressing profound gratification at the honour done to 'one whose name is especially dear and precious to the Catholics of the British Empire and also justly venerated and cherished by his countrymen generally for his high moral and intellectual endowments'. That evening Allies wrote to him:

> For myself I am thankful to have lived long enough to see that done which for twenty years I have desire to see. I have known since May last that the Duke [of Norfolk] and Lord Ripon were striving to make known to the Holy Father what was the wish of so many and I knew that the Duke in December was the first to urge it personally to the Holy Father. But the Holy

A New Life

> Father does not know English, and has had few opportunities of knowing our country's thought and mind. Therefore the success of these efforts was almost beyond one's hope, and gratification is in proportion to preceding fears.
> Though you have thought fit to decline the dignity, the fact remains in all its greatness.[254]

This letter must have crossed in the post with one to him from Newman:

> What the Papers are saying about me implies that I have received a letter from Rome and have replied to it.
> I have ever thought such communications were sacred and that it would be most rude and (so to say) ungentlemanlike to give out 'I have received an offer and refused it'.
> But anyhow what is to be thought of those who instead of letting the Pope himself read his own letter (in the case supposed) letting him read and interpret it, intercept it half way, put their own interpretation upon it and give that interpretation to the world?
> That interpretation was communicated to others long before the supposed letter could have got to Rome.[255]

Allies replied on Friday 21st, 'Your remarks seem to me most just and to apply with great force to those who have rendered themselves subject to them'. Both knew that Manning had assumed responsibility for forwarding Newman's—admittedly somewhat ambiguous—response to the papal offer on to Rome. The next day Allies wrote to him again:

> Last week on Wednesday I think (12 February) rumours reached me that you had received the offer of a Hat, and had declined it. I went to one intimately known both to you and to me, and asked him if he knew the truth. He replied, I know Dr. Gilbert is saying this. As yet I don't believe it.[256]
> What Dr. Gilbert said on such a subject of course spread like wild-fire.
> But I was assured by another person on Tuesday, (18th),

who told me first of the announcement in *The Times*, that Cardinal Manning made no secret of the matter at all.[257]

Daniel Gilbert was the archbishop's Vicar-General. On 20 February a Miss Munro, who knew many London Catholics, had written to Fr Neville of the Oratory: 'Mr. Allies denies *in toto* the Father declined. At Archbishop's House they say he did.' In fact, Newman's letter to Rome had not been a rejection but a rather delicately expressed reluctance to living the remainder of his life in Rome, the normal requirement for cardinals without episcopal responsibilities. Unaware that Manning, who had now arrived there, was himself the source of the confusion, the Duke of Norfolk wrote to him to clarify Newman's thinking. Whereupon the archbishop waited on the Pope and the matter was soon resolved. Before long a committee was established with Allies as one of its secretaries to receive donations for a congratulatory presentation.[258]

As the two men grew older something of their old intimacy was restored, with the cardinal taking an interest in Allies's efforts to encourage his daughter's literary career. Her father had hoped that Mary might edit, with a view to publication, Palmer's journals of his theological travels to Russia and the Levant, as the explanation of why he had found his way not to Orthodoxy but to the Church of Rome. Allies wrote to Newman proposing this, adding that 'from frequent conversations with him during the many years in which he partially lived with us... I often pressed him to draw out a narrative of the course of thought by which at length he became a Catholic'. Newman replied that he too had urged publication and as the manuscripts had been bequeathed to him it was fitting that he should undertake the duty of editor. So it was that in 1882 he published W. Palmer's *Notes of a Visit to the Russian Church*, adding a brief account of the author's life.[259]

On 21 February 1884 Cardinal Newman celebrated his eighty-third birthday, and among the congratulatory letters was one from Thomas Allies, now numbered among the oldest of his friends, who had himself reached the age of seventy-one a few days before. In the light of eternity the differences that had once divided them seemed insubstantial: Allies, who had so many reasons to be grateful to him, was unstinting in his praise:

A New Life

> I have been accustomed to put you in my thoughts with St. Augustine and St. Thomas: because I seem to be more indebted to those three than to any other ... and it is through you that I came to appreciate them. For when I had no guide as an Anglican, and though in orders looked all around in vain for coherent theological instruction, you nursed me, as it were a child, full of errors and false conceptions, and brought me to a better mind—And it was through testing a page of 'Development' that I came to the final enfranchisement of the Faith.[260]

When Allies was eighty-five, Father Neville of the Oratory wrote to him seeking details of the formal addresses to Newman with which he had been associated. Replying, he sought to relieve what might have been a troubled conscience, saying that it was a recurring thought that his greatest friend had been unfairly treated:

> I never lost an opportunity of setting forth to the utmost of my ability what he had done and was then doing. The more so because I felt deeply the bitterness of the jealousy which a certain person felt against him, by whom he was treated as an old coach shunted off the line. I shall never forget the manner in which the suggestion that he should be made a cardinal was that day received.[261]

Political engagement: The Catholic Union

As a representative of the laity Allies took his place in the second rank behind the Catholic nobility, but it was nevertheless an influential place and made more so by his many years on the governing body of the Catholic Union. This sounding board for Catholic opinion was established by Manning in 1870 'to promote by every legitimate means the restoration of the Papal States to the Pope'. Thereafter its perspective and influence gradually widened although always within the limits imposed by the archbishop. Newman had refused to have anything to do with it, despite the urgings of its first secretary, John Wallis, who had owned and edited the *Tablet* until retiring in 1868, disenchanted with the policy of the hierarchy. Writing to Newman he conceded the pomposity of the Union's stated objective of restoring 'the Pope to his legitimate rights as Sovereign of the States of the Church', saying that he had accepted the position as a duty, because 'I was jealous of the honour and character of the English Catholic body'.[262] Newman, whilst sympathising with his self-denial in accepting such 'irksome and thankless' responsibilities, felt no similar calling:

> It is now some years since I came to the conclusion that I should never find myself taking part in any large religious association of any kind. Westminster must be its headquarters in England, and I have an utter distrust of Westminster. Many years ago I was asked to join the Academia. I said I would wait till I was sure that the Pope's temporal power and similar objects were not the real aim of a Society which professed to be of a general literary and theological character—and I think the event has proved I had reason for waiting.[263]

In the years after the Franco-Prussian War, with secularism on the march all over Europe, the Catholic Union widened its perspective. Allies remained intensely interested in the continental Church and in July 1872 at a meeting convened to protest at anti-Church measures in Italy and Germany he made what the *Tablet* described as 'the speech of the meeting, literally bristling with facts and arguments'. The *Saturday Review* took a different view, dismissing his contribution as a piece of 'frothy declamation', a phrase which, according to the *Dublin Review*, exemplified the 'contemptuous and contemptible indifference to things Catholic which characterizes the English Protestant press'.[264] The only exception that the *Dublin* took to Allies's speech concerned a betrayal of his lingering affection for the now excommunicated Döllinger, whom he described as 'the most unhappy of priests', who in old age had destroyed by 'an act of intense pride and overwhelming self-sufficiency the glory of so many years spent as a defender and champion of the Church.'[265] The speech detailing numerous acts of expropriation and suppression was later published as a pamphlet.²⁶⁶

Mass meetings in Willis's rooms did nothing to moderate Victor Emmanuel's government or stop Bismarck in his tracks, nor restrain the anticlerical impulses of French Republicans. Allies read an apocalyptic significance into all this. For example, in 1876 he attended the Austrian Congress of Catholic Unions, and on return reported on the proceedings to his English colleagues, musing on the fact that two years before the first European Congress had been held at a location close to Geneva. It was, he said, 'the very spot where the wicked machinations of Voltaire and his adherents were hatched', and where were sown 'the seeds of crime and misery, the bitter fruit of which was that dreadful revolution which desolated France and even all Europe'. Now Bismarck, the heir of the Enlightenment, had sufficient guns and ammunition to impose by state power the destructive 'false philosophy' that denied the whole supernatural order: 'either this great system of naturalism and positivism must prevail, and the Christian Church must be exterminated; or the Christian Church must win one of its battles ... as important as that battle commenced in the sixteenth century'.²⁶⁷

With the pope a 'prisoner in the Vatican', Allies had no doubt about the reality of 'the Revolution', an amorphous coalition of forces committed to destroying the Church. In 1887 he contributed a chapter to a work edited by Wilfrid Meynell (under the pen-name 'John Oldcastle') celebrating ten years of Leo XIII's pontificate. He identified five characteristics of the enemy's strategy: to widen the division between Church and state; to destroy the indissolubility of marriage; to undermine property rights; to replace the bonds of trust by a 'calculation of expedience'; and underpinning all, the propagation a false philosophy which questioned 'the very basis of belief in all things beyond the senses'. Yet, he concluded, there was no cause for fear, the purposes of God could not be thwarted, had not Pope Leo's concordats already done much to reverse the enemy's gains? Looking back over forty years during which the papal throne had surely received added lustre, Allies was confident of ultimate victory over forces 'neither less numerous nor less destructive than the hordes of Attila'. The Scythian's advance had been providentially checked and now again a 'repetition of the first Leo in another form' was 'an augury of the salvation preparing for the future'.²⁶⁸

Not all Catholics shared his dread of the evolving secular state. At a meeting of the Catholic Union in 1876 the truculent Irish nationalist F. H. O'Donnell questioned why Allies—as chairman of the publication committee—had countenanced a recent pamphlet which was plainly 'an attack on democracy', and therefore on the views of 'the Irish working men of this country'. Such dissension was rare in the Union and the objection was over-ruled, but Allies remained the person he had been in 1832, when he had spoken against democracy in the Oxford Union, and events in Europe since that date had given him no reason to modify his views.[269] And despite many years spent working for the education of the Irish in England, and, despite his son being an Irish landowner, Allies was uncomfortable with Irish culture and political aspirations and strongly opposed home rule. Thus he sought to influence the general election campaign of 1892 by contributing to the *Nineteenth Century* one of a series of ten articles on the theme 'Why I shall vote for the Unionists'. His warnings as to the consequences of devolution seem surprisingly prescient:

> I look upon it as a rapier thrust at the heart of England. Any sort of Parliament now set up at Dublin entails a second parliament at Edinburgh and a third at Caerleon. It is the dissolution of the Empire. One word of Canning dispatches it, 'Repeal the Union; restore the Heptarchy.'
>
> It undoes all the gains of the last hundred years, not to make even Ireland one country, but to plant civil war between its Catholic and Protestant populations.
>
> A Parliament at Dublin inspired by one mind and a Parliament at Westminster inspired by another, would render the Crown itself as great an absurdity as 252 different religions make Christianity a mockery.[270]

England had no Catholic political party, and taking his lead from Cardinal Manning, Allies was quite willing to support the secular state and enter into its political life. His work for the Poor-School Committee had given him confidence in the *bona fides* of successive governments; nevertheless constant vigilance was required, and he remained suspicious of Gladstonian liberalism. Although willing to work with Anglicanism in support of voluntary schools he dismissed it as system established to keep the sheep away from the one true fold. Thus Allies's last contribution to the *Dublin Review* was a bitingly sarcastic review of the Lambeth Conference of 1888, in which he asked what could be expected of an institution established by a king, who 'broke every law, divine and human, to obtain possession of a woman whom he presently beheaded, and by whom he left an adulterine bastard daughter to consummate his work'? In its dismissal of Anglican orders, jurisdiction, doctrine and insularity the article covers familiar ground. But a new claim from the Ritualists—that they possessed the *sacerdotium*, a divine power to offer Christ for the quick and the dead—is dismissed with particular scorn. It was a battle he had been fighting for forty years and still the English Establishment remained unshaken. And so it would continue, for as Allies complained, his opponents would not engage on his chosen ground. The Anglicans ignored his every challenge: 'To take no notice is they think, more profitable than to attempt to refute.'[271]

As a Catholic but also as a patriot Allies took a leading part in the campaign for the beatification of the English Reformation martyrs and to this end made at least one journey to Rome (in 1879) as a member of a delegation of prominent laymen. Their efforts came to fruition on 29 December 1886 when Rome decreed that Thomas More and John Fisher along with fifty-two others were now to be called Blessed. At a meeting of the Catholic Union on 23 February Allies read this address to the pope, which was unanimously endorsed:

> We acknowledge it as a bright spot on an otherwise dark horizon: as a token of moral victories to come in addition to the many the present time has seen. The Holy See, in the person of Leo XIII, acknowledges the martyrs who bled especially for it ... At the hands of Leo XIII, we receive this fresh 'pledge from Rome of Rome's unending love.'[272]

Secretary of the Catholic Poor-School Committee

Allies took up his post on 1 August 1853, at time of crisis for Catholic education. Driven by famine, hundreds of thousands of Irish were moving to England and Scotland, settling mainly in the large towns and cities and adding to an already large number of immigrants. The census of 1851 showed that one quarter of Liverpool's population had been born in Ireland (some 90,000 souls) and in Manchester about 15% (50,000). The number of Roman Catholic children requiring education posed an immense challenge for the Church. They needed to be taught to read and write and they needed nurturing in the faith, an objective—the salvation of souls—which the members of the Committee in appointing Allies as their secretary correctly believed he fully shared.

The state too was concerned for the education of its citizens and in 1833 had begun to fund the elementary schools provided by the Established Church (through the National Society) and the Nonconformist denominations (through the British and Foreign School Society). In 1847 this aid was extended to the Catholic Church. Despite much soul-searching the Vicars Apostolic had accepted that for financial reasons an application for state assistance was unavoidable and had established the Poor-School Committee as their channel of communication with the government (specifically the Education Committee of the Privy Council) and with the districts (dioceses after 1850). It had twenty-four members: one clerical and two lay representatives from each district, with Charles Langdale as chairman[273] and Scott Naysmith Stokes as its first secretary.[274] The latter, a recent convert who had been appointed at Wiseman's recommendation resigned in 1853 to take up a post as the second Catholic Inspector of Schools (Her Majesty's Inspector, HMI). For several months the chairman had to act as secretary, until Allies's success in the July election.

Each morning Allies left his home for 'dull John Street', his office in Grays Inn. Despite some lack of enthusiasm, he must have been aware of the Committee's national importance in shaping the future of Catholic elementary education. As its membership met in full session only once a year their full-time secretary played a key role in implementing policy and in coordinating: between chairman and members and between the bishops and the government. At the end of his first full year in office Allies set out Committee's vision for the future in its Seventh Annual Report (for 1854). His starting point was the desperate unmet need. Using the 1851 census,[275] and from other information, the Catholic

A New Life

population of England and Wales was estimated at 1.2 million, of whom three-fourths could be classified as poor and needing assistance with the education of their children:

> assuming one-fourth as the proportion of those who are of school age, we fix the number who ought to be in attendance at 225,000. The real number for which accommodation is supplied in any Poor Schools, of any kind, inspected or uninspected, appears to be not more than 66,362. There are therefore in the year 1855, upwards of 158,000 Catholic children who, if they are taught anywhere are *not* taught in Catholic schools.

The state had decided that poverty should no longer exclude any child from education. Leaving their children uneducated could no longer be an option for Catholics, notwithstanding that very many were numbered among the very poorest in society: 'the most destitute of the destitute in the richest nation of the world.' This could not continue; the state has 'for the last fifteen years, awakened out of a long neglect, set itself with remarkable zeal and earnestness to the work of educating the poor ... The poor twentieth cannot reverse its (the State's) decision. If they will not educate their own poor, someone else will educate them instead. They will not be left for ever to swarm in courts, and sweep crossings in rags'. Allies noted that Protestants was responding to the challenge with zeal, seeking to sweep up Catholic children into their schools.

> They will provide good schools, wherein kindness will be will be shown to children who have hitherto experienced little of it in the world, wherein a multitude of useful things will be taught them, and last not least, if not the Protestant religion, at least hatred of the Catholic faith.
>
> There was a time when nobody cared to take what we so surrendered. Poor Catholics were then a sort of savage nature, which was left to run wild. It has now been thought wiser as well as more humane, to see whether the taint in their blood, the belief in the Catholic faith might not be

eradicated by general cultivation, and so the *stirps ferina et celtica* (a race of Celtic wild beasts) be humanised into an Anglo-Saxon population.

If we would keep our children, the only means are to provide good schools, wherein secular instruction shall be given with as much ability as elsewhere, whilst religious instruction and the formation of character are *proportionately* attended to.

... there is no argument in the world so strong as a multitude of ignorant Catholic children not taught their duties, and a multitude of Catholic parents of these children not practising them. Such a state of things on a large scale is the converse of what converted the pagan world of old, and instead of 'see how these Christians love one another,' may be said, 'see how little these Catholics care for each other.'

In achieving the desired expansion of Catholic education the Committee's Annual Report identified an underlying deficiency:

institutions for providing trained teachers are wholly wanting. The manager of a school desirous to secure the services of an able master finds himself at a total loss ... If education be a *personal* work, and that most of all in the case of the poor, to whom their teacher must be a living book, it is obvious that education cannot advance without good teachers.

In the building and running of schools and in the training of teachers to mould good citizens, the state was willing to play its part with funds, inspection and encouragement, but for the Church an absolute requirement was for Catholic schools to form good Christians. The Report cited 'the Council of Oscott'[276] as having spoken 'in decided language on this matter': 'While we wish to promote secular instruction equal to what others offer, we consider sound faith, virtue and piety by far the most important elements of education'. And this was Allies's belief, his Committee's philosophy:

We should be the last to depreciate the wonders of God

in the natural world ... But what are these wonders compared to those of the supernatural world, of God deigning to become Man, to have a human Mother, and of the infinite consequences deduced from these facts? These consequences are as interesting to the poorest Irishman's most neglected child, as to the noble blood of Howard or Talbot. But are they likely to assume their due importance in the school, if no note be taken how they are taught ... [to our children] whose inheritance is a faith which can afford matter to exercise the noblest intellect, and devotions to satisfy the most loving heart?²⁷⁷

Given the unmet need an immediate priority for the new secretary was to increase the Committee's annual income. For funds it was heavily dependant on an annual country-wide collection, but according to the 1854 Report almost fifteen percent of missions remitted nothing at all. It was hoped that offenders could be shamed into contributing; for example, one unnamed area was deemed capable of 'rendering a considerable sum' but had for three years failed to respond to all entreaties. Allies's particular concern was the absence of middle-class Catholic contributors: in 1853 only 368 persons contributed £1 or more, with the bulk of the income attributable to the 'Catholic nobility and gentry'. The secretary wrote: it would appear that 'the claims of the Poor-School Committee have hitherto failed to be brought home with efficiency to the far larger portion of the independent, the professional, and the trading classes'. A poor response, which compared most unfavourably with that of the Wesleyans, and raising the question why 'Catholics care so little for their own poor at home, who are the special inheritance of the Lord?' and reinforcing the admonition of the bishops following the First Synod of Westminster: 'No congregation should be allowed to remain without its schools, one for each sex. Where the poverty of the people is extreme, we earnestly exhort you, whom God has blessed with riches ... to take upon yourselves, lovingly, this burthen'.²⁷⁸

Despite these blandishments the Committee's annual income—before exceptional items such as legacies—at about £4,000 did not rise much until the crisis of 1870. From this grants were made for the maintenance of schools, the purchase of text books and occasionally towards building costs; significantly, the Committee funded teacher-training colleges and offered small rewards to teachers and students of distinction.[279] In addition, the salary of the secretary and a clerk had to be paid, which was later to become a matter of some contention. Given its own meagre resources, the Committee was anxious to promote public funds available for the construction of schools and towards defraying their annual running costs, but within the Catholic community there was some suspicion and also misunderstanding. This the Committee sought to allay, by stressing the government's good intentions, that, for example, in making a building grant the Privy Council acquired no rights as regards the management of the school. And it expressed regret that 'many who come freely to this Committee for building grants seem to seek every excuse for not asking one from public money ... They make the loudest professions of poverty, but decline this source of wealth.' Moreover, accepting such a grant involved no obligation to take up grants available for the running of schools which then became subject to HMI inspection. The Committee noted that down to the end of 1853, of £466,081 awarded by the state towards school building, the Catholic share was £2,283.[280]

Reflecting on the four decades that comprised his secretaryship of the Poor-School Committee, Allies singled out the first as a golden period for Catholic elementary education, characterised by good relationships with successive administrations. Overall government policy was encapsulated in the August 1840 Instructions of the Committee of Council for inspectors of schools: 'Their Lordships are strongly of opinion that no plan of education ought to be encouraged in which intellectual instruction is not subordinate to the regulation of the thoughts and habits of the children by the doctrines and precepts of revealed religion.'[281] But before the government's money could be accepted, its role in the management and inspection of schools had to be carefully delineated. This work was largely complete by the time Allies took up office.[282] For example, at its inception the Poor-School Committee had successfully negotiated that inspectors of Catholic schools should themselves be Catholics and that their remit would not extend to religious education. Yet, some Catholics still feared that as paymaster a future government might interfere with

A New Life

the teaching of doctrine. Another source of anxiety was the stipulation that schools built with state funds should adopt the model trust deed the Committee had negotiated with the Privy Council.[283] This required that schools should be managed by a committee so constituted that, except on religious matters, the priest could be out-voted by the lay members. Attempts had been made to safeguard the priest's position by adding 'moral' issues to 'religious' but the Privy Council would not agree. The Poor-School Committee was impatient with any reluctance to cooperate with the state, but suspicions remained, and in 1856 spilled over into the Catholic press. In November, Henry Formby, a priest, wrote to the *Weekly Register*, accusing Allies of being a 'partisan of the Privy Council' and an enemy to freedom of conscience, when he had questioned whether priests who refused state aid should receive funding from the Committee.[284]

Occupying the centre ground between those who opposed any cooperation with the government and more liberal Catholic thinkers pressing for a greater integration of the Church into the life of the nation stood Cardinal Wiseman and most of the bishops, whose objective was simply stated:

> they prefer the establishment of good schools to every other work. Indeed whenever there may seem to be an opening for a new mission, we should prefer the erection of a school, so arranged as to serve temporarily as a chapel, to that of a church without one ... it is the good school that secures the virtuous and edifying congregation.[285]

To this end the bishops looked to the Poor-School Committee and in particular to its well-remunerated secretary, who they believed was familiar with the workings of the Establishment. The burden remained on Allies's shoulders for the next thirty-six years, although for the second half of this term it was shared by his daughter Mary. She wrote 'I was fortunate enough to act as *his* secretary for eighteen years' (1872–90) 'doing for him the mere clerk's work, which would have so palled on him by robbing him of what he was ever most jealous—his working day'.[286]

When Allies recalled his early days as a 'golden period' he perhaps had not entered into the fears of those who remembered the penal days and had experienced the deep reservoir of anti-Catholic sentiment in English society. Foremost among those who doubted the Poor-School Committee's policy was the bishop of Birmingham, William Bernard Ullathorne.[287] In 1857 he set out his concerns in a widely read pamphlet, *Notes on Education*, which questioned whether the state leopard had really lost its spots; perhaps current parliamentarians were sincere, but they could not bind their successors. The Church's ability to educate the young as it deemed appropriate was too precious a possession to be casually thrown aside:

> After ages of exclusion, as Catholics, from the funds at the command of the State, we are beginning to receive its aid towards educating the poor of our Church. And in return for that aid, as a matter of course, we are giving up something of that absolute freedom and independence of action, which, whatever we have suffered, has been our greatest earthly blessing, and has outbalanced even much of our suffering.[288]

Ullathorne did not deny that much had been achieved and congratulated the Poor-School Committee, under the presidency of Mr Langdale, *clarum et venerabile nomen*:

> the improvement in the whole state and progress of education, of which the Committee has been the chief promoter, has been too manifest to need proof or description. And who can deny that the Government aid and the assistance rendered by the inspectors has had an important share in bringing about the results? Or who will say that we could have brought about anything like the same results without this cooperation? Whether we shall pay too dearly for them in the end, is another question.[289]

Although Ullathorne, like Langdale, came from an old Catholic family, of the two he was more aware of grass-roots' opinion. Like Formby, a number of his hard-pressed priests suspected that those who sought to guide them in educational matters and who solicited the hard-earned pennies of their people, university-educated converts like Stokes and Allies could not properly understand their circumstances nor really enter into their fears. They were suspicious that as ex-Anglicans they were too comfortable with the Establishment and too ready to accept its blandishments. Ullathorne understood these fears, however remote and contingent they might be, and considered them sufficient grounds for seriously questioning over-reliance on state assistance. He accepted that inspection had helped to raise standards, but opening school doors to government functionaries would come at a price: 'If at the back of inspection there is no power of action, then inspection itself is as unmeaning as it is ridiculous ... Turn the subject as we will, and we shall find, that ere the balance is finally settled we shall be called upon to pay up liberty in exchange for the public money'. He believed the fundamental fault lay with the trust deed agreed by the Poor-School Committee:

> A school settled in trust upon the model deed, hangs, as respects all acts of proprietorship and transfer, on the finger of the Secretary of State for the Home Department. And we must not for a moment forget, that all schools held on the conditions of the model Trust-deed are placed under lay management, and that out of seven votes the priest has but one. The only exception made respects the question of religious instruction, and to the word *religious* as applied to instruction, the Government refused to allow the addition of the word *moral*.[290]

Writing in the *Tablet* of 4 April 1857 Ullathorne responded to some criticisms of his pamphlet:

> It has been industriously stated that the bishops have formally approved the model Trust Deed, and that even the Holy See has sanctioned the government system. Both statements are incorrect ... During the correspondence between the Poor-

> School Committee and the Privy Council ... I then saw there was something very serious lurking amidst the conditions attached to building grants, and I felt satisfied that no one who did not examine these documents with a theological insight, could detect the difficulties which they presented in anything like their full extent.

The bishop reiterated his belief that there was a threat to the authority of the Church:

> We are to be on the same footing as the Church of England, which recognises in the lay authority the power to limit and define what is and what is not within the competency of a bishop, and what is religion ... When the Poor-School Committee declare that the judgment of what is religious belongs of necessity to the Bishop, the reply is that my lords 'cannot admit modifications *affecting the powers of the Committee of Management* ... We accept a building grant then ... accompanied by the fundamental principle in Church discipline of Calvin, Erastus and the Church of England.

Given Allies's withering criticism of the subjection of the Anglican Church to the appellate jurisdiction of the Crown, he might have sympathised with these fears, but he was sure they were over-blown. One scholar has sought to explain his rather brusque rejection of criticism as stemming from a sense of intellectual superiority compounded by an underlying grievance about the bureaucratic role in which he found himself, believing that his true vocation was as a historian and 'man of letters': 'common sense would suggest that some of his confrontations with the opposition clergy stemmed from social and intellectual discontent'.[291]

If such criticism may seem somewhat gratuitous, an article in *The Rambler* replying to Ullathorne's pamphlet might have reinforced the view of some among an older generation of Catholics that the university converts were out of touch with the fears of 'ordinary Catholics'. Its author, Naysmith Stokes, Allies's predecessor, was a Cambridge convert and as an HMI, a state employee. Having no doubts as the government's good faith he spelled out at length the pressing need for more schools, '74,000 Catholic children who ought to attend school do not attend schools, or at least not Catholic schools'. He dismissed warnings of a Faustian pact as quite hypothetical: 'Dr. Ullathorne … has made no trial of the dangers which he dreads. Years have now passed since other Bishops erected schools, with Government aid, and from none of them has the public heard of disastrous consequences.'[292] The bishop's grounds for concern were ridiculed:

> the supposition, that the majority of a school-committee will become lax, nominal, and rationalising, may be dismissed from consideration … Fears of disputes or litigation about removal of teachers or exclusion of books, apprehensions of dangers from possible lady-visitors, and dread of secret appeals to inspectors, appear quite chimerical; and if on grounds so visionary and intangible we lose every month that passes one new school for two hundred children, which we might have erected with Government aid, we shall certainly in a few years run up a very long score of omissions. How often is it true, that 'the fear of ill exceeds the ill we fear!'[293]

Allies agreed with Stokes but his position was more delicate; ultimately his safeguard was that he was the servant of a Committee whose remit was set by the bishops. Wiseman as their leader was irritated with Ullathorne's perceived disloyalty in repudiating the trust deed the bishops had collectively endorsed and he wrote to the chairman of the Poor-School Committee reaffirming the guidance previously given. The letter was published in the *Tablet* on 2 May 1857:

> Under Providence the Poor-School Committee has been the very right hand of the bishops in combining and concentrating in a uniform plan and a definite action the multiplied relations between themselves, the State, and the Catholic public, in the growing cause of education …

> That jealousy may be felt about any relations between Catholics and Government is a natural result of our past, and even recent history. Vigilance is no doubt to be exercised; all proper caution must be used in the acceptance of such gifts, as we have not been accustomed to. But when these precautions have been taken, apprehension should cease; and the Faithful should not be harassed or perplexed by the raising anew of questions, long since solved after full and deliberate consideration.

Nevertheless, evidence that suspicions remained was seen in the bishops' response to the Newcastle Commission, set up in 1858 to enquire into the provision of elementary education. When it was learnt that there was no Catholic among its membership, liberal Catholic opinion was dismayed. Stokes took again to the pages of *The Rambler*, this time aiming his fire at the Committee, which he said had been caught off-guard:

> Surely, then, it was the duty of the Catholic Poor-School Committee to watch the signs of the proposed commission, to call together its members and debate the question, and ... to demand with all its influence the appointment of a Catholic commissioner ... For many months we have regretted that the ... Committee communicates so rarely with its supporters and the public, and finds so few opportunities to rouse and inform the Catholic body upon educational questions, which never demanded more attentive care than now.[294]

Whatever his sometimes frosty relationship with Allies, Stokes was here was reiterating a long-standing criticism of the Committee; for example, a letter to the *Catholic Standard* in 1855 complained that it was passive and out of touch with wider Catholic opinion.[295] Perhaps Allies should have been doing more? Not quite reconciled to office routine, after the Dublin lecture in December 1854, he had been spending all the hours he could spare reading widely, contemplating the direction that his historical research might take. In 1857 he apologised to Newman for having written no more lectures, complaining that his time was taken up with Committee matters, but adding, 'I have succeeded in removing the rooms of my office one half nearer to my house which is a great point for me.'[296] Writing *The Formation of Christendom* occupied every spare hour he could find, perhaps even above the cause of Catholic education. In 1860 he was able to allocate even more hours to it after securing agreement that his new home in Portman Street could be his office. The first volume of *Christendom* appeared in 1865, the second in 1869 and soon his daughter Mary Helen would be able to contribute to the remaining six volumes by taking over much of the routine office administration. What might have been the impact on the Catholic education had Allies devoted all his energies to this cause alone cannot be judged, but it may be observed that in the period up to 1870 there were no significant initiatives or major increases in expenditure by the Committee.

In support of Catholic schools, Allies did attempt to keep abreast of political developments and to maintain good relationships with the civil servants, although in the wake of Ullathorne's criticisms there was more sensitivity about appearing to be too close to the government. This reflected the policy of the bishops who in November 1859 ruled that the Newcastle Commission inspectors (all of them Protestants) should not be allowed into the Church's schools. Wiseman communicated the decision to his archdiocese as follows:

> Does not official inspection essentially imply authority over whatever is officially inspected and examined? To a Protestant this causes no uneasiness ... for he considers supreme authority over religion to lodge in the State. Not so can it be with a Catholic ... Can this be done without leaving an impression of the State's exercising authority in matters religious?[297]

There was no prohibition on answering the Commission's written questions, and Allies coordinated the Catholic response, from priests as well as that of the Committee itself. The message that he sought to convey was that for the Catholic education was more than instruction, rather 'a moulding of the whole intellectual and moral being,'[298] and he repeatedly referred to the needs of the Catholic poor, particularly in those areas where missions could not raise sufficient funds to pass the threshold for the granting of state aid, 'Catholics as I have stated above, are in too many places simply in the condition of Lazarus, and not even a dog from the Privy Council office comes to lick their sores.'[299]

Despite Catholic fears the Commission recommended no diminution in the freedom from state control enjoyed by the religious bodies, but its 1861 report proposed a system of payment by results, which was to create serious difficulties for Catholic education. The 'Revised Code' of 1862 was the brain-child of Robert Lowe, Vice-President of the Committee of the Council on Education, and intended to secure greater economy and value for money. Amongst other measure, annual payments to schools were to be based on a formula combining recorded attendances with the results of the inspector's examination. Irregular attendance was a particular problem of Catholic schools, and the new system threatened the income of many already under-resourced schools. The Lowe reforms also proved difficult for the Catholic teacher training colleges.

1870 and after

Following the extension of the franchise in 1867 Lowe, who became Chancellor in Gladstone's 1868 government, was supposed to have remarked 'we must educate our masters', and an effective national education system was an important part of the Liberal government's programme. To achieve this, efficiency in the use of public funds was vital, and this inevitably raised the question of the role of the denominations. Could they be trusted to educate the nation? The secularists said 'no' and in 1869 established The National Education League to campaign for universal non-sectarian provision. Pitched against them the denominations coalesced in the Anglican-inspired National Education Union. Manning requested that the Poor-School Committee should fully engage with it.[300] Thus, in November 1869, Allies addressed its national congress in Manchester, arguing the case for Christian education: all that was required was sufficient funding:

> he said no attempt had been made to make the denominational

system universal. He did not complain of the grants allowed in proportion to results but just imagine such a system applied to Eton or Oxford, imagine the college or the tutor fined for the deficiencies of the students. The object was to save the national pocket—but how was that compatible with a system of national education? In districts crowded with the poor the Privy Council ought to offer a more liberal grant than one-third of the cost; and if that were done the people would grow up good Christians and useful to the State, instead of its reproach and its curse.[301]

On 17 November the front page of *The Times* included a notice on behalf of the Union stating its purpose was to secure 'the Primary Education of every child, by judiciously supplementing the present Denominational System'; as evidence of its ecumenical basis, T. W. Allies was named as seconding a resolution moved by Archdeacon Durnford.[302] Archbishop Manning, although not supported by all the bishops urged the need to cooperate with all sects and denominations in support of the voluntary principle. In a pastoral letter (6 June 1869) he sought to prepare Catholics for the crisis that was coming, warning that any scheme of education 'not based on Christianity is an imposture'. Accepting that there could never be a return to the golden age where the Church of Rome and the state were as one, he advocated a civil society in which the Church would be left free to operate its own schools with adequate government support. This objective guided the Poor-School Committee as it responded to Elementary Education Bill introduced in February 1870 by W. E. Forster, the Vice-President of the Council. The legislation proposed that elected local school boards should assess the educational needs of their areas and to the extent that these were under-supplied arrange to provide non-denominational schools, funded by a rate. The denominations were to be given a year to expand their own provision, during which period construction grants would still be available. Denominational schools would continue to be subsidised from the public purse.

The immediate reaction of the denominations to the proposals was one of relief. On 4 March, Allies attended a meeting of the Education Union, where it was resolved that the bill deserves support inasmuch as it aims at supplying the needs of elementary education without prohibiting religious instruction, without prohibiting parental responsibility, and without extinguishing the schools which owe their existence to the costly and persevering labours of the best friends of the education of the people.

However, if Forster's plan did not envisage the national system of 'godless schools' feared by Manning, the bill's passage through Parliament was to look very much like the 'trial of strength between the traditions of Christian England' and the advocates of a secular state having 'supreme control over the education of the people', of which he had warned.[303] To ensure the efficiency of existing Catholic schools and to build more while grants were still available required a coordinated national effort, but the Church's response was initially muted, owing in part to the absence of the bishops who were in Rome attending the Vatican Council. But Manning was not idle, sending letters to Gladstone urging on him two main points: an extended period for grants to be available for opening new Church schools and secondly Catholic freedom from School Board supervision with funding coming directly from the Privy Council. He assured the prime minister that public opinion was behind the voluntary schools and 'with the union of the Anglicans and Catholics you have a great accession of strength'.[304] Whilst Gladstone personally supported Christian education his attitude to Catholic schools was tempered by a suspicion of papal ambition, fuelled by the reports he was receiving from Lord Acton in Rome of Manning's key role in rallying support for the definition of Pio Nono's personal infallibility. This clouded their personal relationship, moreover as leader of a party with a vigorous radical element his room to manoeuvre was limited.

Among Catholics at home there was unpreparedness and disunity, with some accusing the hierarchy of complacency; a view perhaps shared by the Poor-School Committee with Lord Howard of Glossop, its chairman, writing to the press, implicitly criticising the bishops for failing to act collectively.[305] By default, the chairman and secretary were left to coordinate the Catholic response to the bill. On 15 January Lord Howard wrote to the *Tablet* urging Catholics to 'be intelligently awake to the present crisis'. He foresaw great difficulties for the Church: 'we are bad to organise, and consequently feeble in times of danger,' he urged the dioceses to organise and to support the Committee: 'the experiment of local organisation ... would surely be worth trial'. When the parliamentary timetable demanded urgent national coordination this not the call to arms required. Moreover, rather than rising to the challenge some Catholics saw the febrile atmosphere as an opportunity to give vent to long-standing resentments and jealousies. The next issue of the *Tablet* contained this letter from 'A Catholic Curate':

> But with all respect to Lord Howard and the Committee which he represents, I would beg leave to call attention to one fact, which appears inexplicable and calculated to damp the ardour with which the Catholics might otherwise respond to his call. In the Annual Reports which are issued by the Poor-School Committee, there is an item of expenditure which must seem to require either explanation or alteration. It is this—that £400 are awarded yearly as a salary to the Secretary of the Committee. Now, when we consider the nature of the charity, the work done by the Secretary, and the fact that this money is collected from the self-sacrificing contributions of Catholics, and in many cases poor Catholics, it is inexplicable ... that such a sum ... should at once be consumed by such a salary. The Secretary's services are doubtless valuable, but surely similar or equally efficient services might be secured at a less heavy sacrifice.[306]

Somewhat less rancorously the Committee's initial reaction was criticised as halting and uncertain: 'Why do we not have a meeting in every Catholic parish in the country? What is the Poor-School Committee doing? Why do they not arouse the Catholic body'?[307] No one from the Committee answered the attack upon its secretary. Allies himself joined the correspondence by observing that 'anonymous writers in the *Tablet* are continually calling on the Poor-School Committee to be "up and doing" although what they are to do is not specified'. He went on to the offensive: criticising poor diocesan organisation saying that the Committee's recommendations over many years had been accepted but not properly implemented, mentioning in particular inadequate local inspection of schools. 'At the end of 1868 ... I find eight dioceses out of fifteen in which inspectors have been introduced. But in no one have reports as to the state of primary education been published.'[308] The Committee's best response to criticism was to give a clear lead, and following a meeting of clergy and laity at its offices on 22 and 23 February a sub-committee was appointed, including Allies, to monitor the bill through Parliament and to correspond with 'members favourable to the Catholic interest'. A petition was approved praying that Parliament would preserve religious freedom and 'would not pass any measure which would compel the poor of the Catholic community to send their children to schools in which the discipline and course of instruction would be a violation of conscience.'[309] In the ensuing campaign Allies played a key role in defending Catholic interests, demonstrating that his skills did indeed go beyond the merely secretarial. On 7 March, he wrote to the *Tablet* again appealing to the conscience of the government, Mr Gladstone in particular:

> I assume that we have among us more than a million of Irish ... of a practically exhaustless middle-class, with independent incomes, on whom to call for works of charity, we possess few, this fact constitutes for us Catholics an entirely exceptional position in the matter of elementary education ... If we have more children *in proportion* uneducated, than the other three religious bodies, the fact, I conceive, so far from being a cause of shame to us, constitutes the strongest possible claim for an exceptionally kind treatment of us.
>
> Mr Forster's Bill ... professes to continue denominational schools as at present existing, to extend them within a certain time, and then, if need be, supplement them with Board governed and rate paid schools.
>
> As to building new schools, the aid which since the Revised Code has been given by the Privy Council ... amounts to £1 per child to be accommodated ... the expense of building amounts to at least £3 10s. a head ... But this grant ... prohibits

all debt for raising money by mortgage. It is intended still to continue this amount of aid; but it would not be exceeded nor its conditions relaxed, in the most destitute case conceivable, that is to supply schooling for many hundred children, where there is not a single resident proprietor or employer of labour. [If sufficient funds cannot be raised in time] the Bill in Clauses 46–50 provides for erecting Board-governed schools, in which the whole cost of construction shall be raised either by grant of government or by rate.

We have then for building new denominational schools, to be supplied within a year, a grant of one-fourth, with very strict limitations, and no debt incurred; and for the building of proposed Board Schools, a school fund created, to be paid by a rate, which shall meet any deficiency ... A cope of lead for the denominational school; a pair of wings which will carry any body, however weighted, for the Board School ...

... for the annual support, the denominational school may continue to obtain from the Privy Council that one third or thereabouts which is given at present; the rest it must obtain from school pence or private subscriptions. As to the Board School, it need not be under the smallest anxiety, its happy and careless existence is secured for ever.

We have to supply primary education for 150,000 children ... And to help us in this the State offers us as a contribution, a fourth towards building, and a third towards maintenance, under very strict conditions. But the State adds, if all this be not completed in a year's time, I will come with a dragnet such as I have never enabled you to use ... and I will sweep your children by thousands out of the bye-streets, alleys, and courts of the vast cities which my commerce has created, and where they have taken refuge; and I will place them in schools, for the whole building and maintenance of which I will provide by an unfailing fund out of the rates which you will pay in proportion; and wherein they shall be taught, either no religion at all, or such a religion as the managers may chose. These managers, however, will be chosen by a body, which will never elect a Catholic among them; and the religion which they will sanction to be taught in these schools is one, which whatever else it will be, will certainly be in deadly opposition to that faith which the parents of these poor children brought to my shores; will account their greatest nay their only blessing.

Is this, may I ask, the justice which the Ireland that is in England has to expect from that statesman, the glory of whose life we thought it would be to redress the wrongs of the most wronged people on earth, to overthrow the most gigantic iniquity, and to unite England and Ireland in a peace based upon equal treatment, cemented by the Irishman's conviction that England would treat the person, the property and the religion of the Irish, as it would treat all these if they were English.[310]

Not only was Allies correct in saying that the question of Catholic elementary education was principally an Irish question, but approaching the matter in this way was engaging the ruling class at an almost visceral level. Memories were still fresh of Fenian outrages in Manchester (September 1867) and the bombing of Clerkenwell Prison (December 1868). Manning, writing to Gladstone at the time, was fearful that Irish resentment could spark an uncontainable conflagration: 'I have no deeper conviction than that we are preparing, if we go on, our own 1793.'[311] Gladstone replied that he thought their views on Ireland, 'very nearly the same'.[312] The unstated implication of Catholic propaganda was that attempting to drive the children of discontented Irish immigrants into 'Godless schools' was playing with fire.[313] Indeed at the very time Forster's bill was going through Parliament, measures to contain violence in Ireland were being debated and *The Times* was mischievously reporting from Rome that a papal bull condemning Fenianism was under consideration.[314] The secretary of the Poor-School Committee, a strong supporter of the Union, offered denominational schools as the price of stability.[315] Yet, for some parish priests with strong Irish sympathies the Poor-School Committee itself represented an arm of the oppressive Establishment and its secretary's appeals, whether for subscriptions or information were treated with suspicion.

Where there was not active hostility, it was difficult to obtain information from the dioceses that lacked education committees to provide coordination, and in the absence of bishops to give a clear lead, the Committee was driven to using the press. On 26 March in the pages of the *Tablet* Lord Howard pleaded with his fellow Catholics in the face of 'the greatest crisis in which we have ever been placed ... If we can help ourselves, perhaps other will help us. I should be personally, very much obliged by *accurate* statistics from proper sources—not later than the beginning of Low Week—of children of ages from 3 to 12, and of school accommodation, thus showing what more is wanted.'

The faith of thousands of children was at stake: the parishes must bestir themselves. Indeed, he said, a complete moral reformation was required: 'In times of great sickness or calamity, men look more to themselves, they become more careful, steadier, better men. In like manner let us now turn into a benefit what threatens as a calamity: some retrenchment of expenditure, fewer ribbons, less gin, more schools, greater sobriety, more credit to the Catholic body.'[316]

Shortly before the Poor-School Committee's annual meeting the *Tablet* published an editorial demanding more action from it:

> What initiative has it taken to stir up and organize our people? What meetings has it planned? What new interests and sympathies has it striven to excite? What deputations has it sent over the country to awaken and rouse up those who were asleep? What letters, tracts, fly leaves, articles, has it addressed to the rich, the middle class and the poor? What more has it done than it did five and ten years ago, before the clouds gathered and the tempest arose which now threatens us with destruction? The Poor-School Committee may be able to answer these questions, which the public naturally asks itself. We can give no answer. All we know is that the Chairman Lord Howard of Glossop, and the Secretary, Mr Allies have not been wanting in vigilance and have not spared themselves. Others indeed seem to have entered upon a heavy sleep. Is it not now time to awake? Yet a little while longer and death will be upon us.[317]

Indeed, the chairman and secretary had not been inactive. The Committee met with diocesan Vicars-General on 22 February and the terms of the bill analysed in detail. It was pronounced 'dangerous to the faith and religion of poorer Catholics', and the House of Commons was petitioned to continue the 'existing system of denominational schools'.[318] Three weeks later members assembled again to consider their instructions from the bishops in Rome: that 'the engagements of 1847 and the system of education founded on them will remain inviolate'. A few days later Allies and Howard met with Lord de Grey, Lord President of the Council, who fortunately had Catholic sympathies and was to convert four years later. He requested that their representations should be set out in a memorandum; this was drawn up by the secretary and sent to the prime minister and Forster on 19 March. Arguing that education could not be both compulsory and undenominational the document was approved at the annual meting of the Committee and Allies was instructed to send it to the press. As the bill progressed through its committee stage, chairman and secretary met again with Gladstone to discuss his proposed amendments: that the level of Privy Council grant to denominational schools should be up to 50 per cent of their annual cost and that they should remain free of ratepayer control. The latter was one of Manning's key objectives and the prime minister had accepted that the likely composition of School Boards would be unfavourable to the Catholics. He wrote to Manning on 22 June that he now had little cause for complaint: 'Mr Allies told me, if they could make sure of one moiety of the School Charges from the State he thought they could perhaps perform their work; and this moiety will, I apprehend, now be secured for efficient schools by the proposals of the Government.'[319]

Although Manning was reconciled to the dual system, he was unhappy with the parliamentary process, believing that more could have been done to safeguard Christian education. His verdict was: 'The education Bill is decidedly improved ... I still believe the doctrinaire faction prevailed beyond its power ... over the real desire of the country.'[320] Lacking effective parliamentary support—most Catholic MPs were Irish and had little direct interest in the issue—the chairman and secretary had been left to play a poor hand as well as they could. In Allies's opinion the outcome might have been much worse, both as regards funding and the continued freedom of Catholic schools to give religious instruction free from state scrutiny. He was unperturbed that those inspecting Catholic schools no longer had to be Catholics themselves, remaining convinced of the beneficial effect of independent scrutiny. As regards spiritual edification, the Act incorporated a troublesome 'conscience clause', which allowed parents to withdraw their children from religious instruction, while stipulating that it must be taught at the beginning or end of the school day. Catholics, however, could expect nothing from the Board Schools: the passing of the Cowper-Temple clause excluded all denominational religious instruction.

The bill completed its progress through Parliament on 18 July 1870, but not until 9 August—the day the Act received royal assent—did the hierarchy meet the Poor-School Committee. Weeks before this the hard work had begun: the challenge of preventing poor Catholic children being swept up into the Board Schools. There was little time. The period of grace during which building grants would be available for Church schools had been reduced by amendment from a year to six months; and soon the elected boards would begin to decide on the adequacy of denominational provision. An urgent school building and improvement campaign was essential. The Poor-School Committee decided that the desperate circumstances required urgent action, and on Monday 13 June at a crowded meeting of Catholic peers and gentry a fund-raising campaign was instituted. Allies, who was appointed secretary of the Crisis Committee—charged with coordinating the collection and distribution of funds—outlined the scale of the challenge:

> I calculate ... we ought to have under a national system of education 180,000 Catholic children under teaching in Poor Schools. The number at present is not above 110,000 ... [I]n proportion as these 70,000 were taken into the Board School ... that is rated or municipal schools, I feel convinced that the effect upon our Catholic children would be very disastrous indeed. We have therefore not only to maintain our existing schools as far as possible with their existing liberty, and in

as efficient a state, as we can, but we have to supply such a number of additional schools like our present as would prevent our children being driven to the Board Schools.³²¹

Of the total school places estimated by Allies to be available, 25,000 were in uninspected establishments, and in inspected schools average attendance was in the region of 20,00 below available places. This explains a seeming disparity in the figures cited in June 1874 by the bishop of Salford in reporting to his clergy on the great achievements of the Crisis Fund:

> According to the estimate published in the appeal of the Catholic Education Crisis Fund in 1870, the number of Catholic children in Great Britain was 185,000, and the number in average attendance at inspected schools only 64,309 (figure for 1868). According to the official returns just published, the number of Catholic children in average attendance in inspected schools in Great Britain is 99,988. There has therefore been an increase in average attendance of 35,579 Catholic children in the last six years.³²²

Manning's support for the new system, and in particular the encouragement he gave to Catholics to stand in the School Board elections was criticised, but he had no doubt that there was no viable alternative to engagement. As he wrote to Ullathorne,

> The Boards may destroy our lesser schools at once by reporting them insufficient or inefficient. The effect of this in London would be to destroy one-half our schools. By opening relations with the Boards, as I have done with the Privy Council, I hope to save these. By standing aloof from the Boards we should be exposed to the danger of their hostility.³²³

Looking back after sixteen years, in giving evidence to the Cross Commission, and still the Committee's secretary, Allies was sure that the

1870 Act had had a positive effect in stirring up Catholics to accept their responsibility for the street children 'belonging to us'.[324] Asked how much had been raised by the Crisis Fund he replied:

> The accounts have never been finally made up, because they stretched over such a number of years. In 1877 ... I have the amount down as being £342,000. But, however, I have no doubt that a great deal more than that has been spent in certain dioceses, probably in Westminster, and in Liverpool especially, and also, I think, in Glasgow; so that I am unable to say what is the whole amount that has been spent in that way; but it is very large indeed, because I have down here the number of scholars for whom provision was made before the Act of 1870 as 71,000, and now there are 208,000 in average attendance.[325]

Compared with the previous arrangements the Act imposed a heavy burden on the Catholic body. Board schools would be built and maintained wholly from public funds, including the rates paid by Catholic parents. The Church's schools were themselves rated, which money had to be found from voluntary contributions, as supplemented by Privy Council grants. The Poor-School Committee continued to urge the inequity of the arrangements and pressed for more public funding, with Allies playing a key role in presenting the Catholic case. For example, the *Tablet* reported that as a member of a deputation that waited on the President and Vice-President of the Council in February 1876, he had urged

> that at the time of the Act of 1870 ... the intention was only to supplement existing schools; by no means to injure them. The intent of the Act was to take up the population, especially in large cities, which were running wild without education; but increased grants from the parliamentary fund, which should reach 50 per cent, of the cost of maintenance, were expressly promised to voluntary schools. The board schools were not to take their place—were by no means to constitute

the normal schools of the country—but both alike were placed under the inspection of the Privy Council. It was alleged that the increased grant thus promised to be made to voluntary schools would enable them permanently to hold their own ... [I]n fact ...the amount of aid given from public sources—that is from grant and rate—to board schools has been to establish an immense preponderance of such aid in their favour; and ... this preponderance must increase every year, unless a remedy is applied, and must in the end largely endanger the existence of voluntary schools.

Was it right ... that board schools should go on receiving 75 per cent, of their whole cost ... from public sources, while voluntary schools received only 50 per cent? Would not such a preponderance of aid, united to the fact that the subscribers to voluntary schools would be required to pay doubly, first their subscription, and then a heavy rate, lead in the long run to the extinction of voluntary schools, to the very result against which special promises were made by those who passed the Act of 1870?[326]

Equality of treatment remained an aspiration, but things could have been much worse and many Catholics would have endorsed the conclusion of an article in *The Month*:

If the 'Educational Crisis', or any other like occasion for anxiety forces upon us exertions which we have never made before, and an organization which we have never yet attempted, it will not only have obliged us to meet the particular danger of the day, but have fitted us also for future efforts to which we might never dreamt of aspiring, and have turned a host of irregular skirmishers into a compact and disciplined army.[327]

Allies agreed that the crisis of 1870 had administered a necessary shock, leading to a new era for Catholic primary education and that the Government could be trusted to act honourably. He was sure that Catholics in Great Britain enjoyed a much better relationship with the state than did their co-religionists on the Continent, the plight of whom was to absorb his attention as a member of the Catholic Union. By comparison, the granting of preferential financial advantage to schools teaching non-denominational religion might be considered a minor matter. But this view was not shared by all. One sceptic was the Oxford convert Canon Oakeley, who in 1872 published two pamphlets arguing that the practical operation of the Education Act, in particular the conscience clause, and the stance adopted by Government inspectors was tending to the emasculation of the distinctively Catholic character of the Church's schools. Further developments in the legislative framework appeared to support these fears, so that by 1875 a writer in the *Dublin Review* could assert: 'during the last few years very grave attacks have been made upon the religious character of denominational schools ... Secularism in education, planted a few years ago, has already waxed strong and threatens to overshadow the whole of the country'.[328]

The conscience clause limiting and containing the teaching of religion was seen by critics as corrosive. The *Tablet* agreed that caution was required, quoting at length and approvingly from the above article:

> We may therefore anticipate that the Secularist advocates will, before very long, make the discovery that, as a Catholic School must admit non-Catholic scholars, and as neither the priest nor the schoolmaster may teach religion during the ordinary school hours, therefore there can exist no necessity why Catholic Schools as such should be aided with grants of the public money. From the refusal of aid to the Catholic Schools it is a perfectly logical step to the refusal of aid to Catholic training colleges. If the schools are to be undenominational, there can be no reason why the masters should receive a Catholic training. Thus the way is prepared for the total extinction of the Catholic School; the Conscience Clause having been the thin end of the wedge by which the destruction will have been effected.[329]

By implication the Poor-School Committee was criticised for not doing more to raise the alarm. 'Can even a day be spared, when each day witnesses a further advance of that which we have so much reason to dread? The prudence of waiting until something is done positively incompatible with the continued existence of our schools may well be questioned, when we see such a highly organised force steadily advancing against us.'[330]

The context of these fears was the increasing strength of the anti-religious movement on the Continent. Anticlericalism continued unabated: in Germany the *Kulturkampf* was reaching its climax; in France the Third Republic was determinedly anti-Catholic, as was the House of Savoy in Italy. But the Poor-School Committee might well have rejoined that the state had amply proved its disinterestedness by its handling of objections raised by the Protestant Alliance to specifically Catholic content in reading books used during the daily four hours of secular instruction. In December 1872 Allies had to contact the publishers, who withdrew them from circulation, whilst protesting at the 'pecuniary loss' involved. The Alliance, however, was not appeased noting that the objectionable books continued to be used. W. E. Forster asked Allies to take up the matter with the archbishop, who saw justification in the complaints and it required all his political skill to diffuse the crisis. The incident hints at the extent to which Catholic schools strove to maintain their distinctive ethos and at Manning's confidence in the good faith of Gladstone's government.[331]

The Poor-School Committee had more immediate concerns than an imaginary state take-over: in particular the raising of funds and investment in schools. The newly elected School Boards were required to adjudicate on the efficiency of Catholic schools, so that if these were not to be supplanted by Board schools the quality of teaching was key. In November 1870 at a meeting between the hierarchy and the Poor-School Committee Allies urged that additional school places had to be accompanied by more and better trained teachers. In 1874 the bishop of Salford reiterated this point: 'Vain will be the efforts of the priest, useless the expenditure, if the school is not taught by a really efficient teacher.'[332] He observed that effective teacher training could only be provided on a national basis, under the auspices of the Poor-School Committee. Allies himself was a tireless advocate for an integrated national approach to Catholic education: 'As the State deals in its unity with the whole mass of the population, the Church must do the like—consider the needs of the whole body and call upon the whole body to supply them.'[333]

That Catholic Schools flourished in the last decades of the century was considered by the Committee as sufficient vindication of their policy. Good relations with the state were maintained. For example, the Liberal government of 1880 had its radical wing, but the Vice-President of the Council, A. J. Mundella, a celebrated Reformer, was counted a supporter of Catholic education.[334] In 1883, having reached the age of seventy, and having been in post for thirty years, Allies was moved to write to the pope, Leo XIII to celebrate what he believed to be a most satisfactory state of affairs: 'My Committee's Annual Report ... shows that last year, 1882, we received from the Government for the Schools and Training Colleges of Great Britain the sum of £162,887, showing an increase of £13,530 on the preceding year'. He celebrated the achievements of the three teacher training colleges, where 'the most Protestant country in the world' contributed 75 per cent of their costs without any restriction on the religious content of what was taught., and observed 'that the Catholics of Italy, France, Germany and Spain, would give much to have a state of things so favourable to the Church'. As regards Catholic elementary schools, there were many more children attending, reflecting a substantial growth in capacity: in 1870, there were places for 119,156 children, by 1882, 314,595 could be accommodated (compared with the number of children on the Committee's books at 190,540). He said that despite some fears the conscience clause had had a positive impact with the bishops becoming anxious to ensure the efficiency of religious instruction. The Committee had been requested by them to institute a system of rewards for achievement,[335] and the episcopacy had now accepted the need to appoint 'in each diocese one or more priests for the religious inspection of the schools.' Moreover, state inspection of the secular teaching of Catholic schools had not only served to raise standards but 'this free intermingling of mind to mind has removed old prejudices'. Whilst admitting that disparity in funding between Board and voluntary schools had caused many people to be 'fearful about what the future may bring forth' he nevertheless was sure that great gains had been made in the period since the 1870 Act.[336]

The training colleges

Allies believed that the provision of improved teacher education was his most important contribution as secretary: 'Training Colleges in particular have been to a great extent my work: for in 1853 the Bishops took no pains at all about them; the Committee not much.'[337] He recognised that even before the building of new schools it was essential to have trained teachers to serve in them. According to Bishop Ullathorne, its secretary 'ran the policy of the Poor-School Committee on three maxims: 'there can be no sound education without religion, as is the teacher, so is the child, and as is the trainer so is the teacher.'[338] The need for an adequate supply of good teachers was a continual problem. Recruitment of men was particularly difficult. Stokes had sought to address the problem by visiting the Abbé de Lammenais (brother of the editor of *L'Avenir*) at Ploermel in Brittany and agreeing that his congregation, the Brothers of Christian Instruction, would establish a teacher-training college in England. To this end the Order purchased a house in Hammersmith and adapted it for the use of six trainees already undertaking noviateships in France. St Mary's College was founded in 1850, but the Poor-School Committee was disappointed in its hope that eventually Christian Brothers from here would teach the majority of Catholic boys. The Annual Report for 1854 lamented the absence of vocations, and, accepting that lay teachers would have to be enrolled, announced that a department would be added to St Mary's to train pupil-teachers for a Queen's Scholarship qualification, five of whom had already commenced.[339] With a Privy Council grant and £10,000 in donations, building work to provide accommodation for fifty students was begun and by the end of the year the Hammersmith College had become the Committee's property.[340]

Over the years there were to be many difficulties with St Mary's, not least a persistent deficit on annual costs, taxing Allies's patience and ingenuity. It was far otherwise with the college established by the sisters of Notre Dame for young women students at Mount Pleasant, Liverpool. In March 1855 the Committee sent Allies to the mother house of the order in Namur. He was charged with persuading the Mother

A New Life 347

General, Mère Constantine, to establish a training college alongside the schools that the order had already founded in Liverpool. The challenge he put to her was that of 'saving of the Faith of the poor by the saving of Catholic schools'.[341] Despite the considerable cost involved, the challenge was accepted and the newly professed Frances Mary Lescher—a family friend—and three colleagues were sent to England to begin the work. Arriving on 17 October 1855, within six months all had passed the Teacher's Certificate examination, but anticipating this, on 2 February (the Feast of the Purification), twenty-one trainee teachers had arrived to begin their studies. The Liverpool work was to prove very successful and Allies attached by personal as well as professional cords took a particular interest in its progress.

Another college for young women was founded at St Leonards, Sussex, in February 1856, by the new religious order associated with Cornelia Connelly: the Society of the Holy Child Jesus. The nuns began warily: a training school they had sought to establish in Liverpool had proved a costly failure.[342] The new venture, with the strong support of the Poor-School Committee, began well, but the location proved ill-chosen, with insufficient Catholic schools to offer sufficient teaching practice. There were also financial difficulties made worse by changed government funding arrangements introduced in 1862. In particular, the Revised Code deferred grant payment until the trainee had secured a teaching post and continued in it for a stipulated period. There were other problems and it is likely that Committee of Council, seeking to reduce expenditure, used an unfavourable report from Stokes (the HMI) to secure the resignation of Cornelia Connelly as principal, which ultimately led to the work being abandoned.[343]

Both women's colleges were able to attract sufficient numbers of suitable applicants, but this was not the case at Hammersmith, largely because Catholic schoolmasters were very poorly paid. Young men could generally obtain better paid employment, whereas for women there were few other careers available. In 1861, the Oratorian Father James Rowe was appointed principal. His annual reports to the Poor-School Committee for the eight years that he was in office, 'are at once a record of grim struggle and heroic perseverance, and he had unceasingly to complain of the well-nigh impossibility of obtaining suitable material for training.'³⁴⁴ The Revised Code added to the college's continuing financial difficulties, but with Allies's encouragement and practical help the work was eventually put on secure foundations, and in 1874 the Poor-School Committee chairman Lord Howard was able to report that 'it has now attained a very good state and sends out a very good class of master.'³⁴⁵

Whereas the need for male teachers was generally met by Hammersmith, the sisters at Mount Pleasant were unable to provide sufficient women teachers after the 1870 Education Act led to a rapid growth in school places. At the request of the bishops the Committee approached the Sisters of the Sacred Heart, and in 1874 the Order opened a training college at Wandsworth. Allies took a close interest in the work there and would usually speak at the annual prize-giving. In 1881 he told the students that 'that the formation of the Christian life in them was of greater importance than their advancement in secular learning, and greater even than their advancement in religious instruction.' He added that the Vice-president of the Council of Education had assured a Poor-School Committee delegation 'that Catholics have a great power in religious instruction, and Catholic teachers thereby acquire influence which, if rightly used, must secure the well-being of their schools.' Emphasising that the religious element was fundamental to education he observed 'that to teach at all requires authority, and that all authority, especially in religious instruction is a delegation from God.' Their strength and consolation would ever come from frequentation of the sacraments and the other practices of the Christian life which they have been taught while at college.'³⁴⁶

'The chief occupation of my life'

Reflecting in 1883 on his own contribution to Catholic education Allies pointed firstly to the enhancement of the quality of teachers through his Committee's support of the training colleges, and secondly to the establishment of a system of diocesan inspection of Catholic schools (to supplement state inspection and covering religious instruction). In 1875 the Committee decided to discontinue building and maintenance grants and concentrate on funding the inspection of religious teaching with associated rewards. The scheme generated some controversy, not least because of the associated cost with vigorous criticism of the stipends offered to inspectors, and in connection with this one writer to the *Tablet* again criticised the secretary's salary. The journal itself commented on this in a leader (2 August 1878). 'Mr Allies's antecedents, his learning and his labours have, it appears to us, deserved to be otherwise regarded. He is moreover, the official organ between the Catholic Bishops, the Catholic public and the Education Department. He has for years faithfully discharged that office with credit to himself and with satisfaction to the Bishops, the Education Department and the public.' By 1878 all the dioceses had signed up to the scheme, which became a significant drain upon the Committee's resources, and balancing the accounts presented a perennial challenge. In Allies's final year as secretary a small surplus was achieved, but he would have been disappointed that this was through 'a serious curtailment in the grants made for religious inspection.'[347] It was through the standardisation of inspection that the Committee hoped to secure improvements in the diocesan organisation of schools. Allies, however, never achieved his vision of a nationally integrated Catholic elementary education system. This came in 1905 with the establishment of the Council of Education to replace the Poor-School Committee. It was, in his daughter's opinion, the 'realisation of his dream.'[348]

Allies was over seventy when in 1885 the new Conservative government established a royal commission (the Cross Commission) to investigate the state of elementary education. Manning was one of a number of its members who supported denominational schools. Allies, on behalf of the Poor-School Committee, was questioned at some length and his contribution was reflected in the majority report. In endorsing the principle of voluntary schools receiving rate funding without the imposition of the Cowper Temple clause, the commissioners commented: 'We should regard any separation of the teacher from religion as injurious to the morals and secular training of the scholars.'[349] The Commission produced two sets of recommendations (issuing a majority and a minority report) but neither resulted in a new Education Act, although a straw in the wind was the decision of Salisbury's government to replace school fees with state aid of 10s per child.[350]

On 20 May 1890 Allies attended his last annual meeting of the Poor-School Committee. The chairman—the Duke of Norfolk—in announcing their secretary's resignation moved the following resolution, which was agreed unanimously:

> The Committee cannot receive the resignation of their Secretary after nearly forty years of devotion to its service without offering him a warm expression of thanks. In Mr. Allies the Committee had a Secretary of special attainments. Throughout a long and critical period, during which great and eventful changes have taken place in the position of education, and heavy calls have been made upon the energy and resources of the Committee, his great knowledge and experience have been of signal service.

An equally striking endorsement was the voting of a pension of £400 per annum; it was agreed that his replacement should be remunerated at £150 per annum.[351]

As secretary of the Poor-School Committee Allies made enemies. Although some rough edges had been smoothed the truculent rector of Launton could still be seen. He blamed the failure of his vision for a nationally integrated system on a 'want of men'. His daughter commented that he was perhaps, 'too much of a man' and that his tenure in office 'was not always a bed of roses'.[352] A sense of intellectual superiority, never fully mortified, could create avoidable difficulties. The report he prepared for the bishops on Catholic higher education can give a flavour:

> I have never met with an individual Catholic—priest or layman—who did not think and feel that the English Catholics in the matter of education were far inferior to their Protestant fellow country men ... [T]he continuance of our present inferiority tends to encourage even in the minds of Catholics what is a proverb with Protestants—the notion that the profession of the true faith impedes and hampers the cultivation of the intellect; makes men ignorant and slothful.[353]

He complained bitterly about a lack of cooperation from the parochial clergy accusing them, for example, of withholding information about the ability of their parishioners to become subscribers.[354] He found Scott Naysmith Stokes particularly difficult to work with, believing that his inspection reports on St Leonard's College were unfair to the point of dishonesty and had contributed to its failure. He had a better relationship with the first Catholic HMI, Thomas William Marshall, but in comparing his evidence before the Newcastle Commission with that of Allies, Tenbus noted 'pronounced disagreement on various issues'.[355] When Marshall was dismissed from his post and when the same fate befell another Catholic inspector, J. R. Morell, Allies was sure that the ostensible grounds masked an underlying anti-Catholicism within the Education Department. He wrote to Newman: 'Morell is to be dismissed today by an order in council, having refused to resign, upon a charge of disingenuousness and falsehood, of which he is perfectly innocent. I have now witnessed three studied attempts of the Privy Council to prove Catholic Inspectors guilty of precisely that charge'.[356]

Despite this prickliness, and his resentment that he could have made better—meaning more intellectual—use of his time, Allies made a significant contribution to the development of Catholic elementary education. Sufficient for him to merit an entry in the *Dictionary of British Educationists*, which highlights among his achievements: the establishment of ecclesiastical inspection of religious education, and the rapid rise in the number of schools (666 under inspection in 1870, 1562 in 1882) and qualified teachers (799 in 1870, 2943 in 1883).[357] At the age of seventy, reflecting on the thirty years in office he commented 'It is plain therefore that Providence has intended this to be the chief *occupation* of my life. Nine-tenths of it has been the work of a mere clerk; in the other tenth there was something to be done in promoting the task of primary education'.[358] Not eligible for the priesthood, education became his vocation. Schools were his religious work: 'the highest form of charity' in passing on 'knowledge of the faith ... for all is deduced from the House of Nazareth, the Crib of Bethlehem, and the Cross of Calvary'.[359]

Allies the historian

As a young man Allies dreamed of achieving fame and celebrity as a Romantic poet. The ambition for distinction remained and as the author of a magisterial defence of Church of England he attained a certain status among the theologically literate public. Becoming a Catholic was stepping into obscurity; thereafter his publications were largely ignored by the Protestant press. So it was with some feeling that he added to the title page of his apologia, *A Life's Decision* published in 1880, a quotation from Psalm 83: 'I have chosen to be an abject in the house of my God rather than dwell in the tents of sinners.'[360] For Newman it was different: the impact made by the *Apologia* (1864) was widespread and profound. Allies's own work was largely unnoticed, his daughter said that it had 'what the French call a *succès d'estime*, and never met with the circulation it deserved.'[361] The thirst for recognition, his 'thorn in the flesh', was never assuaged; what he wrote in 1855 he could have written forty years later:

> I am this day forty-two years of age. The prevailing feeling with me at every birthday for some time past has been of regret that I was so old. I have been trying to get at the bottom of it, and have little doubt that its root is my natural desire for distinction in literature, which led me to make that the ἔργον [work] of life. If it be so, of course I must feel that I have done little, and especially that most of my time before I became a Catholic was wasted. Of course, I have struggled against this feeling, and I doubt not that it is considerably mortified. I have been long trying to substitute the saving of my soul as the ἔργον of life.[362]

Two years later he was still reflecting on the 'many follies, errors and miseries' of which 'the desire of *genius* rather than *sanctity* has been the cause.'[363] He never thought that being secretary to the Poor-School Committee was enough, just the toil that earned financial security. No doubt the advancement of Catholic education was a praiseworthy cause, but Allies yearned to become a *name* spoken of in intellectual circles. Those who knew of his scholarly achievements and patristic studies never doubted his ability, as Newman wrote to Archbishop Cullen: 'He was the first man of his day at Oxford. He came from Eton with the highest character for scholarship—I suppose he is well versed in philosophy—and, as your Grace knows he is a powerful and eloquent writer—and has of late years devoted himself to the study of the Fathers.'[364] No mention here of Allies's theological expertise, but in the wake of his conversion it was as a Catholic apologist and as a robust advocate of papal supremacy that he was best known. The series of articles in the *Dublin* and the publication in 1852 of *St Peter, his Name and his Office*, have been noted. Perhaps such advocacy could have been his life's work? Rather it was Newman's proposal in May 1854 that he should lecture in the philosophy of history,[365] whilst continuing to work for the Poor-School Committee, that set the future direction of his quest for distinction. *The Formation of Christendom* took the form of lectures, although only the first was ever delivered in Dublin: it became the first chapter of the first volume, published in 1865: *The Christian Faith and the Individual*. There were to be seven more, the last (*The Monastic Life*) appearing in 1896, when the author was in his eighty-fourth year. The whole work had its *terminus ad quem* in the year that, before being deflected by Newman thirty-five years before, Allies had envisaged as the starting point of an analysis of the evolution of the modern religious world. Volume VIII ends with the coronation of Charlemagne by Pope Leo III as marking the establishment of Christendom and Allies finishes with wistful musings on the issues that he might have tackled:

> From his act, which a Pope alone could execute, date five hundred years in which a new Europe, resting on the joint labour and union of religious and civil chieftains, sprang up and was exhibited in a series of Catholic nations. Of these St Peter's See, as it had been the creator, so it was the guide and crown ... Five hundred years of growth and decision which followed that wonderful act of Leo III were followed by a second five hundred years, which have tried to impair and even dissolve, the union of civil government and of spiritual

belief, and the world trembles at the thought that a convulsion may be in store for unbelief which may recall or even surpass, that which attended the breaking up of the great empire.[366]

Allies's *Formation of Christendom* is a formidable achievement. Drawing on the researches of continental scholars and immersed in the patristic sources Allies produced a work of immense industry which illuminates many neglected areas in the evolution of Christendom. But heavily reliant on the publications of officially approved scholars it was not history that satisfied Lord Acton. Allies, however, wrote to make a case: 'It is the voice of all history that God with the most careful providence directs the various and never-ending movements of human affairs. Even against man's intention he makes them serve the advancement of His Church.'[367] In his opinion thoroughness and cumulative detail were justification enough for publication, sure that his evidence would leave an indelible impression: 'The Church of God comes before the thoughtful mind as the vast mass of a kingdom. Its greatest deeds are but parts of something immeasurably greater. The most striking evidence of its doctrines and of its work is cumulative.'[368]

His incessant toil did not go unrewarded: in 1885 Allies was made a Knight Commander of the Order of St Gregory the Great. The papal brief commended him: 'being of keen and active mind, are distinguished in the higher and more difficult branches of human knowledge, while you have gained great merit by earnest action and by esteemed writings on behalf of the Catholic faith.'[369]

In 1894 to honour the publication of a cheap edition Cardinal Vaughan wrote of 'one of the noblest historical works I have read'.

> We have nothing like it in the English language ... No English work that I know exhibits the mission of the Church to the world, to the pagan world, to the civilized world, and I might add to the modern world ... in a more eloquent, a more fascinating, or a more convincing manner.
>
> I am persuaded that nothing wiser could be done than to place this book in the hands of many educated men and women who are enquiring into the claims of the Church, and

are searching for an answer to the problems which stand out before their consciences. They need, not controversy, but the light of history.[370]

Yet *The Formation of Christendom* did not achieve wider recognition, either from his contemporaries or from later generations, whether in the form of academic citation or popular sales. This was despite all the efforts of Ultramontane friends; the *Dublin Review*, for example, hailed the first volume:

> No one can read these lectures without deeply regretting the writer has not given us more, and that the exigencies of practical duty prevent him from devoting his whole time to intellectual pursuits. At such a period as this when the Church so urgently needs the best intellectual efforts of her children, it is lamentable that her cause does not occupy the undivided energies of one, possessing so thoroughly Catholic a spirit, so large a body of learning, both ecclesiastical and secular, so beautiful and attractive a style, and so much power of sustained thought.[371]

The reviewer is sure that only Christianity can provide a coherent philosophy of history, which 'sifts and arranges the facts which it records, and judges them by fixed and eternal principles of right and wrong'. Allies is commended for attributing to 'the influence of Christianity things which a superficial observer may attribute rather to some general progress in the world to a higher civilization.'[372] Each successive volume was eulogised in its turn, the relatively brief notice given to the third (1875) may be taken as an example:

> Mr. Allies treats his subject in a manner unequalled, so far as we are aware, among the English authors who have preceded him ... we cannot help congratulating the Catholic body that the credit of a labour so fitly chosen and so well executed should belong to them.
>
> We say fitly chosen ... because it is always fitting to draw

out the supernatural origin of Christianity as attested by its own history, but also because an inquiry of this sort is pre-eminently opportune at the present moment.

We must add that Mr. Allies—and this is the main value of his book—writes not as a controversialist, but as an historian. His statements are full and impartial, as those of a controversialist can scarcely be, and his proof is all the more convincing because it is indirect and subordinate to the history which it his business to relate.[373]

The *Tablet* was equally enthusiastic; reviewing the second book (1869) it commented 'we feel persuaded that the work is destined to become a classic and an authority on the momentous subject which it treats so ably and so agreeably'. Particularly commendable, from the Ultramontanist viewpoint, was that Allies in blending of history and theology had revealed the 'mystery of iniquity, which it may be remarked is a fact in our history as much as any other human thing and totally independent of the witness given to it by God's revelation.'[374]

The *Spectator*, among the few non-Catholic periodicals to notice the appearance of volume 1, was politely dismissive:

The author has to reconcile two conflicting theories—the theory that there 'sits in Peter's chair one who may well possess and communicate to his children the secret of history', and the theory that the truths of history are to be sought for a patient and diligent observation of the facts. As will naturally be foreseen, the latter goes to the wall, and the writer only pursues the inductive method to the extent that is required for the confirmation of the principles that have emanated from other sources ... It must not, however, be supposed that we consider Mr. Allies' lectures to be wholly without value. He is an accomplished scholar and a good Christian as well as an enthusiastic Roman Catholic and he writes in a style that would command attention for any theory.[375]

There was little scholarly recognition. The *Westminster Review* criticised

Allies's acceptance of traditions about St Peter despite 'insufficiency of testimony'.[376] Most Anglicans dismissed the work as partisan, although in reviewing the third volume in *The Academy*, John Wordsworth[377] was prepared to be generous, welcoming it as 'of service to religious truth in this country' indeed 'about the greater part of his book there is a healthiness of tone that tells of one who in days gone by breathed freer air and even now is not sickly with the malaria of the Vatican'. He regretted the turn Allies's academic career had taken: 'it is impossible to forget that Mr. Allies was once in a position to have done much greater service... Though he may not regret the waste of his powers, others may do so. It is sad for one living in Oxford to reflect how many of her ablest sons, at one critical period of her history, followed Dr. Newman into the desert'.[378] The reviewer may have been provoked by the dedication expressing the author's gratitude to Father Newman, 'once the Hector of a doomed Troy' now 'become in your day and country the Achilles of the City of God'.[379] Wordsworth regrets the author's unwillingness to engage with modern scholarship, for example in a failure to discuss or even acknowledge chronological difficulties with the traditional dating of Peter's visits to Rome: 'Mr. Allies writes as if he were unaware of their existence'.[380]

In fact, Allies did not deny his unwillingness to engage deeply with controverted issues, or that in some cases his conclusions went beyond the available documents. Thus in accounting for the evolution of the Church's structure in its first three centuries, he wrote that in the absence of other evidence the Church itself 'as it met the eye of Constantine must suffice':

> So that, in consequence ... all discussion of certain points of detail, as for instance how the Apostolic power became restricted in the bishop, yet that of the bishop everywhere superior to the priests, must be termed otiose and fruitless. I take the unquestionable result of the Church's development by her own intrinsic power ... as the one fact which I need, and the only one which I think it worthwhile to state. Before it all speculations of infidel criticisms fall to the ground.[381]

The *Union Review*, although sympathetic to non-Ultramontane Catholicism, believed that Allies's evidence was carefully selected:

> The author is a brilliant, not to say reckless, writer, and can give a vivid presentation of one side of a picture—all the more vivid perhaps, from his never being troubled by any suspicion that there may happen to be two sides to it ... While professedly an historian, Mr. Allies invariably writes as a controversialist.[382]

Newman voiced his own disappointment in writing to Canon John Walker, priest at Scarborough, about the second volume:

> I agree with you—it is a thousand pities that a clever man like Allies should sermonise in the way he does. We are reading him in the Refectory—and he always seems in the same place, prancing like a cavalry soldier's horse without advancing, in the face of a mob. He has a noble subject, but I have not gained two ideas from his book—but I must not say so.[383]

To read all eight volumes is to sympathise with Newman. Allies has a basic message regarding the unfolding of Providence, particularly in the miraculous preservation and ultimate triumph of the Holy See. His structure is chronological but he repeatedly returns to the same events, pressing home the same message, so that the overall reaction is one of frustration at the lack of progress and the absence of nuance.

On the Continent, especially in Germany there was a generally positive reaction. For those seeking comfort in the face of corrosive rationalism, and who lamented the concessions that Döllinger and his school were prepared to make, Allies's clear-cut approach was welcome. For example, the confessional review, *Der Katholik* recommended his 1854 lecture as a necessary counter to the dominant 'subjective hypothesis', which entailed 'a denial of our Lord's appearance, of the work of redemption, and of the whole of Christianity'. Allies offered a corrective to Hegel, in whose philosophy 'the conception of freedom, like that of chance is utterly wanting'. The consequences were disastrous: 'Did such lectures on the philosophy of history aim at mere amusement, we might perhaps excuse them by the taste of the age. But we cannot overlook the fact that the most terrible devastation of morality, of religion, and lastly of politic, has proceeded out of this view of history'. In the reviewer's opinion 'the human mind is not moved by conception but by facts. Whoever can turn false conceptions into historic facts has power over it'. Such were the German theologians who had turned truth into myth; Strauss[384] in particular had 'made this power his own by substituting the Hegelian philosophy of history for the gospels and history of the Church'. Such false ideas can be met only by 'the objective principle of the world's history, by a true philosophy of history'. And this Allies had supplied, serving the Church by connecting 'correctness as to form with truth as to matter'.[385]

Even though Newman, always aware of the danger of speculation outrunning fact, might have endorsed this, it is his negative judgment on the *Formation* that has prevailed. Allies's approach was old-fashioned and confessional: chronicling the unfolding of a divine plan for the regeneration of mankind with the Holy See as the source of ultimate authority, and the papal states as the fulcrum of medieval Christendom. There was little engagement with those who saw historical outcomes as a resolution of the contingent, or those convinced by alternative explanations of events. Those sceptical at the beginning remained so, and would have seen ample justification in the 1890 papal brief published as the introduction to volume V (*Throne of the Fisherman*, 1887); Allies is awarded a papal knighthood as a scholar who has gained 'great merit by earnest actions and esteemed writings on behalf of the Catholic Faith'. Allies the apologist is little remembered, Allies the historian is forgotten.

Ordinary Catholic readers were unresponsive. In 1869 the Jesuit *The Month* reviewed volume II and prophesied what was to be the fate of this, Allies's *magnum opus*:

> We most cordially hope that this finely conceived and important work may be carried to its conclusion; and yet it is not without a feeling of sadness that we consider what is too likely to be its reception in the present state of English and Catholic literature. If a work with half its power and half

its research had been produced among Anglicans, it would have been read eagerly by thousands, who will now turn from it on account of the religion of its author. On the other hand, we fear that the taste for works of so high a character has yet almost to be created among English-speaking Catholics, and that an author who would have become famous in Germany or France may meet with but scanty appreciation among our own countrymen. But it is a great thing to have undertaken such a work, and it will be a still greater to complete it—and an author who fully understands the glories of such a subject as the Formation of Christendom can afford to wait some time for a public who will value his labours as they ought to be valued.[386]

Almost twenty years later when volume VI was issued (1888) the *Tablet* confirmed the prophecy:

We believe the English speaking world has not yet learnt the value of this most remarkable work. The volumes have come out irregularly, they have not always been issued by the same publisher, their price is just a little beyond the ordinary sum which a body, not given over to much reading and poor withal, is accustomed to spend upon books... These may have been the reasons that have militated against the widespread sale of these volumes, but they do not embrace the chief reason. The chief and real reason is that their worth is not yet known—the service they are capable of rendering is not yet recognised.[387]

A cheap edition of the first four volumes was published in 1894–5 and again in 1904–6, after which there was a reprint of volumes V to VIII. Yet many of the books seem to have ended in institutions, convent libraries and the like, and it is hard to avoid the conclusion that few readers persevered to the end. The seventh volume (*Peter's Rock in Mohammed's Flood*, 1890) lists all the previous volumes and chapter headings. At the age of seventy-seven Allies, perhaps thinking that the book might be the last, writes: 'I offer this work as a single stone though costing the labour of thirty years, if perchance it may be accepted in the structure of that Cathedral of human thought and action wherein our crucified God is the central figure, around which all has grown'. But he was spared to complete the final volume, *The Monastic Life*, published in 1895. His daughter detected in it 'a suspicion of dust and past ages' and remarked that the long quotation from Athanasius with which it begins is not of 'actual interest'.[388] Even the *Tablet is* somewhat guarded, remarking that 'There is something peculiarly touching in an author's life-long devotion to a great idea ... his vocation, must perforce be found in a work, to produce which the writer is called upon to scorn no mean delights, and live laborious days'.[389]

Scholarly citations from the *Formation* are rare; one such is in *The Ethical Basis of International Law*, by William Francis Roemer, published in 1928. The author in seeking to outline a 'philosophy of history, with regard to the foundations of International Law', draws extensively from the first volume, which he describes as an 'outstanding work'. But Allies and Roemer shared a confessional stance. Then in 2012 appeared a monograph seeking to analyse why Allies failed 'either to create a clear and stimulating product of the Ultramontane historical vision or to achieve an academic or popular reputation as an historian'.[390] The author, C. D. A. Leighton, describes Ultramontanism as 'the most egregious response of Christian churches to the emergence of nineteenth-century secularism', in which history becomes a spiritual battle and the disturbing changes in society the work of the antichrist. According to Leighton Allies lacked confidence, his history did not convey this stark certainty and so lacked resonance with the Catholic public. His apocalypticism was rather obscured, betraying a lack of wholehearted commitment to the cause. This arose from his Ultramontanism having a 'partially positive relationship with that which it struggled against, absorbing too much from it'. Taking his cue from Newman, Allies believed that a painstaking accumulation of facts could reveal a spiritual reality underlying apparent randomness. But what facts and how interpreted? Newman never ceased to value Döllinger as a historian, and Allies could never renounce Newman as mentor and guide. According to Leighton,

> Consistent hostility to the spirit of the age was possible neither to Newman, who had a University that could attract young Irishmen to establish, nor to Allies, who desired academic approval for his work. By training, after all, they were Anglican clergymen ... not field generals warring against society.[391]

It is reasonable for the two men to be linked intellectually up to the time of Döllinger's condemnation but after 1865 they had moved apart, and Allies now saw no need to make concessions to the 'spirit of the age'. The 'sermonising' approach, dismissed by Newman, had Cardinal Vaughan's wholehearted endorsement:

> If any man desire to ennoble his own estimate of the Catholic Church let him read this book. If any man's soul is capable of rising to a lofty ideal of life, as a living member of Catholic Christendom, let him understand the part that Christ has taken (and is still taking) in the formation of Christendom, as is shown from trustworthy sources by the pen of Mr. Allies.[392]

The reasons for Allies's lack of success with the Catholic public lay in his prolixity, and the abstruseness of his subject matter. For example, in the first three volumes there are detailed discussions of the ancient world and its competing philosophies, and in the later volumes lengthy pages are given over to extensive quotations from the Church Fathers. Although persisting with the work would have comforted any reader concerned to see the purposes of God vindicated in history, Leighton is correct in saying that the choice and handling of his subject matter quite blunted Allies's polemical edge. It is unfortunate that with his estrangement from Newman he found no equivalent countervailing intellectual stimulation. He might then have been directed back to a matters of greater interest, Leighton, for example, speculates that Allies might have given the Ultramontane generation a Catholic history of England to replace Lingard's 'timid apologetic whiggery'.[393]

The Formation of Christendom has been disregarded by subsequent scholars. In the twentieth century there were two works with the same title written by eminent historians, neither of which included any reference to Allies.[394] It is a pity, nevertheless, that his prodigious reading and formidable arsenal of textual references remains unquarried, and even for those suspicious of teleology there is much to admire in the eight volumes; not least, the light Allies sheds on the tensions within Christendom arising from the founding of New Rome. In detailing the malign effects of the state's attempts to use religion for its own ends Allies sought to illuminate the religious history of his own land. But for his Catholic readers it was all too much: too many volumes, too many words, too much detail and too much special pleading.

✢ 7 ✢

Home and Family

The next generation

By 1853 all three of Allies's sons were at Labbé's school at Yvetot. It is unclear how long they remained there. The eldest, Edward, never settled, and was soon to return home. He was not academically inclined, and his parents sought some kind of practical training for him, as they later did for Cyril, about whose education somewhat more is known. Basil, however, did settle into the academic routine of the Petit Séminaire, and displayed a great deal more interest in religion than his brothers. In this, Newman as an assiduous godparent played his part, keeping in contact with the growing boy and guiding him in his reading,[1] but the strongest influence upon him was Pierre Labbé, under whose influence he 'adopted the speech and manner of a Frenchman' and discovered a vocation to the priesthood. He went from Yvetot to the seminary of St Sulpice in Paris, but left in July 1865, aged twenty-one. According to his father, for a year he was 'unable to study—their (St Sulpice's) discipline as to the conjoined want of food, air and exercise have undermined his health'.[2] Basil later resumed his theological studies at the University of Louvain and in 1868 was ordained to the priesthood on his own patrimony by Francis Amherst, bishop of Northampton.

Of the three brothers, only Cyril had anything like a conventional English education, being sent to Newman's Oratory School in September 1860 when he was fourteen. When the school was opened the year before Edward was too old to go, but it is unlikely he would have benefited from its public school ethos. Neither was Cyril's time there a success; older than most of the scholars he was disruptive and soon judged ill-fitted to benefit from the curriculum offered. Newman regretted having accepted him; in August 1861 he wrote to the Nicholas Darnell, the headmaster:

Another cause of the infringement of discipline has been the sudden introduction of older boys, who, while from their age they would have greater influence in the School, have not been habituated to our particular rules and ways. Judging by the event, I doubt whether I ought to have let you take Allies. People who see what goes on in Church have told me things of him, which are not nice.[3]

Cyril's behaviour did improve, and given his lack of interest in the classics it was decided that he should concentrate on mathematics with a view to gaining admission to the Royal Woolwich Academy to train as an engineering officer.[4] This was optimistic, as Newman wrote to his parents just three months later in April 1862: 'All boys are wayward but my great perplexity is, that the (basis to work from) is wanting when I would influence him. Religious principle or duty does not commonly act energetically enough in boys, and I find no means of acting upon him, for he does not supply the matter'. He added that, far from being proficient in mathematics, Cyril could not do basic arithmetic; 'It is this want of grounding in the various parts of education which makes it so difficult to do any thing for him. It is not wonderful, that, in consequence, his heart is not in his work, and his influence in the school is not good. I do not see that he is gaining any thing from us; yet I do not know how to advise you'.[5] Cyril was late in returning after the Easter holidays in 1862, and Newman wrote anxiously to assure his father that there was no intention of excluding him. 'Be sure, that if I could be of any use to any boy of yours, I should think it the greatest satisfaction'.[6] He was aware that there were boys from whom Cyril should be kept apart, but unfortunately this was not possible: 'There is a small clique which I should like much to break up'. He suggested another career, 'I had already spoken of land surveying and will try to carry it out, to the best of my power'.[7] A seed must have been planted at Edgbaston because after some false starts, civil engineering proved to be the profession that both he and Edward were to pursue. In August, Mrs Allies, accepting the inevitable wrote to tell Newman that he would not be returning. Probably quite relieved he was still 'very sorry to part with him ... He is a boy with a number of good and taking qualities. He is affectionate and manly, and, if in the course of life he gets into good hands, he may be made a good deal of. I have been very anxious that we should do so.'[8] By November, he was at Havre, 'learning to be a shipbroker'.[9]

Cyril did not take to ship broking, nor had Edward settled into a profession, because by the spring of 1863, their parents decided that the only answer for them was a new start overseas. Their father explained to Cardinal Wiseman that they were going to Australia 'to learn high farming and intend to settle there at least for several years ... Would your Eminence do me the favour to give them a few lines of introduction and recommendation to Dr Quinn the Bishop of Brisbane. Will you likewise give them your benediction as members of your special flock? I trust that before everything they will keep their faith and religion in that new land.'[10] Allies wrote to Newman of the grief of separation; but received little consolation: 'the Antipodes are not further off, than Germany or Poland was 100 years ago, rather not near so far.'[11]

The young men left on Monday 29 June, taking with them the letters of introduction solicited by their father, and doubtless also some of his capital to fund their enterprise. It is likely that they sailed from London to Moreton Bay, Brisbane, and on arrival would have taken advantage of the land order system, whereby each person who paid full passage money was given an order for land in Queensland for £18 (equivalent to 18 acres) and a further order for £12 issuable after two years of residence.[12] What happened to the brothers in Australia cannot now be fully reconstructed. As early as January 1864 their mother was able to assure Newman that for Cyril 'the mysteries of sheep farming' were proving 'an employment he likes better than Latin or Greek.'[13] They appear to have entered into business with a man called Williams and established a sheep farm in the Burnett District of Queensland, several days' journey north of Brisbane. In October 1865 their father updated Newman; the boys, he said, 'have entered into a partnership with a squatter holding a station of 5000 acres within 200 miles of Brisbane. They purchased the half of 7300 sheep, 150 head of cattle, 10 horses etc. Their station will support from 15,000 to 18,000 sheep, and if they are blessed with good seasons they have a good prospect of success'. He then added some more fascinating detail, 'They went to learn their business with a squatter many hundred miles into the

Australian wilderness nearly to the Gulph of Carpentaria ... both had the narrowest possible escape of being killed by a wild tribe of savages. As it was their comrade was killed, instead of them ... Edward buried him, with the fear of the blacks being upon him every moment.'[14]

The brothers worked hard for several years, continuously struggling against the elements, but ultimately they had to admit defeat. On 5 May 1873 the Queensland State Supreme Court granted a Certificate of Discharge to Cyril Allies in the matter of his insolvent estate. By 1875 they had returned to England. One reminder of the brothers' ill-fated venture is the settlement of Allies Creek some 150 miles north-west of Brisbane, which at the last count had a population of 58 souls. Although defeated by drought they had been developed in character by the experience, and on return to England applied themselves to become qualified civil engineers and both found employment with Sheffield Corporation. Of the two Edward appears to have pursued his new career with more enthusiasm and success; he became a member of the Institute of Civil Engineers, and in 1878, already assistant borough engineer in Sheffield, he was appointed—after a rigorous selection process—as Surveyor to the West Derby Local Board (Liverpool) at a salary of £300 p.a.[15] He was to remain there for the next eight years, playing a significant part in Catholic affairs both local and national and in 1880 helped to organise an illuminated address from the Catholics of England congratulating Newman on his appointment to the cardinalate.

Cyril did not pursue his professional career. His father gifted to him the ownership of two islands (and some rocks) off the west coast of Ireland, Shark and Inishbofin the larger; and it was here as landlord, 'the King of Bofin', that he spent almost the rest of his life. The estate had been purchased by Henry Wilberforce in 1854, who two years before—as a married clerical convert—had found a new vocation in Ireland in establishing the Catholic Defence Association to counter the proselytism of the ultra-Protestant Irish Church Missionary Society.[16] The Protestants had established a school and soup kitchen on Inishbofin, but were obliged to retire when Wilberforce let the island to a tenant who pledged to support the Catholic cause. In 1859, Allies, a long-standing friend, provided him with funds by acquiring a mortgage on the property and when Wilberforce died in July 1874, was awarded ownership by the

Home and Family 369

Encumbered Estates Court.[17] It was not an attractive investment; given the poverty endemic to the west of Ireland any income would be small and erratic, and rents were not paid at all or were paid late, but in May 1878 they ceased altogether. Allies's agent informed him that any attempt to evict would be at risk to life. To add insult to this injury in 1882 the guardians of the local Poor Law Union notified him that as owner of 3,140 acres with an estimated rental of nearly £700, he owed £182 in poor rates. Despite his strong protests, which included unsuccessfully asking Gladstone to intervene, Allies was compelled to pay the arrears plus £22 in costs.[18]

It was a very uncomfortable situation and in this extremity Allies turned to his youngest son. Cyril agreed to accept what must have seemed a poisoned chalice, becoming owner of the islands and moving to Inishbofin as resident landlord. He left Sheffield—where he had been actively involved in Catholic social circles[19]—in November 1882. A week later his father wrote to tell Newman what had become of one of his former pupils:

> I venture to mention an Edgbaston school boy who I think should finally earn the blessing of those who bear the yoke in their youth. After twelve years spent fruitlessly in Queensland he has been seven more toiling in Sheffield in a subordinate office, but one carrying a good deal of responsibility, since he had to make an important report every week. I have now been obliged to take him away from this, and to send him as a last recourse to Boffin to see if he can get anything out of five years arrears, £3130. He attempted to cross in an open boat from Westport last Tuesday (14 November) but after eight hours of cold wind and rain got only within 12 miles and had to return. He tried again last Thursday and after seven hours under the same circumstances succeeded in reaching the island.[20]

Cyril rose to the challenge and on Inishbofin found his niche. In 1883 he was visited by friends from Sheffield, who on their return told the local newspaper that 'Mr Allies as a resident landlord is doing much good amongst his tenantry, with whom he is very popular—the best proof of which is the fact that he gets in his rents in a manner which has been unknown for the last five years. In a very short time residence at Boffin will be a pecuniary success to himself as well as a boon to the district.'[21]

According to the historian of Connemara, Tim Robinson, Cyril applied lessons learnt in Australia: he re-arranged holdings and relocated tenants, 'mainly to clear the way for his own expanding sheep farm'. It is recorded that he worked to improve the fishing industry and also co-operated with the Congested Districts Board in the modernisation of the island, particularly in establishing a fish curing station in the harbour. He was instrumental in building St Colman's Church, completed in 1914, where he is memorialised in a plaque. He seems to have felt it his duty to purge his tenants' superstitious beliefs and offered £50 to anyone who could show him a fairy, and £100 if it could be photographed.[22] There is no information as to why Cyril rather than his elder brother was given the island. Perhaps Edward had declined the challenge or perhaps the Australian experience had shown Cyril to have more 'feel' for farming in difficult circumstances? It must have been a lonely existence, but in 1888 Edward retired from his Liverpool position and went to join his brother on the island, recreating their Australian experience. In July 1890 a steamer chartered to survey Irish coastal fisheries anchored off Inishbofin; one of the scientists on board, Alfred Cort Haddon, recorded meeting them:

> The 2 Mr. Allies are Englishmen—some time ago, 8 or 9 years I believe, their father foreclosed on a mortgage on this island and so it and several others some 7 in all—including rocks—became his property and he sent his son to look after it and he has lived there ever since. For about the last 18 months, another brother joined this one and so these 2 middle aged men are living bachelor's lives on this out of the way island—fishing, farming and so forth. They have both spent several years in Australia, mainly in Queensland sheep farming etc. The latter brother is more or less an engineer. The former is the recognised landlord. I got more intimate with Edward

the engineer, and I hope I have got him interested in Folklore and he has promised to collect information for the Royal Irish Academy.

Edward told Haddon about skulls that were displayed in the ruined St Colman's church and they devised a plan to collect a number for scientific research: an expedition that was to inaugurate a significant development in the evolution of scientific anthropology.[23]

The brothers' island life changed dramatically when in January 1891 Cyril married Kathleen, the daughter of the Reverend John Lillie. There was an Australian connection. From 1837 until his return to England in 1858 Lillie was a Presbyterian minister in Tasmania and three years later he returned to the Antipodes, building up large investments in sheep farming in New Zealand and Australia. It may have been in this context that Cyril became acquainted with the family although Kathleen then was still a child. Lillie died in 1866, his widow and daughter returned to England and fifteen years later both converted to Roman Catholicism. As Mrs Allies, Kathleen was to make a significant impression on the island community but tragically died after only three years of marriage, soon after giving birth to a second daughter, leaving her widower to raise his daughters, Monica and Winifred.

Edward had returned to England, but his brother's grief seems to have persuaded Basil to leave parish ministry and move to Inishbofin. It marked the end of an undistinguished priestly career, which had been a sequence of failed experiments, dependent upon his father's cash and influence, but seemingly lacking spiritual direction. After ordination he had transferred to the diocese of Westminster, becoming a curate in High Barnet. The parish priest, George Bampfield, was a convert, an innovator and an evangelist, who founded a school and later formed the Institute of St Andrew, a group of secular priests united in a vision of bringing Catholicism into the surrounding area.[24] Basil did not stay with him long. He is next to be found (1871) as priest at the Catholic chapel of Danesfield House, constructed for the wealthy convert—and friend of T. W. Allies—C. R. Scott-Murray to a Pugin design and completed in 1856.[25] Yet, within a few months he had moved again, joining Canon Walker in Scarborough.[26] Walker died in June 1873 and the following year Basil moved south and for a time was chaplain to the Sacred Heart Convent at Roehampton, which was the order that ran the training school at Wandsworth, and as in his previous posts his father's influence may have played some part in the appointment.[27] Here he came into contact with the Jesuits and in July 1875 entered their novitiate at Manresa House at Roehampton[28] to test whether he had a vocation. He did not, and found living with teenage novices particularly trying. Thereupon he returned to Scarborough to assist the parish priest, his friend Arthur Riddell, who became bishop of Northampton in 1880.[29] It was under his auspices that in 1882 Basil went to become parish priest at Stamford and in 1885 was appointed a canon (Canon Penitentiary) of Northampton Cathedral. His last parish appointment before moving to Ireland was to St Edward's Kettering, from 1894 to 1895.

The final years

Allies continued as secretary to the Poor-School Committee into old age; his family home, which from 1880 was 82 Gloucester Place, served as its registered address and his office. Once retired, in 1890 he Eliza and Mary moved to 3 Lodge Place, St John's Wood, which was then 'quiet as a country parsonage' and close to Our Lady's Church where their last born, Bernard Joseph had been interred.[30] This year saw the death, on 11 August, of Cardinal Newman. Thomas, who with Basil attended the funeral, felt the parting very deeply; in words of his daughter: 'My father survived Cardinal Newman thirteen years, ever the poorer for the loss of his friend, and the richer for the fragrance of that great memory.'[31] His release from daily office hours brought new and perhaps unexpected tensions to the family home. Although he continued until 1895 to work on completing the *Formation of Christendom* his daughter hints that both she and her mother found it difficult to adjust to his unwonted presence: 'Hitherto my father had been a man of books and he had even written on the "Virginal Life" ... If, then, he was a "free man at seventy-seven", he was also *qualis ab initio*; having a heart's desire as well as an intellectual one, he pursued it with all his mind.'[32] In a paragraph not included in the second edition of her biography Mary refers to unhappiness stemming from a clash of expectations:

Home and Family 373

The overweening desire to bring about the happiness of two people did not contribute to the happiness of the many, nor indeed to his own... A great mind may fall into an aberration of heart, for the perfect equilibrium of each would be heaven before its time. It was largely owing to this 'aberration' of my father's that the abode of peace was so full of conflicting wills. He said, 'Peace, peace, and there was no peace.'[33]

Over the final ten years of her life Eliza's hearing deteriorated and it is easy to understand why such a 'free spirit' chafed under the new domestic circumstances.[34] Despite his prayers and agonising Thomas never fully conquered the truculence that came from belief in the rightness of his convictions. Unlike his oldest friend and despite all his sacrificial service to the Church, he was not a candidate for sainthood, not in his own eyes, or those of his daughter. But his services in support of the papacy did not go unrecognised and one of the first acts of Cardinal Vaughan, after being enthroned as archbishop of Westminster was to secure for him the pope's gold medal for merit. This was in April 1893. It was the start of his last decade, years marked by accumulating sorrows; but he battled on to finish *The Formation of Christianity*, the last volume being published in 1896, when he was eighty-three.

Of Thomas's and Eliza's two daughters, Mary Frances (called Mafra by her father) was married in April 1883 to James Lynam Broder; they had two children, Mary Frances, born in 1884, and William in 1888. Her elder sister, Mary Helen, stayed at home to, in her own words, 'feed on my mother's lively wit and the marrow of my father's mind,'[35] and also to chronicle the sorrows of her parent's final years. In August 1893 she travelled with her father to Inishbofin. It was a draining experience; Mary remembered the return journey as 'all but fatal' for him. Just six months later Cyril's wife, his beloved daughter-in-law Kathleen, was dead. And then in the space of little more than a year he and Eliza lost two grandchildren. In November 1895, young Mafra Broder, a pupil at the Convent of the Holy Child, contracted meningitis and died aged 11; twelve months later her cousin Winifrid Mary Allies was also taken. Her aunt described the terrible circumstances:

> My brother Cyril's two little girls, Monica and Winnie, were on a visit to Lodge Place. They arrived from Bofin in September 1896, and there was no suspicion of illness till November 14, the anniversary of Mafra's death, when Winnie fell suddenly sick. Acute gastritis declared itself, and for a whole fortnight Winnie's suffering was excruciating. 'Oh, the pain!' was the constant cry which came from her poor little lips. At last the long agony of twelve hours set in, without one moment of unconsciousness, and Winnie was crowned on the morning of November 29, 1896. She was not quite four years old.[36]

More suffering was to come, Mary wrote: 'My father was 84 on February 12, 1897. He entered on a sorrowful year, which brought for him descent into the valley of the shadow, when earth recedes and heaven seems far off and dim'.[37] He lived six more years, sorrowful years with more tragic losses and increasing bodily infirmity. On 29 April 1897 he suffered a stroke and was never to hear Mass again, 'surely a forecast of purgatory'.[38] Basil returned from Inishbofin to support his sister in caring for their parents. Yet his arrival brought no comfort:

> the support of his presence was much needed; yet, for reasons clear to us afterwards he brought no sunshine. He seemed weighed down by an extreme depression of spirits... He was kind without being resourceful, and as soon as the doctor spoke hopefully of my father, returned to the island home which so fascinated him, but only as it appeared, to die.[39]

Basil died aged 53 in July 1897 and was buried on the island. According to family tradition he succumbed to cholera, but his sister wondered whether his will to resist the disease had already been weakened: 'Coming events cast their shadows before them, and I have always supposed that my brother's approaching end was the shadow apparent in his intercourse with us'.[40] His father mourned him deeply, writing in his diary: 'Next to the gift of Faith itself... comes the gift of a son, my ever dear Henry Basil, endowed with a vocation to the priestly life

... and the ten thousand mercies which sprang out of that vocation to us, his parents.'[41]

Edward died two years later. He had returned to England when his brother's marriage brought their island bachelor life to a close. His health, already poor, continued to deteriorate and early in 1899 his parents decreed that he should stay at their home where for several months he lay 'stretched on a sick bed'. Both Thomas and Eliza were themselves very frail and at length Edward decided that he had recovered sufficiently to return to his Bayswater lodgings. But it was a false dawn, and, very poorly indeed, he was brought back to the family home, where he died 'in a syncope' on the afternoon of Sunday 4 June 1899.[42] Cyril was the only son to outlive his father. In 1900 he married his daughter's governess, and had five more children. Following the death of his second wife he returned to London, but survived her by only a few months, dying in September 1916 at the age of 70. His married sister Mafra had died the year before and so his children were taken in by Mary Helen. They did not inherit the Inishbofin estates, the island holdings having been sold to the Irish Land Commission in 1907.

On the last day of 1900 the Allies's son-in-law, James Broder, died after a brutal and ineffective operation[43] and some days later Thomas became ill enough for him to be anointed, but again he recovered; spared another year to mourn the death of his dear friend and correspondent over many years, the dedicatee of the last volume of the *Formation*, Aubrey de Vere.[44] Then just days later he endured the 'crowning sorrow' of losing Eliza, his companion of sixty years.

> At the end of 1901 she caught a chill which told seriously on a frame weakened by age and cares ... She died, after one week's illness, hardly realising it herself, or only dimly as is the wont of the dying. She passed away at 11.30 am on January 24, 1902. My father who could not see her on account of his own infirmity, was kept in ignorance of his loss until the evening.[45]

In the dedication to *A Life's Decision*, Thomas had acknowledged the great debt he owed to Eliza:

> To my sole partner in these trials, the more helpless and yet the more courageous, the quicker to see the Truth, the readier to embrace it, the first to surrender her home in the bloom of her youth, who chose without shrinking the loss I had brought upon her, and by her choice doubled my gain.

Wilfrid Wilberforce, a family friend wrote of her:

> None who were privileged to know Mrs. Allies could ever forget her. The sparkle of the eye, the keen play of wit, the quenchless spirit of fun—often—it is to be feared, veiling a heart saddened by temporal trials—all this rises before the memory when her name is mentioned. To those who knew her not, no amount of description would reproduce her charming, lovable personality.[46]

Thomas himself had one more year to endure. No better description of his last days can be given than that of the daughter who remained with him:

> On his ninetieth birthday, February 12, 1903, a marked change became apparent in all his being. There seemed to be so little of his personality left, and yet he was quite himself. Cardinal Vaughan came to see him in March, and it was some time before the Cardinal succeeded in conveying his identity. They never met on earth again. His pen had long ceased to write; he could speak only with difficulty; his legs would not carry him. His eyes and ears were affected; he could no longer use his Missal or his Greek Testament. His whole being was silent in the depths of the mysterious valley, and so death found him. On June 13 an attack of *rigor* set in, from which, however, he rallied slightly. After a few days of anxious watching, and two receptions of the Holy Viaticum, he passed away at 2 a.m. on June 17, 1903. There was no spoken farewell, nor anything which I could take to myself as a last word, and I looked upon the silent consummation

as the completion of his work. Six years of infirmity and powerlessness made up what was wanting for the perfection of that noble mind.

He was interred in the same grave as Eliza, his son Edward and granddaughter Winifred, in the little cemetery attached to St Mary Magdalen Church at Mortlake. Their stone incorporated a carved crucifix and Latin inscriptions for *Elisae Hall Allies* and *Thomae Guglielmi Allies*. Many visitors come to the Church to admire the statuary, in particular the tent-shaped mausoleum of Sir Richard and Lady Burton, but sadly the Allies's memorial stone can no longer be traced. From her father's large estate[47] Mary Helen received £5000 in cash, sufficient to give her independence and the leisure to commence work on her biography, which appeared in 1907, with a revised second edition in 1924. She died on 27 January 1927, aged 75.

Reflections on Allies's life

As his life achieved some stability, after the tumultuous years following his conversion, with the Poor-School Committee appointment, Allies rediscovered his poetic gift. He no longer sought recognition or fame, but for recreation would sometimes take up his pen to memorialise, in competent verse, significant times and seasons and the people who were important to him. Others recognised his gift; three weeks after the dogma of the Immaculate Conception was promulgated Newman wrote to him about it: 'A suggestion comes from Rome this morning of our holding an Academia in Dublin in honour of the Immaculate Conception. We *must* have a copy of Greek verses from you. You need not be present, nor your name known as the author.'[48] Much of his poetry has been lost but Mary Helen Allies includes as appendices to her biography two poems dedicated to her younger sister, Mary Frances, one when she was thirteen, the other to her on the eve of her marriage (1883), *To Mafra, A Bride*:

> The Daughter's part is past and gone;
> The Father's prayer still worketh on;

> Parental conquers filial love;
> This dies below, that soars above.[49]

Beyond family, the wellspring of Allies's poetic inspiration was devotion to the Catholic faith. In 1876 he contributed two poems to *The Month*, the Jesuit Review, which since 1865 had been edited by his life-long friend, Father Henry Coleridge.[50] April's number included an ode for St Thomas Aquinas, 'in gratitude and love' and the following month 'a sacred lyric' on the *Magnificat*. With retirement came renewed creativity and in 1894 the *Irish Monthly* published a number of his poems, mostly devotional, but the first (*The Birth, Growth and Suicide of a Heresy*) was starkly polemical: The last echo of an old refrain, it extended to 19 pages, beginning with a quotation from Dryden's *Religio Laici*:

> And this unpolish'd rugged verse I chose
> As fittest for discourse and nearest prose;
> For, while from sacred truth I do not swerve,
> Tom Sternhold's or Tom Shadwell's rhymes will serve.

Old age had not mellowed him. The poem is bitterly vituperative; dismissing the Reformation monarchs with short shrift:

> Men wander'd terror-struck through forty years,
> The desert of Elizabethan rule,
> Of every vice, untruth and fraud, the school,
> Till bastard queen of bastard church the head,
> Died in despair on a sin-haunted bed.

The fruit of Protestantism was inner emptiness, the reality underlying the surface assurance of the Victorian Establishment:

> A church dissolved by its own children's blows
> Bears witness to the source from which it rose,
> And endless error's ever-growing fruit
> Betrays the deadly nature of the root.

> What is the gospel offered to the world
> By power whose teachings from strong fleets are hurl'd?
> Or what the picture of the inward mind
> Whose outward fortune dazzles all mankind?
> Bishops on gravest doctrines disagreed,
> Sects with no bishops, preachers with no creed;
> Synods which call themselves Pan-Anglican,
> And sit and speak, and vote belief in Pan:
> A general residuum undefined,
> Which, each specific lost, remains behind.
> This is the cost of blood, and strife and tears;
> The grand Eureka of three hundred years.[51]

Allies never tired of seeking to open the eyes of the unconverted, whilst oblivious to the ineffectiveness of yet more of his words and the hostility they surely aroused. After completing the poem in 1891 he sent it to Lord Chief Justice Coleridge.[52] Despite the demands and grandeur of his office he took no offence, and in reply reminisced that 'once certainly, at Launton, we fought like Widdrington[53] to the stumps of my intellect at least, if not of yours'. But now he had no heart for further combat:

> the controversies of these times have no present interest for me ... To me an old man to get to heaven is the thing ... and let the rest of it all go its own way; believing that He will in no wise cast out any one who tries earnestly to do right, and quite unable to see either the real Romanism of Newman, or the sham rubbish which imitates it, in the New Testament.[54]

That one of the greatest judicial minds of the nineteenth century could remain satisfied with a religion such as this simply baffled Allies. Newman's 'Romanism' was his faith, the fullness of Christianity. And to mark his esteem sometimes he honoured the Saint's birthday in verse, writing on 21 February 1878:

> Full forty years have passed since words of thine
> First woke in me the thought of things divine,

> How many were the years, how dark the days
> Of wandering spent in labyrinthian ways,
> When 'mid 'stammering lips' of errors old
> Thy voice alone seemed clear, thy accents bold.[55]

The poem goes on on to number his friend with St Thomas Aquinas and St Augustine.[56] There were further verses to mark the cardinal's eightieth birthday in 1881, two sonnets linking him with St Philip Neri. As both men grew older the doctrinal differences that may once have divided them faded into forgetfulness. On 9 October 1885, the fortieth anniversary of his receiving Newman's letter announcing his conversion, Allies reflected that this had 'opened to me a prospect that was terrible.' Adding, 'I must confess that the forty years have been terrible to pass: and again, what might not be expected, that the *retrospect* of them is terrible.'[57] Obedience to conscience had exacted a high price from both: the loss of friends and the comfort of familiar ways. But there was a difference. Although now among a city's teeming poor there was a continuity between Oxford and Birmingham. Newman's days were still devoted to prayer, the priestly ministry, pastoral oversight and writing that would influence Christians of all denominations. His one-time brother-in-arms, Edward Pusey, who had died three years before, had continued as a priest of the Church of England enfolded in the security of and respectability of an Oxford college, but had ended his days an isolated figure in a changing religious landscape. But for Newman the Catholic, secure in Rome's *semper eadem*, incorporation into the *orbis terrarum* had extended his influence far beyond national life. A new generation and a new papacy brought recognition and esteem and old age gifted him a glimpse of the veneration with which future generations would regard his works. Allies was not so favoured. He had left a comfortable rectory, secure income and leisure for study, in order to dwell in an unfamiliar, occasionally hostile, new land. Only after three years of stress and penury did he find employment, as a bureaucrat: 'Pegasus between the shafts of a cart'. As an Anglican his scholarship was widely reviewed and widely influential; as a Catholic, when his academic work had to be squeezed into the margins of the day, his publications never achieved the readership and the impact that he longed for. In 1882 Newman sympathised with him that the Church had 'no public' to supply a market; *The Formation of Christendom* had reached its fourth volume with Allies lamenting the fact that there had been no reaction from any 'competent person'.[58] Undeterred, he continued for two more decades and four more volumes, but could look only to eternity for his reward: 'when I am in safe harbour the look back on the stormy sea will be a pure joy.'[59]

Newman had hoped that in pioneering a new subject, 'the philosophy of history', Allies could open up new intellectual horizons and shine a fresh light on the concerns of contemporary Catholicism. It was an expectation he could not fulfil, despite devoting countless hours to the task, drudgery to set alongside that of serving the Poor-School Committee. If the desire for intellectual recognition had not held him in thrall he might more wholeheartedly have served the cause of education, or burnished his journalistic skills to serve St Peter. Of his polemical output the two volumes of *Per Crucem ad Lucem* (1879) included much valuable material, but as the *Tablet* remarked this pugilism was now shadow-boxing: 'the Anglican controversy is virtually closed. The great office of the Oxford Movement was to make trial of Anglicanism ... and the trial was fatal to its pretensions. Whatever else may be urged in favour of the Church of England, it can never again be defended on the ground of authority.'[60] Granted *Per Crucem* was 'a perfect arsenal of weapons of the finest temper, the greatest keenness and the highest polish', perhaps its author's greatest service to Catholicism was his example:

> Who can estimate the moral influence of the spectacle ... of men most authoritative for character and talent in the National Communion renouncing their false allegiance to it together with all their prospects of worldly advancement and humbly seeking enrolment in the ranks of the host which marches through the ages under the leadership of Peter?

Reflecting on Allies and his fellow converts, the reviewer was reminded of lines from *Rugby Chapel*, 'Ye alight in our van! At your voice, Panic, despair, flee away' men and women whose lives were shaped by a commanding conscience, 'souls temper'd with fire.'[61]

In old age Allies said that with his conversion 'all the glory of the world went at once, irrecoverably. I have ever felt since that I was "an abject"'. This seems overblown.[62] He spent his Catholic years living a comfortable middle-class life and was accepted in the highest ranks of society. He found well-paid employment, without, he said, ever feeling secure, always like Habacuc held by the hair over the lion's den. He was never quite at ease with those who were born into his adopted faith, and exclusion from wider Anglican society produced in him a continuing sadness, his own 'thorn in the flesh'. A recent history of the Newcastle Scholarship observed that the first winner of the prize 'is best remembered for this precocious achievement; nothing in his subsequent career matched it.'[63] A life of devoted study, but so little to show for it, rather a sense of failure that he had 'done little to overthrow the Protestant tradition of the Papacy'. On 2 October 1880 he wrote in his diary:

> Strongly impressed in the night with the false estimate of one's own standing in God's sight, which yearning after intellectual distinction produces. How can I get myself entirely to realise that mental power is of itself no guarantee whatever of Divine acceptance, as little as bodily beauty or material wealth. It seems to me that even now I have not overthrown completely the idolatry in my heart, which quite engrossed me up to the age of twenty-four, and was the root, I think of every error and sin.[64]

Ten years later he reflected on the death of Cardinal Newman, 'I have been thinking again and again of the life which he presented last Monday (11 August 1890) to the all-seeing Judge whom he has so deeply loved and so faithfully served and of the reward he has received for it. Subsidiary to this is the thought that before long I must stand before the same Judge myself.'[65] And on the day of the funeral he wrote, 'I thought how soon I should lie down, as he now lies, and see what he said long ago, that there are but two beings for every man—God and his own soul.'[66] Old age heightened a sense of inner isolation, of unappreciated sacrifice. Evidence to the contrary seemed not to weigh: five years before he

Home and Family 383

had been appointed a papal knight, to be followed by the award of a papal gold medal, according to his daughter, 'the greatest distinction conferred on laymen by the Holy See.'[67] Neither honour brought any enduring sense of fulfilment, just brief respites, glimpses of 'Our Lord on Thabor without his thorns.'[68]

Aged 83 with *The Formation of Christendom* finished, Allies planned one last work to crown his Catholic life, a magisterial defence of the papacy. It was not to be; as Mary remembered,

> I thought God would give him long enough to complete his defence of the Holy See. At this time 1895–6, he did not consider that his life's work was finished ... We were both mistaken. Looking back I can see the process of detachment: how it began in the repeated blows of death, and how it ended in a yet sharper isolation, after his writing and reading days were over, and he had to bear the burden of great infirmities and loneliness of spirit.[69]

On 14 February 1899, 'in a hand, trembling, yet still legible', Allies wrote: 'on September 11, 1850, I frankly gave up all my chance of success in life by becoming a Roman Catholic'. It was a conviction he took to the grave, but never doubting that this was a small price to pay for being the recipient 'from beginning to end' of 'the most unmerited grace of God'; and

> the verification of Our Lord's promise, *Centuplum accipiet* [Matthew 13:23] in one thing most marked from that time to this present time, the gift of inward peace. It is the planting in my heart His own *pax*. No gift of wealth or distinction of any kind, or possessing any friends or relations is equal to that *pax* viewed as the settled habit of the soul and especially as the forerunner and anticipation, so to say, of the future sight of glory, when we shall see our Redeemer as He is.[70]

He lived on into a new century that was to be scarred by the ravages of godlessness of which he had warned. 'He wrote the last entry in his

Diary in 1900. What remained to him of life was sorrow and infirmity; the gradual descent into the valley of death, a lengthened process of leaving and being left.[71] His death, when it came on Wednesday 17 June 1903, attracted little attention; there were few left to mourn, for he had outlived most of his contemporaries. Still a name to some Catholics, in wider British society he was almost forgotten. There was a brief notice in the *Athanaeum*, the *Tablet*'s short memorial was prefaced with the observation that 'he has lived so long in retirement that his death does little to disarrange the course of affairs except in the case of those—of one in particular—who were of his own household. All the same it is an event that stirs—at any rate memories'[72]—memories that were rekindled by his daughter's biography four years later; the *Tablet*'s review was entitled *Thou Hast Great Allies*[73] and her father honoured as the last survivor of the 'old and great Oxford race, Newman, Manning, Ward, Allies, Oakeley, Dalgairns and the rest'.

When the account of his conversion *A Life's Decision* was published Allies added to what he had written a quarter of a century before, an epilogue, entitled 'Paris and Helen'. Written for Anglicans it is a lament for those who had once been bathed in the same light as him and he cited the case of one unnamed clergyman whose published protest against the Gorham judgment he had read to his own congregation. It was Archdeacon Denison, whose *Notes on my Life 1805–1878* had recently been published. Putting this biography aside Allies asked: 'Was this a "Life Worth Living"? Yet it is the life of many thousands who have lived and died between 1850 and 1880 and many thousands more who are detained in Helen's bower.' For himself, he was sure that he had chosen the 'better part':

> O Church of the living God, Pillar and Ground of the Truth, fair as the moon, bright as the sun, terrible as an army in battle array, O Mother of Saints and Doctors, Martyrs and Virgins, clothe thyself in the robe and aspect, as thou has strength, of Him whose Body thou art, the Love for our sake incarnate: shine forth upon thy lost children, and draw them to the double fountain of thy bosom, the well-spring of Truth and Grace.[74]

NOTES

Chapter 1

1. W. J. Pountney, *Old Bristol Potteries*, Arrowsmith, Bristol, 1920, p. 110.
2. Sir John Allies cannot be traced; the individual referred to is probably Sir John Gay Alleyne (1724–1801), a Barbadian politician and slave owner.
3. M. H. Allies, *Thomas William Allies*, Burns & Oates, London, 1907, p. 1.
4. Obituary in the *Bristol Mercury*, 9 March 1843.
5. *The Monthly Repository of Theology and General Literature*, 17, 1822, p. 63.
6. In 1949 the pictures were in the possession of Thomas's great-great-granddaughter, Dorothy Annie Allies Penny, and in January 2008 were sold at Bonhams in 'the contents of a gentleman's library'.
7. The unfortunate under-librarian lost his job. On leaving London the disgraced Dighton moved between Oxford and Cambridge producing satirical portraits of dons. See Dennis Rose, *Life, Times and Recorded Works of Robert Dighton (1752–1814)*, Dennis Rose, Salisbury, 1981, p. 25.
8. She described the 'second Mrs Allies' as 'a stout heretic of the Evangelical School'; Allies, *Thomas Allies*, p. 3.
9. K. Crouan, *John Linnell—A Centennial Exhibition*, Cambridge University Press, Cambridge, 1982, p. xi.
10. At the beginning of the nineteenth century Southampton was rather a spa town than a major port. It developed rapidly with the coming of the railway in 1840, but only acquired city status in 1964.
11. Nicholas Poussin (1594–1665), the French classical painter, a major influence in the development of Western art.
12. Probably Allart van Everdingen (1621–75), the Dutch painter of landscapes, who had two artist brothers—Jan and Caesar.
13. David Linnell, *Blake, Palmer, Linnell & Co.—The Life of John Linnell*, The Book Guild, Sussex, 1994, p. 63.
14. Letter dated 1 November 1819; *ibid*.
15. *Ibid*., pp. 64–6.

16. *Ibid.* Rainier was a noted horticulturalist; the villa and gardens he established in Southampton are still visited.
17. *Ibid.*, p. 79.
18. *Ibid.*, p. 85. Constable was not elected to the Royal Academy until 1828.
19. *Ibid.*, pp. 79–80.
20. Letter dated 17 March 1823; *ibid.*, p. 81.
21. *Ibid.*, p. 82.
22. *Ibid.*, p. 83.
23. Linnell valued it at £50; *ibid.*, p. 375.
24. Allies's step-mother died in 1868 at the age of 87.
25. Allies, *Thomas Allies*, p. 3.
26. *An Account of the Public Charities in England and Wales, by the editor of the 'Cabinet Lawyer'*, Simpkin and Marshall, London, 1828, p. 75.
27. C. P. Hill, *The History of Bristol Grammar School*, Pitman, London, 1951, pp. 66, 67.
28. *An Account of the Public Charities*, pp. 74–6.
29. Sir John Cox Hippisley (1746–1825) was a notorious seeker of public office. As an MP he was a strong advocate of Catholic emancipation and wrote a number of pamphlets in support of the cause.
30. I. Fitzroy Jones, *Some Notes on the Hippisley Family Collected by A. E. Hippisley*, Wessex Press, Taunton, 1952.
31. His will of 1831 (Cornwall RO RH6/2/1).
32. The inscription reads: 'I who was Born a PAGAN and a SLAVE / Now sweetly sleep a CHRISTIAN in my Grave / What tho' my hue was dark my SAVIOR's sight / Shall Change this darkness into radiant Light / Such grace to me my Lord on earth has given / To recommend me to my Lord in heaven / Whose glorious second coming here I wait / With saints and Angels him to celebrate.'
33. Allies, *Thomas Allies*, p. 8.
34. H. C. Maxwell Lyte, *A History of Eton College 1440–1875*, Macmillan, London, 1875, p. 370.
35. *Some Account of the Exhibitions and Scholarships for Superannuated and Other Eton Scholars, with the names of present holders*, N. P. Williams, Eton, 1862, p. x.
36. Maxwell Lyte, *Eton*, p. 370.
37. *Ibid.* A one-time Eton chaplain and Catholic convert, the publisher Charles Kegan Paul, had a more sceptical view of Coleridge: 'a handsome man of

great energy, perhaps it may be said of considerable pretentiousness, who impressed his personality on those who came into contact with him ... The boys in his house and form were disposed to doubt if his scholarship was impeccable.' C. Kegan Paul, *Memories*, Routledge, London, 1899, p. 90.

38. On the basis of annual inflation rates, £250 would be equivalent to £26,000 in today's money.
39. J. Kolb, *The Letters of Arthur Henry Hallam*, Ohio State University Press, Columbus, 1981, p. 288.
40. *Montem* was the custom, formerly practised by the scholars of going every third year, on Whit Tuesday, to Salt Hill and exacting money from passers-by, to support at King's College, Cambridge, the senior scholar of the school.
41. G. F. Waagen, *Treasures of Art in Great Britain*, trans. E. R. Eastlake, Murray, London 1854, p. 416. The visit was some time in the 1830s.
42. Delia Gaze (ed.), *Concise Dictionary of Women Artists*, Fitzroy Dearborn, Chicago, 2001.
43. Also at Eton at this time was another convert, George Beckwith Yard, later blamed by Orlando Forrester for the return of Richard Sibthorp to the Catholic Church in 1865.
44. A student without a scholarship or exhibition.
45. Allies, *Thomas Allies*, pp. 8–9.
46. University College London. 'Legacies of British slave-ownership', ucl.ac.uk/lbs/person/view/2146637328.
47. It was given by his heir to Newman's Magdalen friend, John Morland Rice the grandson of Jane Austen's brother, Edward Knight. See Richard James Wheeler, *The Rice Portrait of Jane Austen*, Richard James Wheeler, Codex Publications, Westerham, 1996.
48. A demy enjoyed a scholarship with emoluments half those of a fellow.
49. W. Tuckwell, *Reminiscences of Oxford*, Dutton, New York, 1908, p. 166; this work has memories of T. H. Newman.
50. Letter dated 13 December 1847; *British Magazine*, 43, 1848, pp. 96–7.
51. 21 May; M. R. D. Foot (ed.), *The Gladstone Diaries*, vol. I, 1825–32, Oxford, 1968, p. 305.
52. *The Bury and Norwich Post*, 25 April 1882. According to his great-nephew, H. M. Croker, he was a gifted amateur painter and connoisseur.
53. 'Eheu! Quanto minus est cum reliques versari quam tui meminisse', reproduced in *Byroniana: The Opinions of Lord Byron on Men, Manners, and Things; with the Parish Clerk's Album, Kept at his Burial Place (Hucknall Torkard)*, Charles Tilt, London, 1834.

54. *Oxford Union Society*, printed by Talboys & Browne, Oxford, 1831.
55. M. H. Allies, *Thomas William Allies—Secundo*, Burns, Oates & Washbourne, London, 1924, p. 5 (this was the second, expanded edition of the biography).
56. Christopher Hollis, *The Oxford Union*, Evans Brothers, London, 1965, p. 46.
57. The recollection of Archdeacon Browne in Wilfrid Ward, *W. G. Ward and the Oxford Movement*, Macmillan & Co., London, 1890, p. 24.
58. Allies, *Thomas Allies*, p. 9.
59. *Ibid.*, pp. 9–10.
60. This confrontation took place at the Clarendon Hotel and was commemorated in a mock Homeric squib called the *Uniomachia*.
61. W. Massie, *Sydenham or the Memoirs of a Man of the World*, Henry Colbourn and Richard Bentley, London, 1830.
62. Allies, *Thomas Allies*, pp. 9–11.
63. Gaggiotti was appointed in 1851. He provided valuable information regarding the Papal States during the crisis of 1859. Clarendon was Foreign Secretary, 1853–9.
64. T. W. Allies, *A Life's Decision*, 2nd edn, Burns & Oates, London, 1894, p. 4. The first edition was published in 1880.
65. Diary, 29 September 1839. Allies's diary for 1839 is in the writer's possession; the first entry is on Monday, 6 May, the last on Tuesday, 31 December; the pages for 2–5 May are not present.
66. Diary, 4 October 1839.
67. Newman had been awarded his MA degree in April 1836.
68. Some months later Allies thought of this as a possibility—perhaps the seeds had been planted by his step-mother? See *A Life's Decision*, p. 5.
69. *Ibid.*
70. *Ibid.*, p. 4.
71. Diary, 31 May 1839.
72. Diary, 18 May 1839.
73. Diary, 29 October 1839.
74. She was christened at Clifton on 20 April 1819.
75. The name 'Goodrest' is said to have originated from the exhausted Cromwell having rested there after the battle of Newbury in 1644; the house is also called Shinfield Park.
76. In 1838 Stonhouse exhibited *Portrait of the Three Younger Children of E. Willes, Esq.* at the Royal Academy. He married the daughter of the celebrated artist, Frederick Christian Lewis. In 1851, he graduated as

Licentiate in Theology from Durham University and until his death in 1883 was rector of Frimley in Surrey.

77. In 1842 following Wilkie's death Willes published a tribute to him, *A Letter to Charles Stonhouse Esq. Formerly Pupil to Sir David Wilkie*, [Lausanne], 1842.

78. Diary, 28 July 1839. Onesimus is the subject of Paul's Letter to Philemon.

79. Poem dated 26 June 1837, it is inscribed from Wordsworth, 'Her eyes as stars of Twilight fair ...' ('Phantom of Delight', 1807).

80. Letter to his son Edward, dated 14 February 1838, Willes Papers, Warwickshire Archives, CR4141/7/652/10.

81. In 1842 Clara married Rev Gilbert Wall Heathcote, the Rector of Ashe in Surrey, the brother of Allies's Oxford friend and religious confidant, William Beadon Heathcote and cousin of Keble's friend and patron, Sir William Heathcote of Hursley.

82. *A Life's Decision*, p. 4.

83. 'Drowned at night in a tank on the Jura mountains', 'Autobiography of Edward Coleridge', BL Add. MS 47555. 'A young Englishman was lately found drowned in a reservoir near a chalet on Mount Tendre, one of the points of the Jura. His knapsack was laid in the chalet, and he had probably gone to the reservoir to draw some water and had fallen in. His watch, money, papers, and other effects were sent to the British Ambassador at Berne. It has since been ascertained that his name was Henry Herbert, a medical student of London, aged 25'; *Bristol Mercury*, 2 September 1837.

84. Allies, *Thomas Allies*, p. 6.

85. For example, 'To the Memory of Bishop Heber' is dated 14 September 1828.

86. *A Life's Decision*, p. 4.

87. *Ibid.*, p. 7.

88. *Ibid.*, p. 284.

89. In particular, John Duke Coleridge. He did not win the 1838 scholarship but was listed among the ten who 'distinguished themselves'; *Standard*, 2 April 1838.

90. M. R. D. Foot (ed.), *The Gladstone Diaries*, vol. II, 1833–9, Oxford University Press, Oxford, 1968, p. 380. Gladstone, only a little older than Allies, had already served as a Junior Lord of the Treasury in Peel's first administration.

91. T. W. Allies, *On the Influence of Practical Piety in Promoting the Temporal and Eternal Interests of Mankind*, D. A. Talboys, Oxford, 1838, p. 10.

92. *Ibid.*, p. 13.

93. *Ibid.*, p. 10.

94. *Ibid.*, pp 34–7.
95. *Ibid.*, p. 38.
96. *Ibid.*, p. 26.
97. In 1830; see Allies's letter to John Duke Coleridge congratulating him on appointment as Lord Chief Justice, 1 December 1880 (Coleridge Family Papers, BL RP 8994).
98. He died in 1843, aged 14.
99. Barrister and merchant, he died in 1876.
100. For a detailed analysis of Dodsworth's London ministry see S. E. Young, 'William Dodsworth 1798–1861: The Origins of Tractarian Thought and Practice in London', Ph.D. thesis, Open University, 2004.
101. Thomas Erskine, born in November 1828; he became rector of Alderley, Cheshire, and died in 1878.
102. Believed to be Henry Leslie Pepys (1830–91); he did not go to Eton.
103. In 1841 Cottenham's brother, Henry Pepys (1783–1860), would become the bishop of Worcester.
104. C. Yonge, *Life of John Coleridge Patteson*, Macmillan, London, 1874, vol. I, p. 5.
105. She was born on 17 December 1821.
106. Diary, 8 June 1839.
107. Probably she was governess to Eliza and her younger sister Julia.
108. Diary, 19 August 1839.
109. Diary, 24 August 1839.
110. Diary, 2 September 1839.
111. Diary, 25 October 1839.
112. Diary, 31 October 1839 (Thursday).
113. Diary, 1 November 1839.
114. When at home Allies occasionally visited Close; see *A Life's Decision*, p. 4; also Allies, *Thomas Allies*, pp. 31, 32.
115. *A Life's Decision*, p. 5.
116. James Marsh, 1794–1842, was a Congregationalist minister, later President of the University of Vermont. In his preface to Coleridge's *Aids to Reflection* (1829) he asserted that philosophies, like those of Locke, that excluded the possibility of spiritual agency were logically defective.
117. Diary 5 August 1839.
118. An annual series of lectures endowed by Robert Boyle with the object of considering the relationship between Christianity and natural philosophy.

119. William van Mildert, *An Historical View of the Rise and Progress of Infidelity, with a Refutation of its Principles and Reasonings. In a series of sermons preached for the lecture founded by the Hon. Mr. Boyle*, printed by T. Combe for J. H. Parker, Oxford, 5th edn, 1839, vol. I, Sermon XI, p. 340.
120. Diary, 29 November 1839.
121. London, 1743. John Ellis (1688–1764?) of Brasenose College was an Anglican clergyman in Dublin. Later editions of his work were additionally titled *Some Brief Considerations upon Mr Locke's Hypothesis*. It was praised by Bishop Horne: 'In this book natural religion is fairly demolished'.
122. London, 1722. John Norris (1657–1711), fellow of All Souls, rector of Bemerton, Platonist theologian.
123. Diary 13 December 1839, Norris opposed John Locke, arguing that eternal truths were discoverable, 'in God'.
124. Diary 23 September 1839.
125. William Cotton (1786–1866) was a successful businessman, who in 1842 became Governor of the Bank of England. He was a prominent Anglican active in establishing new churches in London.
126. Diary, 21 November 1839.
127. Diary, 27 December 1839.
128. See David Sydney Nicholas, 'Derwent Coleridge (1800–1883) and the Deacon Schoolmaster', Ph.D. thesis, University of London, 2007.
129. Blomfield wished to build fifty churches in those parts of London with the densest population; Dodsworth's church, Christ Church, Albany Street, was among the first.
130. Canon 35 of the Church of England requires that the bishop or certain priests appointed by him should diligently examine ordination candidates as to their fitness for office.
131. Allies was at ease in the company of women, and it seems the wives of judges and bishops liked to 'mother' him. Mrs Kent's daughter was present at the soiree; he wrote that she 'rather took my fancy, till I heard she was five or six and twenty'.
132. O. Chadwick, *The Victorian Church—Part One*, Adam & Charles Black, London, 1966, p. 133.
133. G. E. Biber, *Bishop Blomfield and his Times*, Harrison, London, 1857, p. 147.
134. *Ibid.*, p. 102, quoting from Blomfield's primary visitation (1830).
135. *Ibid.*, p. 103.
136. The *Diatesseron* was a harmony of the four gospels believed to have been compiled in the latter half of the second century.

137. H. B. J. Armstrong, *Armstrong's Norfolk Diary: Further Passages in the Diary of the Rev H. B. J. Armstrong, vicar of East Dereham 1850–86*, Hodder & Stoughton, London, 1963.

138. After the Gorham judgment Blomfield did reject two Cambridge graduates because they denied baptismal regeneration. After describing these difficulties, the official historian of the Church Missionary Society writes: 'It rounds off the story well when we find that one of the chaplains who harassed Church Missionary Society students was the Rev. T. W. Allies, who had given Bishop Wilberforce of Oxford much trouble, and who ultimately went over to Rome'; E. Stock, *History of the Church Missionary Society. Its Environment, its Men and its Work*, Church Missionary Society, London, 1890, vol. II, p. 79.

139. G. P. Badger, *The Nestorians and their Rituals with the Narrative of a Mission to Mesopotamia and Coordistan 1842–44*, London, John Masters, 1856. Badger also produced a very successful *History of Malta and Gozo*.

140. When Bennett's ministry ended in 1850 it was at the bishop's request; Spencer had provided him with information on Bennett's 'irregularities'.

141. Letter dated 15 September 1845 (Gladstone Papers, BL Add. MS 44362, f. 316).

142. *A Life's Decision*, p. 8.

143. Diary, 26 September 1839.

144. F. Bennett, *The Story of W. J. E. Bennett*, Longmans, London, 1909, p. 35; his *Guide to the Holy Eucharist* was published in 1842.

145. T. W. Allies, *Sermons on the Epistle to the Romans and Others*, Parker, Oxford, 1844. Page 19 contains the note referring to 'Newman on justification, *passim*; to which work, once for all, the Author begs to acknowledge the greatest obligations'.

146. *Ibid.*, p. 4.

147. *Ibid.*, p. 197.

148. *Ibid.*, p. 266.

149. *Ibid.*, pp. 66–7.

150. *Ibid.*, p. 41.

151. *Ibid.*, p. 111.

152. *The Christian Remembrancer*, 10, July–December 1845, pp. 222–4.

153. *Sermons on the Epistle to the Romans*, p. 406.

154. *A Life's Decision*, p. 7.

155. *Ibid.*, p. 8 Bantam: 'person of diminutive stature and often combative disposition' (Merriam-Webster Dictionary).

156. A. Blomfield, *A Memoir of Charles James Blomfield, Bishop of London*, Murray, London, 1863, vol. II, p. 15.
157. *Ibid.*, p. 19.
158. *A Life's Decision*, p. 10.
159. Letter, Allies to Gladstone, 18 March 1848 (Gladstone Papers, BL Add. MS 44367, ff. 117–18).
160. Blomfield, *Blomfield*, vol. II, pp. 23–4.
161. Circular dated 17 November 1841. See *Churchman's Monthly Review and Chronicle*, January 1842, pp. 70–1.
162. Letter of J. H. Newman to J. R. Hope, 26 November 1841, *Correspondence of John Henry Newman with John Keble and Others 1839–1845*, Longmans, Green & Co., London, 1917, p. 159. Newman speculated as to what these 'ulterior measures' might be: 'I fear few Colleges would have so united a set of fellows as to refuse the College seal to testimonials. It would seem to be spiting other men also' (*ibid.*).
163. 'Some in the new Altitudinarian party have taken the occasion of His Majesty becoming a godfather according to Anglican rites to inveigh against the Lutheran Church as being no church'; *Christian Observer*, ns 50, February 1842, p. 123.
164. 12 February 1842.
165. *A Life's Decision*, p. 10. Here Allies says that he was named to the living on 21 January 1842; the royal christening was on 25 January. Mary Allies, quoting from an 1878 manuscript of her father's, states that it was after Blomfield returned from the ceremony that 'with more sincerity than prudence' Allies stated his scruple to the bishop; Allies, *Thomas Allies*, p. 42.
166. *A Life's Decision*, pp. 10–11.
167. Allies, *Thomas Allies*, p. 42.
168. Usko, a German and a gifted linguist, had been appointed to the living in 1808 by Bishop Porteus in an attempt to inject some scholarship into Anglicanism.
169. B. Clarke, *The British Gazetteer*, H. G. Collins, London, 1852. Using a historical inflation index this stipend would be equivalent to approximately £61,000 in today's money.

Chapter 2

1. J. C. Blomfield's unpublished history of Launton (Bodleian dep. b 63), quoted in P. Tucker, *A History of St Mary's Church, Launton*, Launton

Historical Society, 2005, p. 20.
2. *Ibid.*
3. *Ibid.*, p. 21.
4. *Evangelical Magazine*, 15 August 1807, p. 380.
5. Tucker, *St Mary's Church*, p. 23.
6. Allies, *Thomas Allies*, p. 44. In Anne Pollen's biography of her father, it is recorded that John Hungerford Pollen slept in the haunted room. Although he slept all night in the morning he was discomfited to find that heavy furniture had been moved. Pollen, *John Hungerford Pollen*, John Murray, London, 1912, p. 126.
7. 'Parishes: Launton', in *A History of the County of Oxford*, vol. VI, ed. Mary D. Lobel, Victoria County History, London, 1959. British History Online, http://www.british-history.ac.uk/vch/vol6/pp. 232–43.
8. *A Life's Decision*, p. 62.
9. Tucker, *St Mary's Church*, p. 26.
10. *Ibid.* The altar was removed after Allies's departure; it was later found buried beneath the chancel, and in 1915 installed in the Lady Chapel.
11. *A Life's Decision*, p. 62.
12. Tucker, *St Mary's Church*, p. 26.
13. 19 November 1842 (Lambeth Palace Library, FP Blomfield 34, f. 78).
14. *Leicestershire Mercury*, 5 November 1842. Freeman later summonsed the constable and the magistrates ordered that he pay £2 for wrongful arrest.
15. *Oxford Chronicle*, 28 October 1843.
16. *A Life's Decision*, p. 62.
17. *Bradford Observer*, 22 September 1842.
18. *True Tablet*, 1 October 1842, quoting the *Aylesbury Chronicle*.
19. Letter dated Bicester, 27 September 1842; *True Tablet*, 1 October 1842. The paper had commented on the evidence given by Ferguson to a select committee on the payment of wages ('Mr Ferrand's Truck Committee').
20. Letter from bishop of London dated 19 November 1842 (F. P. Blomfield 34, ff. 75–8).
21. *Ibid.*
22. See Newman's letter to his sister, 10 May 1843; *The Letters and Diaries of John Henry Newman*, multiple editors, 32 vols., Oxford University Press, Oxford, 1961–2008 (henceforth *LD*), vol. IX, p. 333.
23. Reported in the *Bradford Observer*, 22 September 1842.
24. *Leicestershire Mercury*, 8 July 1843.

25. *Oxford Chronicle*, 26 October 1843.
26. *Oxford Chronicle*, 17 January 1846, 28 October 1846.
27. As confirmed in the case of Kemp v. Wickes, 1809.
28. *The Times* 22 July 1842.
29. E. G. K. Browne, *History of the Tractarian Movement*, James Duffy, Dublin, 1856, pp. 70–4.
30. *Oxford Chronicle*, 26 October 1843.
31. *Jackson's Oxford Journal*, 6 July 1844.
32. Letter dated 24 July 1844; *LD*, vol. X, p. 301.
33. For example the *Bradford Observer*, 11 July 1844: 'Frightful Puseyite Outrage at Launton.'
34. W. Ferguson, *The Impending Dangers of our Country*, Ward & Co., London, 1848, p. 69.
35. 'Mr Allies gave his sensible answer to two young persons, Wesleyan Methodists, who wished to have their intended marriage published at his church. "I cannot allow it: if you are Methodists act as Methodists"', *Sheffield Independent*, 2 May 1846.
36. The ceremony was held on 30 November 1845.
37. Allies, *Secundo*, pp. 43–4
38. Letter to Allies dated 18 July 1846. R. K. Pugh (ed.), *The Letter Books of Samuel Wilberforce 1843–68*, vol. XLVII, Oxfordshire Record Society, Oxford, 1970, p. 66. In 1850 a clergyman, Moorhouse James, appeared before the Liverpool assizes on an indictment that he had refused to marry a couple, one of whom was unconfirmed. The case was dismissed on appeal on a technicality regarding the time the request was made, thus whether a clergyman might refuse marriage on religious grounds remained unresolved.
39. W. Ferguson, *Scriptural Rule and Practical Romanism in the Diocese of Oxford. A Letter to the Right Rev. S. Wilberforce, D.D., Bishop of Oxford*, Ward & Co., London, 1848.
40. *Wesleyan Methodist Association Magazine*, October 1849, p. 487.
41. From his epitaph in Ryde Cemetery; he remained at Bicester until 1881 and died in 1889.
42. A. R. Ashwell, *Life of the Right Reverend Samuel Wilberforce D.D.*, John Murray, London, 1880, vol. I, p. 404.
43. Letter dated 22 May 1847; *The Letter Books of Samuel Wilberforce 1843–68*, p. 84.
44. Ashwell, *Life of Wilberforce*, pp. 405–6.

45. Letter dated 22 May 1847; *The Letter Books of Samuel Wilberforce 1843–68*, pp. 84–5.
46. *A Charge Delivered to the Clergy of the Diocese of Oxford by Richard Bagot D.D., Bishop of Oxford at his Fourth Visitation, May 1842*, Parker, Oxford, 1842, pp. 17–18.
47. Allies, *Thomas Allies*, p. 7.
48. *A Life's Decision*, p. 6.
49. 'W. G. Ward conspicuous as one who never shrank from an inference.' L. Stephen, *The English Utilitarians. J. S. Mill*, Duckworth, London, 1900, p. 481.
50. *A Life's Decision*, p. 50.
51. Once when preaching at the Portman Chapel Allies had referred to 'bad principles'; Smith said that he should rather say 'want of principle'; Allies, *Thomas Allies*, p. 71.
52. *Sermons on the Epistle to the Romans*, pp. 365–6.
53. Letter dated 'Littlemore, January 8, 1844'. *A Life's Decision*, p. 41.
54. Quoted in a circular letter dated 5 October 1844, signed by John Griffiths, subwarden of Wadham College; *Christian's Monthly Magazine and Review*, 2, July–December 1844, pp. 590–1.
55. Wall wrote about the anti-Symons campaign in his *Journal of 1844*; see *Oxiensia*, 34, 1959, pp. 82–97.
56. A reference to Pusey's censure; *The Times*, 14 September 1844.
57. In 1844 the Oxford University authorities (Vice-Chancellor and Regius Professor of Divinity) declined to admit R. G. Macmullen as BD, for which he was qualified, because of his known 'Puseyite' opinions. He converted to Roman Catholicism in 1847.
58. *The Times*, 4 October 1844.
59. *Christian's Monthly Magazine and Review*, 2, July–December 1844, pp. 590–1.
60. Wall wrote in his journal: 'Apparently a splendid victory. The Heads of Houses do not think so' (*Oxiensia*, 34, 1959, p. 85).
61. *Christian's Monthly Magazine and Review*, 2, July–Decemeber 1844, pp. 539–40.
62. *The Times*, 18 October 1844.
63. *Ibid*.
64. Correspondence published in *The Times*, 7 October 1844.
65. *A Life's Decision*, p. 21.

66. Allies, *Thomas Allies*, pp. 45–6.
67. *LD*, vol. XXXII, p. 122. The editor comments that she was 'deeply religious, but of a sprightliness which must have been somewhat alarming in the clerical circles of those proper days'.
68. Allies, *Thomas Allies*, p. 44.
69. *Ibid.*, p. 65.
70. C. R. Manning, *A List of Monumental Brasses Remaining in England*, F. & J. Rivington, London, 1846, p. 92.
71. F. W. Faber, *Sights and Thoughts in Foreign Churches and Among Foreign People*, F. & J. Rivington, London, 1842, p. 363.
72. *Ibid.*, p. 381.
73. Mantes-la-Jolie, 50 km west of Paris.
74. *A Life's Decision*, p. 30.
75. *Ibid.*, p. 37.
76. *Ibid.*, pp. 28–9.
77. *Ibid.*, p. 32.
78. *Ibid.*, pp. 34–5.
79. *Ibid.*, p. 35.
80. *Ibid.*, p. 38.
81. *Ibid.*, p. 50.
82. *Ibid.*, p. 60. Newman wrote: 'So the Levites showed themselves truly worthy of the sacerdotal office and were made the sacerdotal tribe, because they steeled themselves against natural affection'; *Meditations and Devotions*, Longmans, Green & Co., London, 1953, p. 229.
83. Allies, *Thomas Allies*, p. 46. Fergusson had accompanied the new Vicar Apostolic of the Western District, Bishop Charles Michael Baggs.
84. *A Life's Decision*, p. 64.
85. T. W. Allies's manuscript commonplace book in the writer's possession, p. 241.
86. *Ibid.*, p. 258.
87. *A Life's Decision*, p. 19.
88. 'In the course of the 18th century a number of box pews were erected—the largest belonging to the Ashby family ... A gallery was erected by the family in compensation for this encroachment ... James Blomfield removed the box pews from the chancel ... Allies removed the gallery and the box pews in the nave, inserted oak pews, a prayer-desk and a new stone altar.' 'Parishes: Launton', in *A History of the County of Oxford*, vol. VI, ed. Mary D.

Lobel, *Victoria County History*, London, 1959, pp. 232–43. British History Online, http://www.british-history.ac.uk/vch/oxon/vol6/pp. 232–43.
89. *A Life's Decision*, pp. 51–2.
90. *Ibid.*, p. 31.
91. The Church was closed for a few weeks; there is no record of whether an alternative meeting place was arranged.
92. W. G. Ward, *The Ideal of a Christian Church Considered in Comparison with Existing Practice*, 2nd edn, 1844, James Toovey, London, 1844, pp. 45, 565. See *The Times*, 16 December 1844.
93. *A Life's Decision*, p. 53.
94. *Ibid.*, p. 52.
95. *Ibid.*, pp. 52–3. Zoar was the city of refuge to which Lot and his two daughters fled to escape death when God destroyed Sodom and Gomorrah (Genesis 19:22–3).
96. Edwin Palmer (1824–95), Corpus Professor of Latin at Oxford (1870–8) and archdeacon of Oxford (1878–95).
97. Allies's diary, quoted in Allies, *Secundo*, p. 40.
98. *Indoles*: meaning nature or character.
99. Allies, *Secundo*, p. 41.
100. Ward had told Henry Wall the secret on 8 February (*Oxoniensia*, 34, 1959, p. 96).
101. Allies, *Thomas Allies*, p. 46.
102. *A Life's Decision*, p. 53.
103. Palmer believed that Anglicanism's future lay in inter-communion with the Orthodox Church. He had already twice visited Russia, but had failed to convince the Metropolitan of Moscow of his communion's Catholicity.
104. Letter dated 27 June 1846 (Gladstone Papers, BL Add. MS 44364, f. 239). It seems that no pupils were forthcoming; perhaps his reputation discouraged parents from entrusting their children to him.
105. *A Life's Decision*, p. 18.
106. Allies, *Thomas Allies*, p. 44.
107. *A Life's Decision*, p. 17.
108. *Ibid.*, p. 18.
109. V. A. McClelland, '"The Most Turbulent Priest of the Oxford Diocese": Thomas William Allies and the Quest for Authority', in V. Alan McClelland (ed.), *By whose Authority. Newman, Manning and the Magisterium*, Downside Abbey, Bath, 1996, pp. 273–90, at p. 278.

110. *A Life's Decision*, p. 61.
111. Recollections of Archdeacon Browne in W. Ward, *William George Ward and the Oxford Movement*, Macmillan, London, 1890, p. 24.
112. For example the Rev. Francis Trench in 1844 and the Rev. J. W. Massie in 1846.
113. In 1844 he published *Du mouvement religieux en Angleterre, ou, Les progrès du catholicisme et le retour de l'église anglicane a l'unité*.
114. C. Wordsworth, *Diary in France Mainly on Topics concerning Education and the Church*, F. & J. Rivington, London, 1845, p. 193.
115. *The Times*, 16 April 1845.
116. Wordsworth, *Diary*, p. 154.
117. *Ibid.*, p. 106.
118. *A Life's Decision*, p. 29.
119. Letter (draft), Manning to Allies, dated 6 December 1848 (Bodleian Lib. MS Eng. Lett. c 657, f. 115).
120. *Ibid.*, f. 117, letter dated 9 December 1848.
121. Allies, *Secundo*, p. 65. Arnold was an ecumenist, believing that all Christians could be united on a few basic principles and that organised Churches were fallible human institutions and thus prone to corruption.
122. *Ibid.*
123. Wordsworth, *Diary*, p. 105.
124. *A Life's Decision* p. 151.
125. Willmott was ordained at St James's, Piccadilly, on 22 May 1842. He found the house 'splendidly furnished' although a little too lonely and too still for one person; Robert Eldridge Aris Willmott, *A Journal of Summer Time in the Country*, Smith, London, 1864, p. 39.
126. *A Life's Decision*, p. 64.
127. Written by Pierre Jean de Beranger (1780–1857).
128. *New Monthly Magazine*, 54/218, 1838.
129. N.-J. Chaline, *Des catholiques normands sous la Troisième République*, Éditions Horvath, Paris, 1985, p. 62.
130. This was not the first time that Allies had visited the church. Among his printed poems is one dated June 1834, entitled 'Written before the altar piece of St Ouen, Rousen, Virgin and Child by Langlois', the tenor of which may be illustrated by one line: 'Not queen of heaven, but happy earthly mother'.
131. T. W. Allies, *Journal in France in 1845 and 1848 with Letters from Italy*

in 1847, of *Things and Persons concerning the Church and Education*, Longmans, London, 1849, p. 22.

132. *Ibid.*, p. 26.
133. Catherine Laboure, canonised in 1947. The medal still worn by millions did much to popularise the doctrine of the Immaculate Conception.
134. Allies, *Journal in France*, p. 61.
135. She remained as superior until 1894 and was canonised in 2007.
136. Allies, *Journal in France*, pp 55–8. Allies says that d'Alzon 'was bent on taking orders'; *ibid.*, p. 41.
137. *Ibid.*, pp. 76–7.
138. *Ibid.*, p. 43.
139. See, for example, J. Morris, *The High Church Revival in the Church of England*, Brill, Leiden, 2016, pp. 156–9.
140. Thomas Bowdler, *Quid Romae faciam? No need to join the Romish Communion; an account of the want of discipline in the Church of England in a letter to a friend*. Rivington, London, 1842.
141. Allies, *Journal in France*, pp 107–8.
142. *A Life's Decision*, p. 65. In his very interesting article, 'British High Churchmen, Continental Church Tourism and the Roman Connection in the Nineteenth Century', *Journal of Ecclesiastical History*, 66/4, 2015, pp. 772–91, Professor Morris speaks of Allies being 'alarmed by the extremism of the Marian liturgies'. He was perhaps not so much alarmed as anxious to understand the explanation of Noirlieu (the curé of St Jacques) of the *culte* of the Blessed Virgin, which perplexed many Anglicans (*Journal in France*, p. 48).
143. *A Life's Decision*, pp. 66–7.
144. *Ibid.*, p. 66.
145. *Ibid.*, p. 67.
146. *Ibid.*, p. 66.
147. Allies, *Thomas Allies*, pp. 48, 49. In 1850 Monro (1815–66) summed up his approach in *Parochial Work*, John Henry Parker, Oxford, 1851. 'An attempt to relate the traditional Anglican approach to pastoral care to Tractarian theology and contemporary needs'; P. Davies, *Raising up a Faithful People*, Gracewing, Leominster, 1997, p. 9.
148. *A Life's Decision*, p. 67.
149. *Ibid.*, p. 68.

Chapter 3

1. Letter from E. B. Pusey, *English Churchman*, 16 October 1845, quoted in H. P. Litton, J. O. Johnston and R. J. Wilson, *Life of Edward Bouverie Pusey*, Longmans, Green & Co., London, 1893, vol. II, p. 461.
2. *The Christian Remembrancer*, 11, January–June 1846, p. 211.
3. Allies, *Secundo*, p. 45.
4. *Ibid.*, pp. 47–50.
5. *A Life's Decision*, pp. 68–9.
6. Journal entry for 5 November 1845, *A Life's Decision*, p. 69.
7. J. H. Newman, *An Essay on the Development of Christian Doctrine*, James Toovey, London, 1845, p. 6.
8. *A Life's Decision*, p. 75.
9. The Vincentian canon is a test of the validity of Catholic doctrine: 'what has been believed everywhere, always and by all'.
10. Newman, *Development of Christian Doctrine*, p. 21.
11. T. W. Allies, *The Church of England Cleared from the Charge of Schism upon the Testimonies of Councils and Fathers of the First Six Centuries*, James Burns, London, 1846, p. 8.
12. Newman, *Development of Christian Doctrine*, p. 170.
13. *Ibid.*, pp. 124–5; the italics are Newman's, who is quoting Bellarmine.
14. *A Life's Decision*, p. 72.
15. Letter dated 20 February; *LD*, vol. XI, p. 121. Joseph Berrington (1746–1827) and John Kirk (1760–1851) published *The Faith of Catholics Confirmed by Scripture and Attested by the Fathers of the First Five Centuries of the Church* in 1813; subsequent editions were published in 1830 and 1846. François Feuardent was a Franciscan Counter-Reformation controversialist, who edited *Adversus Haereses* (1st edn, 1575).
16. *A Life's Decision*, p. 73.
17. Jacques-Bénigne Bossuet (1627–1704), bishop of Meaux, brilliant homilist, defender of the rights of Louis XIV in his dispute with Pope Innocent XI.
18. *A Life's Decision*, p. 77.
19. *The Church of England Cleared*, pp. 55–6.
20. *Ibid.*, p. 76.
21. *Ibid.*, p. 100.

22. *The Christian Remembrancer*, 13, January 1847, pp. 117–265.
23. *Ibid.*, p. 217.
24. *Ibid.*, p. 224.
25. *Ibid.*, p. 247.
26. *Ibid.*, p. 171.
27. *Ibid.*, pp. 172, 173.
28. *Ibid.*, p. 184.
29. *Ibid.*, p. 195.
30. John William Bowden (1798–1844), contributor to *Tracts for the Times*, author of *Life of Gregory VII* (1840).
31. *The Christian Remembrancer*, 13, p. 210.
32. Presumably a reference to the non-juring theologian Jeremy Collier (1650–1726), who wrote the *Rule of Faith*.
33. Letter to Mrs J. W. Bowden, 27 June 1846; *LD*, vol. XI, pp. 186–7. Newman evidently harboured no bad feelings against Allies as he recommended him as a tutor for Mrs Bowden's son, who had just left Eton (letter dated 14 July 1846, *ibid.*, p. 207).
34. Letter dated 4 July 1846; *LD*, vol. XI, pp. 190–1.
35. Edwin Wyndham-Quin, 3rd Earl of Dunraven and Mount Earl (1812–71), a noted archaeologist, who converted to Roman Catholicism in 1855.
36. Letter dated 31 August 1846; *LD*, vol. XI, p. 238.
37. Letter dated 19 November 1849; *LD*, vol. XIII, p. 298. The attribution of addressee is by the editor; Bittleston went to the Oratory soon after this letter and was received on 24 November.
38. *Dublin Review*, 12, March and June 1847, pp. 276, 277.
39. *Ibid.*, pp. 280, 281.
40. *Ibid.*, p. 272.
41. *Ibid.*, p. 275.
42. *Ibid.*, p. 289.
43. *Ibid.*, p. 291.
44. Thompson (d. 1891) became in 1851 editor of the controversial *Clifton Tracts*. His wife Harriett was a popular author; he was the uncle of the celebrated poet Francis Thompson.
45. E. H. Thompson, *The Unity of the Episcopate Considered in Reply to the Work of the Rev. T. W. Allies*, Thomas Richardson, London, 1847, p. 41.
46. *Ibid.*, p. 73.

47. *Ibid.*, p. 144.
48. *Ibid.*, p. 117.
49. *A Life's Decision*, p. 94.
50. These decretals were supposed letters of ante-Nicene and later popes that implied papal supremacy; by the mid-sixteenth century their genuineness was largely disproved.
51. T. W. Allies, *The Church of England Cleared from the Charge of Schism*, 2nd enlarged edn, John Henry Parker, London, 1848, p. xv.
52. *The Rambler*, 1/11, March 1848, pp. 220–1.
53. Allies, *Journal in France*, pp. 258–60.
54. Letter dated 13 March 1849 (Wiseman papers W3/45/13a, Westminster Diocesan Archives).
55. *Ibid.*
56. Letter dated 17 March 1849 (Wiseman papers W3/45/14a, Westminster Diocesan Archives).
57. *A Life's Decision*, p. 90. According to Allies, 'Archdeacon Manning once said wittily that I had got hold of Bossuet by the tail'.
58. *The Church of England Cleared*, p. 177.
59. *Ibid.*, p. 178.
60. *Ibid.*, p. 185.
61. *Ibid.* The 'Gallican Articles' of March 1682 include the provision, 'The Pope has the principal share in questions of faith ... nevertheless his judgment is not irreformable, unless the consent of the Church be added'. The articles which were were signed by Bossuet were pronounced null and void by Pope Alexander VIII in 1690; 'the definition of the infallibility of the Pope has made the doctrinal basis of Gallicanism formal heresy'; W. E. Addis and T. Arnold, *A Catholic Dictionary*, Virtue & Co., London, 15th edn, 1952, p. 363.
62. *The Church of England Cleared*, p. 192.
63. *Ibid.*, p. 193.
64. *Ibid.*, p. 194.
65. P. Le Page Renouf, *The Greek and Anglican Communions. A Letter Respectfully Addressed to the Rev. T. W. Allies, Rector of Launton.*, Jas. Toovey, London, 1847, p. 12.
66. *The Church of England Cleared*, p. 197.
67. *Ibid.*, p. 198.
68. This was a plan agreed in 1841 for the erection of a Protestant bishopric in the Holy Land under the joint aegis of England and Prussia. That the

Church of England was willing to collaborate with the Lutherans (who rejected the Apostolic succession) to intrude a bishop into an existing Catholic diocese was a significant stumbling-block for the Tractarians, and one of the reasons adduced by Newman for his conversion.

69. *The Church of England Cleared*, pp. 201–2.
70. In 1717 Convocation, the collective voice of Anglicanism, was suspended in the wake of the Bangorian controversy (the Lower House's attempt to censure the Latitudinarian views of Bishop Hoadley). It was not restored until 1852.
71. Allies was perhaps thinking of Longley's recent remarks in Leeds.
72. *The Church of England Cleared*, p. 204.
73. *The Greek and Anglican Communions*, pp. 26–7.
74. *A Life's Decision*, p. 81.
75. *Ibid.*, p. 90.
76. *The Christian Remembrancer*, 12, December 1846, pp. 377–98.
77. *The Ecclesiastic*, 2, September 1846, pp. 141–2.
78. *The English Review*, 6, September–December 1846, p. 188.
79. *The English Review*, 8, September–December 1847, p. 108.
80. *A Life's Decision*, p. 114.
81. *Ibid.*, pp. 94–5.
82. *Ibid.*, p. 95.
83. *Ibid.*, p. 100.
84. Anne Pollen, *John Hungerford Pollen*, John Murray, London, 1912, pp. 52–3.
85. *Ibid.*, p. 54.
86. *Ibid.*, p. 45.
87. *Ibid.*, p. 63.
88. A London club established in 1819, where overseas friends could be given hospitality when they visited the city.
89. Pollen, *John Hungerford Pollen*, p. 65.
90. Mary Wollstonecraft Shelly, *Rambles in Germany and Italy in 1840, 1842 and 1843*, vol. II, Moxon, London, 1844, p. 199.
91. A fact that had disappointed W. E. Gladstone when he met Manzoni in 1838. See J. Lindon, 'Alessandro and the Oxford Movement', *Journal of Ecclesiastical History*, 45, 1994, pp. 297–318.
92. Letter from the Earl of Shrewsbury to Ambrose Lisle Phillipps Esq. Descriptive of the Estatica of Caldaro and the Addolorata of Capriana,

Charles Dolman, London, 1842, p. 4.
93. *Ibid.*, pp. 32–5.
94. *Ibid.*, p. 41.
95. Pollen, *John Hungerford Pollen*, p. 76.
96. *Ibid.*
97. Allies, *Journal in France*, p. 135.
98. *Ibid.*, p. 139.
99. *Ibid.*, pp. 148–9.
100. When another opportunity arose to comment, the *Guardian* wrote 'We pass over in silence the description of the Italian miracles. We can see no good end likely to be obtained by placing these narrations in the hands of miscellaneous readers' (28 February 1849).
101. Allies, *Journal in France*, pp. 162, 168.
102. The papal seal of infallibility was bestowed on the doctrine by Pius XII in 1950 (*Munificentissimus Deus*).
103. Allies, *Journal in France*, p. 170.
104. Pollen, *John Hungerford Pollen*, p. 90.
105. *A Life's Decision*, p. 118.
106. *Ibid.*, p. 121.
107. Where McMullen and others of the clergy had converted to Rome.
108. *A Life's Decision*, p. 114.
109. Letter dated 5 July 1848; A. J. Butler, *Life and Letters of William John Butler*, Macmillan, London, 1897, p. 65.
110. In *A Life's Decision*, p. 122, Allies names the church as St Etheldreda's (a church in Holborn which had been known as Ely Chapel and was a centre of Welsh Anglicanism) but this must be a memory lapse or typographical error.
111. Letter to W. E. Gladstone, dated 18 March 1848 (Gladstone Papers, BL Add. MS 44367, ff. 117–22).
112. *Ibid.*
113. *Ibid.*
114. Allies wrote to Gladstone, 22 March 1849, 'I am not a judge of what you think you could with propriety do: but on no account would I seem to ask what limits should be passed' (Gladstone Papers, BL Add. MS 44367, f. 127).
115. J. Godfrey, *Roads to Rome*, Longmans, Green & Co., London, 1901, p. 191.
116. Robert Hussey, *The Rise of Papal Power Traced in Three Lectures*, Parker,

Oxford, 1851, p. ix: 'The facts *do* speak with the voice of truth, against the system of the Roman Communion, as it now is.'

117. Allies, *Journal in France*, pp. 174, 187–8, 210.
118. *Ibid.*, p. 198.
119. *Ibid.*, p. 214.
120. *Ibid.*, p. 295.
121. 'The surgeon said an operation might be performed, but in ninety-nine cases out of a hundred it failed.' The novice was suffering from 'a violent luxation of the cerebral column'; *Journal in France*, p. 206.
122. St Vincent de Paul (1581–1660), noted for his work among the poor; he was canonised in 1737.
123. *Ibid.*, p. 225. 'As we descend the Rue d'Enfer, we find, at No. 74, the Foundling Hospital, founded by the good and celebrated St Vincent de Paule, in 1632. Any child is received at this institution on the mother making a declaration that she has not the means of supporting it, when she receives a certificate signed by a commissary of police; the average number admitted in the last two or three years is rather over three thousand; they are attended by the Sœurs de Charité (Sisters of Charity) in the most praiseworthy manner'; F. Hervé, *How to Enjoy Paris in 1842*, G. Briggs, London, 1842, p. 125.
124. *Journal in France*, p. 225.
125. *Ibid.*, p. 325.
126. *Ibid.*, p. 195. They had been given a letter of introduction to Mgr Pierre Louis Parisis, who had an interest in educational matters and in 1848 was a member of the Assembly.
127. *Ibid.*, p. 251.
128. *Ibid.*, p. 262.
129. *Ibid.*, p. 259.
130. *Ibid.*, p. 264.
131. *Ibid.*, p. 300.
132. *Ibid.*, p. 329.

Chapter 4

1. Letter Manning to Allies, Lavington, 23 September 1848 (Bodleian Lib. MS Eng. Lett. c 657, f. 96).
2. Letter Manning to Allies, 61 Eaton Place, 10 October 1848 (Bodleian Lib. MS Eng. Lett. c 657, f. 97).

Notes

3. Letter Allies to Manning, Launton, 11 October 1848 (Bodleian Lib. MS Eng. Lett. c 657, f. 102).
4. Letter Manning to Allies, Lavington, 13 October 1848 (Bodleian Lib. MS Eng. Lett. c 657, f. 104).
5. Letter Manning to Allies, Lavington, 27 October 1848 (Bodleian Lib. MS Eng. Lett. c 657, f. 106).
6. *A Life's Decision*, p. 124.
7. McClelland, *By whose Authority*, pp. 285, 290.
8. *A Life's Decision*, pp. 123–4.
9. The phrase used by Manning in agreeing with him. Letter Manning to Allies, Lavington, 6 December 1848 (Bodleian Lib. MS Eng. Lett. c 657, f. 115).
10. Letter Allies to Manning, 1 December 1848 (Bodleian Lib. MS Eng. Lett. c 657, f. 113).
11. *The Times*, 17 February 1851.
12. *The Times*, 20 February 1851.
13. *A Life's Decision*, p. 124.
14. Letter Allies to Manning, 1 December 1848 (Bodleian Lib. MS Eng. Lett. c 657, f. 113).
15. *Journal in France*, p. 333.
16. *Ibid.*, p. 339.
17. Letter Allies to Manning, 1 December 1848 (Bodleian Lib. MS Eng. Lett. c 657, f. 113).
18. Letter Manning to Allies, Lavington, 22 December 1848 (Bodleian Lib. MS Eng. Lett. c 657, f. 119).
19. Pollen, *John Hungerford Pollen*, p. 126; the author says that Allies was correcting proof sheets at this time, but as yet a publisher had not been chosen. Allies noted in his diary for 14 December: 'We then walked to Murray's ... [who] asked the object of my *Journal* rather closely.' Allies, *Secundo*, p. 64.
20. Pollen, *John Hungerford Pollen*, p. 127.
21. *A Life's Decision*, p. 123. The italics are Allies's.
22. Letter Allies to Manning, 3 November 1848 (Bodleian Lib. MS Eng. Lett. c 657, ff. 109, 110).
23. *A Life's Decision*, p. 125.
24. Reported in *Bury and Norwich Post*, 28 March 1849.
25. *Guardian*, 28 February 1849.

26. *Journal in France*, p. 349.
27. *Guardian*, 28 February 1849.
28. *The Christian Remembrancer*, 12, January–June 1849, pp. 476–81.
29. *The Christian Remembrancer*, 18, July–December 1849, pp. 151–81.
30. *Ibid.*
31. Letter Coleridge to Allies, 12 April 1849; *A Life's Decision*, pp. 144–5.
32. Letter Easter Monday (9 April 1849); *ibid.*, p. 148.
33. Letter dated 3 March 1849; *ibid.*, pp. 150–3.
34. Letter dated 5 March 1849; *ibid.*, pp. 139–40.
35. Letter dated 19 February 1849; *ibid.*, p. 139.
36. *Ibid.*, pp. 142–3.
37. *Tablet*, 21 April 1849.
38. *Dublin Review*, 26, March 1849, p. 243.
39. Allies, *Journal in France*, p. 298.
40. *Tablet*, 5 May 1849.
41. *Dublin Review*, 26, March 1849, p. 261.
42. *The Examiner*, 21 April 1849.
43. *Dublin Review*, 26, March 1849, p. 243.
44. Letter to Allies, dated 20 February 1849; *LD*, vol. XIII, pp. 59–60.
45. Letter Allies to Manning, Launton, 13 March 1849 (Bodleian Lib. MS Eng. Lett. c 657, f. 122).
46. Letter Allies to Manning, Launton, 21 March 1849 (Bodleian Lib. MS Eng. Lett. c 657, f. 128).
47. Manning begins his letter by quoting Juvenal, *dat veniam corvis* ('the censor forgives the crows'; the quotation continues, *vexat censura columbas*, 'but blames the doves').
48. Letter Manning to Allies, Lavington, 22 March 1849 (Bodleian Lib. MS Eng. Lett. c 657, f. 126).
49. Letter Allies to Manning, Launton, 'Annunciation' (25 March), 1849 (Bodleian Lib. MS Eng. Lett. c 657, f. 132).
50. Letter Allies to Manning, Launton, 3 March 1849 (Bodleian Lib. MS Eng. Lett. c 657, f. 120).
51. *A Life's Decision*, pp. 161–4.
52. *Ibid.*, p. 160.
53. Letter dated 20 March 1849; *ibid.*, pp. 164–9.
54. Henry Wilberforce was vicar of East Farleigh (near Maidstone) in Kent.

Notes

55. Letter dated 21 March 1849 (Bodleian Lib. MS Eng. Lett. c 657, f. 132).
56. With the vagaries of the postal service Allies was reluctant to send letters from Launton to Lavington; this had been a problem with Manning's involvement in editing the *Journal*.
57. Letter dated 'Annunciation' (25 March) 1849 (Bodleian Lib. MS Eng. Lett. c 657, f. 124).
58. Letter Manning to Allies, Lavington, 22 March 1849 (Bodleian Lib. MS Eng. Lett. c 657, f. 126).
59. Letter dated 24 March 1849; *A Life's Decision*, pp. 170–1.
60. Letter dated 28 March 1849 (Bodleian Lib. MS Eng. Lett. c 657, ff. 136–9). Allies said that for the quotations in his letter to the bishop he was indebted to William Palmer's *Harmony of Anglican Doctrine with the Doctrine of the Catholic and Apostolic Church of the East* (1846).
61. Letter dated 27 March 1849; *A Life's Decision*, p. 181.
62. Letter dated 20 April 1849; *ibid.*, p. 144.
63. *Hull Packet*, 6 April 1849.
64. Letter dated 26 March 1849; *The Letter-Books of Samuel Wilberforce 1843–68*, p. 161. The editors note 'Wilberforce preferred not to write to Jacobson, the Oxford Regius Professor'.
65. R. G. Wilberforce, *Life of the Right Reverend Samuel Wilberforce D.D.*, Murray, London, 1881, vol. II, pp. 16–22.
66. Robert Isaac Wilberforce (1802–57, archdeacon of the East Riding) and Henry Wilberforce (1807–73).
67. Letter dated 9 April 1849; *A Life's Decision*, pp. 183–4.
68. Allies, *Secundo*, p. 70.
69. Letter dated St Mark's Day 1849 (25 April), addressed from 7 Marine Parade, Brighton; *A Life's Decision*, pp. 185–8.
70. *Ibid.*
71. Letter dated 27 April 1849. *Life of the Right Reverend Samuel Wilberforce D.D.*, vol. II, pp. 24–5.
72. *A Life's Decision*, p. 190.
73. *Life of the Right Reverend Samuel Wilberforce D.D.*, vol. II, p. 25.
74. Letter dated 3 May 1849 (Bodleian Lib. MS Eng. Lett. c 657, f. 148).
75. Allies, *Secundo*, p. 71.
76. *Ibid.* Allies wrote this in his diary for 11 May.
77. *Ibid.*
78. Letter dated Sunday 4pm (13 May 1849 added later) (Bodleian Lib. MS

Eng. Lett. c 657, f. 150).

79. Letter dated 15 May 1849 (Bodleian Lib. MS Eng. Lett. c 657, f. 152).
80. Letter dated 16 May 1849; *A Life's Decision*, pp. 195–6.
81. *Life of the Right Reverend Samuel Wilberforce D.D.*, vol. II, pp. 26–7.
82. Charles Clerke (1798–1877) was archdeacon of Oxford from 1830 until his death. As a sponsor of the Library of the Fathers series he had been sympathetic to the Tractarians.
83. *Life of the Right Reverend Samuel Wilberforce D.D.*, vol. II, p. 26.
84. Letter dated 23 May 1849 (Bodleian Lib. MS Eng. Lett. c 657, f. 164).
85. *Ibid.*
86. Letter to Manning dated May 23, 1849 (Bodleian Lib. MS Eng. Lett. c 657, f. 162).
87. Bodleian Lib. MS Eng. Lett. c 657, f. 163.
88. *A Life's Decision*, p. 194.
89. According to Allies in his letter to Manning dated Wednesday (6 June 1849?) (Bodleian Lib. MS Eng. Lett. c 657, f. 168).
90. Undated note signed by Allies included among Manning's papers (Bodleian Lib. MS Eng. Lett. c 657, f. 176).
91. Undated note included among Manning's papers and appended to a draft letter to the bishop of Oxford dated Lavington, 23 June 1849 (Bodleian Lib. MS Eng. Lett. c 657, f. 187).
92. *Ibid.*
93. The rubric after the Order of Service for Holy Communion.
94. Letter dated 8 June 1849 (Bodleian Lib. MS Eng. Lett. c 657, f. 172).
95. Letter to Manning dated 15 June 1849 (Bodleian Lib. MS Eng. Lett. c 657, f. 179).
96. *A Life's Decision*, p. 191.
97. Pollen, *John Hungerford Pollen*, p. 129.
98. Letter dated 25 July 1849 (Bodleian Lib. MS Eng. Lett. c 657, f. 189). Penelope's web is a proverbial expression for anything which is perpetually doing and never done.
99. The correspondence was widely published, appearing, for example, in the *Bucks Herald* on Saturday 28 July 1849.
100. For example, *Worcestershire Chronicle*, 22 August 1849. However, to most it was clear that Allies retracted nothing. Writing in the *Essex Standard* (25 August) 'A Protestant' (who claimed to have corresponded with Allies when he was chaplain to the bishop of London) refers to the latter's letter

to the *Tablet* as evidence that he 'does not appear to have retracted the opinions he has published: no, quite the contrary'.

101. *A Life's Decision*, p. 198.
102. *Ibid.*
103. A copy appeared in the sale catalogue of J. R. Smith in 1860; it was described as 'suppressed and very scarce'.
104. *A Life's Decision*, p. 124.
105. In 1846 his late wife's sister Sophia and her husband George Ryder had converted to Catholicism.
106. Letter dated 27 August 1849; Pugh, *The Letter Books of Samuel Wilberforce 1843–68*, p. 175.
107. *Ibid.*
108. *Morning Post*, 3 December 1850. *Life of the Right Reverend Samuel Wilberforce D.D.*, vol. II, p. 68.
109. *Ibid.*, p. 69.
110. *A Life's Decision*, pp. 190–1.
111. J. M. Stone, *Eleanor Leslie. A Memoir*, Art & Book Co., Leamington, 1898, p. 226.
112. From Bishop Wiseman, obtained for Allies by W. G. Ward, who remained a friend (Wiseman papers W3/51/2, Westminster Diocesan Archives).
113. *A Life's Decision*, p. 199.
114. Castel Gandolfo, the summer residence of the pope, is situated on the shore of Lake Albano some 20km from Rome.
115. *A Life's Decision*, p. 201.
116. *Ibid.*, p. 203.
117. On 30 June 1884, Allies wrote the following note about this gift and a later one (preserved by his descendants): 'These two gifts were bestowed upon me by Pope Pius IX. The Cameo of our Lord when I visited him with Fr. Wynne, both of us were Anglican Clergymen, at Gaeta in August 1849. The St. Peter when I first visited him as a Catholic in February 1860, with the words—You have defended Peter: I give you Peter.'
118. Letter dated 2 October 1849 (Bodleian Lib. MS Eng. Lett. c 657, f. 191).
119. *A Life's Decision*, p. 204.
120. *Ibid.*, p. 206.
121. *Ibid.*
122. *Ibid.*, p. 213.
123. In 1847 Pollen had been asked by Pusey to be pro-vicar of his Leeds church,

to replace the vicar, Richard Ward, who had been accused of Romanism. The bishop objected to his continuing the practice of auricular confession, and on Christmas Eve 1850 he was inhibited from practising his ministry. In 1851 Pollen recounted his experiences in *Narrative of Five Years at St. Saviour's*.

124. *A Life's Decision*, pp. 236–43.
125. *Ibid.*, p. 246.
126. Letter dated 27 November 1849 (Bodleian Lib. MS Eng. Lett. c 657, f. 193).
127. Letter from bishop of Worcester, dated 18 October 1849; correspondence published in *Leamington Spa Courier*, 8 December 1849.
128. Letter dated 29 January 1850 (Bodleian Lib. MS Eng. Lett. c 657, f. 195).
129. *Ibid.*, f. 200.
130. Letter dated 6 February 1850 (Bodleian Lib. MS Eng. Lett. c 657, f. 201).
131. *The Things of Caesar and the Things of God. A Discourse preached at Christ Church St. Pancras, on Sunday January 27th, 1850*, J. Masters, London, 1850, p. 12.
132. *Western Times*, 2 February 1850.
133. William Maskell, *A First Letter on the Present Position of the High Church Party in the Church of England, The Royal Supremacy and the Authority of the Judicial Committee of the Privy Council*, William Pickering, London, 1850, pp. 40–1, 46.
134. *A Life's Decision*, p. 250.
135. *Guardian*, 27 February 1850.
136. *A Life's Decision*, p. 255.
137. *Ibid.*, p. 269.
138. Edward Cardwell, *Documentary Annals of the Reformed Church of England*, Oxford University Press, Oxford, 1844; Edward Cardwell, *Synodalia, A Collection of Articles of Religion, Canons and Proceedings of Convocations in the Province of Canterbury*, Oxford University Press, Oxford, 1842.
139. Edmund Gibson, *Codex Juris Ecclesiastici Anglicani: or, the Statutes, Constitutions, Canons, Rubricks and Articles of the Church of England*, Clarendon Press, Oxford, 1761.
140. *A Life's Decision*, pp. 255–6.
141. *Ibid.*, p. 255.
142. *Ibid.*, p. 269.
143. *Ibid.*
144. The papal bull issued by Pope Pius V on 25 February 1570, declaring

Elizabeth I to be a heretic and releasing her subjects from any allegiance to her.

145. Letter dated 28 February 1850 (Bodleian Lib. MS Eng. Lett. c 657, f. 208).
146. Maskell Papers, BL Add. MS 37284, f. 146.
147. Bodleian Lib. MS Eng. Lett. c 657, f. 209.
148. *A Life's Decision*, p. 267. Manning was referring to the lamentation for the dead.
149. Report in *Guardian*, 4 April 1850.
150. Bodleian Lib. MS Eng. Lett. c 657, f. 211. Privately Manning was less sanguine having been much influenced by a letter from James Hope (29 January 1850), arguing that Erastianism was integral to the Anglican system. E. S. Purcell, *Life of Cardinal Manning*, Macmillan, London, 1895, vol. 1, pp. 524–7.
151. T. W. Allies, *The Royal Supremacy Viewed in Reference to the Two Spiritual Powers of Order and Jurisdiction*, William Pickering, London, 1850.
152. *Ibid.*, p. 23.
153. *Ibid.*, pp. 34–5.
154. David Lewis, *Notes on the Nature and Extent of the Royal Supremacy*, James Toovey, London, 1847.
155. 'They had no more right to consecrate an Archbishop of Canterbury, than they had to consecrate one for Milan.' *Ibid.*, p 72 (quoted in Allies, *Royal Supremacy*, p. 45).
156. *Ibid.*, p 76 (quoted in Allies, *Royal Supremacy*, pp. 48–9).
157. *Ibid.*, pp. 86–7.
158. Allies, *Royal Supremacy*, p. 55.
159. *Ibid.*, pp. 54–6.
160. *Ibid.*, p. 60.
161. *Ibid.*, p. 63.
162. *Ibid.*, p. 64.
163. Letter dated 16 April 1850 (Bodleian Lib. MS Eng. Lett. c 657, f. 213).
164. Letter dated 1 March 1850 (Maskell Papers, BL Add. MS 37284, f. 146).
165. Article 37: 'Of the Civil Magistrates: 'The Queen's Majesty hath the chief power in this Realm of England, and her other Dominions, unto whom the chief Government of all Estates of this Realm, whether they be Ecclesiastical or Civil, in all causes doth appertain, and is not, nor ought to be subject to any foreign Jurisdiction ... they should rule all states and degrees committed to their charge by God, whether they be Ecclesiastical

or Temporal, and restrain with the civil sword the stubborn and evil-doers. The Bishop of Rome hath no jurisdiction in this Realm of England.'

166. Letter dated 16 April 1850 (Bodleian Lib. MS Eng. Lett. c 657, f. 213).
167. Letter dated 18 April 1850 (Wiseman papers W3/51/2, Westminster Diocesan Archives).
168. Letter dated 22 April; *A Life's Decision*, p. 257.
169. Letter dated 24 May 1850; *ibid.*, pp. 262, 264.
170. Letter to Manning dated 10 May 1850 (Bodleian Lib. MS Eng. Lett. c 657, f. 217).
171. Letter from the bishop of Brechin, 16 May 1850; *A Life's Decision*, p. 267.
172. Letter dated Ascension Day (9 May,1850); *ibid.*, p. 265.
173. H. P. Liddon, J. O. Johnston and R. J. Wilson, *Life of Edward Bouverie Pusey*, 3rd edn, Longmans, Green & Co., London, 1895, vol. III, pp. 95–6.
174. E. B. Pusey, *The Royal Supremacy not an Arbitrary Authority but Limited by the Laws of the Church of which Kings are Members*, Parker, Oxford, 1850.
175. Letter to Manning dated 29 April 1850 (Bodleian Lib. MS Eng. Lett. c 657, f. 215).
176. The introduction to Pusey's book was finished on 21 April. Allies was reading it on 10 May.
177. *A Life's Decision*, p. 268.
178. Pierre François le Courayer, *A Dissertation on the Validity of the Ordinations of the English and of the Succession of Bishops in the Anglican Church*, John Henry Parker, Oxford, 1844. *A Life's Decision*, p. 247.
179. Antonio Pereira, *Tentativa Theologica Episcopal Rights and Ultra-Montane Usurpations*, trans. Rev. E. H. Landon, Joseph Masters, London, 1847, p. vii.
180. *Ibid.*, pp. 215–16.
181. Purcell, *Life of Cardinal Manning*, vol. I, p. 474.
182. Letter to Manning dated 10 May 1850 (Bodleian Lib. MS Eng. Lett. c 657, f. 218).

Chapter 5

1. *A Life's Decision*, p. 271.
2. *Ibid.*
3. Allies, *Thomas Allies*, p. 166. The reading was in 1862, two years before Gillis died in office as Vicar Apostolic of the Eastern District of Scotland.

4. *A Life's Decision*, p. 271.
5. Ibid., p. 273.
6. *LD*, vol. XIII, pp. 473–4.
7. Allies, *Thomas Allies*, p. 64.
8. Letter to Mrs Allies, dated 25 June 1850; *LD*, vol. XIII, p. 478.
9. 'When I consented, without further delay, to my wife's becoming a Catholic, I had no thought of remaining an Anglican myself'; *A Life's Decision*, p. 277.
10. W. Maskell, *A Second Letter on the Present Position of the High Church Party in the Church of England*, William Pickering, London, 1850, p. 23.
11. Letter dated 16 April (Bodleian Lib. MS Eng. Lett. c 657, f. 211). On page 32 of Maskell's 'Second Letter' there is reference to resolutions signed by Manning and others on 19 March 1850 as an immediate response to the Gorham decision, one of which was as follows: 'That, inasmuch as the Faith is one, and rests upon one principle of authority, the conscious, deliberate, and wilful abandonment of the essential meaning of an Article of the Creed destroys the "Divine foundation upon which alone the entire Faith is propounded by the Church".' 'That any portion of the Church which does so abandon the essential meaning of an Article of the Creed, forfeits, not only the Catholic doctrine in that Article, but also the office and authority to witness and teach as a member of the Universal Church.' 'That by such conscious, wilful, and deliberate act, such portion of the Church becomes formally separated from the Catholic body, and can no more assure to its members the grace of the Sacraments and the Remission of Sins.' Maskell commented, 'Now I demand of those who subscribed these resolutions sufficient proof how far, and in what way, they do not apply to, and are not fatal to the claims of, the reformed Irish Church.'
12. Maskell, 'Second Letter', p. 11.
13. In his pamphlet *A Letter to the Rev. E. B. Pusey on the Position he has taken in the Present Crisis*, Pickering, London, 1850 (7 May), Dodsworth writes of Allies's work on the Royal Supremacy as 'most ably and learnedly treated' (p. 19).
14. H. E. Manning, *A Letter to the Right Reverend Ashurst-Turner, Lord Bishop of Chichester*, John Murray, London, 1850, p. 47. It appeared in July 1850.
15. Purcell, *Life of Cardinal Manning*, vol. I, p. 551.
16. March 1849; *A Life's Decision*, p. 100.
17. Ibid., p. 119.
18. Pusey, *The Royal Supremacy not an Arbitrary Authority*. The work is dated 21 April 1850.
19. W. Dodsworth, *A Letter to the Rev. E. B. Pusey, D. D. on the position which*

he has taken in this present crisis, William Pickering, London, 1850, p. 9. The work is dated 7 May 1850.

20. *Ibid.*, p. 20.
21. Letter dated 17 May 1850 (Bodleian Lib. MS Eng. Lett. c 657, f. 223).
22. Letter dated 9 May 1850; later published in W. Maskell, *A Letter to Rev. Dr. Pusey on his Practice of Receiving Persons in Auricular Confession*, Pickering, London, 8 October 1850, p. 13.
23. In 1867 Maskell annotated a copy of this letter, saying that he had 'quite forgotten' to what Pusey was referring.
24. Pusey's letter is undated (Maskell Papers, BL Add. MS 37284, ff. 218–21).
25. Letter dated 17 May 1850 (Bodleian Lib. MS Eng. Lett. c 657, f. 223).
26. Undated letter, Pusey to Allies (Maskell Papers, BL Add. MS 37284, f. 222, 223).
27. Letter dated May 16, 1850; published in Maskell, *A Letter to Rev. E. B. Pusey*, p. 15.
28. Undated letter Pusey to Allies (Maskell Papers, BL Add. MS 37284, f. 225).
29. Undated letter Pusey to Allies (Maskell Papers, BL Add. MS 37284, f. 225).
30. Letter dated Whitsunday 1850 (19 May) (Maskell Papers, BL Add. MS 37284, f. 224).
31. Maskell, *Letter to Pusey on Auricular Confession*, p. 15.
32. Dodsworth, *A Letter to the Rev. E. B. Pusey on the Position he has taken in the Present Crisis*, p. 16.
33. *Western Times*, 31 August 1850.
34. Published in *The Times*, 1 May 1850. Pusey's letter is undated (Maskell Papers, BL Add. MS 37284, ff. 218).
35. 'If these men mean nothing personal ... they will not be in such a hurry, they will consent to wait a little, and let the matter be thoroughly discussed in private before they publish.' Letter to Pusey, Whitsunday Eve (18 May) 1850; Liddon *et al.*, *Life of Edward Bouverie Pusey*, vol. III, pp. 265–6.
36. *Ibid.*, p. 265.
37. Undated letter Pusey to Allies (Maskell Papers, BL Add. MS 37284, ff. 222–3).
38. E. B. Pusey, *The Church of England leaves her children free to whom to open their griefs—A Letter to the Rev. W. U. Richards*, Parker, Oxford, 1850. Canon Liddon's comment is: 'To the ordinary reader this letter might appear at first sight an undigested mass of out-of-the-way learning directed to the establishment of a point which could only interest the mind of a schoolman. In reality, Pusey never in his life wrote anything more practical in its drift'; Liddon *et al.*, *Life of Edward Bouverie Pusey*, vol. III, p. 266.

39. Pusey, *The Church of England*, p. 1.
40. *Ibid.*, p. 133.
41. *Ibid.*, p. 103.
42. *Ibid.*, pp. 120–1.
43. Letter dated 11 October 1850; *LD*, vol. XIV, p. 101.
44. Henry of Exeter, who wrote in a pastoral letter (9 April 1851): 'For that the Church of England has always holden, and does hold "auricular confession to be a means of grace" is a proposition too manifest to admit dispute:— what the Church of England does not hold, but is held by the Church of Rome, is, that "auricular confession" is necessary to salvation' (p. 56). 'What I deprecate is, that this (confession) should be made a regular observance,—still more that any priest should advise it as such' (p. 57). H. Philpott, *A Pastoral Letter to the Clergy of the Diocese of Exeter on the Present State of the Church by Henry, Lord Bishop of Exeter*, John Murray, London, 1851, pp. 56–7.
45. Liddon et al., *Life of Edward Bouverie Pusey*, vol. III, pp. 268–9.
46. Letter dated 15 October 1850 (Maskell Papers, BL Add. MS 37284, f. 274).
47. 'Common sense, however, usually carries the day in the end with her Schoolmen ... and a very little study of them will be sufficient to make a cautious thinker pause before he allows a technical difficulty to master his practical conclusions.' *The Christian Remembrancer*, 21, January–June 1851, p. 456.
48. *A Life's Decision*, p. 268.
49. *Devizes and Wilts Gazette*, 17 October 1850.
50. Biber, *Bishop Blomfield*, pp. 361–2.
51. Liddon et al., *Life of Edward Bouverie Pusey*, vol. III, p. 295.
52. Letter dated 9 November 1850 (Maskell Papers, BL Add. MS 37284, f. 301).
53. E. B. Pusey, *A Letter to the Right Hon. and Right Rev. the Lord Bishop of London in Explanation of Some Statements Contained in a Letter by the Rev. W. Dodsworth*, John Henry Parker, Oxford, 1851. The letter is dated 2nd week in Epiphany, 1851. By this time Dodsworth was no longer a clergyman, having converted on 1 January 1851.
54. T. W. Allies, *The See of St. Peter, The Rock of the Church, The Source of Jurisdiction, and the Centre of Unity*, Burns & Lambert, London, 1850, pp. xi–xiv.
55. 'A few days after her (Eliza), Mrs Foljambe had been received, and Case; and as I was with them, they made incessant efforts to determine me at once.' *A Life's Decision*, p. 277.

56. *Hants and Sussex Chronicle*, 6 July 1850 (quoted in the *Church and State Gazette*, 1850).
57. *Cheltenham Chronicle*, 8 August 1850 (quoted in the *Church and State Gazette*, 1850).
58. *A Life's Decision*, p. 277. He communicated in a building in Great Titchfield Street, temporarily occupied by Margaret Street Chapel, which had closed on Easter Monday, 1850, whilst a new church (All Saints) was built to replace it.
59. *Ibid.*, p. 279.
60. *Ibid.*, p. 278.
61. Letter dated 19 June 1850. *Ibid.*, p. 280.
62. Letter dated 24 June 1850. *Ibid.*, p. 281–2.
63. *Ibid.*, p. 97.
64. *Ibid.*, p. 277.
65. The book may be seen at Gladstone's Library, Hawarden.
66. Mentioned in letter from Dodsworth to Allies, 24 May 1850 (Maskell Papers, BL Add. MS 37284, f. 231).
67. Godfrey, *Roads to Rome*, pp. 191–3.
68. *Ibid.*
69. *A Life's Decision*, p. 282.
70. Letter received by Allies on 24 June 1850. *A Life's Decision*, p. 281.
71. *Ibid.*, p. 282.
72. *Ibid.*, p. 96.
73. *Ibid.*
74. Bolgeni (1733–1811) was a Jesuit theologian. According to Thompson his work 'seems singularly calculated to remove the prejudices of those who reject the claims of the Papal See, on the ground of their interfering with the rights of the Episcopate' (Thompson, *Unity of the Episcopate*, p. 49). According to *The English Review* (8/16, 1847), Bolegni's 'work on the Episcopate appears to be a text book with Romanists at present'.
75. *L'Episcopato*, quoted by Thompson, *Unity of the Episcopate*, p. 94.
76. *A Life's Decision*, pp. 282–3.
77. W. E. Gladstone, *Remarks on the Royal Supremacy, as it is Defined by Reason, History and the Constitution. A Letter to the Lord Bishop of London*, John Murray, London, 1850, pp. 16–17.
78. *See of St. Peter*, p. iii.
79. *Ibid.*, p. 22.

80. *Ibid.* 3rd edn, Burns, Lambert & Oates, London, 1866, p. 99.
81. *Ibid.*, p. 124.
82. *Ibid.*, p. 129.
83. *Ibid.*, p. 237.
84. *Ibid.*, p. 246.
85. *The Morning Post*, Saturday 21 September 1850. Allies had written: 'How are the Father and the Son one?—By the Holy Spirit, which is their love.' *See of St. Peter*, p. 43.
86. *The Christian Remembrancer*, 21, 1851, p. 36.
87. Allies, *The Church of England Cleared*, 1848 edition, p. vi.
88. *The See of St. Peter*, 1850, p. xii.
89. *The Christian Remembrancer*, 21, 1851, pp. 46, 47.
90. The second edition was therefore dedicated to Pius IX and dated 'Feast of the Immaculate Conception [8 December] 1854'. The translator was the Jesuit priest G. Costa. On 3 December 1850 he dined with Gladstone, who remarked, 'He is able and pleasant, but I felt when with him, that a Jesuit is as it were shut up against the access of truth in those things in which he has it not'; M. R. D. Foot and H. C. G Matthew (eds.), *The Gladstone Diaries*, vol. IV, 1848–54, Clarendon Press, Oxford, 1974, p. 281. The second edition noted that the *See of St. Peter* had also been translated into Armenian.
91. Carlo Passaglia, *De Praerogativis Beati Petri, Apostolorum Principis*, Manz, Ratisbon, 1850. Passaglia, was reputed the best theologian of his day and helped to formulate the dogma of the Immaculate Conception. He subsequently took the Piedmontese side regarding the Pope's temporal supremacy seeking to negotiate with Pius IX on behalf of Cavour. He met with no success and became alienated from the Catholic establishment.
92. T. W. Allies, *St. Peter, his Name and his Office as set forth in Holy Scripture*, Richardson & Son, London, 1852; preface, pp. vii, viii, ix.
93. *Ibid.*, p. ix.
94. *The Month: A Magazine and Review*, 15, July–December 1871, p. 176.
95. J. Chapman, *Studies in the Early Papacy*, Sheed & Ward, London, 1928, p. 72.
96. C. L. Young (Mrs Bertram Currie), *Some Side-Lights on the Oxford Movement by Minima Parspartis*, Art and Book Company, London and Leamington, 1895, pp. 167, 168.
97. *The Church of England Quarterly Review*, vol. XXXIV, William Edward Painter, London, 1853, p. 84.
98. *Ibid.*, p. 280.

99. *A Life's Decision*, p. 282.
100. *LD*, vol. XIV, pp. 31, 34, 48.
101. *A Life's Decision*, p. 283.
102. Typhus fever claimed the life of the Rev. Henry Holland, fellow of New College, and serving as curate of Pattishall in Northants. He was aged 37.
103. 'Remember, most loving Virgin Mary, never was it heard that anyone who turned to you for help was left unaided. Inspired by this confidence, though burdened by my sins, I run to you for protection for you are my mother'; *A Life's Decision*, p. 276.
104. *Ibid.*, p. 292.
105. Letter from Newman to Allies dated 22 August 1850; *LD*, vol. XIV, p. 48.
106. *A Life's Decision*, p. 284.
107. Cotton Hall was the gift of the Earl of Shrewsbury to Frederick Faber, who had renamed it St Wilfrid's. Before long he and the group of young men who had followed him had built a church there and filled it with Catholic converts. These 'Wilfridians' having united with Newman's group moved to London to establish an Oratorian work there, leaving the problem of what to do with such large and isolated property, which could not be sold for any secular purpose.
108. *A Life's Decision*, p. 290.
109. *Stamford Mercury*, 20 September 1850.
110. *The Catholic Magazine and Register*, 12/68, October 1850, pp. 198–9.
111. Letter dated 16 September 1850; *LD*, vol. XIV, p. 68. Maskell was drafting his letter to Pusey.
112. *The Household Narrative of Current Events 1850* (28 August – 28 September).

Chapter 6

1. Allies wrote in his diary for 21 October 1850, 'I reached Nelmes, having posted in London the formal and legal resignation of my living—too soon as it turned out, for I ought first to have recovered the rents due, of which one half year on one farm, £162, 10s, have been lost by my relinquishing the powers of a landlord'. *A Life's Decision*, p. 300.
2. Allies, *Secundo*, p. 80.
3. Hitherto there had been eight English districts ruled by Vicars Apostolic; in 1850 these were replaced by thirteen dioceses: Westminster (archbishopric), Southwark (London District), Hexham (Northern District), Beverley (Yorkshire), Liverpool and Salford (Lancashire), Menevia/Newport and

Shrewsbury (Welsh District), Clifton and Plymouth (Western), Nottingham and Birmingham (Central) and Northampton (Eastern District).

4. The Woottens had been committed Tractarians; after Frances was widowed in August 1847 Pusey sought to stop her from pursuing her wish to convert. However, under the guidance of Fr Robert Newsham (formerly priest at St Clement's, Oxford) she made her profession on 10 March 1850. Although there is no evidence it is possible that her conversion spurred Eliza Allies into action.
5. *A Life's Decision*, p. 292.
6. *Ibid.*
7. Letter dated 21 September 1850; *LD*, vol. XIV, p. 75.
8. *Ibid.*
9. 'At last it was determined to take the large room at Hawkins's and deposit the books and furniture there'; *Life's Decision*, p. 298.
10. *LD*, vol. XIV, p. 95.
11. *A Life's Decision*, p. 298.
12. Bicester station had just opened.
13. *A Life's Decision*, p. 299.
14. *Ibid.*
15. Writing to Newman on 11 June 1863, Allies wrote of Edward as 'the youth whom I brought to you nearly thirteen years ago to make his baptism sure' (Birmingham Oratory Archives 043, A003).
16. Letter dated 1 April 1851, quoted in P. Adams, *English Catholic Converts and the Oxford Movement—The Cost of Conversion*, Academica Press, Palo Alto, 2010, p. 107.
17. Letter to J. Spencer Northcote, dated 10 October 1850; *LD*, vol. XIV, p. 95.
18. Letter to Newman dated 15 March 1852 (Birmingham Oratory Archives 043, A002); *English Catholic Converts*, pp. 107–8.
19. *English Catholic Converts*, p. 108.
20. Allies, *Thomas Allies*, p. 67.
21. *LD*, vol. XIV, p. 80.
22. Journal entry, 5 November 1850; *A Life's Decision*, p. 301.
23. Journal entry, 6 November 1850; *ibid.*
24. Father John Morris wrote in his obituary of Scott-Murray that 'Danesfield became one of those centres of Catholic influence and edification, the multiplication of which is almost as important an element in the conversion of England as the multiplication of her priests and religious communities.

This was one of the Catholic houses in which Cardinal Wiseman felt at home, and it was here that he was first received with the state belonging to his rank on his return to England as its first Cardinal Archbishop'. *Tablet*, 2 September 1882.

25. Letter Newman to Allies dated 25 July 1851; *LD*, vol. XIV, p. 317. Pauline Adams writes, 'The Allies family for whom rooms were found near Wiseman's house in Golden Square had to vacate them on Tuesday afternoons when the Westminster chapter met in their dining room'. *English Catholic Converts*, p. 170.

26. Allies, *Secundo*, p. 83. It is not possible from Mary Allies's brief notice to identify which member of the extensive Weld family is referenced. It may have been Jane Charlotte Weld (1806–71), or Teresa Weld-Blundell (1818–89). The Carrington Smythes of Wootton House were old Catholics, Richard was the brother of Sir Charles Frederick Smythe, of Acton Burnell, and his wife, Eleanor Mary was the daughter of Lord Stourton.

27. Letter dated 13 July 1851; Raleigh Addington (ed.), *Faber: Poet and Priest, Selected Letters 1833–1863*, D. Brown & Son, Cowbridge, 1974, p. 229.

28. *LD*, vol. XV, p. 10.

29. Allies, *Thomas Allies*, p. 164.

30. *Ibid.*, p. 80. The church had been founded by Jessie and Lousie Gallini, daughters of the famous eighteenth-century impresario and dancing master, Sir John Gallini.

31. Letter Allies to Newman 23 March 1858 (Birmingham Oratory Archives 043, A002).

32. Birmingham Oratory Archives 043, A002. John Bethell (1804–67) practised as a solicitor in London, but achieved some fame as an inventor. In 1850 he followed his wife in becoming a Roman Catholic. His brother Richard was a prominent Liberal politician, created the first Baron Westbury, Lord Chancellor (1861–5).

33. 'Few houses in London, it has been remarked, have been the scene of stronger and more interesting emotions than the Priory, 21, North Bank, Regent's Park, a dwelling-place differing little in outward appearance from others in the district. It was to this house that George Eliot came with George Henry Lewes in 1864, and it remained the great novelist's home until her marriage with Mr John Cross in 1880, seven months before her death. The Priory is closely associated with the writing of "Felix Holt", "Middlemarch," and "Daniel Deronda." Here, too, George Eliot held her famous Sunday afternoon at homes, which were attended by most of the literary celebrities of the time'. See *The Queen's London: A Pictorial and*

Descriptive Record of the Streets, Buildings, Parks and Scenery of the Great Metropolis, Cassell & Co., London, 1896, p. 276.
34. Allies, *Thomas Allies*, p. 61.
35. *A Register of St. Nicholas College, Lancing, from its Foundation at Shoreham in August 1848 to the Commencement of the Month of November 1900*, privately printed, 1900, no author, p. 28.
36. Allies, *Secundo*, p. 83.
37. There is no record of how frequently they were visited.
38. Allies, *Thomas Allies*, p. 76.
39. *Ibid.*, p. 73.
40. *LD*, vol. XIV, p. 313.
41. Allies, *Thomas Allies*, p. 69.
42. Allies, *Secundo*, p. 86.
43. Allies was guided by Newman, who was no gothicist. Letter dated 6 July 1851, M. Belcher, *The Collected Letters of A. W. N. Pugin*, vol. V, 1851–2, Oxford, 2015, pp. 281–2. The encounter was five days previously.
44. Letter dated 10 February 1851; *LD*, vol. XIV, p. 208.
45. Allies, *Thomas Allies*, p. 68. In 1854, Henry Wilberforce, who as a married Catholic convert was also cast adrift in his new church, acquired the *Standard* and became its editor.
46. Letter to Allies dated 28 December 1852; *LD*, vol. XV, p. 231.
47. *LD*, vol. XIV, p. 125, n. 1. There is no information as to where the appeal originated, how extensively it was distributed or with what result.
48. J. H. Newman, *My Campaign in Ireland*, privately printed, 1896, p. xii.
49. The Belgian bishops established a new Catholic university at Mechelin in 1834, it moved and became the Catholic University of Louvain the following year.
50. 'The Catholic University was to cater for the *youth of Ireland*. It was to provide for the daily professional needs of Irish society'; V. A. McClelland, *English Roman Catholics and Higher Education 1830–1903*, Clarendon Press, Oxford, 1973, p. 94.
51. Newman's reply to Cullen, dated 16 April 1851; *LD*, vol. XIV, p. 257.
52. Letter dated Easter Sunday (20 April 1851); *LD*, vol. XIV, p. 262.
53. Letter dated 28 April 1851; *ibid.*, p. 268.
54. *My Campaign in Ireland*, p. xiii. Leahy was parish priest at Thurles and professor of theology at St Patrick's College in the town; he later became vice-rector of the Catholic university and in 1857 archbishop of Cashel.

O'Reilly was a lay Catholic scholar, who had returned from studying in Rome to assist in relief work during the famine. He later fought with the Irish Brigade in defence of the papacy during the campaign of 1860.

55. R. Ornsby, *Memoirs of James Robert Hope-Scott*, Murray, London, 1884, vol. II, p. 199. Hope, who converted in 1851, was a contemporary of Allies in Coleridge's house at Eton.
56. Letter dated 23 July 1851; *LD*, vol. XIV, pp. 315–16.
57. Letter dated 15 March 1852, Wootton House, Henley in Arden (Birmingham Oratory Archives 043, A002).
58. Letter dated 14 April 1852; *LD*, vol. XV, p. 65.
59. Letter from Cullen dated 25 April 1852; *LD*, vol. XV, p. 74, n. 2.
60. Letter dated 27 April 1852; *LD*, vol. XV, p. 75.
61. Quoted in *LD*, vol. XVI, p. 567 (Appendix 2).
62. *Tablet*, 30 December 1854.
63. McClelland, *English Roman Catholics and Higher Education*, p. 138.
64. Allies, *Thomas Allies*, p. 68.
65. In a letter to Father John Gordon, 13 May 1852, Newman wrote, 'tell F. Ambrose that Allies told me he *was prepared* to make nothing at all by pupils the first year. If after this he does not pay his rent, I won't say much for his confessor'; *LD*, vol. XV, p. 87.
66. 14 April 1852, *LD*, vol. XV, p. 65.
67. Allies, *Secundo*, p. 86.
68. *Ibid.*, p. 87.
69. The post was advertised in *The Times* on 5 July 1853.
70. Allies, *Thomas Allies*, p. 69.
71. It is doubtful whether the *Dublin* paid very well: 'The big quarterlies paid their writers handsomely but the Catholic publication was always pulling the devil by the tail and at best doled out a mere token-payment to a few contributors.' P. J. McLaughlin, 'Dr. Russell and the *Dublin Review*', in *Studies: An Irish Quarterly Review*, 41/162, June 1952, p. 176.
72. J. L. Altholz, *The Liberal Catholic Movement in England, the 'Rambler' and its Contributors, 1848–1864*, Burns & Oates, London, 1962, p. 9.
73. 'Archdeacon Wilberforce on Erastianism', *The Rambler*, 8/45, September 1851, pp. 216–34.
74. Charles William Russell (1812–80), from 1857 president of St Patrick's College, Maynooth, was a friend and collaborator with Cardinal Wiseman and a strong influence on Newman.

75. *Dublin Review*, 29, December 1850, pp. 476–507, reprinted in T. W. Allies, *Per Crucem ad Lucem, The Result of a Life*, C. Kegan Paul & Co., London, 1879, vol. II, pp. 17–18.
76. Allies, *Per Crucem ad Lucem*, vol. II, pp. 51–2.
77. *Ibid.*, p. 54.
78. Article II: 'The Greek Church—A Sketch by the Author of a "Proposition for Christian Union"', *Dublin Review*, 30, March 1851, pp. 24–32; Article VIII: 'The Anglican Universities as Ecclesiastical Training Schools—The Royal Commission for Visiting the Universities', *ibid.*, pp. 208–53. This latter article was republished in Allies, *Per Crucem ad Lucem*, vol. II, pp. 57–110.
79. *Ibid.*, 'The Greek Church', pp. 31–2.
80. *Ibid.*, 'The Anglican Universities', pp. 67, 69.
81. *Ibid.*, p. 83.
82. Article VII: 'Address of the Irish Bishops on the Catholic University', *Dublin Review*, 31, December 1851, pp. 529–88; reprinted in Allies, *Per Crucem ad Lucem*, vol. II, pp. 113–82.
83. Allies, *Per Crucem ad Lucem*, vol. II, pp. 123–4.
84. *Ibid.*, pp. 119, 120.
85. *Ibid.*, p. 137.
86. *Ibid.*, p. 143.
87. Letter to Allies dated 18 May 1854; *LD*, vol. XVI, p. 136. Newman noted Allies's acceptance in his University Journal for 6 June (*ibid.*).
88. Letter to Allies dated 3 September 1854; *LD*, vol. XVI, p. 244. After reading the *Philosophy of History* of the polymath, Romantic poet, philosopher and philologist Karl Wilhelm Schlegel (1772–1829), Allies wrote, 'There is to my mind a painful confusion in the method of this work, the more tantalizing because individual passages give one glimpses of so much promise.' Commonplace book, p. 157. For a discussion of Newman's contribution to the philosophy of history see, J. D. Holmes, 'Cardinal Newman on the Philosophy of History', *Tijdschrift voor filosofie*, 32/3, 1970, pp. 521–35.
89. Letter to Newman dated 10 November 1854 (Birmingham Oratory Archives 043, A002).
90. T. W. Allies, *The Formation of Christendom*, vol. I, *The Christian Faith and the Individual*, Burns & Oates, London, 1896, pp. 32–3.
91. *Ibid.*, p. 11.
92. *Ibid.*, pp. 21–2.
93. Allies, *Thomas Allies*, p. 78.

94. Henry Hart Milman (1791–1868), whose *History of the Jews* was published in 1829.
95. J. H. Newman, *The Idea of a University, Defined and Illustrated*, Pickering, London, 1873, pp. 85–6.
96. Allies, *The Formation of Christendom*, vol. I, p. 18.
97. *Ibid.*, p. 19.
98. T. W. Allies, *Per Crucem ad Lucem*, vol. II, p. 123.
99. François Guizot (1787–1874), a French historian and statesman.
100. Allies, *The Formation of Christendom*, vol. I, p. 29.
101. Allies, *Per Crucem ad Lucem*, vol. II, p. 128.
102. F. W. Faber, *Spiritual Conferences*, Thomas Richardson, London, 1859, pp. 254, 281.
103. M. Wilkinson, *Frederick William Faber, A Great Servant of God*, Gracewing, Leominster, 2007, p. 141.
104. *Ibid.*, p. 148.
105. See his letter to Edward Badeley, 22 March 1864; *LD*, vol. XXI, p. 86. This he gave as a reason why convert priests in London failed to sign a letter of support when he was attacked by Kingsley.
106. Newman's letter to him dated 5 June 1854; *LD*, vol. XVI, p. 143 and n. 2. Acton had met him whilst visiting the United States. Brownson's son was a fellow student in Germany.
107. Johann Joseph Ignaz von Döllinger (1799–1890). In 1858 he was Professor of Ecclesiastical History at Munich, well known as a scholar of the Reformation and Luther. His developing liberalism finally led him to reject the declaration of papal infallibility and his excommunication.
108. T. A. Howard, *The Pope and the Professor*, Oxford University Press, Oxford, 2017, p. 91.
109. *Ibid.*, p. 94.
110. D. Mathew, *Lord Acton and his Times*, Eyre & Spottiswoode, London, 1968, p. 149.
111. Lord Acton, *Essays on Church and State*, Hollis & Carter, London, 1952, pp. 58, 65; the article on 'Ultramontanism' reprinted from *Home and Foreign Review*, July 1863.
112. Letter to J. H. Newman, 7 January 1858 (Birmingham Oratory Archives 043, A002).
113. In a report for the English bishops in 1872. Allies, *Thomas Allies*, p. 101.
114. Altholz, *The Liberal Catholic Movement*, p. 43.

Notes

115. Letter Acton to Simpson, 6 October 1862; J. Altholz, D. McElrath and J. Holland, *The Correspondence of Lord Acton and Richard Simpson*, Cambridge University Press, Cambridge, 1975, vol. III, p. 25.
116. Letter Acton to Simpson, 28 February 1858; J. Altholz and D. McElrath, *The Correspondence of Lord Acton and Richard Simpson*, Cambridge University Press, Cambridge, 1971, vol. I, p. 13.
117. He said that Allies 'has moved so much in the business that I fear he made sure of it'. Letter dated 25 July 1858, Altholz and McElrath, *Acton and Simpson*, vol. I, p. 66. Edward Bellasis, a prominent lawyer and his wife were personal friends of Thomas and Eliza. Allies was Bellasis's godfather when he was received into the Church on 28 December 1850. See Edward Bellasis, *Memorials of Mr. Serjeant Bellasis (1800–1873)*, Burns & Oates, London, 1893, pp. 80, 90.
118. Letter dated 26 July 1858; *LD*, vol. XVIII, p. 427, n. 1.
119. Letter to Acton, dated 2 August 1858; *LD*, vol. XVIII, p. 433.
120. Letter dated 18 October 1858; *LD*, vol. XVIII, p. 488.
121. 26 March 1858, Altholz and McElrath, *Acton and Simpson*, vol. I, p. 19.
122. Allies, *Thomas Allies*, p. 108.
123. *The Rambler*, ns 10, October 1858, pp. 268–79.
124. Evan Baillie, 'A Letter to the Parishioners of Lawshall', *The Rambler*, ns 10, November 1858, pp. 356–9.
125. Letter dated 26 November 1858; Altholz and McElrath, *Acton and Simpson*, vol. I, p. 97.
126. Letter Simpson to Acton, 27 November 1858; *ibid.*, p. 98.
127. Letter to Newman, 2 March 1859; *LD*, vol. XIX, p. 60.
128. Letter Simpson to Acton, 19 January 1859; Altholz and D. McElrath, *Acton and Simpson*, vol. I, p. 136.
129. Letter to Newman, 30 September 1861; *LD*, vol. XX, pp. 47–8.
130. Edward Healy Thompson, 1813–91, Anglican priest, converted to Catholicism in 1846, and thereafter devoted his life to religious literature.
131. Letter to R. Simpson, 10 September 1861; Abbot Gasquet, *Lord Acton and his Circle*, Burns & Oates, London, n.d., p. 194.
132. Letter dated 5 April 1862; *ibid.*, p. 267.
133. Letter to R. Simpson, 26 April 1862; *ibid.*, p. 274.
134. Altholz, *The Liberal Catholic Movement*, p. 190. W. G. Ward was appointed editor of the *Dublin Review* in 1863; the first issue of the new series appeared in July of that year.

135. Letter Acton to Simpson, 8 March 1864; Altholz, *The Liberal Catholic Movement*, p. 224. The Munich Congress (28 September to 1 October 1863) was a gathering of mainly German theologians, during which Döllinger spoke on the 'Past and Present of Catholic Theology', which was seen as a challenge to the prevailing orthodoxy. The papal brief was issued as a letter to the archbishop of Munich, 21 December 1863.
136. Letter Acton to Simpson, 22 January 1859; Altholz and D. McElrath, *Acton and Simpson*, vol. I, p. 141. 'The Paternity of Jansenism' appeared in *The Rambler*, ns 10, December 1858, pp. 362–3.
137. Altholz and D. McElrath, *Acton and Simpson*, vol. I, p. 144 (27 January 1859).
138. Letter to Newman 12 June 1862; *LD*, vol. XX, p. 206.
139. Commonplace book.
140. Letter to Newman, 8 March 1862 (Birmingham Oratory Archives 043, A003).
141. Juan Donoso Cortès (1809–53), Spanish conservative, political theorist and theologian.
142. Allies, *Thomas Allies*, p. 108.
143. *Ibid.*, p. 110.
144. Note on Lecture 12 of the *Philosophy of History*, in Allies's commonplace book (p. 151).
145. Constantin von Höfler (1811–98), German Church historian.
146. Allies's manuscript note on von Höfler, *Kaiserthum und Papstthum, Ein Beitrag zur Philosophie der Geschichte*, 1862; Commonplace book, p. 301.
147. Letter dated 9 November 1860 (Birmingham Oratory Archives 043, A003).
148. Letter dated 22 November 1860; Allies, *Thomas Allies*, pp. 112–13.
149. Letter dated 29 November 1860; *ibid.*, pp. 114–19.
150. Letter dated 4 December 1860; *ibid.*, pp. 120–4.
151. *Ibid.*, p. 126.
152. Letter dated 5 March 1861; *ibid.*, pp. 130–2.
153. Faber, *Spiritual Conferences*, p. 354. See C. D. A. Leighton, 'Finding Antichrist: Apocalypticism in Nineteenth-Century Catholic England and the Writings of Frederick Faber', *Journal of Religious History*, 37/1, March 2013, pp. 80–97. See also C. D. A. Leighton, 'Thomas Allies, John Henry Newman and Providentialist History', in *History of European Ideas*, 38/2, 2012, pp. 248–65.
154. Allies, *The Formation of Christendom*, vol. I, p. 55.
155. Letter to Newman dated 26 October 1863 (Birmingham Oratory Archives 043, A003).

156. Letter dated 10 November 1863; *LD*, vol. XX, pp. 557–9.
157. Letter dated 8 November 1863; *LD*, vol. XX, pp. 553–6.
158. Allies, *The Formation of Christendom*, vol. I, p. 91.
159. Letter from Newman dated 26 October 1863; *LD*, vol. XX, p. 547, n. 3.
160. Letter to Allies, 26 October 1863; *LD*, vol. XX, p. 548.
161. Allies, *The Formation of Christendom*, vol. III, p. v.
162. Letter dated 18 January 1864; *LD*, vol. XXI, p. 22.
163. Letter dated 20 January 1864; *LD*, vol. XXI, p. 23.
164. Letter dated 11 February 1864; *LD*, vol. XXI, p. 48, n. 2.
165. Letter to Allies, 12 February 1864; *LD*, vol. XXI, p. 48.
166. Letter dated 30 November 1864; *LD*, vol. XXI, p. 327.
167. The Oxford University Act 1854 and the Cambridge University Act 1856.
168. Letter dated 30 November 1864; *LD*, vol. XXI, p. 327.
169. This is contested by J. Pereiro, *Cardinal Manning*, Oxford University Press, Oxford, 1998, p. 237, although he cites a letter from Wiseman about his needing to avoid the impression that he was receiving all his inspiration from Manning.
170. Letter dated 8 October 1864, cited in *LD*, vol. XXI, pp. 308–9, n. 3.
171. 'Christian and Antichristian Education', in Allies, *Per Crucem ad Lucem*, vol. II, p. 179.
172. Letter dated 3 December 1864; *LD*, vol. XXI, p. 327, n. 2.
173. Letter to Newman, 10 December 1864; *LD*, vol. XXI, p. 340, n. 1.
174. 'The Questions about University Education for Catholics'; *LD*, vol. XXI, Appendix 2, pp. 510–11.
175. *LD*, vol. XXI, p. 380.
176. The syllabus of eighty condemned propositions was an annex to the encyclical *Quanta Cura*, issued by Pius IX on 8 December 1864, the Feast of the Immaculate Conception.
177. Letter to Henry Nutcombe Oxenham, 25 January 1865; *LD*, vol. XXI, pp. 391–2.
178. Letter to Newman, 10 December 1864; *LD*, vol. XXI, p. 340, n. 1.
179. *LD*, vol. XXI, p. 410.
180. Letter to Newman dated 22 February 1865 (the day of Wiseman's funeral) (Birmingham Oratory Archives 043, A004).
181. *LD*, vol. XXI, p. 440, n. 2.
182. Letter dated 23 May 1865; *LD*, vol. XXI, p. 488.

183. Letter to Allies, 24 May 1865; *LD*, vol. XXI, p. 475.
184. Letter dated 25 May 1865; *LD*, vol. XXI, p. 483, n. 1. The incident referred to was the plan to appoint Newman to a bishopric in connection with his leadership of the Catholic University.
185. 'Excuse others.' Letter dated 26 May 1865 (Birmingham Oratory Archives 043, A004).
186. Letter dated 3 June 1865 (Birmingham Oratory Archives 043, A004).
187. Letter dated 4 June 1865; *LD*, vol. XXI, p. 483.
188. Letter dated 10 October 1865 (Birmingham Oratory Archives 043, A004).
189. E. B. Pusey, *Case as to the Legal Force of the Judgment of the Privy Council, in re Fendall v. Wilson*, J. Parker & F. H. Rivington, Oxford, 1864.
190. *Ibid.*, pp. 3–4. See H. P. Liddon, J. O. Johnston, R. J. Wilson and W. C. E. Newbolt, *Life of Edward Bouverie Pusey*, Longmans & Co., London, 2nd edn, 1897, vol. IV, pp. 95–6.
191. H. E. Manning, *The Workings of the Holy Spirit in the Church of England, A Letter to the Rev. E. B. Pusey D.D.*, Longman Green, London, 1864, p. 30.
192. E. B. Pusey, *The Church of England, A Portion of Christ's One Holy Catholic Church, and a Means of Restoring Visible Unity, An Eirenicon in a Letter to the Author of 'The Christian Year'*, Parker, Oxford, 1865, p. 237.
193. Letter to Newman, 17 October 1865 (Birmingham Oratory Archives 043, A004).
194. *Dublin Review*, ns 6, January–April 1866, pp. 189–90.
195. T. W. Allies, *Per Crucem ad Lucem*, vol. I, p. 294.
196. *Ibid.*, p. 304.
197. *Ibid.*
198. *Ibid.*, p. 321.
199. *Ibid.*, p. 339.
200. *Ibid.*, p. 419.
201. *Dublin Review*, ns 8, January–April 1866, p. 117.
202. *The Union Review*, 4 (ns 1), January–December 1866, p. 578.
203. Letter to Allies, 11 October 1865; *LD*, vol. XXII, p. 72.
204. *A Letter to the Rev. E. B. Pusey D.D., on his Recent Eirenicon*, Longmans, Green, Reader & Dyer, London, 1866.
205. *Ibid.*, p. 105.
206. Allies to Newman 15 February 1866 (Birmingham Oratory Archives 043, A004).

207. Letter to Newman, 15 February 1866; *LD*, vol. XXII, p. 158, n. 2.
208. Letter to Allies, 19 February 1866; *ibid.*
209. Letter to Rev. H. P. Liddon, D.D., 31 March 1878; Liddon *et al.*, *Life of Edward Bouverie Pusey*, vol. IV, p. 307.
210. Letter from Liddon to Newman, 1 April 1878; *ibid.*, p. 308.
211. Presumably a reference to what Allies regarded as a patched-together theology.
212. Letter dated 4 March 1880; *LD*, vol. XXIX, p. 244. Newman was equally concerned by what he deemed Allies's harshness in *A Life's Decision* in recalling Charles Marriott's shortness of temper and requested that he should attribute this to his frail health.
213. Oxenham (1829–88) was an Anglican priest, who converted in 1857; an ecumenist who disliked Ultramontanism, he came increasingly under the influence of Döllinger.
214. Johann Joseph Ignaz von Doellinger, *The First Age of Christianity and the Church* (1863); Oxenham's translation appeared in 1866. The dedication read 'To the Very Reverend John Henry Newman D.D. whose illustrious name is alone a passport to the hearts and a secure claim on the intellectual respect of all his countrymen both within and without the Church, this Translation of a Work The Great Catholic Divine of the Continent, is with his kind permission, very respectfully dedicated by the Translator. March 1866.'
215. Letter dated 8 March 1866 (Birmingham Oratory Archives 043, A004). The *Atlantis* was the organ of the Irish Catholic University.
216. Letter to Allies, 9 March 1866; *LD*, vol. XXII, p. 175. The 'former work' was John J. I. Döllinger, *The Gentile and Jew in the Courts of the Temple of Christ. An Introduction to the History of Christianity*, trans. N. Darnell. Longman, Green, Longman, Roberts & Green, London, 1862.
217. Letter to Newman dated 10 March 1866 (Birmingham Oratory Archives 043, A004).
218. Letter to Allies, 13 March 1866; *LD*, vol. XXII, p. 180.
219. Letter to Newman dated 15 March 1866 (Birmingham Oratory Archives 043, A004).
220. 13 April 1866; *LD*, vol. XXII, p. 212.
221. Letter to Allies dated 9 July 1866; *LD*, vol. XXII, p. 257.
222. *Ibid.*, n. 3.
223. William George Ward, *The Authority of Doctrinal Decisions*, Burns, Lambert & Oates, London, 1866, p. xxvii.

224. H. I. D. Ryder, *Idealism in Theology*, Longmans, Green, Reader & Dyer, London, 1867, p 5.
225. 'The Gods of the Nations when Christ Appeared', *Dublin Review*, ns 9, 1867, pp. 80–109; 'The First and Second Man', *ibid.*, pp. 441–72; 'The Second Man Verified in History', *Dublin Review*, ns 10, 1868, pp. 177–210; 'The First Age of the Martyr Church', *ibid.*, pp. 362–95.
226. Letter dated 19 October 1866 (Birmingham Oratory Archives 043, A004). See *LD*, vol. XXII, p. 303, n. 1.
227. Letter to Allies, 21 October 1866; *ibid.*, pp. 302–3. The sermon, 'The Pope and the Revolution', was preached at the Oratory on 7 October 1866. 'This sermon is given to the world having been made the subject in the public prints of various reports and comments, which both friendly and fair to the author, have proceeded from information inexact on points of detail.'
228. Letter to Newman dated 22 October 1866 (Birmingham Oratory Archives 043, A004). In 1859, after his withdrawal from Italy Napoleon III had advised the pope to cede the Papal States to Victor Emmanuel II. Pius IX declared that the French emperor was a 'liar and a cheat'. Although the emperor agreed to defend Rome, there was a continual fear that his troops would be withdrawn.
229. Letter to Allies, 23 October 1866; *LD*, vol. XXII, p. 305.
230. Letter dated 26 October 1866 (Birmingham Oratory Archives 043, A004).
231. Matthew Arnold in the preface to *Essays in Criticism*, 1865. Macmillan & Co., London, 1865, pp. xviii, xix.
232. Letter to Allies, 3 March 1867; *LD*, vol. XXIII, p. 71.
233. Letter to Newman dated 6 March 1867 (Birmingham Oratory Archives 043, A004), quoted in *LD*, XXIII, p. 75, n. 1.
234. *LD*, vol. XXI, p. 380, n. 1. The address (7 January 1865) with Allies's signature attached, was printed in the *Morning Post*, 2 February. The newspaper contrasts this address with that of the 'Ultramontane' Dr Cullen, who had delivered a vigorous speech attacking 'mixed education'.
235. Letter dated 7 March 1867; *LD*, vol. XXIII, p. 76.
236. Letter to Newman dated 8 March 1867 (Birmingham Oratory Archives 043, A004).
237. As noted by the editors of *LD*; letter dated 18 September 1872; *LD*, vol. XXVI, p. 172.
238. Letter to Hope-Scott dated 25 September 1867; *LD*, vol. XXIII, p. 343.
239. Allies, *Thomas Allies*, p. 99.
240. *Ibid.*, p. 99–100.

241. *Ibid.*, pp. 101–2.
242. Letter to Emily Bowles, dated 8 June 1872; *LD*, vol. XXVI, p. 110.
243. Newman was also nominated but he declined because the new institution would present students for examination by London University, he wrote to Manning, 'I could not without a great inconsistency take part in an Institution, which formally and 'especially' recognizes the London University, a body which has been the beginning, the source and the symbol of all the Liberalism existing in the educated classes for the last forty years.' Letter dated 24 November 1873; *LD*, vol. XXVI, p. 390.
244. V. A. McClelland, *Cardinal Manning, His Public Life and Influence, 1865–92*, Oxford University Press, London, 1962, p. 109.
245. *LD*, vol. XXVI, Introductory Note, p. xvi.
246. Letter dated 11 October 1868; *LD*, vol. XXIV, p. 158. Edgar Edmund Estcourt was an Anglican clergyman, who in 1845 followed Newman to Rome, in 1850 he was appointed *oeconomus* of the newly established diocese of Birmingham.
247. Letter dated 28 January 1870; *LD*, vol. XXV, p. 20.
248. Letter dated 28 January 1870; *LD*, vol. XXV, pp. 18, 19.
249. 'Definition of Infallibility: To the Editor of the Vatican', dated Palm Sunday 1870; printed in the *Tablet*, 16 April 1870, reprinted in Allies, *Per Crucem ad Lucem*, vol. II, p. 11.
250. Letter to his friend Miss Holmes, dated 22 May 1870; *LD*, vol. XXV, p. 132.
251. Letter dated 21 January 1875; *LD*, vol. XXVII, p. 202 (Birmingham Oratory Archives, 043, A004).
252. T. W. Allies, *The Formation of Christendom*, vol. III, *The Christian Faith and Philosophy*, 1897, Burns & Oates, London, pp. v, vii.
253. Allies's letter received by Newman 2 February 1875; *LD*, vol. XXVII, p. 209, n. 1.
254. Birmingham Oratory Archives 043, A004.
255. *LD*, vol. XXIX, p. 29.
256. According to Meriol Trevor, Allies's informant was probably Oakeley; *Newman Light in Winter*, Macmillan, London, 1962, p. 558.
257. Birmingham Oratory Archives 043, A004.
258. *Pall Mall Gazette*, 14 March 1879. On 29 April 1880, £2628 18s 5d was paid to Cardinal Newman from the Presentation Fund; *LD*, vol. XXIX, p. 266, n. 2.
259. Letter from Allies dated 6 July 1880 (Birmingham Oratory Archives 043, A004) and letter to Allies dated 7 July 1880; *LD*, vol. XXIX, pp. 150–1.

260. *LD*, vol. XXX, p. 313, n. 2.
261. Letter dated 30 January 1898 (Birmingham Oratory Archives 043, A004).
262. Letter to Newman dated 21 August 1873; *LD*, vol. XXVI, p. 355, n. 3.
263. Letter dated 24 August 1873; *LD*, vol. XXVI, p. 356.
264. *Tablet*, 27 July 1872; *Dublin Review*, ns 19, July–December 1872, p. 349.
265. Döllinger's rejection of papal infallibility; the *Tablet* thought his impact on the Church far more baleful than Allies allowed.
266. T. W. Allies, *Germany, Italy and the Jesuits, A Speech Delivered before the Catholic Union, July 1872*, Burns & Oates, London, 1872.
267. *Tablet*, 29 January 1876. Allies was reporting to the general committee of the Catholic Union on 14 January, having just returned from the Continent.
268. John Oldcastle (ed.), *Life of Leo the Thirteenth*, Burns & Oates, London, 1887, p. 84. Allies's reference is to the threat posed to Rome by Attila's invasion forces in 452, the first Pope Leo intervened leading to a withdrawal of the Hun's army.
269. Had Allies lived to read O'Donnell's book *Paraguay on Shannon* (Hodges & Figgis, Dublin, 1908) he would have felt vindicated; it was a sustained attack on the hierarchy of the Irish Catholic Church, who were accused of diverting into ecclesiastical building projects government funds meant for economic development.
270. 'Why I shall vote for the Unionist Candidate', *The Nineteenth Century*, 185, July 1892, pp. 172–3.
271. *Dublin Review*, third series, 20, 1888, pp. 291–311.
272. *Tablet*, 26 February 1887.
273. Langdale was born in 1787 In 1815 he inherited the name and the estates at Houghton Hall of his mother's cousin, Philip Langdale. Having promoted Emancipation, he was one of the first Catholic MPs, being returned as the Whig member for Beverley in 1832. He served as chairman of the Committee until his death in 1868. He is remembered as the biographer of Maria Fitzherbert, wife of George IV.
274. Stokes, a convert of 1845, was a scholar of Trinity College, Cambridge, and secretary of the Camden Society.
275. The 1851 census noted that from 'the return as to "birth place" it appears as many as 519,959 of persons resident in England at the time of the census were born in Ireland: these would be nearly all Roman Catholics' (quoted on p. 15 of the *Seventh Annual Report*.)
276. The first Provincial Synod of the restored hierarchy of Westminster took place at Oscott in the summer of 1852.

Notes

277. *Seventh Annual Report of the Catholic Poor-School Committee*, pp. 15–26.
278. Charlotte Hansen, 'Roman Catholic Education in England in the Nineteenth Century with Special Reference to William Bernard Ullathorne', Ph.D. thesis, University of Durham, 1998 (Durham E-Theses Online: http://etheses.dur.ac.uk/4643), p. 47.
279. Summary taken from: John P. Marmion, 'Cornelia Connelly's Work in Education, 1848–79', University of Manchester, Ph.D. thesis, 1984, p. 86.
280. *Seventh Annual Report of the Catholic Poor-School Committee*, p. 8.
281. Quoted in W. B. Ullathorne, *Notes on the Education System*, Richardson & Sons, London, 1857, p. 17. See Hansen, 'Roman Catholic Education', p. 71.
282. Hansen, 'Roman Catholic Education', p. 63.
283. Referred to as the Kemerton Trust Deed.
284. Mary Griset Holland, 'The British Catholic Press and the Education Controversy', Washington, DC, 1975, pp. 250–1.
285. First Synod of Westminster, 1852, synodical letter, quoted in Marmion, 'Cornelia Connelly', p. 87.
286. Allies, *Thomas Allies*, p. 93.
287. Ullathorne's commitment to Catholic education was undoubted; in the early years of the Poor-School Committee he was the only bishop whose name appeared on the list of subscribers.
288. Ullathorne, *Notes on the Education System*, p. 7.
289. *Ibid.*, p. 12.
290. *Ibid.*, pp. 61–2.
291. Holland, 'British Catholic Press', p. 241.
292. *The Rambler*, ns 7, 1857, p. 338.
293. *Ibid.*, p. 344.
294. *The Rambler*, ns 11, January 1859.
295. Letter from Gaisford dated 19 May, quoted in Holland, 'British Catholic Press', p. 236.
296. Letter dated 19 March 1857 (Birmingham Oratory Archives 043, A002). In 1853 the office was in John Street (Holborn); in 1858 it moved to Duke Street, closer to Allies's home at 44 Abbey Road, St John's Wood.
297. *The Rambler*, ns 1, 1859, p. 121.
298. *Answers to the Circular of Question*, Sessional Papers 1861, Education—General, 25 July 1859, vol. VII, p. 39. Quoted in E. G. Tenbus, *English Catholics and the Education of the Poor, 1847–1902*, Pickering & Chatto, London, 2010, p. 24.

299. Quoted in Marmion, 'Cornelia Connelly', p. 405.
300. J. von Arx, 'Cardinal Manning and his Political Persona', in S. Gilley (ed.), *Victorian Churches and Churchmen*, Catholic Record Society, London, 2005, pp. 5–7.
301. Report in the *Tablet*, 6 November 1869.
302. Both men were Etonians. Durnford was Edward Coleridge's brother-in-law. Both had married daughters of the headmaster, John Keate.
303. H. E. Manning, *Denominational Education. A Pastoral Letter*, Burns, Oates & Co., London, 1869, pp. 7, 11.
304. Letter dated 25 March 1870, P. C. Erb (ed.), *The Correspondence of Henry Edward Manning and William Ewart Gladstone*, vol. III, 1861–75, Oxford University Press, Oxford, 2013, pp. 197–8. See *Cardinal Manning, His Public Life and Influence, 1865–92*, p. 68.
305. Published in the *Catholic Times*, 22 January 1870; *Cardinal Manning, His Public Life and Influence, 1865–92*, p. 78.
306. *Tablet*, 29 January 1870.
307. *Catholic Times*, 5 February 1870.
308. *Catholic Times*, 26 February 1870.
309. *Ibid.*
310. *Tablet*, 12 March 1870.
311. Letter dated 22 September 1867; Erb, *Correspondence of Manning and Gladstone*, p. 101.
312. Letter dated 13 October 1867; *ibid.*, p. 102.
313. It has been estimated that living within 50 miles of Manchester there were at this time 50,000 Fenian sympathisers. See P. Rose, *The Manchester Martyrs, the Story of a Fenian Tragedy*, Lawrence & Wishart, London, 1970, p. 13.
314. 17 February 1870.
315. See M. J. Hickman, 'Catholicism and the Nation-State in Nineteenth Century Britain', in M. Eaton, J. Longmore and A. Naylor (eds.), *Commitment to Diversity. Catholics and Education in a Changing World*, Cassell, New York, 2000.
316. *Tablet*, 26 March 1870.
317. *Ibid.*, 23 April 1870.
318. *The Twenty-Third Annual Report of the Catholic Poor-School Committee*, p. 2.
319. Erb, *Correspondence of Manning and Gladstone*, pp. 209–10.

320. Letter to Gladstone dated 10 July 1870; *ibid.*, p. 211.
321. *Tablet*, 18 June 1870. In the Crisis Fund's appeal, the English Catholic population was given as 1,242,000, of whom 185,000 were assumed to be of school age. See Joan Bland, 'The Impact of Government on English Catholic Education, 1870–1902', *The Catholic Historical Review*, 62/1, 1976, pp. 36–55.
322. *Tablet*, 13 June 1874.
323. Shane Leslie, *Henry Edward Manning: His Life and Labours*, Burnes, Oates & Washbourne, London, 1921, p. 174.
324. *Tablet*, 18 September 1886.
325. *Ibid.*
326. *Ibid.*, 26 February 1876.
327. 'Catholic Interests and the Late Session of Parliament', *The Month*, ns 2, July–December 1870, p. 390.
328. 'Secularism in Elementary Education', *Dublin Review*, 25, July–October 1875, pp. 63–82.
329. *Tablet*, 21 August 1875.
330. *Ibid.*
331. This incident is described in V. A. McClelland, 'The Protestant Alliance and Roman Catholic Schools, 1872–4', *Victorian Studies*, 8/2, 1964, pp. 173–82.
332. *Tablet*, 13 June 1874.
333. 'The Bearing of the new Education Act on the Catholic Population', *The Month*, ns 2, July–December 1870, p. 611.
334. *Tablet*, 17 December 1881.
335. A bronze Marian medal was awarded for good conduct.
336. Allies, *Thomas Allies*, pp. 87–92. The letter was written in Italian; according to J. Bland, 'an attempt to find the Italian original in the Vatican archives was unsuccessful'. See Bland, 'The Impact of Government', p. 48.
337. Allies, *Thomas Allies*, pp. 83–4.
338. Hansen, 'Roman Catholic Education', p. 76.
339. *Seventh Annual Report of the Catholic Poor-School Committee*, 1854. At Appendix G of this report was included a paper that Manning had submitted to the bishops on the 'necessity of training schools for lay teachers'; evidently there was some reluctance to accept that the teaching force could not be comprised principally of the religious.
340. W. O'Dea, 'The Catholic Education Council, its History and Work', *Tablet*, 12 June 1915.

341. A Sister of Notre Dame, *Sister Mary of St. Philip (Frances Mary Lescher) 1825–1904*, Longmans, Green & Co., London, 1922, p. 102.
342. The prime mover in this design was Emily Bowles, the friend of J. H. Newman, who joined the Society of the Holy Child in 1846. Six years later she was the Order's superior in Liverpool, and was responsible for the over-borrowing which encumbered the Society for many years. In 1856 she renounced her vows and left the order. See Marmion, 'Cornelia Connelly', p. 286.
343. *Ibid.*, p. 239.
344. J. J. Doyle, 'Catholic Training Colleges', *Tablet*, 5 October 1929.
345. Letter dated 3 March 1874; *Tablet*, 7 March 1874.
346. *Tablet*, 17 December 1881.
347. *Tablet*, 24 May 1890.
348. Allies, *Thomas Allies*, p. 83.
349. McClelland, *Cardinal Manning, His Public Life and Influence, 1865–92*, pp. 85–6.
350. *Ibid.*, p. 86.
351. *Tablet*, 20 June 1903, has an interesting account of the proceedings, evidently written by somebody present. 'In May 1890, the annual meeting of the School Committee took place ... There was a full attendance in view of the business to be considered—the retirement of the Secretary. The Duke of Norfolk in expressing the regret of the Committee at the loss of so valued a colleague proposed that a pension of £350 a year be voted to him. The proposal was received with cries of 'Four Hundred!' from various parts of the room; the Duke of Norfolk and the Marquis of Ripon both stating that, although they personally would have preferred the amount to be £400 they thought unanimity very important and they hoped to secure it by naming the lesser sum. Mgr. Gilbert and Mgr. Clarke encouraged by further cries of 'Four Hundred!' and by remarks from Mr. Fitzherbert, put the rival sums to the vote, when the majority was found to favour the larger amount. The proposition that a pension of £400 a year (the full amount of his former salary) should be granted, was, therefore, carried unanimously.'
352. Allies, *Thomas Allies*, p. 83.
353. *Ibid.*, pp. 103–4.
354. 'I must say the vast majority have treated the Poor-School Committee with utter indifference'; letter to J. H. Newman, 17 December 1860 (Birmingham Oratory Archives 043, A003).
355. Tenbus, *Education of the Poor*, p. 153. Marshall had been Anglican incumbent of Swallowcliffe, Wiltshire, who after converting in 1845 became an Inspector of Schools.

356. 1 March 1864; *LD*, vol. XXI, p. 65, n. 2.
357. R. Aldrich and P. Gordon, *Dictionary of British Educationists*, Routledge, London, 1989, p. 7.
358. Allies, *Thomas Allies*, p. 83.
359. *Ibid.*, p. 85.
360. *A Life's Decision*. After Allies's death, when a third edition was published (1913), the motto was removed and replaced by a quotation from St Augustine (*Diligite homines, interficite errores*, 'Love the people, but destroy the mistakes') which perhaps reflected Mary Allies's opinion that her father had been too unforgiving towards Bishop Wilberforce.
361. Allies, *Thomas Allies*, p. 165. Mary meant that the book had almost no public impact, but that those who were interested in the Catholic movement in the Church of England read it with interest (and perhaps some irritation). According to the prologue the book was written in 1853 for the author's children when the events were still fresh in his mind. It 'lay in a drawer for twenty-five years' until a son asked him to publish it.
362. 12 February 1855; *ibid.*, p. 77.
363. *Ibid.*, pp. 106–7.
364. Letter dated 28 April 1851, from Newman to Archbishop Cullen, recommending Allies's appointment to the Catholic University; *LD*, vol. XIV, pp. 267–8.
365. Letter to Allies dated 18 May 1854; *LD*, vol. XVI, p. 136. Newman noted Allies's acceptance in his University Journal for 6 June (*ibid.*).
366. T. W. Allies, *The Formation of Christendom*, 8 vols., 1865–96, vol. VIII, *The Monastic Life: From the Fathers of the Desert to Charlemagne*, Kegan, Paul, Trench & Trubner, London, 1896, p. 374.
367. Allies, *The Formation of Christendom*, vol. VII, *Peter's Rock in Mohammed's Flood*, Burns & Oates, London, 1890, p. vii.
368. *Ibid.*, p. v.
369. Allies, *The Formation of Christendom*, vol. VI, *The Throne of the Fisherman*, Burns & Oates, London, 1887, p. viii.
370. Allies, *The Formation of Christendom*, vol. I, Burns & Oates, London, 1897, pp. v, vi.
371. *Dublin Review*, ns 4, January–April 1865, p. 547.
372. *Dublin Review*, ns 5, July–October 1865, pp. 425–53.
373. *Dublin Review*, ns 24, January–April 1875, pp. 513–15.
374. *Tablet*, 2 February 1869.
375. *The Spectator*, 20 October 1866, p. 22.

376. *The Formation of Christendom*, vol. III, reviewed in *The Westminster Review*, ns 48, July and October 1875, p. 213.
377. John Wordsworth (1843–1911) was a classical scholar, appointed in 1883 Oriel Professor in the Interpretation of Holy Scripture; he was made bishop of Salisbury in 1885.
378. *The Academy, A Weekly Review of Literature, Science and Art*, 14 August 1875, pp. 160–1.
379. Allies, *The Formation of Christendom*, vol. III, p. vii.
380. *The Academy*, 14 August 1875, p. 160–1.
381. Allies, *The Formation of Christendom*, vol. III, pp. 428–9.
382. *Union Review*, January–December 1869, pp. 278–9 (vol. II).
383. Letter dated 6 June 1869; *LD*, vol. XXIV, p. 265.
384. D. F. Strauss, *Das Leben Jesu*, Osiander, Tübingen, 1840; George Eliot's translation: *Life of Jesus, Critically Examined by Dr David Friedrich Strauss*, Chapman Brothers, London, 1846 (translator's name not given).
385. 'Selections from Foreign Catholic Periodicals', *The Month and Catholic Review*, 9 (28), September–December 1876, pp. 358–61, 496–508.
386. *The Month*, 10, 1869, p. 397.
387. *Tablet*, 17 November 1888.
388. Allies, *Thomas Allies*, p. 146.
389. *Tablet*, 18 April 1896.
390. C. D. A. Leighton, 'Thomas Allies, John Henry Newman and Providentialist History', *History of European Ideas*, 38/2, 2012, pp. 248–65.
391. *Ibid.*, p. 264.
392. Letter to an unnamed 'head of one of our Colleges' in *Tablet*, 9 June 1894.
393. Leighton, *Providentialist History*, p. 257. Despite his rejection of Catholicism, Gladstone in 1853 described Allies's writing as 'very powerful' (Pollen, *John Hungerford Pollen*, p. 244).
394. Christopher Dawson, *The Formation of Christendom*, Sheed & Ward, New York, 1967, and Judith Herren, *The Formation of Christendom*, Fontana Press, London, 1989.

Chapter 7

1. In January 1858 Newman complained, 'I have heard nothing at all of Basil for an age' and had it in mind 'to get some of my *opuscula* bound up for him. He might be interested in some of them now'; *LD*, vol. XVIII, p. 224.

2. Letter to J. H. Newman, dated 26 October 1866 (Birmingham Oratory Archives 043, A004).
3. Letter to Nicholas Darnell, August 29, 1861; *LD*, vol. XX, p. 39.
4. Letter to Allies, 26 January 1862; *LD*, vol. XX, p. 135.
5. Letter to Allies, 15 April 1862; *LD*, vol. XX, pp. 186–7.
6. Letter dated 29 April 1862; *LD*, vol. XX, p. 193.
7. *LD*, vol. XX, p. 194.
8. Letter dated 30 August 1862; *LD*, vol. XX, p. 264.
9. Letter to J. H. Newman, dated 24 November 1862 (Birmingham Oratory Archives 043, A004).
10. Letter dated 25 June 1863 (Wiseman papers W3/51/13, Westminster Diocesan Archives).
11. Letter dated 14 June 1863; *LD*, vol. XX, p. 468.
12. 'Immigration and the Immigrant Ships', lecture by A. G. Davies, read at a meeting of the Historical Society of Queensland, 26 March 1935.
13. Letter from Eliza Hall Allies to J. H. Newman, 21 January 1864 (Birmingham Oratory Archives 043, A003).
14. Letter dated 17 October 1865 (Birmingham Oratory Archives 043, A004). The account of this encounter with the indigenous people is consonant with research into clashes between settlers and Aborigines which has established that the loss of life on both sides was higher in Queensland than in any other colony in Australia.
15. *Liverpool Mercury*, 19 June 1878. The following year Allies gave a lengthy lecture to the Liverpool Engineering Society on sewers and sewage. 'He advocated agricultural irrigation as the least expensive mode of disposing of town sewage when there is no direct outlet to the sea'; *Liverpool Mercury* 7 November 1879.
16. The founder of the ICMS was an Anglican clergyman, Alexander Dallas, who had laid hands on Henry Wilberforce at his Anglican ordination.
17. Estate Record: Allies—Landed Estate, NUI Galway (landedestates.nuigalway.ie/LandedEstates/jsp/estates-show.jsp?id=788). The Court was established in 1849, it could authorise the sale of indebted estates, giving the new owner clear title.
18. *The Manchester Courier and Lancashire General Advertiser*, 12 August 1882.
19. On 13 February 1882, Cyril acted as a steward at the Sheffield Catholic Ball; *Sheffield Daily Telegraph*, 14 February 1882.
20. Letter dated 21 November 1882 (Birmingham Oratory Archives 043, A004).

21. *The Sheffield Weekly Telegraph*, 15 September 1883.
22. T. Robinson, *Connemara 'The Last Pool of Darkness'*, Penguin Books, London, 2009, p. 170.
23. See https:/ballymaclinton.wordpress.com/2015/07/18/what-happened-on-inisbof-in-in-July-1890-three-days-that-changed-the-history-of-anthropology-in-ireland-and-britain
24. Stewart M. Foster, 'Et in Suburbia Ego: Father George Bampfield and the Institute of St Andrew', *Recusant History*, 23, 1996, p. 444.
25. *Catholic Directory*, 1871, p. 180.
26. Allies, *Secundo*, p. 168.
27. *Ibid.*
28. The Jesuits acquired the property in 1861 and named it after the town in Spain where St Ignatius developed his Spiritual Exercises. Among the early novices was Gerard Manley Hopkins, and at the time of Allies's studies he was a member of staff teaching classics and writing some of his most celebrated poems, including *The Wreck of the Deutschland*.
29. Allies, *Secundo*, p. 169.
30. *Ibid.*, p. 177. Thomas had taken the lease on another property, and when he discovered that it was haunted he agreed to pay a fine of £80 to be released from the obligation.
31. *Ibid.*, p. 179.
32. Allies, *Thomas Allies*, p. 176.
33. *Ibid.*
34. In a letter dated 9 October 1885, Allies told Newman that Eliza was deaf (Birmingham Oratory Archives 043, A004).
35. Allies, *Thomas Allies*, p. 164.
36. Allies, *Secundo*, pp. 187–8.
37. *Ibid.*, p. 189.
38. *Ibid.*, p. 189.
39. *Ibid.*, p. 190.
40. *Ibid.* According to Wilfrid Wilberforce (youngest son of Henry Wilberforce) 'it was said at the time... that he gave his life in the cause of charity by going to attend a dying man... at a time when he himself was so ill that it was an evident danger for him to leave his bed.' Review article, 'Thomas William Allies', *The Catholic World*, 86, October 1907 – March 1908, pp. 318–31.
41. Allies, *Secundo*, p. 191.
42. *Ibid.*, p. 192. 'Syncope' refers to the loss of consciousness rather than to the underlying cause of death.

43. Performed by the celebrated surgeon, Sir F. Treves; *ibid.*, p. 194.
44. Aubrey Thomas de Vere (1814–1902), received into the Catholic Church by Manning in 1851, was a critic and recognised poet, particularly of devotional verse. According to Allies's dedication he 'welcomed my first effort to trace the work of Christ in a single human soul, and year after year has cheered me with a mind which knows, and a heart which feels, the scope of the task pursued by me'.
45. *Ibid.*, p. 195.
46. W. Wilberforce, *The Catholic World*, 86.
47. 'The will of the late Mr. T. W. Allies has been sworn at £39,357–13–1d' (some £4.75m in today's money); *Tablet*, 1 August 1903.
48. Letter dated 30 December 1854; *LD*, vol. XVI, p. 338.
49. Allies, *Secundo*, pp. 206–8, 210–11.
50. Henry James Coleridge (1822–93), second son of Sir John Coleridge, converted in 1852, and entered the Jesuit novitiate in 1857.
51. *The Irish Monthly*, 22/247, January 1894, pp. 33–51.
52. John Coleridge, 1st Baron Coleridge (1820–94), first son of Sir John Coleridge, Lord Chief Justice from 1880; he was in office at his death.
53. The allusion is to the *Ballad of Chevy Chase*, quoted by Samuel Butler in *Hudibras*: 'But Widdrington in doleful dumps / When legs were off fought on his stumps.'
54. 'M. R.' 'The First Lord Coleridge and His Brother', *The Irish Monthly*, 23/25, January 1895, pp. 1–15.
55. *The Irish Monthly*, 15/169, January 1894, p. 385.
56. The poem was entitled 'February 21st 1878'; *LD*, vol. XXVIII, p. 318, nn. 1 and 2.
57. *LD*, vol. XXXI, p. 85, n. 3.
58. Letter to T. W. Allies 21 May 1882; *LD*, vol. XXX, p. 89 and n. 1.
59. Letter to Newman dated 9 October 1885 (Birmingham Oratory Archives 043, A004).
60. *Tablet*, 22 November 1879.
61. Review of *Per Crucem ad Lucem*, *Tablet*, 22 November 1879. Matthew Arnold, *New Poems*, Macmillan, London, 1867. Of course, the irony is that the Tractarians considered the poet's father an apostle of liberalism and a sworn enemy.
62. Allies, *Thomas Allies*, p. 162. His daughter observed 'some people remarked that they would not have objected to be an abject if he was one'.

63. H. Eyres, 'The Perils of Precocity', *The Financial Times*, 27 December 2013.
64. Allies, *Secundo*, pp. 172–3.
65. *Ibid.*, p. 179.
66. *Ibid.*
67. Allies, *Thomas Allies*, p. 179.
68. *Ibid.*, p. 170. Mount Tabor was the traditional site of the Transfiguration.
69. *Ibid.*, p. 187.
70. *Ibid.*, pp. 193–4.
71. *Ibid.*, p. 195.
72. 20 June 1903.
73. From Wordsworth's 1802 poem, *To Toussaint L'Ouverture*, 'thou hast great allies; / Thy friends are exultations, agonies; / And love, and man's unconquerable mind'.
74. *A Life's Decision*, C. Kegan Paul, London, 1st edn, 1880, p. 364.

BIBLIOGRAPHY

This bibliography covers manuscript sources and lists the published works of Thomas William Allies. Bibliographical details of other works cited are given in the chapter notes.

PRINCIPAL MANUSCRIPT SOURCES

Coleridge Papers, British Library
Commonplace book (owned by the author)
Correspondence with W. E. Gladstone, British Library
Correspondence with H. E. Manning, Bodleian Library, Oxford
Correspondence with W. Maskell, British Library
Correspondence with J. H. Newman, Birmingham Oratory
Correspondence with N. Wiseman, Westminster Diocesan Archives
T. W. Allies, Diary 1839 (owned by the author)

PUBLISHED WORKS OF T. W. ALLIES

Poems for Private Circulation, D. A. Tallboys, Oxford, 1837
On the Influence of Practical Piety in Promoting the Temporal and Eternal Interests of Mankind, D. A. Tallboys, Oxford, 1838
Sermons on the Epistle to the Romans and others, John Parker, Oxford, 1844
Holiness of Consecrated Places (A chapter in 'Sermons for Sundays, Festivals and Fasts contributed by Bishops and other clergy of the Church', ed. A. Watson), Joseph Masters, London, 1846
The Church of England Cleared from the Charge of Schism upon the Testimonies of Councils and the Fathers of the First Six Centuries, James Burns, London, 1846
The Church of England Cleared from the Charge of Schism by the Decrees of the Seven Ecumenical Councils and the Tradition of the Fathers. Second Edition, enlarged, John Henry Parker, Oxford, 1848

Journal in France in 1845 and 1848, with Letters from Italy in 1847, of Things and Persons concerning the Church and Education, Longman, Brown, Green and Longmans, London, 1849

The Royal Supremacy Viewed in Reference to the Two Spiritual Powers of Order and Jurisdiction, William Pickering, London, 1850

The See of St. Peter, the Rock of the Church, the Source of Jurisdiction and the Centre of Unity, Burns & Lambert, London 1850

St. Peter, his Name and his Office as set forth in Holy Scripture, Richardson & Son, London, 1852

The Formation of Christendom, Part First, Longman, Green, Longman, Roberts & Green, London, 1865

Dr. Pusey and the Ancient Church, Longmans, Green, Reader, & Dyer, London, 1866

The Formation of Christendom, Part Second, Longmans, Green, Reader and Dyer, London, 1869

The Formation of Christendom, Part Third, Longmans, Green, Reader and Dyer, London, 1875

Per Crucem ad Lucem: The Result of a Life, 2 vols., C. Kegan Paul & Co., London, 1879

A Life's Decision, C. Kegan Paul & Co., London, 1880

Church and State as Seen in the Formation of Christendom, Burns & Oates, London, 1882

The Throne of the Fisherman Built by the Carpenter's Son, the Root, the Bond, and the Crown of Christendom, Burns & Oates, London, 1887

Teacher of the Church: Peacemaker among Nations (Chapter IX in 'Life of Leo XIII', edited by John Oldcastle), Burns & Oates, London, 1887

The Holy See and the Wandering of the Nations from St. Leo I to St. Gregory I, Burns & Oates, London, 1888

Peter's Rock in Mohammed's Flood from St. Gregory to St. Leo III. Being the Seventh Volume of the Formation of Christendom, Burns & Oates, London, 1890

The Monastic Life from the Fathers of the Desert to Charlemagne, Kegan Paul, Trench, Trübner & Co., London, 1896

PUBLISHED ARTICLES BY T. W. ALLIES

The Dublin Review
'Testimony of Grotius and Liebnitz', 29, 1850, pp. 476–507
'The Greek Church: A Sketch; Nationalism and Catholicism. A summary and review with textual excerpts', 30, 1851, pp. 24–32
'The Anglican Universities as Ecclesiastical Training Schools', 31, 1851, pp. 208–53
'The Catholic University: A Justification and Defence', 31, 1851, pp. 529–88
'The Jesuits in India: A Work by Father Strickland, a Missioner Working in India. A Summary with Textual Extracts', 32, 1852, pp. 386–406
'Dr. Pusey's Apology for Anglicanism along with Letter to Dr Pusey by Mr Allies' (with W. G. Ward), ns 6, 1866, pp. 188–239
'Dr. Pusey on Ecclesiastical Unity', ns 8, 1867, pp. 83–118
'English Catholic Poor Schools' (authorship inferred), ns 8, 1867, pp. 299–315
'The Gods of the Nations when Christ Appeared', ns 9, 1867, pp. 80–109
'The First and Second Man', ns 9, 1867, pp. 441–72
'The Second Man Verified in History', part 2, ns 10, 1868, pp. 179–210
'First Age of the Martyr Church', ns 10, 1868, pp. 362–95
'Catholicity in Germany' (authorship inferred), ns 19, 1872, pp. 335–51
'The Lambeth Conference', ns 20, 1888, pp. 291–311

The Rambler
'Archdeacon Wilberforce on Erastianism', 8, 1851, 216–34
'Catholic and Protestant Missionary, Book and Education Societies', ns 10, 1858, pp. 268–79

The Nineteenth Century
'Why I shall vote for the Unionist', 9, July 1892, pp. 172–3

INDEX

Abbaye aux Bois, Paris 94
Abraham, C. J. (1814–1903), first bishop of Wellington 128
Academia of the Catholic Religion 277, 314
The Academy, monthly review (1869–1902) 357, 440
Acland, Thomas Dyke, 11th baronet (1809–98), educational reformer and politician 17, 39
Acton, Lord John Dalberg-Acton, 1st baron (1834–1902), Catholic historian and politician 270–8, 284, 298, 299, 308, 332, 354, 426–8
Adare, Lord Edwin Wyndham-Quin (1812–71), archaeologist, Catholic convert (1855) 112
Affre, Denis-Auguste (1793–1848), archbishop of Paris 138, 140
Aldenham, Salop seat of Lord Acton 271, 274
Alderson, Baron Edward Hall (1787–1857), commercial judge 33–5, 39–42, 125, 135, 136, 166–9, 172, 174, 177, 180, 241
Alderson, Edward Packenham (1830–76), Allies's pupil, merchant and barrister 33
Alexander VI, Roderick de Borgia (1431–1503), pope 278
Alexander VIII, Pietro Vito Ottoboni (1610–91), pope 403

Alleyne, John (1724–1801), Barbadian slave owner 385
Allies, Bernard Joseph (b. & d. 1855), Allies's fifth son 83, 248
Allies, Caroline (1821–53), Allies's half-sister 4, 8, 243
Allies, Caroline *née* Hilhouse (*c.*1781–1868), Allies's step-mother 3, 4–6, 8, 23, 36, 243, 386, 388
Allies, Cyril (1846–1916), Allies's fourth son:
childhood 82, 180, 247–9, 271, 365–7
Australia 285, 367–9
civil engineer 366, 368, 369, 441
landlord of Innisbofin 368–71, 373–5
death 375
Allies, Edward Hall (1841–99), Allies's first son
childhood 41, 45, 185, 244, 249, 365, 421
Australia 285, 367, 368
civil engineer 366, 368, 370, 441
Innisbofin 370, 371
death 375, 377
Allies, Edwin (b. 1782), Allies's uncle 1, 2
Allies, Eliza Hall *née* Newman (1821–1902), married T. W. Allies 1 October 1840
courtship 35–7, 41, 390

rector's wife 56, 57, 62, 76, 77, 82, 83, 93, 165, 168, 180, 181
becomes a Roman Catholic 203–6, 223, 225, 237–9
life as a Catholic 241–3, 247–9, 285, 286, 291, 300, 310, 372, 373, 417, 421, 427, 441, 442
personality 76, 77, 203, 204, 206, 285, 376
death 372, 373, 375, 377
Allies, Frances Elizabeth *née* Fripp (1791–1813), Allies's mother 2, 3, 10
Allies, George, mayor of Worcester, Allies's uncle 1
Allies, George Hilhouse (b. & d. 1819), Allies's half-brother 5
Allies, Hannah *née* Duddon Allies's grandmother 1, 4, 10
Allies, Henry Basil (1844–97), Allies's third son
childhood 81, 82, 180, 244, 247–9
studies 365, 440
priestly ministry 371, 372
death 374
Allies, Henry Edward (b. & d. 1842), Allies's second son 57, 77
Allies, James, Allies's grandfather 1, 4
Allies, Kathleen *née* Lillie (d. 1894), married Cyril Allies (1891) 371, 373
Allies, Mary Anne (1818–87), Allies's half-sister 4, 8, 243
Allies, Mary Helen Agnes (1852–1927), Allies's first daughter and biographer vii, 13, 70, 76, 82, 83 87, 204, 245, 248, 249, 274, 312, 329, 372, 373, 374, 375, 377, 383, 393, 422, 439

Allies, Monica Mary (1892–1970), Allies's granddaughter 371, 374
Allies, Thomas (1785–1838), Allies's father
early years and marriages 1–3
connoisseurship 4–8
rector of Wormington 10–11
death 11, 23
Allies, Thomas William (1813–1903)
childhood and schooling 4, 8–13
Oxford 14–17, 23–4, 30
the call to be a poet 14, 16, 18–20, 24, 26–9
early travels on the Continent 18, 21–3
first conversion (1837) 23–7, 29–30
On the Influence of Practical Piety 30–3
London (1838–40) 33–5, 39–41
courtship 35–7
the making of a Tractarian 37–9, 46–7, 76, 81–3
Sermons on the Epistle to the Romans 47–9, 71–2
examining chaplain to bishop Blomfield (1840–2) 41–6, 49–52
rector of Launton (1842– 50) 52–69, 83–4, 86–9, 97–9, 135–6
controversy at Oxford 69–71, 73–5, 84–6
Continental travel (1843–9) 77–81, 89–97, 128–34, 137–42, 180–3
relationship with J. H. Newman 30, 37, 46–9, 65–6, 69–72, 81–3, 86, 91, 97–9, 101, 103–7, 155, 184, 206, 218, 237–9, 242–8, 251–7, 259, 264, 265, 269–75, 277, 279–93, 295–314, 328, 351–3, 357–9, 361, 362, 365–7, 372, 377, 379–82, 384

Index

The Church of England Cleared from the Charge of Schism 106–28
relationship with E. B. Pusey 46, 74, 75, 86, 102–3, 129, 134, 135, 138, 144, 145, 148, 153, 160, 163, 167, 171, 172, 176, 178, 182, 185, 197, 199, 200, 208–24, 239, 292–7
The Journal in France 78–80, 116, 130, 137, 139–80
relationship with bishop Wilberforce 66–9, 128, 134, 135, 139, 140 156–80, 246, 260, 392, 439
relationship with H. E. Manning 71, 91, 118, 125, 134, 142–5, 147–9, 153, 156, 157, 160–2, 164, 165, 167–77, 182, 184–7, 192, 193, 197, 198–201, 205, 207, 208, 210, 213, 214, 223, 270, 276, 277, 290–3, 300, 305, 307, 311, 312, 316, 330–2, 338, 349
the Gorham Judgment 161, 165, 185–209, 215, 222, 227, 234, 239, 246, 259, 293, 294, 384, 415
jurisdiction 108, 114–19, 141, 188–202, 205, 208–33, 239
The Royal Supremacy 188, 191–7, 200, 206, 208–10, 222, 226, 228, 230, 294
absolution 45, 81, 196, 201, 210–20, 239
second conversion (1850) 206–9, 222–5, 237–40
The See of St Peter 226–34
St Peter, his Name and his Office 234–7
seeking employment (1850–3) 241–53
the Catholic University of Ireland 253–8

writing for Catholic Reviews 258–64
the philosophy of history 264–9
liberalism and ultramontanism 269–77, 285–6, 289–92, 298–302, 307–13
The Formation of Christendom 277–85, 352–63
Catholic higher education 286–9, 302–7
Dr Pusey and the Ancient Church 292–7
Catholic Union 313–17
Catholic Poor-School Committee 317–51
family life 365–72
final years and death 372–7
reflections on his life 377–84
Allies, Winifrid Mary (1893–6), Allies's granddaughter 373, 374
Ambrose of Milan (*c.*339–*c.*397) 182
Amherst, Francis Kerril (1819–83), Catholic bishop of Northampton 365
Appleyard, Ernest Silvanus (1804–76), Anglican clergyman and writer 261
Aquinas, Thomas (1225–74) 378, 380
Armstrong, Benjamin (1817–90), vicar of East Dereham 43, 44, 392
Atlantis, journal of the Catholic university of Ireland 274, 275, 298, 431
Augustine of Canterbury (d. 604) 225
Augustine of Hippo (354–430) 49, 82, 108, 137, 147, 182, 217, 265, 275, 277, 278, 281, 294, 297, 313, 380, 439

Austen, Jane (1775–1817), novelist 15, 387

Austen, Thomas (1775–1859), soldier and politician 15

Bacon, Francis 1st Viscount St Alban (1561–1626), philosopher and statesman 263, 265, 268

Badeley, Edward Lowth (1803/4–1868), ecclesiastical lawyer, Catholic convert (1852) 71, 426

Badger, George Percy (1815–88), Anglican missionary and Orientalist 44, 392

Bagot, Richard (1782–1854), bishop of Oxford and Bath and Wells 69, 70, 396

Baillie, Evan, Anglican clergyman, Catholic convert (1858) 427

Bampfield, George (1827–1900), Anglican clergyman, Catholic convert (1856), priest 371, 442

Bathurst, Philip (1815–1900), Anglican clergyman, Catholic convert (1850), Oratorion 255

Bellarmine, Robert (1542–1621), Jesuit theologian and cardinal, canonized (1930) 117, 118, 401

Bellasis, Edward (1800–73), lawyer, Catholic convert (1850) 273, 427

Bennett, W. J. E. (1804–86), Anglican high churchman 45–7, 392

Berrington, Joseph (1746–1827), Catholic priest and scholar 105, 401

Biddulph, Thomas Shrapnel (1789–1866) 2, 3

Biddulph, Thomas Tregenna (1763–1838), Evangelical clergyman in Bristol 2, 3

Birmingham 237, 239, 242, 243, 245, 270, 271, 287, 291, 300, 310, 380, 421

Bittleston, Henry (1818–86), Anglican clergyman, Catholic convert (1849), Oratorian 112, 402

Blomfield, Charles James (1786–1857), bishop of London 40–6, 49–53, 55, 57, 60, 62, 66, 135, 136, 161, 163, 220, 221, 391, 392, 393, 394, 417

Blomfield, Dorothy, second wife (m. 1819) of bishop Blomfield 42, 391

Blomfield, George Becher (1801–85), rector of Stevenage 42

Blomfield, James (1794–1877), rector of Launton and Orsett, Essex 42, 52, 55, 56, 59, 62, 397

Blomfield, James Charles (1821–95), rector of Launton, antiquary 55, 57, 393

Bolgeni, Giovanni Vincenzo (1733–1811), Jesuit theologian and controversialist 227, 418

Boniface I (d. 422), pope 108

Bonnetty, Augustin (1798–1879), French writer and Catholic apologist 89, 94

Borghese, Gwendoline, Princess née Talbot (1817–40) 21

Borghese, Marcantonio, Prince (1814–86) 21

Bossuet, Jacques-Bénigne (1627–1704), French theologian and orator 107, 116, 118, 119, 401

Bourges 142

Bowden, Charles Henry (1836–1906), Oratorian 250, 402

Bowden, Elizabeth (1805–96) 111, 206, 250, 402
Bowden, John William (1798–1844), Anglican writer on church matters 111, 250, 402
Bowdler, Thomas (1780–1856), Protestant controversialist 96, 400
Bowyer, George Sir (1811–83), Catholic lawyer and philanthropist 304
Bramford Speke, Devon 239
Brancker, Thomas (1812/13–1871), rector of Limington 17
Bristol 1–4, 9–11, 21, 25, 36, 37, 385
Bristol Grammar School 9–12, 386
British Museum 5
Broder, James Lyman (1843–1900), Allies's son-in-law 373, 375
Broder, Mary Frances (1884–95), Allies's granddaughter 373
Broder, Mary Frances née Allies (1853–1915), Allies's second daughter 83, 248, 373, 377
Broglie, Albert de (1821–1901), French historian and statesman 271
Brown, Richard Lewis (1811–83), Eton scholar, first class cricketer 13
Browne, Edward George Kirwan, historian of Tractarianism 64
Browne, Robert (1809–95), archdeacon of Bath and Wells 388, 399
Browne, William Frederick (1755–1837), rector of Launton 55, 56, 77
Brownson, Orestes (1803–76), American, Catholic convert

(1844), writer on theology and philosophy 270, 426
Buckle, Henry Thomas (1821–62), historian 273
Bulteel, Henry Bellenden (1800–66), Calvinist seceder from the Church of England 16
Burns, James (1808–71), publisher, Catholic convert (1847) 273, 275, 276
Butler, Joseph (1692–1752), Anglican bishop and theologian 44, 110
Butler, Samuel (1835–1902), novelist 443
Butler, William John (1818–94), vicar of Wantage 135, 405
Butterfield, William (1814–1900), Gothic revival architect 128
Byron, George Gordon, 6th baron Byron (1788–1824), romantic poet 14, 16, 19, 70, 387

Calmet, Antoine Augustin (1672–1757), French Benedictine bible scholar 49
Cambridge University 5, 262, 271, 272, 286, 303, 326, 385, 392, 429
Campbell, Augustus (1786–1870), rector of Liverpool 42
Capalti, Annibale (1811–77), Italian priest created cardinal (1868) 287
Capes, John Moore (1812–89), writer, Catholic convert (1845) 259, 274
Capri 21, 182
Cardwell, Edward (1787–1861), Camden professor of ancient history at Oxford 190, 412
Caroline Divines 162, 163, 224

Carpenter, Lant (1780–1840), educator and Unitarian minister 3

Carpenter, Mary (1807–77), artist and educational and social reformer 13

Carrington Smythe, Eleonora *née* Stourton (1820–99) 247, 422

Carron, L'Abbé, Parisian churchman 94

Castel Gandolfo, papal residence 411

Chapman, John (1865–1933), scholar, Abbot of Downside 235, 419

Charlemagne (747–814), king of the Francs 279, 353

Chateaubriand, François-René de (1768–1848), French author and diplomat 94

Cheltenham 23, 35, 36

Christ Church, Albany Street 34, 391

Christ Church College, Oxford 16, 29, 129

Christian Remembrancer, High Church periodical (1819–68) 48, 101, 106, 109, 111, 125, 132, 151, 219, 232, 233, 392, 417

Chrysostom, John (347–407) 48, 137, 217

Church and State Gazette, Anglican newspaper (1842–56) 418

Clerke Charles Carr (1798–1877), archdeacon of Oxford 170, 171, 177, 410

Clevedon, Somerset 36

Clifton, Bristol 4, 25, 36, 236, 242, 246, 388, 421

Close, Francis (1797–1882), Evangelical rector of Cheltenham 23, 24

Cockerell, Charles Robert (1788–1863), architect, writer, traveller 130

Cohen, James, Anglican clergyman 45

Coleridge, Derwent (1800–83), principal of St Mark's College, Chelsea 41, 391

Coleridge Edward (1800–83), assistant master at Eton College 10, 12, 13, 29, 33, 34, 37, 39, 40, 46, 71, 79, 106, 115, 128, 135, 143, 167, 206, 241, 386, 389, 424, 436

Coleridge, Frederick William (1829–43), Allies's pupil 33

Coleridge, Henry (1822–93), Catholic convert (1852), Jesuit priest 289, 378, 443

Coleridge John (1790–1876), judge of the Queen's Bench 33, 34, 35, 39, 40, 71, 128, 136, 152, 167, 198, 224, 408, 443

Coleridge, John Duke (1820–94), Lord Chief Justice 33, 379, 389, 390, 443

Coleridge, Samuel Taylor (1772–1834), poet and philosopher 38, 390

Collier, Jeremy (1650–1726), non-juring divine 402

Connelly, Cornelia (1809–79), American religious 347, 435, 436, 438

Constable, John (1776–1837), landscape painter 7, 8, 386

Constantine (c.272–337), emperor of Rome 199, 357

Cortès, Juan Donoso (1809–53), Spanish political theorist,

Index

diplomat and politician 279, 428
Cotton Hall, Staffordshire 239, 420
Cotton, William (1786–1866), governor of the Bank of England 40, 50, 391
Courayer, Pierre Francis le (1681–1776), French theologian 200, 414
Cross Commission 340, 349
Cullen, Paul (1803–78), archbishop of Dublin, created cardinal (1866) 253, 255, 257, 353, 423, 424, 432, 439
Cyril of Jerusalem (c.313–86) 137

d'Aglie, Carlo Ludovico, Piedmontese patriot 131
d'Alzon, Emmanuel (1810–80), French ecclesiastic, founder of the Assumptionist order 95, 400
Danesfield House, Marlow 246, 371, 421
Darnell, Nicholas (1817–92), Catholic convert (1848), headmaster of the Oratory school 365, 431, 441
Darwin, Charles (1809–82) 272
Dayman, Alfred Jeken (1820/1821–57), Anglican clergyman, Catholic convert (1850) 186
De Beranger, Pierre Jean (1780–1857), French poet and song writer 399
De Fresne, Marcellin (1793–1869), French scholar 130, 131
De Lisle, Ambrose Phillipps (1809–78), Catholic convert (1823), founder of Mount St Bernard

Abbey 131, 250, 404
Dean, Edward (b.1814), Anglican clergyman, Catholic convert (1855) 243, 249, 300
Der Katholik, German journal (1821–1918) 358
des Billiers, M., canon of Langres 141
Dickens, Charles (1812–70) 240
Dighton, Richard (1795–1880), artist 4
Dighton, Robert (1752–1814), portrait painter and caricaturist 5, 385
Dodsworth, William (1798–1861), Anglican clergyman, Catholic convert (1851) 34, 40, 41, 46, 53, 86, 91, 134, 135, 160, 187, 208–10, 214–16, 221, 222, 247, 390, 391, 415–18
Döllinger, Johann Joseph Ignaz von (1799–1890), German priest, theologian and historian 270, 271, 274, 277, 279, 284, 286, 289, 298–300, 314, 358, 361, 362, 426, 428, 431, 434
Dublin 255–7, 265, 268, 269, 270, 272, 274, 286, 303, 307, 316, 328, 353, 377, 391
Dublin Review, Catholic periodical (1836–1969) 113, 154, 155, 259–61, 268, 270, 273, 275, 276, 289, 293, 295, 300, 301, 314, 317, 343, 353, 355, 402, 408, 424, 425, 427, 430, 432, 434, 437, 439, 447
Durnford, Richard (1802–95), bishop of Chichester 331, 436
Dyson, Charles (1788–1860), rector of Dogmersfield, Oxford professor of Anglo-Saxon 79

Ecclesiastic Anglican review 126, 404
Edgbaston 257, 366, 369
English Review, Anglican review 126, 404, 418
Erskine Thomas (1788–1864), judge, president of the Trinitarian Bible Society 34, 35
Erskine Thomas (1828–78), Allies's pupil, rector of Alderley 34, 390
Escott Thomas Sweet (1801–56), vicar of Gedney 63, 64
Estcourt Edgar Edmund (1816–84), Anglican clergyman, Catholic convert (1845), canon of Birmingham cathedral 307, 433
Eton College 10–13, 16, 21, 26, 27, 29, 30, 33, 39, 40, 42, 46, 79, 87, 93, 128, 129, 136, 206, 241, 271, 331, 353, 386, 387, 390, 402, 424, 436
Everdingen, Allart Van (1621–75), Dutch painter and printmaker 6, 385

Faber, Frederick William (1814–63), Anglican clergyman, Catholic convert (1845), founded the London Oratory 77, 78, 239, 247, 250, 269, 270, 273–5, 277, 279, 283, 285, 397, 420, 422, 426, 428
Fenian outrages 336, 436
Ferguson, William, Congregationalist minister at Bicester 59–62, 65, 67, 394, 395
Fergusson, Thomas Tierney (b. 1818), soldier, Catholic convert (1838), priest 81, 397
Feuardent, François (1539–1610), French patristic scholar 106, 401

Fleury, Claude (1640–1723), French priest and ecclesiastical historian 264
Florence 21, 109
Forbes, Alexander Penrose (1817–75), bishop of Brechin 141, 199, 226
Formby, Henry (1816–84), Anglican clergyman, Catholic convert (1846), priest 323, 324
Forster, William Edward (1818–86), industrialist and Liberal politician 331, 332, 334, 336, 338, 344
Freeman, James, farmer of Launton 58, 394
Fripp, Alfred Downing (1822–95), watercolourist 2
Fripp, Edward Bowles (1787–1870), brother of Frances Elizabeth Allies 2, 3
Fripp, George Arthur (1813–96), watercolourist 2
Fripp, Samuel (1755–1810), father of Frances Elizabeth Allies 2
Fripp, Samuel Charles (1785–1843), Anglican clergyman, Unitarian convert (1822) 2, 3, 8
Froude, James Anthony (1818–94), historian and novelist 154, 155

Gaeta Italy 181, 411
Gaggiotti, Gustavo (1793–1874), Italian nobleman, British vice-consul in Ancona 21, 388
Gallicanism 90, 96, 107, 118–20, 142, 201, 301, 403
Gallini, Giovanni (1728–1805), dancer and theatre manager 248, 422

Index

Garbett, James (1802–79), Oxford Professor of Poetry (1841) 51
Gasquet, Francis Aidan (1846–1929), Benedictine monk, scholar, created cardinal (1914) 427
Genoa 131, 182
Gentili, Aloysius (1801–48), Italian Rosminian cleric 79, 131
Gibson, Edmund (1669–1748), bishop of London 190, 412
Gilbert, Daniel (1827–95), Catholic priest, canon of Westminster 311, 312, 438
Gillis, James (1802–64), vicar-apostolic of the Eastern District of Scotland 204, 414
Gist, Samuel (1717 or 1723–1815), English-American slave owner and financier 10, 11
Gladstone, William Ewart (1809–98) 16, 31, 39, 40, 45, 46, 50, 71, 87, 125, 136, 137, 153, 225, 228, 309, 330, 332, 334, 336, 338, 344, 369, 387, 389, 392, 393, 398, 404, 405, 418, 419, 436, 437, 440
Gladstone's Library, Hawarden 418
Godley, John Robert (1814–61), Anglican founder of a settlement in New Zealand 129
Golden Square, London 247, 250, 422
Golightly, Charles Pourtales (1807–85), anti-Tractarian Anglican clergyman 50
Gondon, Jules (1816–79), French Catholic writer and political commentator 89
Gonville and Caius College, Cambridge 43
Goodenough, John Joseph (1779–1856), Anglican clergyman, headmaster of Bristol Grammar School 9, 10, 12
Goodrest, Berkshire seat of Edward Willes 25, 26, 388
Gorham, George Cornelius (1787–1857), Calvinist Church of England clergyman 161, 165, 185, 187, 188, 190, 192, 193, 196, 199, 204, 205, 207–9, 215, 222, 227, 234, 239, 246, 259, 293, 294, 384, 392, 415
Görres, Johann Joseph von (1776–1848), German philosopher, theologian and historian 131
Grant, Thomas (1816–70), rector of the English College Rome 181
Grey, George Robinson de, 1st Marquess of Ripon (1827–1909), Liberal politician, Catholic convert (1874) 310, 338, 438
Griffiths, John (1806–85), warden of Wadham College 74, 75, 396
Grotius, Hugo (1583–1645), Dutch humanist, theologian and jurist 259, 260, 263
Guardian, Anglican newspaper (1846–1951) 133, 150, 151, 159, 161, 189, 190, 252, 405, 407, 408, 412, 413
Guéranger, Prosper (1805–75), French priest, restorer of Benedictine monasticism 89, 95, 271
Guizot, François Pierre Guillaume (1787–1874), French historian and statesman 268, 426

Haddon, Henry Cort (1855–1940), anthropologist and ethnologist 370, 371

Hale, William (1795–1870),
    Anglican clergyman, master of
    Charterhouse 42
Hallam, Arthur Henry (1811–33),
    dedicatee of Tennyson's *In
    Memoriam* 13, 387
Hallam, Henry (1777–1859),
    historian 13, 278
Hampden, Renn Dickson (1793–
    1868), bishop of Hereford 16
Hanmer, Anthony John (1817–1909),
    curate of Tidcombe Wilts,
    Catholic convert (1849) 186
Heathcote, Clara Rosalie *née*
    Stonhouse-Vigor (1818–96) 25,
    26, 28, 389
Heathcote, Gilbert Wall (1806–93),
    rector of Ash, Hants 389
Heathcote, William, 1st baronet
    (1801–81), politician, Tractarian,
    patron of Hursley 389
Heathcote, William Beadon (1812–
    62), Anglican clergyman, warden
    of Radley College 129, 135, 145,
    148, 153, 160, 162
Henbury, Bristol 3, 11
Herbert, Henry (d. 1837),
    Eton scholar drowned in
    Switzerland 13, 27, 389
Hilhouse, George (1778–1848),
    shipbuilder of Bristol 11
Hilhouse, James Martin (1749–1822),
    founder of Bristol shipbuilding
    company 3, 4
Hippisley, Sir John Cox (1747–
    1825), Whig politician and
    diplomat 10, 386
Hody, Humphrey (1659–1707),
    scholar and theologian 14, 30
Höfler, Konstantin von (1811–
98), German ecclesiastical
    historian 280, 428
Holden, Henry (1814–1909),
    headmaster of Uppingham
    School 45, 46
Home and Foreign Review Catholic
    periodical (1862–4) 276, 287,
    426
Hook, Walter Farquhar (1798–1875),
    vicar of Leeds 51, 71, 75, 102
Hope-Scott, James (until 1853 Hope)
    (1812–73), Catholic convert
    (1851), ecclesiastical lawyer 255,
    304, 424, 432
Hotwells, Bristol 3
Howard, Lord Edward Fitzalan-
    Howard, 1st baron (1818–83),
    Liberal politician, chairman of
    Catholic Poor-School Com-
    mittee 321, 332, 333, 337, 338, 348
Hucknall Torkard,
    Nottinghamshire 16, 387
Hussey, Robert (1801–56), Oxford
    professor of ecclesiastical
    history 138, 405

Immaculate Conception 250, 270,
    377, 400, 419, 429
Inishbofin island 368–71, 373–5
Innocent XI, Benedetto Odescalchi
    (1611–89), pope 401

Jenner-Fust, Herbert (until 1842
    Jenner) (1778–1852), judge and
    Dean of Arches 63, 160, 161,
    163, 165, 185, 186
Jurisdiction 108, 114–16, 118, 119,
    141, 188–98, 200–2, 205, 208–11,
    213, 216–21, 227–9, 233, 239, 260,
    269, 283, 308, 317, 326, 413, 414

Kaye, John (1783–1853), bishop of Lincoln 163
Keate, John (1773–1852), headmaster of Eton 12, 436
Keble, John (1792–1866), vicar of Hursley 33, 48, 49, 51, 71, 82, 89, 93, 102, 145, 153, 163, 197, 216, 389, 393
King's College, Cambridge 387
Kirk, John (1760–1851), Catholic divine and antiquary 105, 401
Knight, Edward Austen (1767–1852) 387

Labbé, Pierre (d. 1871), French priest, founded Yvetot *Petit Seminaire* 93, 94, 238, 239, 249, 365
Labbé, Xavier, French priest, teacher at Yvetot *Petit Seminaire* 94
Lacordaire, Jean-Baptiste Henri (1802–61), French priest, journalist and political activist 90, 95, 96, 116, 117, 141
Lamennais, Félicité de (1782–1854), French Catholic priest, philosopher, theologian 89, 90, 95
Lamennais, Jean Marie Robert de (1780–1860), French priest of Ploërmel 346
Langdale Charles (1787–1868), MP, chairman of Catholic Poor-School Committee 318, 324, 434
Launton, Oxfordshire 42, 52, 53, 55–71, 75–8, 83–9, 92, 97, 99, 134, 135, 144, 157, 161, 163–5, 168, 169, 172, 175, 179, 181–3, 185, 204, 206, 207, 221–3, 225, 226, 231, 237, 238, 240, 241–4, 249, 257, 379, 393–5, 397, 403, 407–9

Lazzari, Maria Domenica (1815–48), *l'addolorata di Capriana*, Italian mystic 131–3, 180, 404
Leahy, Patrick (1806–75), president of St Patrick's College, Thurles, archbishop of Cashel 254, 255, 423
Leamington Spa 25
Leeds 51, 71, 75, 102, 135, 183, 404, 411
Leo I (400–61), pope 108, 434
Leo III (d. 816), pope 353
Leo XIII, Vincenzo Pecci (1810–1903), pope 310, 315, 317, 345, 434
Lear, Edward (1812–88), artist and poet 181
Leibniz, Gottfried Wilhelm (1646–1716), German philosopher and mathematician 259–61
Lescher, Frances Mary, Sr Mary of St Philip (1825–1904), principal of Notre Dame college, Liverpool 347, 438
Lewis, David (1814–95), Anglican clergyman, Catholic convert (1846) 194, 195, 275, 304, 413
Liddon, Henry Parry (1829–90), Anglican theologian 296, 297
Lillie, John (1806–66), Presbyterian minister 371
Lingard, John (1771–1851), Catholic priest and historian 362
Linnell, John (1792–1882), engraver, landscape and portrait painter 5–8, 385, 386
Liverpool 318, 341, 346, 347, 368, 370, 395, 420, 438, 441
Locke, John (1632–1704), empiricist philosopher 38, 390, 391

Lockhart, William (1819–92), Catholic convert (1843), priest 79

Longley Charles Thomas (1794–1868), bishop of Ripon, archbishop of Canterbury 102, 103, 183, 404

Lowe, Robert, 1st Viscount Sherbrooke (1811–92), Liberal MP, cabinet minister 17, 330

Lushington, Stephen (1782–1873), judge and MP 163, 166, 178

Lyall, John Edwardes (1811–45), lawyer, Advocate-General of Bengal 17

Magdalen College, Oxford 15, 24, 85, 310

Manning, Henry Edward (1808–92), archdeacon, Catholic convert (1850), archbishop of Westminster 71, 89, 91, 118, 125, 134, 142–9, 153, 156, 157, 160–2, 164, 165, 167–75, 177, 182, 184–7, 192, 193, 197–201, 205, 207, 208, 210, 213, 214, 223, 270, 276, 277, 287, 288, 290–3, 300, 301, 304, 305–7, 311–13, 316, 330–2, 336, 338, 340, 344, 349, 384, 399, 403, 406–10, 413–15, 429, 430, 433, 436–8, 443

Manresa House, Roehampton 372

Manzoni, Alessandro (1785–1873), Italian poet, novelist and philosopher 130–2, 404

Marseilles 182

Marsh, James (1794–1842), American philosopher 38, 390

Marshall, Thomas William (1818–77), Anglican clergymen, Catholic convert (1845), HMI 351, 438

Marriott, Charles (1811–58), Tractarian clergyman, Oxford academic 16, 17, 82, 89, 90, 93–6, 98, 99, 128, 145–7, 153, 431

Maskell, William (1814–90), Anglican clergyman, liturgical scholar, Catholic convert (1850) 188, 191, 193, 197, 207, 208, 210, 214–16, 218–22, 239, 246, 259, 412, 413, 415–18, 420

Massie, Edward (b. 1805/1806), Anglican clergyman 17, 18

Massie, James William (1799–1866), Independent minister 399

Mathew, David (1902–75), Catholic bishop and historian 271, 426

Mathison, Gilbert Farquhar (1803–54), secretary of Royal Mint, Anglican educational reformer 39

Maurice, Frederick Denison (1805–72), Anglican theologian 40

Maurice, Peter (1803–78), vicar of Yarnton 57

Maynooth Seminary 90

Meynell, Wilfrid (1852–1948) ('John Oldcastle'), newspaper publisher 315

Midsomer Norton, Somerset 3

Mildert William Van (1765–1836), last prince-bishop of Durham 38, 391

Mill, John Stuart (1806–73), philosopher, economist and politician 272, 396

Milleret de Brou, Marie-Eugénie (1817–98), French religious, canonized (2007) 95

Index

Milman, Henry Hart (1791–1868), Anglican historian, dean of St Paul's 267, 426
Moberly Charles Edward (1820–93), headmaster Park House School Shoreham 185
Möhler, Johann Adam (1796–1838), German Catholic priest, theologian 279
Monro, Edward (1815–66), vicar of Leeds 98, 400
The Month, Jesuit review (1864–2001) 235, 342, 378, 419, 437, 440
Moore, Daniel (1809–99), vicar of Holy Trinity Paddington 45
Moore, Thomas (1779–1852), Irish poet, friend of Byron 14
Morell, John Reynell (1821–91), Catholic convert, HMI 351
Morl, Maria (1812–68), *Ecstatica*, Italian mystic bearing the stigmata 131, 132, 180, 404
Morris, John (1826–93), Jesuit priest, secretary to Cardinal Wiseman 276, 288, 421
Morris, John Brande (1812–80), Anglican clergyman Catholic convert (1846) 73
Mount Tabor 444
Mozley, James Bowling (1813–78), Oxford Regius Professor of Divinity 101, 102
Mundella, Anthony John (1825–97), Liberal MP, cabinet minister 345
Munro, Miss G. (d. 1913), Catholic convert (1846), J. H. Newman was her spiritual director 312

Naples 21–3, 181, 182, 234
Napoleon III (1808–73), Emperor of the French 301, 302, 432
Nelmes, Essex 14, 36, 221, 239, 243, 244, 246, 420
Neville, William Paine (1824–1905), Catholic convert (1851), Oratorian 312, 313
Newcastle Commission 275, 328, 329, 351
Newcastle scholarship 12–14, 27, 30, 382
Newman John Henry (1801–90) 30, 37, 46–51, 64–6, 69–72, 79, 81–3, 86, 89, 91, 93, 95, 97–9, 101–13, 124, 127, 129, 131, 133, 134, 154, 155, 164, 180, 184, 206, 208, 218, 224, 227, 231, 237–9, 242–4, 246–8, 250–7, 259, 264, 265, 268–75, 277, 279–93, 295–314, 328, 351–3, 357–9, 361, 362, 365–9, 372, 377, 379–82, 384, 392–4, 397, 398, 401, 402, 404, 420–34, 438–43
Newman, Richard Harding (1757–1808) 14
Newman, Thomas Harding (1779–1856) of Nelmes, Allies's father-in-law 15, 36
Newman Thomas Harding (1811–82) of Magdalen College, Oxford 14–16, 18, 20, 21, 23, 24, 85, 86, 387, 388
Norfolk, Henry Fitzalan-Howard, 15th duke (1847–1917) 309, 310, 312, 350, 438
Norris, John (1657–1712), theologian and philosopher 39, 391
Northcote, James Spencer (1821–1907), Anglican clergyman,

Catholic convert (1846),
president of Oscott College 421

Oakeley, Frederick (1802–80),
Anglican clergyman, Catholic
convert (1845), canon of
Westminster 343, 384, 433
Odescalchi, Livio (1805–85), prince
of ancient Italian family 181
O'Donnell, Frank Hugh (1846–1916),
Irish journalist and nationalist
politician 316, 434
O'Reilly, Myles (1825–80), Irish
soldier, MP and writer 255, 424
Orleans 142
Oscott College 239, 244, 249, 320,
434
Our Lady's Church, St John's
Wood 248, 372
Oxenham, Henry Nutcombe
(1829–88), Anglican
clergyman, Catholic convert
(1857), ecclesiologist and
translator 289, 298–300, 429,
431
Oxford Movement 33, 34, 37, 38,
46, 47, 50, 51, 52, 107, 133, 134,
164, 245, 254, 381, 384, 396
Oxford Union Society 16, 17, 316,
388
Oxford University 13–16, 18, 19, 21,
23, 24, 26, 30, 32, 42, 51, 53, 69,
70, 73, 74, 77, 86, 89, 93, 96, 97,
99, 103, 129, 134, 136, 161, 165,
172, 176, 177, 183, 190, 215, 241,
243, 244, 256, 262, 271, 272, 286–
90, 302–6, 331, 353, 357, 380, 385,
396, 429

Palmer, Edwin (1824–95), Corpus
Professor of Latin at Oxford,
archdeacon 85, 398
Palmer, Roundell first earl of
Selborne (1812–95), twice Lord
Chancellor 17
Palmer, William (1811–79) of
Magdalen, scholar of Orthodoxy,
Catholic convert (1855) 53, 85,
92, 107, 153, 168, 173, 301, 309,
310, 312, 398, 409
Palmer, William (1803–85) of
Worcester College, theologian
and liturgical scholar 44, 86,
107
Palmer, William Jocelyn (1778–1853),
rector of Mixbury 53, 241
Paris 18, 19, 23, 89, 94, 95, 128, 130,
138, 139, 142, 214, 243, 251, 365,
406
Parisis, Pierre Louis (1795–1866),
bishop of Langres 406
Passaglia, Carlo (1812–87), Italian
Jesuit theologian 234, 235, 419
Patterson, James Laird (1822–1902),
Catholic convert (1850), auxiliary
bishop of Westminster 138–41,
160, 225
Pattison, Mark (1813–84), rector of
Lincoln College 17, 31
Pelham-Clinton, Henry, 4th duke of
Newcastle (1785–1851) 12
Pepys, Charles, 1st earl of
Cottenham (1781–1851), Lord
Chancellor 34, 390
Pepys, Henry (1783–1860), bishop of
Worcester 390
Pepys, Henry Leslie (1830–91),
Allies's pupil 34, 390
Pereira, Antonio de Figueiredo
(1725–97), Portuguese priest,

Index

historian, theologian 200, 201, 414
Petre, William Bernard, 12th baron (1817–84), Catholic philanthropist 304
Phillpotts, Henry (1778–1869), bishop of Exeter 161, 185, 188, 192, 210, 417
Pickering, Miss 36, 390
Pius V, Antonio Ghislieri (1504–72), pope 191, 412
Pius IX, Giovanni Maria Mastai Ferretti (1792–1878), pope 180–2, 234, 242, 250, 269–71, 274, 307, 309, 332, 411, 419, 429, 432
Pocock, Nicholas (1740–1821), marine artist 2
Pollen, Anne Gertrude Mary (1856–1934), biographer of her father J. H. Pollen 176, 394, 404
Pollen, John Hungerford (1820–1902), Anglican clergyman, Catholic convert (1852), writer on crafts and furniture 13, 128–30, 134, 135, 137, 138, 144–6, 148, 157, 160, 177, 183, 203, 210, 225, 226, 243, 244, 394, 404, 405, 407, 410–12, 440
Pollen, Laura Susan (1818–51) 129
Pollen, Richard Hungerford, 3rd baronet (1815–81), Catholic convert (1853), artist 13, 129
Portman Chapel 46, 396
Pountney, William (d. 1852), Bristol potter, historian of ceramics 1
Poussin, Nicholas (1594–1665), painter 6, 385
Poynder, Frederick (1816–99), Anglican clergyman, master of Charterhouse School 45

Prendergast, Lennox Guy (1830–1907), army officer, educationalist 176
Pugin, Augustus Welby Northmore (1812–52), Catholic convert (1835), architect and designer 239, 250, 251, 371, 423
Pusey, Edward Bouverie (1800–82), Regius Professor of Hebrew at Oxford 46, 51, 71, 72, 74, 75, 86, 101–3, 129, 134, 135, 138, 144, 145, 148, 153, 160, 163, 167, 171, 172, 176, 178, 182, 185, 197, 199, 200, 207–11, 213–24, 239, 289, 292–8, 300, 380, 396, 401, 411, 414–17, 420, 421, 430
Puseyism 53, 56, 65, 71, 74, 191, 240, 245, 272, 395, 396

Quanta Cura (1864) 289, 429
Queens' College, Cambridge 2
Queensland 285, 367–70, 441
Quinn, James (1819–81), Catholic bishop of Brisbane 367

Rainier, Peter (1784–1836), naval captain and horticulturalist 7, 386
Rambler Catholic periodical (1848–62) 116, 259, 270, 272–6, 286, 287, 326, 328, 403, 424, 427, 428, 435
The Ramblers, Oxford University debating society 17, 18, 89
Ravignan de, Gustave Delacroix (1795–1858), French Jesuit preacher and author 141
Read, David Charles (1790–1851), painter and etcher 5–8
Récamier, Juliette (1777–1849), French socialite 94

Renouf, Peter le Page (1822–97), Catholic convert (1842), Egyptologist 121, 124, 403
Rice, John Morland (1823–97), rector of Bramber 387
Richards, William Upton (1811–73), Tractarian clergyman 167, 216, 219, 416
Richardson, Mr 78
Richardson, Thomas (1797–1875), Catholic publisher 252
Riddell, Arthur George (1836–1907), Catholic bishop of Northampton 372
Robert, Charles, French priest 93
Rodwell, John Medows (1808–1900), Anglican clergyman, scholar of Islam 136, 137
Roemer, William Francis (1894–1971), writer on legal matters 361
Rolls, S., lay preacher of Bicester Congregational Church 62
Rosmini-Serbati, Antonio (1797–1855), Italian priest and philosopher 131, 152
Rouen 78, 93, 94, 139
Routh, Martin (1755–1854), classical scholar, president of Magdalen College 310
Rowe, James Boone (1824–88), Catholic convert (1845), Oratorian, principal of St Mary's College Hammersmith 347
Royal Academy 7, 386, 388
Royal Irish Academy 371
Royal Military Academy, Woolwich 366
Ruskin, John (1819–1900), writer, philosopher and art critic 5

Ryder, George Dudley (1810–80), Anglican clergyman, Catholic convert (1846) 411
Ryder, Henry Ignatius Dudley (1837–1907), priest of the Birmingham Oratory 300, 432
Ryder Sophia Lucy (1814–50), Catholic convert (1846) 411

Schlegel, Karl Wilhelm Friedrich (1772–1829), German poet, philosopher, philologist 264, 279, 425
Scott, Linlithgow, Anglican high churchman 236
Scott, Robert (1811–87), Anglican clergyman and philologist 31
Scott-Murray, Charles (1818–82), Catholic convert (1844), Conservative politician 246, 371, 421
Selwyn, George Augustus (1809–78), Anglican bishop of New Zealand and Lichfield 41, 46
Seyer, Samuel (1757–1831), Anglican clergyman, historian of Bristol 10
Shaftesbury, Lord Anthony Ashley-Cooper, 7th earl (1801–85), social reformer, Protestant zealot 179–80
Shelley, Mary Wollstonecraft (1797–1851), novelist 131
Shrewsbury, John Talbot, 16th earl (1791–1852), prominent Catholic layman 131, 132, 404, 420
Sibthorp, Charles (1783–1855), ultra-Tory MP for Lincoln 90
Sibthorp, Richard Waldo (1792–1879), Anglican clergyman twice a Catholic convert 387

Index 465

Simeon, John, 3rd baronet (1815–70), Liberal politician, Catholic convert (1851) 288
Simpson, Richard (1820–76), Anglican clergyman, Catholic convert (1846), polemicist and literary scholar 272–5, 277, 298, 299, 427, 428
Sinclair John (1797–1875), archdeacon of Middlesex, theologian 42, 45
Smith, Sydney (1771–1845), Anglican cleric, wit and writer 71
Sorrento 21, 182
Southampton 5–8, 82, 93, 385, 386
Spencer, C. C., rector of Benefield, Northampton 45, 392
St Augustine's College, Kent 128, 135
St Clement's church, Oxford 421
St Edmunds College, Ware 214
St Edmund's Hall, Oxford 1, 2
St John, Ambrose (1815–75), Anglican clergyman, Catholic convert (1845), Oratorian 257, 424
St John's Wood, London 248, 249, 285, 372, 435
St James church, Bristol 2, 3
St Leonards-on-Sea, East Sussex 347, 351
St Margaret's church, Westminster 2
St Mary Magdalen church, Mortlake 377
St Mary's church, Marylebone 38, 41, 216
St Saviour's church, Leeds 102, 135, 183, 412
St Thomas's church, Oxford 138

Stanley, Arthur Penrhyn (1815–81), Anglican clergyman, ecclesiastical historian 16
Stanton, Vincent John (1817–91), Anglican clergyman, linguist, missionary in Hong Kong 44
Stella, Joseph, chamberlain to Pius IX 181
Stokes, Scott Naysmith (1821–91), Catholic convert (1845), HMI 275, 318, 325–8, 346, 347, 351, 434
Stonhouse, Charles (1807–83), artist and clergyman 25, 388, 389
Stonhouse-Vigor, Timothy (1765–1831), archdeacon of Gloucester 25
Sumner, Charles Richard (1790–1874), bishop of Winchester 164
Sumner, John Bird (1780–1862), archbishop of Canterbury 44, 216
Symons, Benjamin Parsons (1785–1878), warden of Wadham College 72–5, 396

The Tablet, Catholic journal founded in 1840 59, 60, 154, 174–6, 178, 183, 234, 256, 304, 307, 308, 314, 325, 327, 332–4, 337, 341, 343, 349, 356, 360, 361, 381, 384, 394, 408, 411, 422, 424, 433, 434, 436–40, 443
Tabor, Robert Stammers (1819–1909), Anglican clergyman, headmaster of Cheam School 45
Tait, Archibald Campbell (1811–82), archbishop of Canterbury 15, 16
Tharp, Eliza Mary (1755–1831), owner of slaves in Jamaica 15

Thompson, Edward Healy (1813–91), Anglican clergyman, Catholic convert (1846), writer and polemicist 114–18, 142, 227, 275, 276, 289, 402, 418, 427

Thring, Edward, headmaster of Uppingham school 46

Thurles, Co. Tipperary 253, 255, 423

Tournay, William (1762–1833), warden of Wadham College 14

Tractarianism 15, 33, 34, 37, 41, 45–7, 49–53, 65, 69–71, 73–6, 78, 79, 82, 86, 89, 90, 93, 95, 98, 101, 102, 104, 106, 107, 129, 134, 135, 138, 145, 153, 160, 161, 164, 165, 176, 180, 183, 185, 192, 197, 199, 208, 215, 222, 225, 226, 293, 390, 395, 400, 404, 410, 421, 443

Trench, Francis Chenevix (1805–86), Anglican clergyman, writer 399

Trench, Richard Chenevix (1807–86), Anglican archbishop of Dublin 135

Trevelyan, Walter (1763–1830), vicar of Henbury Bristol, slave owner 11

Treves, Frederick, 1st baronet (1853–1923), prominent surgeon 443

Trinity College, Cambridge 13, 434

Trinity College, Dublin 257

Trinity College, Oxford 51, 138

Turner, Joseph Mallord William (1775–1851), painter 5, 13, 16

Ullathorne, William Bernard (1806–89), Catholic bishop of Birmingham 239, 287, 288, 292, 302, 308, 324–7, 329, 340, 346, 435

Union Review journal advocating corporate reunion (1863–1921) 295, 358, 430, 440

Unionism 316, 434

University College, Kensington 307

University College, London 387

University College, Oxford 17

Usko, John Frederick (1760–1841), rector of Orsett in Essex 53, 393

Vaughan, Herbert Alfred Henry (1832–1903), archbishop of Westminster 307, 354, 362, 373, 376

Vaughan, James (1774–1857), rector of Wraxhall Somerset 2

Venice 132, 133

Vere, Aubrey Thomas de (1814–1902), Irish poet and critic 375, 443

Vincent de Lerins (d. 434?), Gallic monk and author 104, 401

Vincent de Paul (1581–1660), French priest canonized (1737) 94, 140, 406

Voltaire, François-Marie Arouet (1694–1778), French Enlightenment writer 93, 315

Waagen, Gustav Friedrich (1794–1868), German art historian 13, 387

Wadham College, Oxford 14, 17, 19, 23, 30, 45, 51, 52, 72, 74, 396

Wakefield, Edward Gibbon (1796–1862), proponent of colonisation 129

Walker, John (1800–73), Catholic priest at Scarborough 358, 371

Wall, Henry (1810–73), Wykeham Professor of Logic at Oxford 73, 128, 396, 398

Index

Wallis, John E. (1821–88), barrister, edited *The Tablet* 314
Ward, Richard (1813–69), Anglican clergyman, Catholic convert (1851) 412
Ward, William George (1812–82), Anglican clergyman, Catholic convert (1845), polemical writer edited *Dublin Review* 16, 17, 37, 70, 71, 75, 76, 77, 84–6, 113, 114, 247, 275–7, 288, 289, 291, 293, 300, 301, 304, 384, 388, 396, 398, 399, 411, 427, 431
Watson, Joshua (1771–1855), prominent high churchman 42
Watts, John William (1806–89), Evangelical vicar of Bicester 67–9, 243, 395
Weld, Alfred (1823–90), Jesuit Provincial 304
Weld, Mrs 247, 422
Westminster Review quarterly journal (1823–1914) 356
Wheeler, William (1808–89), vicar of Old Shoreham, Catholic convert (1855) 45
White, F. G., Anglican clergyman 128
Wilberforce, Henry (1807–73), Anglican clergyman, Catholic convert (1850) 31, 91, 111, 144, 145, 147, 168, 179, 190, 191, 205, 254, 304, 368, 408, 409, 423, 441, 442
Wilberforce, Robert Isaac (1802–57), archdeacon, Catholic convert (1854) 199, 259, 409, 424
Wilberforce, Samuel (1805–73), bishop of Oxford and Winchester 66–9, 128, 134, 135, 138–40, 156, 157, 160–8, 170–3, 175, 176, 178–80, 246, 260, 297, 392, 395, 396, 409–11, 439
Wilberforce, Wilfrid Ignatius (1850–1910), writer 376, 442, 443
Wilds, William (1768–1854), Catholic priest 206
Wilkie, David (1785–1841), painter 25, 389
Willes, Edward (1787–1847), landowner of Newbold Comyn, Warwickshire 21, 25–7, 388, 389
Willes, Edward (b. 1820), Allies's pupil 26, 27
Williams, Isaac (1802–65), Tractarian clergyman, poet and theologian 51, 52
Williams, Mr, Australian sheep farmer 367
Willmott, Robert Eldridge Aris (1809–63), Anglican cleric and author 45, 92, 399
Wilson, Daniel (1778–1858), Anglican bishop of Calcutta 50
Wiseman, Nicholas Patrick Stephen (1802–65), appointed cardinal and archbishop of Westminster (1850) 198, 237, 242, 246, 250–2, 269, 270, 273, 276, 277, 287–92, 318, 323, 327, 329, 367, 411, 422, 424, 429
Wood, Charlotte (1789–1873), Catholic covert (1845) 180
Wood, Granville Francis (1818–56), naval officer, Catholic convert (1849), Jesuit priest 180
Woodard, Nathaniel (1811–91), Anglican clergyman, educationalist 45, 185, 244, 249
Wootten, Frances (d. 1876), Catholic convert 1850, matron of the Oratory School 204, 242, 421

Wootton House, Wootton Wawen Warwickshire (Wootton Hall) 247, 248, 250, 422, 424
Worcester 1, 4
Wordsworth, Christopher (1807–85), bishop of Lincoln 89, 90, 92, 94, 399
Wordsworth, John (1843–1911), classical scholar, bishop of Salisbury 357, 440
Wordsworth, William (1770–1850), Romantic poet 389, 444
Wormington, Gloucester 10, 11
Wraxhall, Bristol 2
Wynne, Charles Griffith (1815–74), Tory MP for Caernarfon 129
Wynne, John Henry Griffith (1819–93), Anglican cleric, first-class cricketer, Catholic convert (1850), Jesuit priest 13, 128–31, 133–5, 137, 138, 145, 146, 157, 160, 181, 182, 203, 225, 411
Wynter, Philip (1793–1871), president of St John's College Oxford 71, 73–5

Yard, George Beckwith (1812–73), Anglican clergyman, Catholic convert (1863) 387
Yonge, Charlotte Mary (1823–1901), novelist 34, 390
Young, Caroline Louisa (Mrs Bertram Currie) (1836–1902), Catholic convert (1862), writer 236
Young, Miss 94
Yvetot, commune in Normandy 93, 94, 139, 238, 249, 365

www.ingramcontent.com/pod-product-compliance
Lightning Source LLC
Chambersburg PA
CBHW030330240426
43661CB00052B/1584